**steam '80**

*'Steam Past' Books from Allen & Unwin*

THE LIMITED by O. S. Nock
THE BIRTH OF BRITISH RAIL by Michael R. Bonavia
STEAM'S INDIAN SUMMER by George Heiron & Eric Treacy
GRAVEYARD OF STEAM by Brian Handley
PRESERVED STEAM IN BRITAIN by Patrick B. Whitehouse
MEN OF THE GREAT WESTERN by Peter Grafton
TRAVELLING BY TRAIN IN THE EDWARDIAN AGE by Philip Unwin

STEAM '80 edited by Roger Crombleholme and Terry Kirtland

# steam '80

A complete enthusiasts' handbook to railway preservation activities and minor railways in the British Isles

Edited by **Roger Crombleholme** and **Terry Kirtland**

London
GEORGE ALLEN & UNWIN
Boston          Sydney

First published in 1980

GEORGE ALLEN & UNWIN LTD
40 Museum Street, London WC1A 1LU


© George Allen & Unwin (Publishers) Ltd, 1980

**British Library Cataloguing in Publication Data**

Steam – (Steam past).
  '80
  1. Locomotives – Great Britain – History
  – Periodicals
  I. Crombleholme, Roger
  II. Kirtland, Terry   III. Series
  385'.36'105        TJ603.4.G7

  ISBN 0–04–385077–4

Typeset in 9pt Univers and
printed in Great Britain by
Unwin Brothers Ltd, Old Woking, Surrey

# FOREWORD

by Dr John Coiley
*Keeper of the National Railway Museum*

1980 promises to be a fascinating year for the railway enthusiast. It will see celebrations associated with the 150th anniversary of the opening of the Liverpool and Manchester Railway, the return to steam for several famous locomotives and the introduction to passenger service by British Rail of their exciting Advanced Passenger Train.

It is therefore all the more appropriate that in 1980 this well established handbook should be given a new lease of life with new publishers who hopefully will see it and railway preservation go from strength to strength. Nevertheless, despite the significance of 1980 for railways, past and present, it is not going to be an easy year. During the past twelve months the economic situation, and the fuel crisis in particular, resulted in noticeably fewer visitors for most railways and museums with the usual effect on financial performance. While some of the reasons are obvious, the almost universal need for heavier and more expensive repairs to faithful workhorses is perhaps more insidious. While some of the larger lines have newly restored locomotives ready to plug gaps, others were not so fortunate. Although there is no easy answer to this problem, one way to minimise its effects is to arrange, where possible, short-term exchanges. Other obstacles, which private railways have so far overcome, include the need for more volunteers for jobs of all kinds and the effects of increasingly stringent safety measures.

Despite the continuing problems of railway preservation, it is surely encouraging that the last few years have seen an increasing interest in the wider aspects of railway operation. Carriage preservation and restoration attracts a greater following, including on-train catering, aided in no small measure by TV and filming activities. Diesels are gradually gaining acceptance with visitors as well as with operators although so far major maintenance remains something of an unknown factor. More and more lines are introducing more sophisticated signalling systems to improve safety and allow a more frequent train service at peak periods, although it is perhaps unfortunate that it is usually so difficult to arrange for visitors to be shown the workings of signal boxes and the elements of train control. Against this background it is clear that 1980 will be both an eventful and demanding year. The actual 'Rocket 150' event at Rainhill and Liverpool will stretch to the full most of the organisations concerned, with only a brief respite before the normal peak season, ending for many with more 150 celebrations at Manchester in September. It is of course hoped that these official celebrations will stimulate further interest and visits to member organisations of ARPS as well as generate more passengers for SLOA charter and BR steam specials on the main line. The success of all these events depends upon support which in turn relies on accurate communication of information, much of which is to be found in this important handbook (and updated in the ARPS Newsletter). I should therefore like to take this opportunity to congratulate those concerned in every way with its past and to wish the new team every success in the future.

# INTRODUCTION

It's great to be back! Yes, we're proud to present *Steam '80* with a new crisp image, wider coverage, and a firm commitment to move forward into the new decade on the still rising tide of railway preservation.

During the past ten years, the Steam Year Book has become established as the firm favourite encyclopaedia for steam freaks everywhere. We're really chuffed at the encouragement we have always received from enthusiasts, railway managements and, of course, the great British steam-loving public who have all helped to make our book the 'Bible of railway preservation'.

Now it's great to have our enthusiasm spurred on by our new publishers, George Allen & Unwin Ltd, who have set a clear road for Steam in the 'eighties!

### The 'Steam Past' Award

Above all, it's your book. You've always told us your views on the steam scene – now we can involve you even more. We know you enjoy your visits to the multitude of steam centres up and down the country, so here's your chance to make positive recommendations for our 'Steam Past' award. This prize, which is to be presented annually by our Publishers in connection with their 'Steam Past' series of railway books, will go to the railway which *you* have voted as the one which has achieved the highest standards of professionalism in bringing enjoyment to the public.

Every line will be in with a chance, from the big boys to the smallest of the miniatures. But what will count will be their enthusiasm, their standards and, above all, their service to you, the public. For without your support, live steam could not survive.

### Rainhill

And talking of live steam, the 'eighties open with a significant landmark in railway history — the sesquicentennial celebrations commemorating the opening of the Liverpool and Manchester Railway. Highlight of the proceedings will, of course, be the re-staging of the Rainhill trials involving the freshly built working replicas of the original contestants: *Rocket*, *Sans Pareil* and *Novelty*. British Railways are masterminding the entire 'Rocket 150' celebrations and promise us a spectacle which will linger in our memories for many years to come.

So the scene has been well set for some exciting new chapters in the book of steam. Rest assured that, with your support, we will keep bringing you, year by year, the rich panorama of our new railway heritage, as it happens!

Yes, it's great to be back . . .

# Alphabetical list of contents

## KEY TO ABBREVIATIONS USED IN THIS BOOK

Classification of preservation sites into types:

A   Fully-operational for public traffic, offering train rides with steam motive power.

B   Fully-operational for public traffic or demonstration purposes using internal combustion, electric, cable or horse motive power.

C   Privately-operated railways using any form of motive power.

D   Live steam centres where locomotives are steamed and rides given on special open days.

E   Museums of preserved locomotives and rolling stock or static public exhibits. Non-operational.

F   Preservation sites where stock is gathered for eventual use on a preserved line. Check on public access before visiting.

G   Private premises on which steam locomotives are housed. PLEASE OBTAIN PERMISSION FROM THE OWNER BEFORE VISITING.

H   Groups owning rolling stock used on operating lines.

I   Industrial steam locations. No public access without permission.

## LOCOMOTIVE TYPES

The Whyte notation for wheel arrangement has been used throughout this book to designate steam locomotive types. The same system is also used for electric and internal combustion locomotives with driving wheels coupled by outside rods. Small locomotives with non-coupled wheels are shown as 4W or 6W to indicate four- or six-wheel drive. The following abbreviations are also used to indicate locomotive type:

T    Side tank. Tanks mounted on the frame, usually on each side of the boiler

CT   Crane tank. Side tank locomotive fitted with a crane

PT   Pannier tank. Side tanks slung, pannier fashion, either side of the boiler

ST   Saddle tank. Tank mounted above the boiler

WT   Well tank. Tank mounted between the frames

TG   Geared tank. Locomotive drive transmitted by gears and/or chains

VB   Vertical boiler

F    Fireless thermal storage steam locomotive

DM   Diesel locomotive with mechanical transmission

DE   Diesel locomotive with electric transmission

DH   Diesel locomotive with hydraulic transmission

PM   Petrol locomotive with mechanical transmission

BE   Battery powered electric locomotive

PH   Petrol locomotive with hydraulic transmission

E    Electric locomotive

R    Railcar

# AREA A

## South West

Cornwall
Devon
Somerset
Dorset
Wiltshire
Avon

---

### 1 Dart Valley Railway     A

Buckfastleigh Station, Devon

*Access:* Buckfastleigh Station is just off the A38 trunk road, halfway between Exeter and Plymouth
Tel: Buckfastleigh 2338
OS Ref: SX 747663

Passenger-carrying standard gauge railway, 7 miles in length from Buckfastleigh to Totnes Riverside.
Services operate over Easter week, May Day Holiday week-

Skirting the banks of the River Dart, GWR No. 1450 hurries along with a luncheon party special, with the *Devon Belle* to the fore

---

end then daily from mid-May to mid-September.
Facilities for visitors include free car parking, riverside picnic area complete with miniature railway (see Group No. 50), restaurant, toilets, transport museum and book and souvenir shops.
The Dart Valley Railway is a portion of the old GWR Totnes–Ashburton branch which was closed by BR in 1962. Services were restored between Totnes and Buckfastleigh in May 1969 by Dart Valley Light Railway Ltd who operate the line on GWR principles but as a commercial proposition rather than as a preservation organisation. As such, it is the only standard gauge railway in the country to adopt this method of operation (BR excepted!).
Passengers can enjoy excursions through the heart of South Devon's wonderful countryside behind gleaming Great Western steam locomotives and can join trains at Buckfastleigh and Staverton Bridge stations. The railway operates to a point north-eastwards of Ashburton Junction at Totnes where a new station is under construction. Access at Buckfastleigh is recommended, as there is no car park or public transport at Staverton Bridge and no access whatever to trains at the Totnes end of the line.

**Stock**
[2]GWR 2–6–2T No. 4555 (Class 45XX) built 1924
[3]GWR 0–6–0PT No. 1369 (Class 1366) built 1934
[4]GWR 0–6–0PT No. 1638 (Class 16XX) built 1951
[5]GWR 0–6–0PT No. 6430 (Class 64XX) built 1937
[5]GWR 0–6–0PT No. 6435 (Class 64XX) built 1937
[6]GWR 0–4–2T No. 1420 *Bulliver* (Class 14XX) built 1933
[7]GWR 0–4–2T No. 1450 *Ashburton* (Class 14XX) built 1935
[8]BR 2–6–4T No. 80064 (Riddles Class 4MT) built 1953
LSWR 2–4–0T No. 30587 Beyer Peacock 1412 built 1874
[1]Peckett 0–4–0ST No. 1 2031 built 1942
Peckett 0–4–0ST *Lady Angela* 1690 built 1926
Fowler 0–4–0DM 4210141 built 1958
BR/Drewry 0–6–0DM No. 2 (BR Class 03 No. D2192) built 1961
Hunslet 0–6–0ST *Glendower* 3810 built 1954

Hunslet 0–6–0ST *Maureen* 2890 built 1943
Bagnall 0–6–0ST 2766 built 1944
GWR Auto-trailers Nos 225, 228 & 232 built 1951
GWR Auto-trailer No. 240 built 1954
GWR open 3rd coaches Nos 1285 & 1295 built 1937
[1]GWR Super Saloon No. 9111 'King George' built 1932
GWR Dynamometer Car No. 7 built 1901
GWR Directors Saloon No. 249 built 1894
GWR Engineers Saloon No. 6479 built 1910
Pullman Observation Car No. 280 'Devon Belle' rebuilt 1947
GWR 4-wheel coach body built 1835
GWR 'Toad' 20-ton goods brake van No. 68479 built 1947
[1]GWR 'Toad' 20-ton goods brake van No. 68777 built 1939
SR Goods Van No. S 65495 built 1939
'Shell' tank wagon built 1924
[1]LMS Open Wagon PLA No. C19 built 1944
[1]GWR Fruit van No. 95979
GWR 'Mink B' van No. 125814 built 1939
GWR 'Damo B' van No. 42223 built 1939
GWR Breakdown tool van No. DW146 built 1910
GWR 30-cwt Traffic Department Crane No. 610 built 1893
[1]GWR Banana van No. 5575 built 1929
[1]GWR Shunters truck No. 41873 built 1896
[1]GWR iron 'Mink A' covered van No. 59119 built 1896
GWR 'Mica B' insulated van No. 79740 built 1925
[1]GWR open wagon No. 102776
[1]GWR 'Mink' covered van No. 104700 built 1930
GWR 'Mink' covered van No. 105658
'Renwick Wilton & Dobson' 10-ton coal wagon
[1]LMS Box van built 1923
GWR 'Fruit D' van No. W92091
[1]GWR 4-wheel Mess Van No. 215 built 1900
Ten Wickham petrol rail trolleys
*Note:* Rolling stock may be interchanged between the Totnes–Buckfastleigh and Paignton–Kingswear sections from time to time as traffic demands.

[1]Property of Dart Valley Railway Association.
[2]Withdrawn from Lairashed, Plymouth in December 1963 and purchased privately for preservation.
[3]Withdrawn from Wadebridge shed in November 1964. A modified version of the 1361 class, six locomotives (1366–71) were built to replace old Cornwall Minerals Railway saddletanks. The class was divided between Swindon and Weymouth depots for much of its existence, those at Weymouth often being used to haul the boat trains through the street to the quay. In 1962, the three survivors, Nos 1367–9, were sent to Wadebridge to work on the Wenford Bridge branch, for so long the preserve of the LSWR 2–4–0TS. No. 1369 worked the last steam-hauled train over the branch and thus became the last steam engine to work on BR in Cornwall.
[4]Withdrawn from Croes Newydd (Wrexham) in August 1966 as BR No. 1638. Although pure GWR in design, the first of the class did not appear until 1949. Many lines being too restricted to allow for workings by the standard 57XX class, something lighter was required and the result was the 16XX class. It was the last class of pannier tank to be designed and built at Swindon.
[5]Withdrawn from Yeovil shed in October 1964 and purchased for preservation.

[6]Withdrawn from Gloucester shed in November 1964 and purchased for the DVR.
[7]Withdrawn from Exmouth Junction shed in May 1965 and purchased for the DVR.
[8]Owned by the 80064 Locomotive Group.

**Dart Valley Railway Association**      **H**
*Headquarters:* GWR Super Saloon No. 9111 'King George', Buckfastleigh Station, Dart Valley Railway, Devon
*Details from:* D. Hine, 89 Queensholm Crescent, Down End, Bristol
*Membership:* 2,000

The DVRA is the only Supporters' Society that offers the choice of helping with two separate railways – the original Totnes–Buckfastleigh line and the Paignton–Kingswear section. Membership privileges include unlimited free travel (except on specified peak trains) between Buckfastleigh and Totnes and up to six journeys per year on the Torbay line.

## 2   Torbay and Dartmouth Railway     A

Paignton Park Station, Paignton, Devon

*Access:* Torbay and Dartmouth line station is next door to BR Paignton station and the bus station. From South Hams area, make for Dartmouth, then take the ferry to Kingswear station. By public transport: rail from Exeter or beyond, Newton Abbot and Torquay to Paignton BR. There are frequent local buses to Paignton from the Torbay area itself.
Tel: Paignton 55872
OS Ref: SX 889606

The seven-mile former GWR Paignton–Kingswear line was purchased when it was closed by British Rail in October 1972. From mid-April until October a full daily steam service is operated. The Torbay line runs through some spectacular scenery offering panoramic views of Torbay and the Dart Estuary, high viaducts and a 492-yard tunnel. Gradients up to 1 in 60 prevail in both directions. DVRA members are able to assist in running the railway in the same way as at Buckfastleigh.
Both lines are run as far as possible with Great Western traditions in mind, with GWR type locomotives. Although some fine specimens of Great Western coaches have been acquired, most of the service trains are formed of former BR Mk 1 coaches, particularly on the Torbay line where summer crowds require the use of high-capacity trains. All trains are normally steam-operated.

**Stock**
[1,2]GWR 4–6–0 No. 7827 *Lydham Manor* built 1950
GWR 2–6–2T No. 4588 (Class 4575) built 1927
GWR 2–8–0T No. 5239 *Goliath* (Class 52XX) built 1924
[3]GWR 4–6–0 No. 4920 *Dumbleton Hall* built 1929
Hudswell Clarke 0–6–0DM *Enterprise* D810 built 1953
GWR Super Saloon No. 9116 *Duchess of York* built 1932
GWR Engineers Saloon No. 9035 built 1896
GWR Auto-Trailer No. 238 built 1954
GWR Hawksworth BCK coach No. 7377 built 1948
LNER Gresley Buffet Car No. 9129 built 1937
BR Standard Mk1 2nd class open coaches Nos 4046, 4166, 4256, 4275, 4288, 4289, 4317 & 4507 built 1954–57

Photo: Tim Stephens

'Twixt country and sea. With the rolling Devon hills as a backdrop, GWR Prairie tank No. 4588 crosses Maypool viaduct with an afternoon train from Paignton to Kingswear

---

BR Prototype 1st class open coaches Nos 3081 & 3084 built 1957, later rebuilt 1972 as Disco/Dancing car
GWR Steam Crane No. 2 built Ransomes & Rapier 1908
GWR Match truck No. ADW150434
Three BR non-gangwayed 2nd class coaches
Two Wickham petrol rail trolleys

[1]Property of Dart Valley Railway Assocation.
[2]Withdrawn in 1965 and sold to Woodham Bros., Barry, for scrap. Purchased by the DVRA and moved to Buckfastleigh in June 1970. Fully restored to working order and transferred to the Torbay line.
[3]Owned by the Dumbleton Hall Preservation Society. Withdrawn from Bristol Barrow Road in 1965. Sold to Woodham Bros., Barry, for scrap and purchased for preservation in 1973. Moved to Buckfastleigh by road in 1976 and is now undergoing a thorough overhaul which is expected to take several years. When complete, it will enter service on the Torbay and Dartmouth line.

## Dumbleton Hall Preservation Society     H
*Headquarters:* Buckfastleigh Station, Dart Valley Railway, Devon
*Details from:* R. Elliott, 25 Queens Road, St Thomas, Exeter

Restoring and rebuilding former GWR 'Hall' class 4-6-0 No. 4920 *Dumbleton Hall* at Buckfastleigh for eventual use on the Torbay and Dartmouth line.

## 3   East Somerset Railway     A

East Somerset Railway Co. Ltd., Cranmore Station, Shepton Mallet, Somerset

*Access:* Cranmore is 3 miles east of Shepton Mallet on A361 Frome Road. Bus: 'Crown Tours' Shepton-Frome service
Tel: Cranmore 417
OS Ref: ST 664429

Standard gauge railway preservation centre. The first 1¼ miles of track from Cranmore westwards to Merryfield Lane, Doulting has been purchased by the ESR and an application made for a Light Railway Order so that a public service can be run. The Depot is open daily except Christmas Day. Steaming on Sundays and Bank Holidays, mid-March to the end of October. Opening hours 9 am-6 pm April-October and 9 am-4 pm November-March.
Facilities for visitors include car parking, refreshments, souvenir shop, museum, toilets, picnic area and art gallery in the station signal box.
The development of the East Somerset Railway project has been motivated by railway and wildlife artist David Shepherd. Originally part of the broad gauge East Somerset Railway from Witham to Shepton Mallet, Cranmore station was closed to passenger traffic in 1963, but goods traffic remained, enabling the fledgling project to get established there. In addition to the renovation of the station buildings, a brand new two-road engine shed to authentic Victorian design was built. Since 1973, the collection of locomotives has been steadily growing in number, and Cranmore 'works' is gaining a fine reputation for the engineering standards it sets in restoring them to working order. The inauguration of passenger services on the railway, which is now imminent, is awaited with a keen sense of anticipation.

### Stock
[2]BR 2-10-0 No. 92203 *Black Prince* (Riddles Class 9F) built 1959
[3]BR 4-6-0 No. 75029 *The Green Knight* (Riddles Class 4MT) built 1954
[4]SR 4-4-0 No. 928 *Stowe* (Maunsell Class V) built 1934
[1]LMS 0-6-0T No. 47493 (Class 3F) Vulcan Foundry 4195 built 1927
[1]RSH 0-6-0ST No. 68005 (Class J94) 7169 built 1944
[1]Barclay 0-4-0ST *Lord Fisher* 1398 built 1915
[1]Barclay 0-4-0ST *Glenfield* 1719 built 1920
[1]Dubs 0-4-0CT 4101 built 1901
[5,][1]LBSCR 0-6-0T No. 32110 Class E1 built 1877
BR BSO Bogie coach No. 9241 built 1955
BR brake/2nd coach No. 43231 built 1957
BR brake/2nd coach No. 43289 built 1955

Photo: Rex Coffin

BR 2nd class experimental all-fibreglass coach No. 1000 built 1962

BR (LNER design) 2nd class sleeping car No. 1767 built 1951

LMS 1st class saloon coach No. 3322 built 1929 rebuilt 1973

WD 20 ton goods brake van No. 49028 built 1959

LSWR Road van No. 12424 built 1900

[1]LSWR box van No. 9128

[1]LSWR flat wagon No. 6095

[1]LNWR 20 ton goods brake van No. 49026

SR PMV 4-wheeled utility vans Nos 1137 & 1396

MR tank wagon No. 82620 built 1916

LMS Box van No. 47760

LSWR Box van No. 47754

Esso fuel tank wagon No. 1800 built 1939

LMS 7-plank open wagons Nos 72403, 72426, 73039, 73178 & 73226

[1]MR March truck No. 82620

[1]Owned by Lord Fisher Locomotive Group.

[2]Withdrawn from Birkenhead shed in December 1967 and purchased for preservation by David Shepherd. No. 92203 worked the last steam-hauled John Summers Bilston-Shotwick iron ore train on 6 December 1967. Stored at Longmoor, Liss and Eastleigh before being moved to Cranmore in 1973.

[3]Withdrawn from Stoke-on-Trent shed in August 1967 and purchased for preservation by David Shepherd. Subsequently repainted in BR green livery and named. Stored at Longmoor,

One of the driving forces behind David Shepherd's East Somerset Railway is the enthusiasm of the Lord Fisher Locomotive Group. And speaking of driving forces, here's *Lord Fisher* himself piloting the freshly restored LMS *Jinty* No. 47493

Liss and Eastleigh before being moved to Cranmore in 1973.

[4]Withdrawn from Brighton shed in November 1962 as BR No. 30928. Purchased by Lord Montagu for static display at the head of three Pullman cars in the grounds of Beaulieu (the Montagu Motor Museum). In 1973 the locomotive was transferred to Eastleigh works for restoration in SR green livery and subsequently moved to Cranmore. It is now jointly owned by David Shepherd and Lord Montagu.

[5]Built at Brighton Works in 1877 as No. 110 *Burgundy*. Sold in 1927 to Cannock & Rugeley Colliery Company and became No. 9 *Cannock Wood*.

Withdrawn in 1963 and purchased for preservation by the RPS (Chasewater Light Railway). Purchased by Barry Buckfield, Dean Knights and Dick Bellchambers and arrived at Cranmore on 11 September 1978.

## East Somerset Railway Co.

*Details from:* General Manager, Cranmore Station, Shepton Mallet, Somerset

*Membership:* Male Adults £1.50 p.a., Ladies and Juniors 75p

*Number of members:* 850

**Lord Fisher Locomotive Group**

The Group supports the East Somerset Railway in all its activities

*Details from:* B. G. Buckfield, Newtown Gardens, Park Road, Paulton, Bristol BS18 5NF

*Progress 1979:* The Jinty and Austerity are in service after general overhaul, the Crane Tank continues to give good service with works trains and in lifting operations. 'Lord Fisher' and 'Glenfield' are undergoing general overhauls in Cranmore Works and 32110 is stored pending overhaul. Now that access to the line has been obtained at Merryfield Lane, there is plenty of work for the Group members, their locomotives and wagons.

## 4  West Somerset Railway                    A

Minehead Station, Minehead, Somerset

*Access:* By road, off the main A39 near the seafront
Tel: Minehead 4996
OS Ref: SS 984464

Passenger carrying standard gauge railway, 20 miles in length, operating from Minehead to Bishops Lydeard. Diesel multiple-unit trains operate all the year round (except Sundays), whilst steam trains run daily in the summer season. Facilities for visitors include car parking, souvenir and book shops, refreshments and toilets.

The original West Somerset Railway opened as a Broad Gauge branch line from Taunton to Watchet in 1862. It was extended to Minehead in 1874 by a separate Company (The Minehead Railway), and both parts of the line were worked by the Bristol and Exeter Railway until all were absorbed into the Great Western. The whole branch was converted to standard gauge in 1882, ten years before the last Great Western broad gauge train of all. The Minehead branch had an uneventful history thereafter, until final closure by British Railways in 1971.

Shortly after closure, a new West Somerset Railway Company appeared on the scene with the object of purchasing and re-opening the line. Protracted negotiations, which also involved Somerset County Council, took place, followed by

**Presenting the Pannier tank that found fame and fortune on the West Somerset as *The Flockton Flyer*. No. 6412 raises steam at Minehead**

Photo: Paul Barber

the application for a Light Railway Order and bringing the line back up to a standard ready for passenger trains. The official re-opening ceremony took place at Minehead on 28 March 1976 and inaugurated the initial service to Blue Anchor (3½ miles).

In successive seasons, services have been extended further and further along the line, until trains now run through to Bishops Lydeard, making the West Somerset Railway the longest privately owned passenger railway in the British Isles. Williton Station (9¾ miles from Minehead) marks the limit of operation for steam hauled summer tourist trains, but the year round dmu service runs the remaining ten miles to Bishops Lydeard. Problems still surround the re-entry of West Somerset trains into Taunton BR station, but in the meantime the section of line down to the junction at Norton Fitzwarren will be brought up to a standard where it can be used by through excursions by BR trains.

## Stock

GWR 2-6-2T No. 4561 (class 45XX) built 1924
GWR 2-6-2T No. 5521 (class 4575) built 1927
GWR 2-6-2T No. 5542 (class 4575) built 1928
[1]GWR 0-6-0PT No. 6412 (class 64XX) built 1934
[2]LBSCR 0-6-0T No. 78 Knowle (A1X Class) built 1880
[3]Bagnall 0-6-0ST Vulcan (2994) built 1950
[3]Bagnall 0-6-0ST Victor (2996) built 1951
[4, 8]S & DJR 2-8-0 No. 53808 S & D No. 88 (Stephenson 3894) built 1925
[5, 8]Hawthorn Leslie 0-6-0ST Isabel (3437) built 1919
[8]Avonside 0-6-0ST No. S3 Portbury (1764) built 1917
[6, 8]Peckett 0-4-0ST Kilmersdon (1788) built 1929
Peckett 0-4-0ST No. 1163 'Whitehead' 1163 built 1908
[8]Bagnall 0-4-0F No. 12473 built 1932
[8]Ruston Hornsby 4WDM No. 24 (Class 80/88HP) (210479) built 1941
[7]BR Bo-Bo DH No. D7017 (Hymek Class) built 1962
BR/Park Royal dmu power cars Nos W50413 and W50414 built 1958
BR/Park Royal dmu trailer cars Nos W50168 and W50169 built 1958
Six BR Mk 1 bogie coaches built 1951-59
Two BR Mk I Suburban compartment coaches
Three GWR 'Toplight' ex-camping coaches
Esso four-wheeled oil tank wagons Nos 1326 (built 1918) and 1822 (built 1939)
[8]Mess & Tool Van (ex-GWR Composite)
[8]LMS 6-wheeled Brake Parcels Van No. M32994 built 1938
[8]BR (WR) 'Fruit D' van
[8]GWR 'Fruit D' van No. W3450W built 1955
[8]GWR Gunpowder van
[8]BR (SR) Standard van
[8]Two 10-ton open wagons
[8]GNR brake/first coach No. 3178 built 1910
[8]LSWR brake/third bogie coach No. S3204 built 1926
[8]LMS CCT van No. ADM396003 built 1938
[8]SR box van No. 48949
[8]LNER 20-ton goods brake van built 1952
[8]MR eight-ton open wagons Nos. 112 and 1402 (ex-PBA)
[8]LTSR tank wagon (Shell Mex/BP) No. 401 built 1902
[8]GNR six-wheeled goods brake van built c.1880

Photo: Diesel and Electric Group

Neat enough to be mistaken for a 00 gauge model, but Hymek No. D7017 is real enough to be put to good use on the West Somerset Railway. Nice paint job, lads!

[8]NCB six-plank 12-ton open wagon No. 72395 (registered in 1936 as LMS 137495)
[8]NCB five-plank 12-ton open wagon No. 72399 (LMS 239195)
[8]NCB seven-plank 13-ton open wagon No. 72401 (registered as LMS 138934, possibly owned by James More)
[8]NCB seven-plank 13-ton open wagon No. 72402 (LMS 607324)
[8]NCB seven-plank 13-ton open wagon No. 73031
[8]NCB seven-plank 13-ton open wagon No. 73152
[8]NCB eight-plank 13-ton open wagon No. 79515 (built Cambrian Wagon Works, Cardiff)
[8]Stothert and Pitt steam crane (10-ton capacity) No. 312
[8]Wickham 4WPMR Nos 6168 and 6967 (built 1932)

[1]Withdrawn from Gloucester shed in November 1964 as BR No. 6412 and purchased for preservation. Used on the Dart Valley Railway until 1972 then transferred to the Torbay Steam Railway, from whom it was bought in 1976.
[2]Originally LBSCR No. 78 Knowle. Sent to Isle of Wight as SR No. W4 Bembridge in 1929 and returned to the mainland in 1937 as SR No. 2678. Withdrawn in 1963 and restored to LBSCR livery at Eastleigh Works. Put on display 1964.
[3]Ex-British Leyland Motor Corporation, Austin-Morris Division, Longbridge, Birmingham, 1973.
[4]Built 1925 by Stephensons as S & DJR No. 88. Renumbered twice by the LMS, firstly as 9678 in 1930 and then as 13808 in 1932. After nationalisation in 1948 it became BR No. 53808. Reboilered in 1953; withdrawn from service in March 1964; saved from Barry scrapyard and moved back to Radstock in 1970.
[5]Built 1919, this locomotive worked at Blackley Dyestuffs factory near Manchester for 50 years. Purchased in 1969 by the Keighley and Worth Valley Railway but was unsuitable for the heavy trains there. Bought by three members of the Trust and arrived at Radstock in 1971. First steamed over the Spring Bank Holiday 1972 and has been in regular use since.

[6]Built 1929, this locomotive worked at the nearby Kilmersdon Colliery hauling coal from the pithead to a gravity-operated incline connecting with the GWR Frome to Bristol line. Made redundant when the colliery closed in October 1973. It is now on permanent loan from the NCB.

[7]The Hymeks were the most numerous of the Western Region hydraulics and were used on both main-line passenger and freight services. They were soundly engineered and soon became popular with management and operating crews alike. Their light weight and rugged reliability also helped in the success of the preservation appeal, it being the first successful appeal in this country for a main-line diesel locomotive. The locomotive was purchased, in working order, in April 1975 and was moved from Old Oak Common to Taunton on 30 July. Locomotive owned and maintained by the Diesel and Electric Group (q.v.).

[8]Rolling stock owned and maintained by the Somerset and Dorset Museum Trust (q.v.).

## Somerset and Dorset Museum Trust                          H
Rolling stock in store on the West Somerset Railway, Washford Station, Somerset
*Access:* By West Somerset Railway train to Washford.

The Trust is a rolling-stock owning group with its own base on the WSR at Washford. It actively supports the WSR in all its activities. The Trust's headquarters are open to the public at weekends and Bank Holidays. Short steam rides are available from time to time – see local press for details.
*Details from:* M. J. Palmer, The Haven, Chandlers Lane, Edington, Bridgwater, Somerset.

## Diesel and Electric Group                                 H
Minehead Station, West Somerset Railway

*Details from:* John M. Crane, 7 Robert Close, Potters Bar, Herts EN6 2DH
Tel: 0707 43568

The Diesel and Electric Group was formed with two main aims: the preservation of interesting items of diesel or electric motive power and the fostering of interest in modern railway practice.
The Group owns two BR Class 35 'Hymek' Diesel hydraulic locomotives. D7017 is based on the West Somerset Railway and D7018 is at Didcot Railway Centre (see Group No. 456). Plans are also in hand to preserve BR Class 14 locomotive No. D9526, at present owned by Blue Circle Cement.
The second aim of the Group is met by the magazine *Inter-City Express*, which is published every other month.

## 5   Lappa Valley Railway                                  A

St Newlyn East, Newquay, Cornwall

*Access:* Via the A3075 road, 5 miles from Newquay
Tel: Mitchell 317
OS Ref: SW 839564

Passenger-carrying 15 in. gauge light railway, 1 mile in length. Daily operation from Easter to October.
Facilities for visitors include car parking, shop, refreshments, toilets, picnic area, boating and a nature trail.

The railway is laid along the trackbed of the former GWR Newquay–Chacewater line, commencing from Benny Mill, about 1 mile north of St Newlyn East, and running to East Wheal Rose Mine. The line was opened on 16 June 1974 and it is hoped to extend it at both ends at some future date. At East Wheal Rose there is a characteristic ruined engine house and chimney. Trains negotiate a turning circle at the mine, whilst the locomotive is turned on a 10 ft turntable at Benny Mill so that it always works chimney-first.

### Stock
Curwen/Berwyn 0-6-0 *Muffin* built 1967
Curwen/Severn-Lamb 0-6-2T *Zebedee* built 1974
Minirail Bo-BoE *Lappa Lady* plus diesel generator trailer built 1965
Lister 4WDM *Pooh* 20698 built 1942
Booth/Villiers 4W-4PM powered service vehicle
Five semi-open bogie coaches (built Jays Gates 1974)

## 6   Bird Paradise                                         A

Hayle, Cornwall
OS Ref: SW 555365

Passenger-carrying 15 in. gauge railway, 240 yards in length in the form of a continuous circuit.
Operates daily throughout the summer season.
Trains start from, and return to, Cockatoo Halt – a ride comprising two circuits of the track.

### Stock
Heiden 0-4-0WTT *Chough* built 1968
Barlow 4-6-2DE *Princess Anne* built 1962
Lister 4WDM *Zebedee* 101080 built 1938
Two articulated bogie coaches

## 7   Bicton Woodland Railway                               A

Bicton Gardens, East Budleigh, Budleigh Salterton, Devon

*Access:* On A376 Newton Poppleford-Budleigh Salterton Road, slightly north of St Mary's Church. Nearest BR station Exmouth, thence by No. 40 bus on Exmouth–Sidmouth route
Tel: Budleigh Salterton 2820
OS Ref: SY 074862

Passenger-carrying 1 ft 6 in. gauge line 1¼ miles in length. Facilities for visitors include car parking, souvenir shop, refreshments, Countryside Museum and Hall of Transport displaying vintage cars and motorcycles.

The railway was opened in 1963 and a 537-yard branch to the Hermitage added in 1976. Although a product of the steam preservation age, the Bicton Woodland Railway has much period charm and slips well into its lush surroundings. Bicton Gardens themselves were laid out in 1735 to the designs of André le Nôtre, who was landscape gardener at the Palace of Versailles. Much of the railway's equipment hails from the 18 in. gauge system at the Woolwich Arsenal and is of First World War vintage; whilst a finishing touch is added by the former LSWR lower-quadrant signals, shortened to dwarf stature to fit the scale of their new surroundings.

**Stock**
Avonside 0-4-0T No. 1 *Woolwich* 1748 built 1916
Ruston Hornsby 4WDM No. 2 *Bicton* (20DL class) 213839 built 1942
Hunslet 0-4-4-0D No. 3 *Carnegie* 4524 built 1954
Ruston Hornsby 4WDM No. 4 *Budley* (20DL class) 235624 built 1945
Four open bogie coaches
Five covered bogie coaches
4-wheeled passenger brake van
Woolwich Arsenal Rly bogie wagon built 1914

## 8   Longleat Railway                                A

Longleat Park, near Warminster, Wiltshire BA12 7NW

*Access:* Just off A362 between Frome and Warminster. British Rail stations at both places, then buses 253 or 254. Longleat is permanently signposted on all major surrounding roads
Tel: Maiden Bradley 579
OS Ref: ST 808432

Passenger-carrying 15 in. gauge railway 1¼ miles in length. The railway operates from Easter to the end of October. The railway shop remains open until Christmas.
Other facilities for visitors include car parking, refreshments, toilets, picnic area, amusements and, of course, the famous lions of Longleat and its stately home.
The railway was opened in 1967 and came under the control of Lord Weymouth, the son of the Marquis of Bath, the present owner of Longleat, in 1975. The track was then extended from the original ½-mile run through a cutting, out on to a high embankment, curving back to run through wooded parkland, beside a waterfall, to return to the main station.

**Stock**
Severn-Lamb Bo-BoDHR No. 1 *Lenka* 7322 built 1973
Severn-Lamb 2-8-0PH No. 2 *Ceawlin* R7 built 1975 (steam outline)
Curwen/Severn-Lamb 0-6-2T No. 3 *Dougal* built 1970
Four enclosed 16-seat bogie coaches built by Severn-Lamb 1975
Four enclosed 16-seat bogie coaches built at Longleat 1977-79
3-ton bogie wagon
4-wheel ballast hopper wagon

## 9   Bristol Suburban Railway                        A

Bitton Station, Bristol, Avon

*Access:* Bitton Station is on the A431 near Willsbridge
OS Ref: ST 670705

Bristol Suburban Railway steams back to life with a brilliant display by Avonside 0-6-0ST *Edwin Hulse*

Standard gauge railway preservation centre, featuring steam-hauled train rides on open days.
Facilities for visitors include car parking, museum of railway relics and souvenir shop.
The Bristol Suburban Railway Society has relaid all the track within station limits at Bitton on the former Midland Railway Bristol-Bath line and also leases a mile or two of trackbed to the north.

**Stock**
[1]LMS 4-6-0 No. 45379 (Stanier Class 5MT) Armstrong Whitworth 1434 built 1937
[2]Avonside 0-6-0ST No. 2 *Edwin Hulse* 1798 built 1918
Peckett 0-6-0ST *Fonmon* 1936 built 1924
[3]Fox Walker 0-6-0ST No. 3242 built 1874
[4]Ruston Hornsby 4 WDM Class 48DS 235519 built 1945
LMS goods brake van No. 294176 built 1928
BR Mk1 CK bogie coach 15447 built 1953
LMS 12-ton covered vans Nos 26 & 29
MR open wagon

GWR 'Toad' 20-ton goods brake van No. DW 17391 built
c 1940
[3]GWR open wagons Nos 10931 and 86582 built 1912

[1]Withdrawn from service in July 1965 and sold to Woodham
Brothers, Barry, for scrap. Purchased for preservation 1974
and undergoing restoration by the Bristol Black 5 Society.
[2]Ex-Imperial Smelting Corporation Ltd, Avonmouth 1971.
[3]Owned by Bristol Industrial Museum (Group No. 21).
[4]Ex-Keynsham Paper Mills Ltd, Bristol (at one time BR
No. DS1169).

Society details from: R. J. Marsh, 14 Dial Lane, Downend,
Bristol BS16 5UH.

## 10 Crowlas Woodland Railway        A

'Age of Steam', Rospeath Lane, Crowlas, near Penzance,
Cornwall TR20 8DU

*Access:* By road and rail to Penzance or St Erth, thence
various buses
Tel: Cockwells 631 (STD 0736 74)

Passenger-carrying 10¼ in. gauge railway over 1 mile in
length.
The railway operates from Easter to October inclusive. First
trains run at 10.30 am.
Facilities for visitors include car parking, picnic areas, refreshments, model railways and model displays, children's paddleboats, croquet lawn, gift shop, picture gallery and toilets.
Excellent toilets are also provided for disabled visitors who in
any event are always admitted free.
'Age of Steam' is a comprehensive project which sets out
to echo the qualities of pleasure and elegance, leisure and
learning that were the hallmarks of the historic and great
age of steam. Within its rural surroundings, visitors can not
only ride behind live steam locomotives, but can also study
five models, see working model railways, view rare prints
and paintings, and even drive their own model trains and
model steam paddleboats. The Crowlas Woodland Railway
was opened in the spring of 1977 and makes little pretence
at hiding its similarity in livery and initials to the famous
Great Western Railway. The C.W.R.'s special claim to fame
is that it is both the first and last steam railway in England
– being only some 12 miles from Land's End!

### Stock
Curwen 4WDM No. 1 *Kingsley* built 1954
Guest Bo-BoPM No. 2 *Sir Humphry Davy*
Minimum Gauge Railways 0-6-2T No. 3 *Trevithick* built
1975
Curwen 2-6-0 No. 4 *Isambard Kingdom Brunel* built 1977
Six saloon bogie coaches built 1976–77

## 11 Forest Railroad Park        A

Dobwalls, Liskeard, Cornwall

*Access:* Nearest BR station, Liskeard
OS Ref: SX 216650
*Operator:* John Southern

Passenger-carrying 7¼ in. gauge railway, 1 mile in length
featuring intensive steam operation.

A trainload of cheerful visitors enjoys the 1¼ mile run
on the 'Age of Steam's' light railway at Crowlas, near
Penzance. This delightful little line is steam-hauled by
two engines named *Trevithick* and (seen here) *Isambard
Kingdom Brunel*

Photo: 'Age of Steam'

The railway operates at Easter, then Wednesdays and Sundays to Spring Bank Holiday, then daily until October.
Facilities for visitors include car parking, picnic area, cafe, forest walk, children's playground, waiting room and toilets. This is the most arduous and spectacular 7¼ in gauge railway in the country. It has severe gradients, high embankments, deep cuttings and three tunnels ranging from 60 to 85 ft in length. The track layout is in the form of three continuous, intertwined ovals and up to four trains can use the circuit at once. Operation is protected by automatic, four-aspect colour-light signalling installed by BR signal engineers and follows North American practice. In concept and in fact, the Forest Railroad is a spectacular railway entertainment for its visitors – plenty of moving trains to watch and ride, complete with all the atmosphere conjured up by steam, hot oil and chime whistles. But don't just take our word for it; go and see John Southern's achievements for yourselves. As if all these distinctions weren't enough, the Forest Railroad's principal claim to fame lies in the most massive of its steam locomotives – the Union Pacific *Big Boy* No. 4008. This is, quite simply, the largest and most powerful 7¼ in gauge steam locomotive anywhere in the world.

**Stock**
Union Pacific 4-8-8-4 No. 4008 *William Jeffers* built Severn-Lamb 1978
Union Pacific 4-8-4 No. 818 *Queen of Wyoming* built Curwen/Severn Lamb 1974
Rio Grande 2-8-2 No. 488 *General Palmer* K36 class built Curwen 1971
Rio Grande 2-8-2 No. 498 *Otto Mears* K36 class built Curwen 1979
Hudswell Clarke 2-6-0 No. 7 *David Curwen* built Curwen 1972
Union Pacific Do-DoDH 'Centennial' class built Curwen 1979
Rio Grande Bo-BoPM No. 108 built Curwen 1971
32 Cromar White 'sit-astride' bogie coaches

## 12　Beer Heights Light Railway　A

Peco Ltd, Underleys, Beer, near Seaton, Devon

OS Ref: SY 230892

Passenger-carrying 7¼ in. gauge line, half mile in length.
Operates on weekdays and Saturday mornings during the summer season.
Facilities for visitors include car parking, picnic area and Peco Model-land.
The Beer Heights Light Railway was opened on 14 July 1975 and is the principal attraction at the Peco Modelrama which is a permanent exhibition of model railways by the Pritchard Patent Product Co. Ltd. The line starts near the factory at Much Natter station and winds through a deep cutting to Upsan Down, where the loco shed is situated. Trains are then propelled round a curve and into the open countryside, offering passengers scenic views across the bay. A large expansion of the railway is planned, to incorporate two-train operation.

**Stock**
Curwen 0-4-2TT *Dickie* built 1979
Hunslet 0-4-0STT *Thomas Jnr* built Richards Eng. 1975
Cromar White 4WBE No. E7039 *Little Nell* built 1975
Five 4-seat open bogie coaches built 1975-77
One 'sit-astride' bogie coach
Two open wagons

*Standard gauge static exhibit:*
BR Pullman car 'Orion' built 1950

## 13　Oakhill Manor Miniature Railway　A

'The World of Models', Oakhill Manor Museum, Oakhill, near Bath, Somerset BA3 5AW

*Access:* Off A37 road, 4 miles north of Shepton Mallet. Turn at The Mendip Inn
Tel: Oakhill 840210
OS Ref: ST 641474

Passenger-carrying 10¼ in. gauge railway 1 mile in length. Operates daily from 12 noon to 6 pm Easter to 31 October. Facilities for visitors include car parking, refreshments, toilets, souvenir shop, picnic area and railway walk, historic country house featuring displays of fine models, N gauge model railway and gardens.'
The home of Mr and Mrs Walter Harper, Oakhill Manor is a pleasing example of England's smaller country estates of about 45 acres. In this beautiful environment, high in the Mendip Hills, has been created an unusual and fascinating project incorporating a superb collection of models and pictures relating to transport, a furnished mansion house set in landscaped gardens and a very fine miniature railway. The railway itself is an outstanding feature with close-to-scale track, locomotives and rolling stock and pretty stations in Mendip stone. It has an air of authenticity reminiscent of a cross-country main line in the days of steam.

**Stock**
SR 4-6-0 No. 772 *Sir Percivale* N15 class built 1979
LMS 4-6-0 No. 6100 *Royal Scot* built Bassett-Lowke 1938
Hunslet 0-4-0STT *Nelly* built Richards Engineering 1977
Cromar White Bo-BoBE No. E7045
Five SR-styled saloon bogie coaches including one full brake
NER brick and sulphate bogie wagons
Four articulated open bogie coaches

## 14　New Cornish Riviera Lido　A

Carlyon Bay, Par, Cornwall

Passenger-carrying 10¼ in. gauge line 1,000 ft in length operated by Mr Lovett.

**Stock**
LMS 4-4-2 No. 1 built 1949
Dove Bo-BoPM *Texas Ranger*
Hunt Bo-BoP No. 50 A451
Cromar White bogie coaches

## 15 Little Western Railway          A

Trenance Park, Newquay, Cornwall

Passenger-carrying 7¼ in. gauge line in the form of a 300-yard circuit.

**Stock**
LMS 4–6–0 No. 6100 *Royal Scot* built Maldon SME
Freelance 0–4–0T *Midge*-type
Cromar White Bo-BoP built *c* 1969
Open bogie coaches

## 16 Seaton and District Electric Tramway B

Seaton, Devon

*Access:* Axminster BR Station, thence by bus
OS Ref: SY 247901

Passenger-carrying 2 ft 9 in. gauge electric tramway operating along the trackbed of the former LSWR Seaton branch.
Half-hourly service of trams at peak periods from Seaton to Colyton throughout the holiday season.
This 2½-mile line was opened on 28 August 1970 using trams from the former Modern Electric Tramways line at the Crumbles, Eastbourne.

*General Manager:* A. J. V. Gardner.

**Stock**
Seven bogie tramcars, four being double-deck, open top types
Ruston Hornsby 4WDM (48DL class) 435398 built 1959
Mobile tram shop car No. 01
Engineering car No. 02
Two ex-Bournemouth single-deck trams

## 17 Dodington Park Light Railway          B

Dodington House, Park and Carriage Museum, near Chipping Sodbury, Bristol, Avon BS17 6SF

*Access:* Main gate is 200 yards north of Junction 18, M4 on the A46 Bath-Stroud road
Tel: Chipping Sodbury (0454) 318899
OS Ref: ST 750799

Passenger-carrying 2 ft gauge line, 1,065 yards in length. The railway operates daily from 1 April to the end of September between 11 am and 5 pm.
Facilities for visitors include the classically designed Dodington House containing much of its original furnishing together with paintings by Rembrandt, Titian and others; the Carriage Museum with its live exhibition of over 30 coaches; carriage rides; refreshments, model aviation collection, 700 acres of parkland landscaped by Capability Brown, gift shops, car parking, toilets and children's Adventureland.
The railway runs in a woodland setting through the 4-acre Adventureland part of the grounds, passing through a Red Indian village!

**Stock**
Hunslet 4WDM *Dodington Dragon* 4395 built 1952
Hunslet 4WDM 4394 built 1952
4-wheel open coaches

## 18 Morwellham Open Air Museum          B

Dartington Amenity Trust, Morwellham Quay, near Tavistock, Devon

Passenger-carrying 2 ft gauge railway, nearly ½-mile in length.
Operates daily throughout the year, except Christmas Day, from 10 am to 6 pm or during November–March from 10 am to dusk.
Trains run at 15-minute intervals or as required.
Facilities for visitors include car parking and subterranean floodlit display of mine interior.
The railway was brought into operation in August 1978 to give visitors to the Mining Museum the chance to ride into the old George and Charlotte copper mine, closed for over 100 years. Trains start from the Old Quay, running through the woods for over ¼ mile along a ledge cut in the hillside above the River Tamar and into the mine for a further 150 yards. At the end of the journey into the adit, the working face of the mine is floodlit to show working conditions and mining equipment of 100 years ago.

**Stock**
Wingrove & Rogers 4WBE No. 6298 W227 class built 1960
Wingrove & Rogers 4WBE No. G7124 W227 class built 1967
Wingrove & Rogers 4WBE No. H7197 W227 class built 1968
Six passenger coaches

## 19 Somerset Railway Museum          E

Bleadon and Uphill Station, near Weston-super-Mare, Avon

*Access:* Situated on the main A370 Highbridge road approximately three miles from Weston-super-Mare
OS Ref: ST 325578

Static display of steam locomotives and railway equipment. In the station building there is a display of relics, including locomotive chimneys, signalling equipment, signs, etc. Open on Saturday afternoons only, between 2 pm and 6 pm, June to October.
*Details from:* B. K. Kinsey, 15 Brookland Road, Weston-super-Mare, Avon.

**Stock**
[1]Cardiff Rly. 0–4–0ST No. 5 (Preserved as GWR 1338) Kitson 3799 built 1898
[2]Hunslet 0–4–0T 1684 built 1931
[3]Sentinel 4WVBTG No. 1 9374 built 1947
[4]Hibberd 4WDM 3057 built 1946
BR 4WDM Railbus No. W 79976 built by AC Cars Ltd 1958

[1]Withdrawn from Swansea East Dock shed as BR No. 1338 in 1963. This locomotive spent most of its working life

shunting in the Docks owned by the GWR and its constituents, having served at Cardiff, Bridgwater and Swansea. It was the last of the pre-grouping GWR engines in BR service and the ultimate surviving GWR 0-4-0ST. Owned by the 1338 Preservation Fund.
[2]Ex NCB Kilmersdon colliery, Somerset. Owned by the 1338 Preservation Fund.
[3]Ex Roads Reconstruction (Quarries) Ltd, Frome, Somerset.
[4]Ex Plymouth Tar Distillery.

Details of the 1338 Preservation Fund may be obtained from: John B. True, 119 The Avenue, Kennington, Oxford OX1 5QZ.

## 20   Great Western Railway Museum      E

Thamesdown Borough Council, Museums Division, Faringdon Road, Swindon, Wilts

*Access:* Swindon BR station
Tel: Swindon 26161 Ex. 562
OS Ref: SU 145846

Static steam locomotive exhibits as well as other relics and displays of GWR items.
The museum is open Monday–Saturday 10 am–5 pm and Sundays 2 pm–5 pm throughout the year. Closed Christmas Day, Boxing Day, New Year's Day and Good Friday.
Facilities for visitors include museum shop, toilets and parking nearby.

### Stock
[1]GWR 0-6-0 No. 2516 (Class 2301) built 1887
[2]GWR 4-4-0 No. 3717 *City of Truro* built 1903
[3]GWR 4-6-0 No. 4003 *Lode Star* built 1907
[4]GWR 0-6-0PT No. 9400 (Class 94XX) built 1947
GWR 2-2-2 (replica) *North Star* built 1837 (broad gauge)

[1]William Dean's standard goods engine for the GWR totalling 260 engines built 1883–99. Large numbers of the class were sent overseas during both world wars and many were destroyed in action. They were to be found at home working throughout the entire GWR system.
[2]Churchward 'City' class, originally numbered 3440. Withdrawn in 1931, restored and placed on display in York Railway Museum. Returned to traffic in 1957 for use on special excursions until withdrawn in 1961 and placed on display in 1962. The first British locomotive reported to have exceeded 100 m.p.h. whilst hauling the 'Ocean Mail' special from Plymouth to Paddington in 1904.
[3]Withdrawn from Laudore (Swansea) shed in July 1951 as BR No. 4003. The 'Stars' were the first four-cylinder locomotives built in this country. When new, some were constructed as 4-4-2s and all locomotives were designed for easy conversion to and from 4-6-0. The 4-6-0 type proved itself and modifications were incorporated into successive batches until 1922. Built for express passenger work, the class remained so employed virtually until the end of its existence.
[4]Withdrawn from Old Oak Common (Paddington) shed in December 1959 as BR No. 9400. The largest pannier tanks and final GWR class appearing prior to nationalisation, the

class is virtually a tank version of the 2251 class 0-6-0 but with smaller wheels. Originally designed as carriage pilots and trip goods and shunting locomotives, the type was never as popular as the more numerous 57XX class. Orders for 200 of the type were placed by the GWR and the last engine was not in traffic until 1956.

## 21   Bristol Industrial Museum      AE

Princes Wharf, Bristol, Avon BS1 4RN

*Access:* 5 minutes walk from the centre of Bristol. Nearest BR station, Bristol Temple Meads. Car parking adjacent to site in Wapping Road
Tel: Bristol (0272) 299771 Ext. 290
OS Ref: ST 583722

The Museum houses machinery and vehicles associated with Bristol's industrial past. At intervals throughout the summer season, a standard gauge steam railway operates in conjunction with the Museum, offering a ⅓ mile ride as far as the Great Western drydock where Brunel's famous ship, the SS 'Great Britain', is on display.
The Museum is open Saturdays–Wednesdays throughout the year from 10 am–12 noon and 1–5 pm. Admission free. Facilities for visitors include a museum shop, car parking and toilets.
Bristol Industrial Museum was opened in March 1978, in what was once a transit warehouse in the heart of the City Docks. The exhibits on display are only a part of the technology collection, and are chosen for their particular connections with the Bristol region. Outstanding amongst these is the 1880 Grenville steam carriage – the world's oldest self-propelled passenger vehicle still in working order.

### Stock
Peckett 0-6-0ST No. S9 *Henbury* 1940 built 1937
[1]Avonside 0-6-0ST No. S3 *Portbury* 1764 built 1917
[2]Fox Walker 0-6-0ST No. 3 242 built 1874
[3]GWR 6-wheel tri-composite coach No. 820 built 1886
GWR 'Toad' goods brake van built 1941
GWR 'Mogo' Motor car van built 1946
Various sections of GWR Broad gauge coach bodies

[1]Located at Washford, West Somerset Railway.
[2]Located at Bitton, Bristol Suburban Railway.
[3]In store pending restoration.

## 22   China Clay Industry Museum      E

Wheal Martyn, Trenance Valley, St Austell, Cornwall
OS Ref: SX 009549

Static steam locomotive exhibits plus display of machinery and equipment representing the history of the china clay mining industry in Cornwall.
Facilities for visitors include car parking and a museum shop.
A long-term aspiration of the museum is to restore and operate about one mile of the adjacent ex-GWR Trenance Valley branch.

**Stock**
[1]Bagnall 0–4–0ST *Judy* 2572 built 1937
Peckett 0–4–0ST *Lee Moor No. 1* 783 built 1899 (4 ft 6 in. gauge)
Wooden clay wagons (2 ft gauge)

[1]Ex English Clays Company, Par, 1974.

## 23   South Devon Railway Museum                E

Dawlish Warren Station, Dawlish, Devon

*Access:* Dawlish Warren BR station

A museum of small railway relics open daily between 11 am and 5 pm from April to September.
Exhibits include locomotive name and number plates, photographs, signs, notices, tickets, documents, paperwork and many items connected with railways.

## 24   Tolgus Tin Mine Museum                E

Portreath Road, Redruth, Cornwall

OS Ref: SW 689443

2 ft 2 in. gauge static diesel locomotive exhibit in a museum devoted to the history of the Cornish Tin Mining industry.

**Stock**
Ruston Hornsby 4WDM LA class 371547 built 1954. Ex British Gypsum Ltd, Glebe Mines, Nottinghamshire, 1972.

## 25   Wendron Forge Museum                E

Wendron, near Helston, Cornwall
Tel: Helston 3173 and 3531

Standard gauge static steam locomotive exhibit in newly-opened museum of rural machinery. Also features underground tin mine.
The museum is open from 1 April to 31 October between 10 am and 6 pm.

**Stock**
Peckett 0–4–0ST No. 6 1530 built 1919.
Ex Falmouth Docks & Engineering Co. 1978. To be restored to exhibition finish (non-operational).

## 26   Plymouth Railway Circle                E

Saltram House, Plympton, Plymouth, Devon

OS Ref: SX 521556

4 ft 6 in. gauge static exhibits from the former Lee Moor Tramway. The Lee Moor Tramway was the last of the privately-owned mineral railways built to the 'Dartmoor' gauge of 4 ft 6 in. It was built to carry china clay and other produce from the pits and works on the southern slopes of Dartmoor to the quays of Plymouth. From 1899 to 1947 three different forms of traction – steam, gravity and horse – were needed to convey a train the full length of the line. From 1947 until final closure in 1960 only the lower part of the line remained open, where horses were used and which thus outlasted the other forms of motive power.

**Stock**
Peckett 0–4–0ST *Lee Moor No. 2* 784 built 1899. Lee Moor Tramway china clay wagon

Locomotive withdrawn in 1945. Purchased for preservation in 1964 and kept in original shed leased from English Clays Limited. Now restored to exhibition condition for display at Saltram House.

PRC details from: R. E. Taylor, 32 Honicknowle Lane, Pennycross, Plymouth, Devon.

## 27   Tiverton Museum                E

Tiverton, Devon

*Access:* Near centre of town, on St Andrew Street (near Bethel Assembly of God, which is signposted)

OS Ref: SS 960127

Static steam locomotive exhibit. Other small exhibits include a large model of a GWR broad-gauge 4–4–0T *Lalla Rookh* which was built *c* 1870.

**Stock**
GWR 0–4–2T No. 1442 Class 14XX built 1935. Withdrawn from service in 1965 and purchased by Lord Amory who presented it for display.

Soon to get a roof over its head is GWR 0–4–2T No. 1442 pictured here opposite the site of its former haunts, Tiverton Station, Devon

Photo: Graham Scott-Lowe

## 28  British Rail, Newton Abbot                                    E

Newton Abbot Station, Devon

OS Ref: SX 867712

7 ft ¼ in. gauge static steam locomotive exhibit.

**Stock**
South Devon Railway 0–4–0VBWT No. 151 *Tiny* built Sara & Co., Penryn, 1868. Withdrawn in 1883 as GWR No. 2180 and used as a stationary engine at Newton Abbot Works until placed on display in 1927. This is the sole surviving engine representing the GWR Broad Gauge era which came to an end in 1892.


## 29  Frome Rural Council                                           E

Welshmill Adventure Playground, Frome, Somerset

OS Ref: ST 778486

Standard gauge steam locomotive on static display.

**Stock**
Sentinel 4WVBTG 9387 built 1948. Ex Roads Reconstruction (Quarries) Ltd, Vallis Vale, Frome, 1972.


## 30  Newlyn, Cornwall                                              E

Amey Roadstone Corporation, Penlee Quarry, Newlyn

OS Ref: SW 467281

2 ft gauge static steam locomotive exhibit.

**Stock**
Freudenstein 0–4–0WT *Penlee* 73 built 1901. Formerly used on quarry railway system at Penlee.


## 31  Cornish Steam Locomotive                                      D
##      Preservation Society

Imperial Sidings, Bugle, near St Austell, Cornwall

*Access:* British Rail Bugle station. Alongside A391 Bodmin – St Austell road

OS Ref: SX 014580

The depot is open on the last Sunday in each month from April to September, plus every Sunday during August and Bank Holiday Mondays, Easter, May Day, Spring and August between 11 am and 5.30 pm.
Facilities for visitors include train rides, railway shop, refreshments, car parking, toilets and picnic area.
The Society was formed in 1973 and leases sidings from English Clays Ltd which once joined the Goonbarrow mineral branch. Although the branch was lifted in March 1979, it is hoped eventually to relay part of it. On the closure of the GW Society depot at Bodmin in October 1977, much of the stock there was moved to Bugle to form the nucleus of the Society's collection.
Passengers are given short rides in a brake-van along the

sidings which are situated amongst old clay drying kilns. Future projects include the provision of a new platform at the end of the line and a new shed where locomotive restoration can be carried out.

**Stock**
[1]Bagnall 0–4–0ST *Alfred* 3058 built 1953
[2]Bagnall 0–4–0ST No. 19 2962 built 1950
[3]Peckett 0–4–0ST *Progress* 1611 built 1923
[4]Bagnall 0–4–0F 3121 built 1957
[5]GWR Churchward 'Toplight' 3rd class coach No. 2434 built 1910
LMS 20-ton Goods Brake Van No. 294315 built 1930
LNER 12-ton Fruit Van No. 222814 built 1938
GWR 12-ton Ventilated Van No. 103999 built 1926
[6]LSWR 4-wheel velocipede *Camel* built 1875

An item of particular interest is the outer fire box wrapper of Liskeard and Caradon Railway locomotive *Caradon* which had been in use at Moorswater as a toilet until rescue in 1971.

[1]Ex English Clays Ltd, Park Docks 1978.
[2]Ex Devonport Dockyard.
[3]Ex Albright & Wilson Ltd, Portishead.
[4]Ex English Clays Ltd, Marsh Mills, Plymouth.
[5]Converted to mess vehicle 1956. Now used as Mess, sales and refreshments.
[6]Ex Wenford Mineral branch.

Society details from: M. Orme, 24 Margaret Gardens, Eglashayle, Wadebridge, Cornwall. Tel: 2335.


## 32  Swanage Railway                                               F

Swanage Railway Co. Ltd, Swanage Station, Dorset

*Access:* BR Wareham Station, thence Hants and Dorset bus to Swanage.

Standard gauge railway preservation scheme. A growing number of items of rolling stock is gathered at Swanage station pending the relaying and reopening of the line.

Open every weekend of the year from 10 am to 5 pm.
Facilities for visitors include a display of rolling stock and a railway shop.
The former LSWR Wareham–Swanage branch was closed by BR in January 1972. Since that time, the Swanage Railway Society has been active in gaining a foothold at Swanage station and encouraging Dorset County Council to modify its road plans which would have otherwise eaten up a major part of the branch trackbed. It's a daunting prospect to try to reopen any closed railway line, let alone one which needs 6½ miles of track relaying before trains can run again. But that is the magnitude of the task before the Swanage Railway Society.
The project is first concerned with restoring a public amenity service from Swanage to Wareham and the BR network. The secondary object is to form a working railway museum in an authentic setting to recreate the atmosphere of Southern Steam. In this, the Society is supported by a number of rolling-stock owning groups, principally the Southern Steam Trust.

[1]BR 2-6-4T No. 80078 (Riddles class 4MT) built 1954
GWR 0-6-2T No. 6695 (Class 56XX) built 1928
Barclay 0-4-0ST No. ED10 *Richard Trevithick* 2354 built 1954
Fowler 0-4-0DM No. 2 *May* 4210132 built 1957
[1]Hibberd 4WPM *Beryl* 2054 built 1938
[1]SR Bulleid Brake/3rd coach No. 4365 built 1947
[1]SR Scenery Van No. 4594 built 1938
[1]SR Luggage Van No. 1234 built 1935
[1]LSWR Coach No. 0695 (body only) built 1885
[1]WD 4-wheel dropside open wagon No. 45020

[1]Owned by the Southern Steam Trust.

Details of the Swanage Railway Society are available from: The Secretary, 109 Bay Crescent, Swanage, Dorset BH19 1RA.

*Progress 1979*
The Swanage Railway Co. Ltd (the Company formed by the SRS to purchase and operate the line) have been granted interim possession of the railway formation between Swanage and Herston, subject to a full licence being granted by the end of the year. The operation of trains over the first ¾-mile of the Swanage Railway has been agreed by the County Council's Transportation and Planning Committee.

**Southern Steam Trust**                                    H
Headquarters: Swanage Station, Dorset
Details from: M. D. Stone, 96 Worplesdon Road, Guildford, Surrey GU2 6RT

The Trust was formed as the Southern Steam Group in 1972. Since then, charitable status has been obtained.
The object of the Trust is to preserve locomotives, rolling stock and other apparatus associated with the LSWR, the Southern Railway and the Southern Region of BR for operation on the Swanage-Wareham branch when it is reopened. In this regard, it supports the Swanage Railway Company who plan to restore both vintage steam and amenity services over the branch. A fund to acquire SR 'U' class 2-6-0 No. 31638 from Barry scrapyard has been set up by members of the Trust who are hopeful they will complete the purchase by the end of 1979. Similarly, another group is hoping to add 'Merchant Navy' Pacific No. 35022 'Holland-America Line', also at Barry, to the Trust's collection.

## 33   Bournemouth Steam Centre                           F

Standard-gauge locomotive preservation organisation seeking to purchase and restore SR Bulleid Pacific No. 34058 *Sir Frederick Pile* from Barry scrapyard.
The Society, which was formed in 1975 to establish a steam centre in the Bournemouth area, has experienced difficulty in obtaining a suitable site. A great deal of work has been carried out on No. 34058 and it has now been protected from rust until it is moved from Barry to the Steam Centre. The Society hopes to go on to purchase 'Merchant Navy' Pacific No. 35027 *Port Line* from Barry and is issuing shares in this locomotive.

*Details from:* C. C. Timms, 44 Glenferness Avenue, Bournemouth, Dorset. Members receive bi-monthly newsletters giving news of locomotive progress and of working parties.

## 34   Taff Vale Restorations                             G

Standard gauge preservation group restoring a former Taff Vale Railway bogie coach body.

*Details from:* Steve Erlicher, 2 Hay Hill, Bath, Avon BA1 5IZ.

The body was built in 1912 by the Gloucester Railway Carriage and Wagon Company to replace a seven-compartment 3rd Class body destroyed in the Coke Ovens Yard crash on the TVR in 1911. The new body was a three-compartment brake/3rd and was mated with the original 1889 chassis of 8-wheeled semi-rigid design. After renumbering into GWR stock as No. 1775 in 1926, this unusual arrangement was sold to a farmer near Bath and the chassis presumably scrapped. It was acquired for preservation in 1974 and moved to its present site in 1975.

**Stock**
TVR Brake/3rd coach body No. 203 built 1912

## 35   Swindon and Cricklade                              F
##      Railway Society

Standard gauge railway preservation society seeking to reopen a portion of the old Midland and South Western Junction Railway between Moredon and Cricklade station. Another organisation faced with the herculean task of relaying several miles of track on a disused trackbed before trains can run again. However, a diesel locomotive has been obtained on free loan to the Society for five years with the option of purchase afterwards and members are keen to make a start on the project.

**Stock**
Fowler 0-4-0DM No. 2 4210082 built 1953

## 36   Old Delabole Slate Co. Ltd                         E

Lower Pengelly, Delabole, Cornwall
OS Ref: SX 075836

1 ft 11½ in. gauge rolling stock restored for static display in a small museum devoted to the Cornish slate industry.

**Stock**
Motor Rail 4WDM 3739 built 1925
[1]Motor Rail 4WDM 4534 built 1928
Various narrow gauge slate wagons

[1]Not yet on display.

## 37   Falmouth Shiprepair Ltd                    I

Falmouth Docks, Cornwall

OS Ref: SW 822324

Industrial steam location featuring occasional steam working.

**Stock**
Hawthorn Leslie 0–4–0ST No. 3 3597 built 1926
Hudswell Clarke 0–4–0ST No. 5 1632 built 1929
Sentinel 0–4–0DH No. 129 built 1963


## 38   British Rail Engineering, Swindon          G

BREL, Swindon Works, Wilts

Standard gauge diesel locomotives on static display outside the works, grouped round the turntable and visible from passing trains.

**Stock**
[1]BR Bo-BoDH No. D818 *Glory* built 1960
[2]BR Bo-BoDH No. D821 *Greyhound* built 1960
[2]BR Bo-BoDH No. D7029 Beyer Peacock 7923 built 1962
BR Co-CoDH No. D1041 *Western Prince* built 1962

[1]Owned by BR Research and Development Division.
[2]Owned by Modern Traction Ltd.


## 39   Wimborne Model Town
Wimborne, Dorset                                 E

10¼ in. gauge steam locomotive on static display

**Stock**
Kitson 2–6–6–2T *Jason* built 1938
The locomotive formerly ran on Sir Thomas Salt's Shillingstone Light Railway in Dorset and was originally built for the Surrey Border & Camberley Railway


## 40   Inny Valley Railway                        C

Trecarrell Mill, Trebullett, Launceston, Cornwall

OS Ref: SX 320772

Private 1 ft 10¾ in. gauge light railway ½ mile in length owned by Mr J. J. A. Evans.

**Stock**
Hudswell Clarke 0–4–2ST *San Justo* 639 built 1902
Hudswell Clarke 0–4–2ST *Santa Ana* 640 built 1902
Hunslet 0–4–0ST *Velinheli* 409 built 1886
Bagnall 0–4–0ST *Sybil* 1760 built 1906
Planet 4WDM No. 2 1896 built 1935
Simplex 4WDM No. 3 9546 built 1950
Three 4-wheel verandah-end coaches based on Lister truck

chassis and incorporating seats built from pews from a church at Probus.


## 41   Poole Miniature Railway                    B

Poole Park, Poole, Dorset

Passenger-carrying 10¼ in. gauge line, ¾ mile in length

**Stock**
Longfleet Co-BoP No. D1007
Southern Min. Rlys Bo-BoP No. D7000 built 1965
Six open bogie coaches


## 42   Buscot Light Railway                       C

Buscot, Wiltshire

Private 11½ in. gauge light railway 101 yards long operated by Mr K. Peacock.
The railway is used for hauling logs from a dump to the house. Visitors are welcome, but a maximum of four is recommended, the land being under the care of the National Trust.

**Stock**
PTR 4WBE built 1963
Two tipper wagons
Flat truck
Water wagon


## 43   Bowleaze Cove Railway                      B

Bowleaze Cove, Weymouth, Dorset

A 7¼ in. gauge passenger-carrying line 150 yards long operated by Mr Pat Henshaw.
The railway operates daily during the summer season.
The line is arranged as a continuous circuit with a two-road engine shed adjoining the main station, access to which is via a footbridge.
Earthworks include a 4 ft deep cutting and a tunnel. The railway was opened in May 1975.

**Stock**
Smith Bo-BoBE built 1975
Two covered bogie coaches built by T. Smith 1975


## 44   Blaise Castle Miniature Railway            B

Blaise Castle, near Bristol, Avon

*Access*: 4 miles North-West of City, off B4057

A 10¼ in. gauge passenger-carrying line.

**Stock**
Haynes/Cromar White Bo-BoBE (steam outline)

## 45  Brean Central Miniature Railway                    B

Mid-Somerset Leisure Centre, Brean, Somerset

Passenger-carrying 1 ft 6 in. gauge line

**Stock**
Deacon Bo–BoPM built 1975
Three articulated bogie coaches


## 46  Kingsbridge Miniature Railway                      B

The Quary, Kingsbridge, Devon

*Access:* Totnes British Rail, then bus (three times a day); or
Kingswear (Torbay and Dartmouth Railway), ferry to Dartmouth, then bus.

Passenger-carrying 7¼ in. gauge line running round three
sides of the quay car park alongside the estuary at Kingsbridge and giving an out-and-back ride of about ½-mile.
The railway operates for Easter week, then daily from mid-
May to mid-September.
The line was built in stages from 1969 and was originally
steam-worked with a GWR 0–6–0ST. A new 0–4–0 battery
electric locomotive (built by Cromar-White) was added to
stock in 1976 while the petrol locomotive, which had run
for two years, was rebuilt as a diesel-hydraulic.
Sorry about the modern image motive power, chaps, but
many of our passengers, who are in the one-to-ten year old
range – if they travel by train at all – have never seen steam
in its native habitat. They see diesels and electrics on BR
and like to see the same thing in miniature. Let's get the
youngsters on the trains, whatever the power, for they are
the enthusiasts of tomorrow.

**Stock**
Willbro Precision B–BDH No. 1 *Little Bear* built 1974 as
petrol loco
Cromar-White 0–4–0BE No. 2 *Heidi* E7050 built 1976
Freelance Bo–BoBER under construction
Control trailer coach (to work in conjunction with *Heidi* or
the electric railcar)
Sit-astride bogie coaches


## 47  Butlins, Minehead                                   B

Butlins Ltd, Minehead Holiday Camp, Somerset

Adjacent to Minehead Station, West Somerset Railway
OS Ref: SS 984464

Passenger-carrying 2 ft gauge line

**Stock**
Chance 4–2–4DH No. 30 *C. P. Huntingdon* 64–5031–24
built 1964 (steam outline)
Open bogie coaches


## 48  Towans Railway                                      B

Hayle, Cornwall

Passenger-carrying 10¼ in. gauge line, ¼ mile in length, laid
in a figure 8.
The railway operates daily in summer and on Sunday afternoons in winter.

**Stock**
LMS 4–6–0P No. 6100 *Royal Scot* built by Carland (formerly
steam powered but now with power tender)
Cromar White Bo–BoP No. D7028 built 1972
Three open bogie coaches

It is hoped to return the *Royal Scot* to steam power
eventually.


## 49  Clevedon Miniature Railway                         B

Salthouse Fields, Clevedon, Avon

Passenger-carrying 9½ in. gauge line

**Stock**
Severn-Lamb 2–8–0PH (steam outline) built 1976


## 50  Riverside Miniature Railway                        AB

Buckfastleigh Station, Dart Valley Railway, Devon

*Access:* Just off A38 trunk road, halfway between Exeter
and Plymouth
Tel: Buckfastleigh 2338
OS Ref: SX 747663

Passenger-carrying dual 7¼ in. and 10¼ in. gauge railway.
Operates from Easter to October from 11 am to 5 pm.
The line runs alongside the standard gauge Dart Valley
Railway (see Group No. 1) round part of the riverside picnic
area and forms a continuous circuit. Different forms of motive
power operate on the two different gauges (mixed-gauge
track).

**Stock**
Lynton and Barnstaple 2–6–2T built Milner Eng. 1979,
7¼ in. gauge
Shepperton Bo–BoDH 10¼ in. gauge
Shepperton 4 WDM 10¼ in. gauge
Double articulated set of coaches 10¼ in. gauge

# AREA B

# South East

**Kent
Surrey
Sussex
Hampshire
Isle of Wight**

---

## 51 Sittingbourne and Kemsley Light Railway A

Sittingbourne, Kent

*Access:* By road in Sittingbourne by 'The Wall' near Milton Creek. 5 minutes walk from Sittingbourne BR station and bus stops.
Tel: Sittingbourne 24899 or 0634 32320
OS Ref: TQ 905643

Passenger-carrying 2 ft 6 in. gauge light railway, 2 miles in length running from Sittingbourne to Kemsley Down.
The railway operates passenger services on Saturdays, Sundays and Bank Holidays from Easter to mid-October, also Tuesdays, Wednesdays and Thursdays in August and certain days over the Christmas period.

Facilities for visitors include refreshment and sales kiosk at Sittingbourne; refreshment room and picnic area at Kemsley Down. Special facilities for parties by prior arrangement, including set meals and guide, etc. Large free car park at Sittingbourne SKLR station in Milton Road (close to Sittingbourne BR station and A2 road). *Note:* There is no road access to Kemsley Down.

Running between Sittingbourne and Kemsley in Kent, the railway was built by Edward Lloyd Ltd to a gauge of 2 ft 6 in. and was used by them to transport paper and other material (also employees) between their mills and Ridham Dock on the banks of the Swale. In 1948, Edward Lloyd Ltd was taken over by the Bowater Group. In 1969 the Locomotive Club of Great Britain (LCGB) leased from the Bowater Corporation a two-mile section of the line. This lease has now been passed to the Sittingbourne and Kemsley Light Railway Ltd, incorporated on 30 December 1971 to give added protection to members, who are all members of the Company. The Company, limited by guarantee and not having a share capital, is a non-profit making enterprise. Policy matters are controlled by a board of directors and day-to-day running is in the hands of responsible officers on a departmental basis. The Company has at present about 460 members and all work is undertaken on a voluntary basis.

All trains are hauled by vintage steam locomotives and pasengers normally have the choice of travelling in open or covered coaches. At Kemsley Down, the locomotives not in use are on display, together with other industrial equipment.

*Secretary:* N. J. Widdows, 51 Russell Drive, Whitstable, Kent CT5 2RG

**Stock**
Bagnall 0-6-2T *Alpha* (2472) built 1932
Bagnall 0-6-2T *Triumph* (2511) built 1934
Bagnall 0-6-2T *Superb* (2624) built 1940
Bagnall 2-4-0F *Unique* (2216) built 1924

---

It seems like only yesterday that the Sittingbourne and Kemsley Light Railway got under way. But ten years have elapsed since these two stalwarts steamed together on what was Bowaters Railway

Photo: A. Luke

Kerr Stuart 0-4-2ST *Premier* (886) built 1905
Kerr Stuart 0-4-2ST *Leader* (926) built 1905
Kerr Stuart 0-4-2ST *Melior* (4219) built 1924
Ruston Hornsby 0-4-0DH *Edward Lloyd* (LH Class) (435403) built 1961
Hunslet 4WDM *Victor* (4182) built 1953
Three Chattenden and Upnor bogie coaches
Six saloon bogie coaches
Two standee passenger coaches
Thirty-three bogie pulp trucks
Two clay hopper wagons
Four tipper wagons
Two rubbish box bogie wagons
One high-capacity bogie wagon
Nine flat bogie wagons
Two coal box bogie wagons

The railway also has on display the following standard gauge steam locomotives:
Hawthorn Leslie 0-4-0ST *Swanscombe No. 4* (3718) built 1928
Peckett 0-4-0ST *Bear* (614) built 1896
Barclay 0-4-0F No. 1 (1876) built 1925

## 52   Bluebell Railway                                    A

Sheffield Park Station, Uckfield, Sussex

*Access:* Sheffield Park station is exactly nine miles from both Lewes and East Grinstead on the A275 road, 2 miles north of its junction with the A272.
Horsted Keynes station is situated at the foot of the hill which leads from the West Hoathly to Horsted Keynes road at Great Oddynes turning. Car parking facilities are available at both stations.
Frequent trains operate to Haywards Heath. Services also operate to Lewes, Uckfield and East Grinstead. Southdown express bus service 769 departing from Haywards Heath

Bus Station.
Tel: Newick 2370
OS Ref: TQ 403238

The Bluebell Railway is a standard-gauge passenger-carrying line operating services at weekends throughout the year and weekdays in the summer between Sheffield Park and Horsted Keynes (five miles).
The railway operates during Easter week, on Sundays in January, February and December, on weekends in March, April and November, on weekends and Wednesdays in May and October, daily June–September inclusive and on Bank Holidays.
Facilities for visitors include buffet, souvenir shops, car parking and toilets at both stations. Picnic area at Horsted Keynes.
Established in 1960 as a living museum for the steam train in a rural branch-line setting, it has become one of the major attractions of South-Eastern England. From small beginnings with two locomotives and two coaches, the Bluebell Railway is now the home of the largest and most comprehensive collection of Vintage Railway Locomotives, Carriages, and Wagons, that operated in the South of England. Situated in the heart of the Sussex Weald and running through 5 miles through some of its most beautiful countryside, the line offers the ideal setting for the operation of vintage steam trains.
The stations and equipment too are not without their interest, dating from the construction of the line in 1882. At Sheffield Park at the southerly end of the line the pre-1923 atmosphere of the London Brighton and South Coast Railway still is strong, with the oil-lit platform lamps, and slowly restoration work to make the atmosphere more accurate and complete is being put in hand. At Horsted Keynes at the northerly end of the line the emphasis is on the period immediately following 1923 when the Southern Railway had taken over; and again restoration work is in hand to modify and enhance this image.
The journey on the vintage train is naturally the high-light of any visit, giving the passenger the opportunity to re-live (or perhaps enjoy for the first time) the joy of being hauled by a steam locomotive in vintage coaches. Sometimes the train may be formed of elderly non-corridor 'branch-line' coaches dating back to the early years of this century hauled by a locomotive that could be 100 years old. Other times the train may be formed of main-line coaches introduced by the Southern Railway hauled by an 'express' or secondary locomotive such as was in use on British Railways until relatively recently. Nevertheless, whichever is the locomotive you travel behind or the coach you travel in, you can be sure that this is an experience that can no longer be appreciated on the British Rail system.
For those not so interested in railways as such, there is always the delight of the Victoriana, Edwardiana and Pre-war relics gained by a peep into, for example, the Signal Box at Sheffield Park or by studying the collection of enamel signs, or simply by appreciating the sheer size and magnificence of Horsted Keynes station, set in the middle of nowhere, and the impact building on this scale must have had on a rural 19th Century community. The excursion on the line too is not without interest for the non-railway minded

Step up young man and enjoy the good old days of steam! You can do it Stroudley style with *Fenchurch* on the famous Bluebell Railway

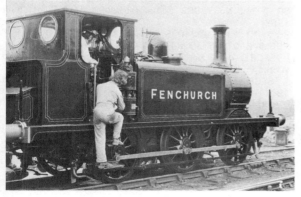

Photo: John Gardner

**Bluebell Railway has always maintained the highest standards in railway preservation. Here is one of the Standard Class Four No. 75027 with a heavy train arriving at Horsted Keynes**

on the 200 ft climb from Sheffield Park, on the river Ouse, out of the valley and up to Horsted Keynes. Wild flowers abound in their season and wild life of all kinds can be spotted from the train windows by the quick-sighted.

The Bluebell Railway collection of steam locomotives, coaches and wagons reflects mainly the Southern Railway and its pre-1923 constituent companies. It is a large and diverse collection of over 75 items, some over 100 years old. The Bluebell Railway's policy is to restore vehicles to an authentic livery which the particular vehicle carried at some time during its life, although of course not all vehicles will represent the same period in time.

**Stock**

[1]LBSCR 0-6-0T No. 55 *Stepney* (Stroudley AIX Class) built 1875

[2]LBSCR 0-6-0T No. 72 *Fenchurch* (Stroudley AIX Class) built 1872

[3]LBSCR 0-6-2T No. 473 *Birch Grove* (Billington E4 Class) built 1898

SECR 0-6-0T No. 27 (P Class) built 1910 (BR No. 31027)

SECR 0-6-0T No. 323 *Bluebell* (Wainwright P Class) (BR No. 31323) built 1910

SECR 0-6-0T No. 178 *Pioneer II* (Wainwright P Class) (BR No. 31178) built 1910

[4]LSWR 4-4-2T No. 488 (Adams 0415 Class) (BR No. 30583) built Neilson 1885

[5] [13]SR 2-6-0 No. 1618 (Maunsell 'U' Class) built 1928

BR 2-6-4T No. 80100 (Riddles 4MT Class) built 1955

[5]SR 4-6-0 No. 30847 (Maunsell S15 Class) built 1936

[6]SR 0-6-0 No. 30541 (Maunsell Q Class) built 1939

SR 4-6-2 No. 34059 *Sir Archibald Sinclair* built 1947

BR 4-6-0 No. 73082 *Camelot* (Riddles 5MT Class) built 1955

BR 2-10-0 No. 92240 (Riddles 9F Class) built 1958

[13]SR 0-6-0T No. 30064 (USA Class) built 1943

[7] [14]SECR 0-4-4T No. 263 ('H' Class) constructed at Ashford Works in 1905

[8] [15]SECR 0-6-0 No. 592 ('C' Class) (BR No. 31592) built 1901

[9] [16]SR 4-6-2 No. 21C23 *Blackmore Vale* built 1946

[9] [17]SR 0-6-0 No. C1 (Class Q1) built 1942

[9] [18]LSWR 0-4-0T No. 30096 *Normandy* (Class B4) built 1893

[10]NLR 0-6-0T No. 2650 built 1880

[11]GWR 4-4-0 No. 3217 *Earl of Berkeley* built 1938

BR 4-6-0 No. 75027 (4MT Class) built 1954

Fletcher Jennings 0-4-0T *Baxter* (158) built 1877

Aveling Porter 2–2–0TG *Blue Circle* (9449) built 1926
Howard 4w PM *Britannia* (957) built 1926
Avonside 0–6–0ST No. 24 *Stamford* (1972) built 1927
LBSCR directors' saloon No. 60 built 1913
LSWR third-class coach No. 320 built 1900, rebuilt SR 1935
GNR saloon coach No. 706E built 1897
LNWR observation car No. 1503 built 1913
SR Bulleid open third-class bogie coach No. 1481 built 1951
Metropolitan Railway bogie coaches Nos 512, 515, 516 and 518 built 1898–1900
SECR bogie coach No. 971 built 1923
SR third-class bogie coach No. 1050 rebuilt 1927
SECR brake composite coach No. 1061 built 1909
SECR third-class bogie coach No. 1098 built 1923
LSWR third-class corridor coach No. 494 rebuilt as camping coach No. S39S in 1953
SR Maunsell third-class open coach No. 1365 built 1927
BR 3rd-class sleeping coach No. M623M built 1952 to LMS design
SR Maunsell TPO Van No. S4922 built 1939
SR Bulleid Open 3rd coach No. 1464
LCDR six-wheel brake/third-class coach (SECR No. 2781) built 1894
SR Bulleid brake/third-class bogie coach No. 4279 built 1948
SR Maunsell BCK bogie coach No. 6575 built 1927
SR Maunsell buffet bogie coach No. 7864 built 1927
BR composite compartment coach No. E43010 built 1954
BR brake/second No. E43172 built 1954
BR open second-class bogie coach No. E48015 built 1955
LMS dormitory coach No. DM395584 built 1924
LMS 12-wheeled first-class sleeping coach No. M398M built 1952
SR Maunsell BSO bogie coach No. 4441 built 1933
SR Maunsell brake/third corridor coach No. 2356 built 1931
SR Maunsell third-class saloon coach No. 1309 built 1930
SR Bulleid third-class saloon coach No. 1482 built 1946
SR Bulleid BTK semi-open coach No. 2515 built 1946
⁹SR Bulleid CK bogie coach No. 5768 built 1947
SR Maunsell BCK coach No. 6686 built 1935
SECR 10-ton high-roofed van No. 15750 built 1920
SECR six-wheeled passenger brake van No. 719 built 1905
LSWR four-wheeled express luggage van No. 5498 built 1920
GWR 'Toad' 20-ton goods brake van No. 17908 built 1913
LNER Wickham petrol rail trolley built 1932
⁹BR goods brake van No. 49027 built 1959 for Army use
SR eight-plank open goods wagon PBA No. 58164 built *c.* 1923
SECR eight-plank open goods wagon PBA No. 58162
SR five-plank open goods wagon No. 59425 built 1931
'Cory' 12/13-ton mineral wagons Nos 67 and 68 (BR Nos P91344 and P383095)
SR 'Borail' SA wagon SR No. 57949S
SR BY parcels brake van No. 653 built 1937
SR BY parcels brake van No. 442 built 1937
SR 'Covcar' four-wheeled utility van No.2276 built 1929
LBSCR milk van No. 270 built 1908
SECR four-wheeled utility van No. 153 built 1922
GWR flat wagon PLA No. E2 built *c.* 1890

SR 12-ton six-wheeled hand-crane No. DS1748 built 1943
SR match truck No. 1748SM built 1943
Shell petrol tank wagon No. 4497 built 1930
LSWR covered van No. 8112 built 1912
LSWR 20-ton road van No. 5706 built 1898
LMS open wagon No. 474558 built 1937
LMS banana van No. 570027 built 1946
BR Palvans Nos B761349, 772970 and 772972 built 1954–6
⁹LSWR tool van No. 47773 built 1912
⁶GWR tool van No. 92 built 1920
4 wheeled brake coach No. 404
Two Chaldron wagons built 1869
LMS 'Medfit' open wagon No. 480222 built 1948
BR 'Medfit' open wagon No. DB458525 built 1951
BR 'Medfit' open wagon No. DB461224 built 1955
LBSCR eight-ton open wagon No. 3346 built 1914
CPR *Sylvester* 4WPM permanent way trolley
BR Wickham 4WPMR No. PWM 3962 6947 built 1955
SR covered van No. 47588 built 1931
BR 'Lowmac' wagon No. B904134 built 1957
Esso tank wagon No. 1921 built 1942

**Historical notes**

¹Built at Brighton in December 1875. Renumbered 655, it became SR No. B655 and was withdrawn from traffic in 1925, being placed in store. Reinstated in 1927, it eventually became SR No. 2655 and was ultimately withdrawn from Eastleigh shed in May 1960 as BR No. 32655. Purchased for preservation by the Bluebell Railway and restored to Stroudley yellow livery.

²Built at Brighton in September 1872, this was the first of William Stroudley's 'Terriers'. The engine was built at a cost of £500 and was sold to the Newhaven Harbour Company in 1898 for the same sum. The Stroudley livery and name were retained until 1902, when it was repainted black with two red lines. The Westinghouse brake, removed when the engine was sold, was refitted in 1913, when *Fenchurch* was rebuilt to A1X Class at Brighton. In 1925, the Newhaven Harbour Company was taken over by the SR and the engine was taken into stock as No. B636, later No. 2636. Finally withdrawn from Eastleigh shed in November 1963 as BR No. 32636 and sold to the Bluebell Railway. The engine is restored in lined black livery with *Fenchurch* on the left-hand side tank and 'Newhaven Harbour Co.' on the right-hand side.

³Built at Brighton in July 1898 and withdrawn from Nine Elms in October 1962 as BR No. 32473. Seventy-five locomotives of this class were constructed for mixed traffic work and in their early days they did a fair amount of passenger work, but were gradually displaced, spending the latter part of their lives on shunting and cross-London freight workings. Purchased by the Bluebell Railway and restored in the umber livery used by that company in its latter years.

⁴Withdrawn from Exmouth Junction shed in July 1961 as BR No. 30583. This is the sole survivor of a class of 71 engines built for suburban passenger work between 1883 and 1885, but most of the class were withdrawn and broken up between 1921 and 1928. It is appropriate that No. 488 should be the survivor, since it has quite a remarkable

history. It was sold out of service by the LSWR in September 1917 and bought by the Ministry of Munitions for £2,104. After a repaint at Eastleigh it was sent to work at Ridham Salvage Depot, Sittingbourne, where it remained until April 1919, when it was again sold, this time to the East Kent Railway for £900, becoming EKR No. 5. The engine worked on the EKR until 1939, when it was laid aside at Shepherds-well and, like many a Colonel Stephens engine, started to slowly decay in open storage. Its slumbers were awakened in 1946, however, when it was sold to the Southern Railway for £800 and thoroughly overhauled for use on the tortuous Lyme Regis branch alongside the two other survivors of its class. The trio continued to work this line until 1960, when replaced by LMS 2-6-2 tanks, and, happily, the Bluebell Railway intervened and saved this elegant and historic engine from the scrapheap in the following year.

[5]Owned by the Maunsell Locomotive Society (q.v.).

[6]Owned by the Southern Railway 'Q' Class Locomotive Fund (q.v.).

[7]Owned by the 'H' Class Trust (q.v.).

[8]Owned by the Wainwright 'C' Class Preservation Society (q.v.).

[9]Owned by the Bulleid Society Ltd. (q.v.).

[10]Outside-cylinder goods and shunting locomotive built at Bow Works in 1880 as North London Railway No. 116. On absorption by the LNWR in 1909 it became No. 2650, and, after the Grouping, LMS No. 7505. A few of this class migrated to Rowsley during their career for working the mountainous Cromford and High Peak line, where they were often employed in pairs and made a stirring sight belching out masses of smoke as they stormed the banks, their exhaust beats echoing across the valleys. No. 2650 was one of these exiles, and apart from receiving a LNWR-pattern chimney. has remained in original condition. Withdrawn from Rowsley in 1960 as BR No. 58850.

[11]This double-framed 4-4-0 was reconstructed at Swindon in March 1938 using frames from 'Bulldog' No. 3425 and officially replacing 'Duke' Class No. 3258 The Lizard. With-drawn from Machynlleth shed in October 1960 as BR No. 9017 and purchased privately for preservation. Many of the 'Dukes' (built in 1895) spent several years working on the Cambrian section of the GWR, where they were the heaviest permitted engines. Between 1936 and 1938 the frames from newer 'Bulldogs' – these latter engines having been replaced by 'Halls' and 'Castles' – were used to rebuild 29 of the 'Dukes' in order to extend their working lives. No. 3217 was the last of its class to survive and was the last double-framed engine in regular traffic on BR.

[12]Withdrawn from Guildford shed in 1964 as BR No. 31618 and sold to Woodham Brothers, Barry, for scrap. Purchased for preservation in 1969 and stored at New Hythe, Kent, until moved to Tenterden in 1972.

Originally ordered as 'K' Class 2-6-4T locomotives, the 20 'U' Class engines numbered 1610-1629 were being assembled when No. A800 River Cray was involved in the Sevenoaks disaster. As a result of this mishap all the 'K' Class tanks were rebuilt as 2-6-0 tender locomotives and instructions were given for Nos 1610-1629 to be similarly completed. Had No. 1618 been built as a tank engine it would have been named River Hamble.

As tender engines, the class resembled the existing 'N' Class moguls with the exception of larger cylinders and driving wheels and greater overall weight. The 2-6-0s were at the time of their construction a new generation of locomotives, capable of working the heaviest goods trains over the whole Southern system, whilst at the same time being able to assist with express passenger work when necessary.

[13]This locomotive was built by the Vulcan Ironworks, Wilkes-Barre, Pennsylvania, USA, in 1943 (Works No. 4432) for use in Europe by the US Transportation Corps. At the end of the war, several European railways acquired this class, in particular the SNCF. Of those which remained in England, most were stored at Newbury Racecourse until 1946 when the Southern Railway purchased 14 of them for use in Southampton Docks. No. 30064 remained active until the end of steam on the Southern Region in July 1967, when it was withdrawn from Eastleigh shed and taken to Salisbury for disposal. Happily, the Southern Locomotive Preservation Co. Ltd intervened at this point and purchased the engine for preservation. The engine appeared in the film Young Winston and immediately afterwards was moved to Sheffield Park to take up regular duties on the Bluebell Railway.

[14]Withdrawn from Three Bridges shed as BR No. 31263 in 1964 and purchased for preservation and restoration to SECR livery. Returned to steam in summer 1967 and has since attended BR and other open days and been featured on TV. The 66 Wainwright 'H' Class engines were a highly successful design and were used on branch line and secondary duties throughout the Eastern and Central Sections of the SR. They were also one of the most handsome of Edwardian tank engine designs.

[15]Withdrawn as BR Departmental Locomotive No. DS239 in 1966 and purchased for preservation in 1967. Altogether 109 engines of this class were built between 1900 and 1908 and remained the backbone of the SECR fleet of freight engines until the 'N' Class 2-6-0s appeared. Like most 0-6-0s, they were more powerful than their appearance suggests, in addition to which they were very speedy machines when occasion demanded, taking almost anything into their stride, including the 'Night Ferry' and 'Thanet Belle', besides numerous hop-pickers' specials. This loco-motive is notable as being the only Longhedge-built engine in existence.

[16]Bulleid 'West Country' class light Pacific built at Brighton Works. Withdrawn from Nine Elms shed in 1967 as BR No. 34023. One-hundred-and-ten of these engines (including the identical 'Battle of Britain' class) were built, making this the largest class of Pacific locomotive ever built in this country. Originally built with many of Oliver Bulleid's unorthodox features, such as 'air-smoothed' casting, chain-driven valve gear and BFB cast steel wheel centres, many were reconstructed by BR on more orthodox lines during the late 1950s. 34023 was the final unrebuilt engine in traffic and worked a special 'Farewell to Southern Steam' railtour on 18 June 1967. Moved to Sheffield Park in 1971.

[17]Bulleid Q1 Class 'Austerity' goods engine built for wartime work but lasting until the mid-60s hauling heavy goods, engineer's trains and occasional passenger trains. Like Blackmore Vale No. C1 was built at Brighton, and for about the

last ten years it has been in store at Preston Park Pullman shed, Brighton. It is part of the national collection and is on loan to the Bulleid Society and Bluebell Railways as custodians.

[18]Adams dock tank, formerly LSWR No. 96. Sold to Corrals Ltd, Dibbles Wharf, Southampton, and renamed *Corrall Queen*, the locomotive was purchased by the B4 Group of the Bulleid Society and moved to the Bluebell Railway in 1972.

## The Bulleid Society Ltd                                           H

The Society was formed in 1966 by a group of railwaymen at Nine Elms (London) locomotive depot, who wanted to see one of the famous Bulleid Pacifics preserved in full working order. The designer O. V. S. Bulleid agreed to become President.

It took nine long years for 'Blackmore Vale' to emerge as 21C123 pristine in her original Southern Railway livery, with six restored Southern coaches to haul. However, the long wait was justified on 15 May 1976, when replica 'Atlantic Coast Express' trains drew crowds of thousands to the Bluebell Railway. The following year the scene was repeated, when the Bulleid and Bluebell Societies were presented with the SR Q1 Class on loan from the National Collection.

*Membership:* 350
*Annual Subscription:* £2.75
*Details from:* Mrs S. Noel, 19 Bramble Twitten, Estcots Oaks, East Grinstead, West Sussex.

---

Look at the cut, the style, the line . . . It's altogether the finest train the Southern ever ran. The ace of the Bluebell steam stud must be Bulleid Pacific No. 21C123 *Blackmore Vale*

Photo: Brian Stephenson

Photo: Tom Heavyside

Meanwhile, back in Frankenstein's engine shed lurks Bulleid's other monster, the powerful Q1 Class 0–6–0 No. C1

### Maunsell Locomotive Society                    H
The Society incorporates the interests of the Southern Mogul Preservation Society and the 847 Locomotive Preservation Fund, each of whom have secured a locomotive for use on the Bluebell Railway.

*Secretary:* R. Packham, 132 Church Road, Swanscombe, Kent DA10 0HP

### 'H' Class Trust                                H
The Trust owns and maintains SECR 'H' Class 0–4–4T No. 263.

*Details from:* E. R. C. Oades, 5 Senlac Way, St Leonards-on-Sea, Sussex

### Wainwright 'C' Class Preservation Society      H
The Society was formed in 1962 to preserve an example of Wainwright's SECR goods locos which became the last class of steam engine used in Kent. The chosen locomotive (ex BR No. 31592) was withdrawn from Capital Stock and transferred to Ashford Works as DS 239. Final withdrawal came in December 1966 and the engine was purchased through a package deal arranged by ARPS. 592 was kept at Ashford running shed until 1970 when it was transferred to the Bluebell Railway. Working parties have continued restoration to full SECR condition and livery.

*Membership:* 60
*Annual Subscription:* Ordinary £1.50, Junior 50p, Life £25.
*Details from:* I. H. De Maid, 69 Bromley Gardens, Bromley, Kent BR2 0ES

### Southern Railway 'Q' Class Locomotive Fund     H
An independent fund to secure SR 'Q' Class 0–6–0 No. 30541 for future use on the Bluebell Railway.

*Annual Subscription:* £1.50.
*Details from:* D. Preece, 8 Podsmead Place, Gloucester GL1 5PD.

## The Bluebell Railway Preservation Society

The Society exists to support the Railway, to operate and maintain it, to restore its vehicles and often purchase them. The Society elects Trustees who are the Directors of the Bluebell Railway Limited, the owning and operating company of the Railway.

Society members can assist in operating the Railway by joining:

(*a*) the Traffic department which covers Signalmen, Guards and Shunters as well as the staffing of the stations (including shops and car parks).

(*b*) the Carriage and Wagon department, working on restoration and maintenance of the Railway's fleet of some sixty vehicles.

(*c*) the Locomotive department which provides the Engine Crews and Cleaners and assists with locomotive maintenance and restoration now carried on in the new works.

(*d*) the Signal and Telegraph department which provides staff for the enormous tasks of maintenance, repair and extension of this unsung area of the railway.

(*e*) the Engineering department maintaining track and bridges, etc.

Vacancies exist in all these departments and training is given to all. If you feel that what is being done is worthwhile and you would like to help, there is a welcome waiting. Should you wish to help but are unable to come to the line you are very welcome as a member of the Bluebell Railway Preservation Society and thereby assist in preserving our Steam Heritage.

Membership has other advantages too, privilege rates of travel and free admission to the Bluebell Railway, discount on purchases at Bluebell Railway shops, the quarterly magazine Bluebell News, and the knowledge that you are helping to run the line.

Full details of membership are available by post, please send a stamped self-addressed envelope, from The Membership Secretary, Bluebell Railway Preservation Society, 27 Inholmes Park Road, Burgess Hill, Sussex RH15 0JJ. Or from either station booking office.

## 53 Kent and East Sussex Railway A

Tenterden Town Station, Tenterden, Kent

*Access:* Headcorn and Ashford BR stations, then by Maidstone and District bus services Nos 12 and 400
Tel: Tenterden 2943
OS Ref: TQ 882336

Standard gauge passenger carrying light railway, four miles in length from Tenterden Town to Wittersham Road. The line is being reopened in stages to Bodiam (10 miles). Rolling stock located at Bodiam, Tenterden Town and Rolvenden Stations.

*Operating days:* Weekends and Bank Holidays, March–October; Sunday afternoons in November and

Photo: Brian Stephenson

**Deep in the weald of Kent the Colonel Stephens' traditions are still alive on the Kent and East Sussex Railway. Norwegian Mogul No. 19 attacks Tenterden Bank with a northbound train**

December; Wednesdays in June and July; daily from the end of July to the end of August; Sundays only in November. Special steam events take place in mid-September and around Christmas.

The Kent and East Sussex Railway is perhaps the most famous of all British standard-gauge light railways, being the first such line to be built under the Light Railways Act 1896 and now is almost the last survivor. Its principal claim to fame lies in its being engineered and operated by the late Colonel Holman F. Stephens, the uncrowned king of British light railways. Opened in stages from 1900 from Robertsbridge on the Hastings line, through Tenterden to Headcorn on the Tonbridge–Ashford main line. Closures and track-lifting by British Railways have left ten miles intact between Tenterden and Bodiam. The preservation organisation was set up in 1961 immediately following the closure for all traffic of the Tenterden–Robertsbridge section and has faced many severe obstacles since then in its struggle to reinstate services over all or part of this portion of the line. Sheer dogged perseverance and enthusiasm finally won the day and the K & ESR jubilantly reopened for passenger traffic on 3 February 1974, almost exactly 20 years after the last BR passenger train over the line. An official reopening ceremony was performed on 1 June by the Rt Hon. William Deeds, MC, DL, MP, and by the end of the year over 37,000 passengers had travelled over the operating section to Morghew Crossing, half-a-mile west of Rolvenden. On 22 March 1975 a special ceremony was held at Rolvenden to celebrate the 75th anniversary of the opening of the original Rother Valley Railway from Robertsbridge, when No. 3 *Bodiam* hauled two 'birdcage' coaches conveying guests in period costume.

**Stock**

[2]LBSCR 0-6-0T No. 3 *Bodiam* (Stroudley A1X Class) built 1872
[3]LBSCR 0-6-0T No. 10 *Sutton* (Stroudley A1 Class) built 1876
[4]SECR 0-6-0T No. 11 *Pride of Sussex* (Wainwright P Class) built 1909
Peckett 0-4-0T No. 12 *Marcia* (1631) built 1923
Manning Wardle 0-6-0ST No. 14 *Charwelton* (1955) built 1917
Hunslet 0-6-0ST No. 15 *Hastings* (469) built 1888
BTH Bo-Bo DE No. 16 built 1932
Manning Wardle 0-6-0ST No. 17 *Arthur* (1601) built 1903
Peckett 0-6-0ST No. 18 *Westminster* (1378) built 1914
NSB 2-6-0 No. 19 (NSB No. 376) (Nohab 1163) built 1919
GWR/AEC Bo-Bo DM railcar No. 20 built 1940
[5]SR 0-6-0T No. 21 *Wainwright* (USA Class) built 1943
[3]SR 0-6-0T No. 22 *Maunsell* (USA Class) built 1943
Hunslet 0-6-0ST No. 23 *Holman F. Stephens* (3791) built 1952
Hunslet 0-6-0ST No. 24 *William H. Austen* (3800) built 1953
Hunslet 0-6-0ST *Linda* 3781 built 1952
RSH 0-6-0ST 7086 built 1943
Manning Wardle 0-6-0ST No. 38 *Dolobran* (1762) built 1910
Manning Wardle 0-6-0ST No. 41 *Rhyl* (2009) built 1921
RSH 0-6-0ST No. 26 (7667) built 1950
[1]Fox Walker 0-6-0ST *Minnie* (385) built 1878
Manning Wardle 0-4-0TG *Gervase* (1472) built 1900
RSH 0-4-0DH *Baglan* (8377) built 1962
Hunslet 0-6-0DM No. 28 *Dahlech* (4208) built 1958
North London Poly. 4WPM built 1979
Ruston Hornsby 4WDM (48DS Class) (252823) built 1947
SR Maunsell BSO R1 bogie coaches Nos 53 and 54 built 1930 (formerly SR Nos 4432 and 4443)
SR Maunsell CK R1 bogie coaches Nos 55 and 56 built 1930 (formerly SR Nos 5153 and 5618)
SR Maunsell SK RO bogie coach No. 59 built 1931 (formerly SR No. 1020)
SR Maunsell SO R1 bogie coach No. 58 built 1931 (formerly SR No. 7798)
SR Maunsell FK RO bogie coach No. 57 built 1931 (formerly SR No. 7400)
LSWR bogie tricomposite coach No. 62 built *c.* 1900 (formerly SR No. 318)

SECR 'birdcage' brake/third bogie coaches Nos 60 and 61
Four BR MK1 bogie coaches
BR restaurant-kitchen car No. E1955
GNR Clerestory Brake/Composite No. 127 (body only)
SR Pullman coaches Nos 184 *Barbara* and 185 *Theodora* built 1926
LNWR four-wheeled brake/third coach No. 101 built 1910
Shell-Mex oil tank wagon No. 7522 built 1943
Smith Rodley diesel crane No. 12019 built 1935
Five eight-ton open wagons
Two covered goods vans
SR 25-ton goods brake van No. 103 built 1941
SECR six-wheeled goods brake van No. 102
LNWR 20-ton goods brake van No. 104
Three Wickham petrol rail trolleys
Two flat wagons Nos. 115 and 116 (converted from tank wagons)
A 12 cu. yd bogie tipper wagon No. 117 built in USA

[1]Owned by the Industrial Locomotive Preservation Group
[2]Built at Brighton as No. 70 *Poplar* in November 1872. Sold to the Rother Valley Railway, becoming their No. 3 *Bodiam* in 1901. Absorbed by BR in 1948 as No. 32670, it was finally withdrawn from Eastleigh in November 1963. Purchased privately for use on the K & ESR, *Bodiam* has returned to the Rother Valley and hauled the reopening special train on 3 February 1974.
[3]Built at Brighton as No. 50 *Whitechapel* in December 1876. Renumbered 650 by the LBSCR, becoming Southern No. B650, it went to the Isle of Wight in 1930 as W9 *Fishbourne*. When returned to the mainland in 1937 the name was removed and it entered service stock as 515S for shunting at Lancing Carriage Works. Converted for oil burning in 1946 and reconverted to coal firing in 1947, it returned to ordinary service in October 1953 as BR No. 32650. Withdrawn from Eastleigh in November 1963, the locomotive was sold to Sutton Borough Council, who have loaned it to the K & ESR.
[4]Built at Ashford as SECR No. 753 and renumbered A556 by the Southern Railway in 1925. Became BR No. 31556 and was withdrawn in June 1961 and sold to James Hodson (Millers) Ltd of Robertsbridge who named the engine *Pride of Sussex*. Purchased for the K & ESR in 1969 and has since been overhauled and repainted.
[5]Both locomotives built by the Vulcan Ironworks, Wilkes-Barre, Pennsylvania, USA, in 1943 for the US Army Transportation Corps. They were taken into SR stock in December 1946 and on nationalisation became BR Nos 30070 and 30065 respectively. Both were withdrawn in October 1962 and transferred to SR service stock as DS238 and DS237 when they acquired their present names. Final withdrawal came in September 1967 and they were purchased for preservation a year later.

## 54 Romney Hythe and Dymchurch Railway

*Headquarters:* New Romney Station, Kent

Photo: Mike Wood

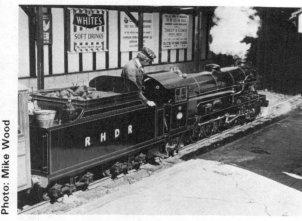

Masterpiece in miniature. One of Henry Greenly's RH & DR 4–8–2s No. 6 *Samson* shows its strength at the head of an express at New Romney

*Access:* The RH & DR is easily reached by road along the A259. Folkestone Central BR Station, thence by East Kent bus to Hythe RH & DR Station.
Tel: New Romney 2353
OS Ref: TR 074249

Passenger-carrying 15 in. gauge railway 13¾ miles long.
The railway operates daily from Easter to the end of September, also on Saturdays and Sundays in March, October and November.
*Details from:* The Manager, RH & DR, New Romney Station, Kent
*Facilities:* Car parks and refreshments at main stations. Model exhibition with large working 'O' gauge model railway at New Romney. Cheap return fares available on Friday mornings. Parties catered for.
The RH & DR is the only miniature railway in the British Isles to be authorised by a Light Railway Order. The railway was built by the late Captain J. E. P. Howey to serve a hitherto untapped part of the Kent coast and was opened to all traffic in stages between 1927 and 1929. At first, passenger and goods services operated all the year round, but the winter service did not pay and was withdrawn in 1948, whilst goods traffic ceased in 1951. During the war the railway was taken over by the military and after hostilities ceased the New Romney to Dungeness section was singled. Captain Howey died in 1963, but operation of the railway was continued by local business interests until arrears of maintenance forced them to contemplate closure in 1971. Happily this was forestalled by sale to a new consortium headed by Bill McAlpine and Brian Hollingsworth in February 1972. The RH & DR Association is a subscriber to the consortium and assists in publicising the railway and supplying volunteer labour.

*RH & DRA details from:* L. A. Adams, 43 Eliot Road, Dagenham, Essex RM9 5XT
**Stock**
Davey Paxman 4–6–2 No. 1 *Green Goddess* (21499) built 1925
Davey Paxman 4–6–2 No. 2 *Northern Chief* (21500) built 1925
Davey Paxman 4–6–2 No. 3 *Southern Maid* (22070) built 1926
Krauss 0–4–0 No. 4 *The Bug* (8378) built 1926
Davey Paxman 4–8–2 No. 5 *Hercules* (22071) built 1926
Davey Paxman 4–8–2 No. 6 *Samson* (22072) built 1926
Davey Paxman 4–6–2 No. 7 *Typhoon* (22073) built 1926
Davey Paxman 4–6–2 No. 8 *Hurricane* (22074) built 1926
Yorkshire Engine Co. 4–6–2 No. 9 *Winston Churchill* (2294) built 1931
Yorkshire Engine Co. 4–6–2 No. 10 *Doctor Syn* (2295) built 1931
Krupp 4–6–2 No. 11 *Black Prince* (1664) built 1937
Motor Rail 4WDM 7059 built 1938
RH & DR 4WPM No. PW2 built 1949
Forty-eight bogie saloon coaches
Four semi-open bogie coaches
Twelve open bogie coaches
Two Eaton Hall Railway coaches
Various works stock, approximately 40 units

## 55 Mid-Hants Railway                    A

(The 'Watercress' Line)
Alresford Station, Alresford, Hampshire SO24 9JG

*Access:* Close to the main A31 Guildford to Winchester Road, or by Alder Valley buses from Alton, Winchester or Southampton.
Tel: Alresford 3810, during operating days only.
OS Ref: SU 588325

Passenger carrying standard gauge railway, three miles in length from Alresford to Ropley.
The railway operates on Saturday afternoons, Sundays and Bank holidays from the end of March to the end of October. Facilities for visitors include car parking (at Alresford only), souvenir ship, refreshments and toilets.
The original Mid-Hants 'Watercress' line from Alton to Winchester Junction (17 miles) was closed by British Rail in 1973. Efforts to save the line started at once with Winchester and Alton Railway Ltd being successful in raising sufficient capital in 1975 to secure the land from Alton to Alresford (10 miles) and the track from Alresford to Ropley (3 miles). Valuable support is given by the Mid-Hants Railway Preservation Society whose membership is growing steadily. Opening of the Alresford-Ropley section took place on 30 April 1977, and since then the railway has become one of the fastest growing lines in the country. The locomotive shed at Ropley was constructed during 1979 and plans are now well in hand for the extension of the line from Ropley to Alton. Not only has all the land been bought but the necessary Light Railway Order has already been obtained.

Despite the appearance of the rustic fire brigade, the Mid Hants. Railway does in fact have its own water supply to top up its engines. Southern Mogul No. 31874 *Aznar Line* steams past on the railway's inaugural train

---

The 'Watercress' line is the only preserved section of the former London and South Western Railway.

**Stock**
[1]SR 2-6-0 No. 31806 ('U' Class) built 1928 – previously 'K' Class 2-6-4T No. A806 *River Torridge*, built 1926
[2]SR 2-6-0 No. 31874 ('N' Class) built 1925. Now named *Brian Fisk*
[3]SR 4-6-2 No. 34016 *Bodmin* ('West Country' Class) built 1945, rebuilt 1958
[4]BR 4-6-2 No. 34105 *Swanage* ('West Country' Class) built 1950
[5]LSWR 4-6-0 No. 30506 (Urie S15 Class) built 1920
LMS 0-6-0T No. 47324 (3F Class) North British Loco. Co. 23403 built 1926
BR 2-6-0 No. 76017 (Riddles 4MT Class) built 1953
[6]Hunslet 0-6-0ST No. 196 (3796) built 1953
[7]Hudswell Clarke 0-6-0ST *Slough Estates No. 3* (1544) built 1924
[8]Bagnall 0-4-0ST No. 2 (2842) built 1946
[9]Fowler 4WDM No. 4 (22889) built 1939, rebuilt 1958
BR tourist open second-class coaches Nos E4549 and E4600 built 1956
BR corridor composite coach No. W15798 built 1955

BR brake corridor composite coaches Nos E21077 built 1955 and E21092 built 1956
BR First open coach No. 3043 built 1954
BR First class corridor coach No. 13088 built 1954
BR Brake/Second corridor coach No. 34618 built 1955
BR Lavatory Composite coach No. 43012 built 1954
BR Brake/Second coach No. 43161 built 1955
BR Brake/Second coach No. 43190 built 1954
BR Second class coach No. 46069 built 1954 (To be converted into an office)
BR Second class coach No. 46116 built 1954
SR Bulleid Brake/3rd corridor coach No. 2850 built 1945
SR Maunsell Brake/3rd corridor coach No. 3190 built 1923
SR Maunsell Brake/2nd open coach No. 4449 built 1933 (Being converted to a handicapped persons saloon).
SR Maunsell Post Office Stowage van No. 4958 built 1939 (used as a workshop/stores van)
SR Bulleid Corridor Composite coach No. 5761 built 1947
SR Maunsell Brake Composite corridor coach No. 6601 built 1930
SR Bulleid brake third-class coach No. 4211 built 1947
SR Maunsell brake third-class coach No. 3719 built 1930
SR parcels brake van No. 765 built 1939
SECR parcels van No. 1995 built 1922
SR parcels vans Nos 1851 built 1940 and 2196 built 1934
LSWR Dining car No. 64 built 1905
LSWR Dining car No.76 built 1908
SR CCT van No. 1768 built 1938
SR Parcels van No. 2188 built 1934

LMS 'Stove R' 6-wheel van No. 32990 built 1938
BR (to LNER design) 6-wheel brake van No. 70692 built 1950
GWR 'Toad' 20-ton goods brake van No. 35907 built 1944
Tar tank wagon No. 95 (ex South Western Tar Distilleries) built 1939
LMS Flat wagon No. 202 built 1935
SR Box van No. 46011 built 1939
LSWR open wagon No. 46102
MR open wagon No. 46270 built c1920
Hurst Nelson open wagon No. 47081 built c1920
Woolwich Arsenal open wagon No. 47096 built c1920
NER Box van No. 47764
SR Box van No. 47777 built 1940
SR 25 ton Brake Van No. 55506 built 1926
Woolwich Arsenal open wagon No. 55858 built c1920
Threlkeld Granite Co. open wagon No. 57117 built c1920
SR Bogie Flat wagon No. 57849 built 1924
LMS Box van No. 91395 built 1933
LNER Box van No. 110504 built 1928
LMS Box van No. 513212 built 1940
SR Box van (for LMS) No. 514791 built 1942
LMS Box van No. 517317 built 1942
LMS Box van No. 523671 built 1945
LMS Box van No. 524430 built 1945
BR Pallet van No. 776446 built 1957
Wickham 4WPMR No. 1 8267 built 1934
Wickham 4WPMR No. DS339 6642 built 1953
Wickham 4WPMR No. AD9023 8087 built 1958
Isles, Stanningley self-propelled steam crane built 1886

[1]Originally built at Brighton in 1926 as a 'K' Class tank locomotive named *River Torridge*, it was rebuilt two years later as a 'U' Class tender engine. After World War II, No. 31806 was based at Faversham, Kent, but moved to Nine Elms, London, in October 1954 and to Basingstoke in June 1955. For nearly eight years this locomotive worked mainly semi-fast passenger services to and from the south coast until in March 1963 it was transferred back to Guildford, where it had been sent when new. Ten months later it was withdrawn and sent to Woodham Brothers scrapyard until purchased by two MHRPS directors in July 1975. The tender to be used with No. 31806 in future worked until 1960 with 'King Arthur' Class locomotive No. 30797 *Sir Blamor de Ganis* and latterly with S15 Class locomotive No. 30847.

[2]Mixed-traffic locomotive built from parts made at Woolwich Arsenal to relieve unemployment after World War I. The boiler came from the North British Locomotive Company in Glasgow and assembly of the complete locomotive took place at Ashford, Kent, in September 1925. One of its first tasks was the handling of passenger services from Waterloo to Bournemouth and Exeter, but in September 1933 transfer to Hither Green in South London took place. For 28 years the locomotive worked between London and the Kent coast, but when the lines in Kent were electrified, No. 31874 was sent to Exmouth Junction in Devon. From February 1961 it was frequently used on the North Cornwall line from Exeter to Padstow until withdrawn in April 1964. The journey to Woodham Brothers scrapyard at Barry then followed, but on 28 April 1973, No. 31874 was purchased by Mr John

Bunch, a director of the Mid-Hants Railway Preservation Society.

[3]One of 110 Pacific locomotives built to Southern Railway design after the last war which received 'West Country' and 'Battle of Britain' names. No. 34106 was built at Brighton and entered traffic at Exmouth Junction, near Exeter, in November 1945. The locomotive was rebuilt to its current form in February 1958 and transferred to Ramsgate. During the summer of 1959 the first stage of railway electrification in East Kent was introduced, and *Bodmin* was transferred to Bricklayers Arms depot in South-East London. A further move took place in May 1961 when No. 34016 became based at Eastleigh, but in June 1964 it was withdrawn from traffic and used for safety-valve setting at Eastleigh until despatched to Woodham Brothers scrapyard. Mr John Bunch saved No. 34016 from destruction in 1971, and on 29 July 1972 the locomotive completed a move by road from the scrapyard to Quainton Road Station, near Aylesbury, where restoration work commenced. Now owned by John Bunch and Richard Heather.

[4]After being built at Brighton in February 1950, *Swanage* was based at Bournemouth for all its comparatively short working life, and regularly handled express workings on the Waterloo–Southampton–Bournemouth route. Unlike many similar locomotives, including *Bodmin* (above), *Swanage* remained in its original form until withdrawn in October 1964. Four months later it was towed to South Wales for cutting up at Woodham Brothers scrapyard, but like most engines sent there No. 34105 enjoyed a stay of execution, and in April 1976 was purchased by a group of 'Watercress' line supporters. The tender bought to run with this engine was last used with 'Merchant Navy' Class locomotive No. 35018 *British India Line*.

[5]Withdrawn in 1964 and sold to Woodham Brothers, Barry, for scrap. Purchased for preservation in April 1973. The Urie S15 Class represented an important landmark in locomotive development. No. 30506 is the only preserved locomotive to represent the work of Robert Wallace Urie, the Chief Mechanical Engineer of the LSWR between 1912 and 1922. Twenty of these 4-6-0 engines were built to Urie's design at Eastleigh during 1920–21, and with their 5 ft 7 in. driving wheels provided the main source of power for fast freight duties from Feltham and later throughout the Southern Railway system. At busy periods they were also to be found on passenger duties, being able to produce speeds of 65–70 mph if occasion demanded. This locomotive is owned by the Urie S15 Preservation Group (q.v.).

[6]A fine example of a popular class of 0-6-0 saddletank locomotive built in large quantities during and after World War II. Constructed by the Hunslet Engine Company of Leeds in 1953, No. 196 was included in a batch of 14 destined for the War Reserve. Three are still operated by the Army, whilst several others are still in use on private railways in England. Our locomotive is believed to have been stored near here, at Liphook, until September 1955, when it was transferred to Honeybourne in Worcestershire, arriving on 16 September. Further transfers took place on 26 July 1957 to nearby Long Marston, and on 7 November 1960, when it was sent for general overhaul to the Central Workshops

at Bicester. In November 1964 it returned to Hampshire, destined for the 16th Railway Regiment, Royal Engineers, at Longmoor. Shortly afterwards, on 22 January 1965, No. 196 entered service on the Longmoor Military Railway and worked regularly until the line closed at the end of October 1969. Whilst there, on 8 January 1968, No. 196 was named *Errol Lonsdale* after the Transport Officer-in-Chief, Major General Lonsdale.

[7]Built by Hudswell Clarke at Leeds in 1924, works number 1544, this locomotive worked for 49 years at the Slough Trading Estate hauling freight around the extensive system there. In 1973 the last two locomotives were withdrawn and the one in the best condition was offered to Winchester and Alton Railway Limited on free permanent loan, together with a large quantity of spares, by Slough Estates Limited. It became the second locomotive to appear at Alresford for our project, arriving on 18 August 1973, and will be seen in action next year, shunting at Alresford and Ropley.

[8]Built by W. G. Bagnall at Stafford in 1946, works number 2842, this small tank locomotive was purchased in 1973 by a group of 'Watercress' line supporters from the CEGB Croydon Power Station. Transfer to Alresford by road was completed on 24 July 1973. No. 2 will eventually be used on light shunting duties here.

[9]This useful locomotive was built by John Fowler and Company in Leeds during 1939, works number 22889, and was one of many used by the War Department. In 1958 it was completely modernised and received a new Maclaren six-cylinder 150 hp engine. When renumbering of Army locomotives took place in 1968, the number 242 was allotted in place of 852, but 224 was applied in error and the number was never amended. Latterly No. 224 was used at HM Victualling Depot at Botley, near Southampton, but earlier this year it was bought in working order by G. A. Day Limited who presented it on permanent loan to Winchester and Alton Railway.

Details of the Mid-Hants Railway Preservation Society Ltd may be obtained from the Membership Secretary at Alresford Station.

*Membership:* 2,300
*Annual Subscription:* Adult £3, Child/OAP £1.50, Family £5, Life £40, OAP Life £10.

### Urie S15 Locomotive Preservation Group    H

Alresford Station, Mid-Hants Railway

*Membership and shares:* Hon. Treasurer, Flat 4, 'Lingfield', Elvetham Road, Fleet, Hampshire GU13 8QW
*Subscriptions:* Annual £1.50; junior (under 18) and senior (over 65) 75p; life £30; joint (husband and wife) £2.25
*Membership:* 675

## 56   Isle of Wight Steam Railway    A

Haven Street Station, near Ryde, Isle of Wight

*Access:* Service 3 Southern Vectis bus operates from Ryde Esplanade or Newport and stops outside Haven Street

Steam on the Wight lines. Hawthorn Leslie 0–4–0ST No. 37 *Invincible* looks at home in this rural setting

Photo: Mike Wood

Station. Inclusive through 'Awayday' tickets available from a number of Southern Region stations, Portsmouth Harbour and Southsea (Clarence Pier)
Tel: Wootton Bridge 882204
OS Ref: SZ 556898

Passenger-carrying standard gauge steam railway, 1¾ miles in length, from Haven Street to Wootton.

The railway operates on Easter Sunday and Monday, on Sundays from May to September, on Thursdays in July and August and on Spring and Summer Bank Holidays.

Facilities for visitors include car parking, museum, souvenir shop, refreshments and toilets.

The Wight Locomotive Society was formed in 1966 to preserve a selection of Isle of Wight rolling stock, together with the locomotive *Calbourne*. After several years storage at Newport, the stock was moved over the closed line to Haven Street in January 1971 and, following negotiations with the IWCC, the Haven Street–Wootton section of single line was leased. The Society subsequently formed the Isle of Wight Railway Company Limited to operate and administer the steam railway, which has become a popular tourist attraction with holidaymakers and day visitors alike. Haven Street Station, rebuilt by the SR in 1926, was a former passing place on the Ryde–Newport line. The original station at Wootton was closed in 1953 and demolished soon after and, although it was hoped to reopen the former station, an extensive earth-slip on the site made this impossible. Consequently, a new terminal station has been built at Wootton.

A workshop is being built at Haven Street to speed the process of restoring the growing collection of historic rolling stock. The Isle of Wight Steam Railway is alone amongst the standard gauge preserved railways in the British Isles in using exclusively pre-grouping carriages to form its trains.

## Stock

[1]LBSCR 0–6–0T No. W8 *Freshwater* (Class A1X) built 1876
[2]LBSCR 0–6–0T No. W11 *Newport* (Class A1X) BR No. 32640 built 1878
[3]LSWR 0–4–4T No. W24 *Calbourne* (Class O2) built 1891
[4]Hawthorn Leslie 0–4–0ST No. 37 *Vectis* (3135) built 1915
[5]Andrew Barclay 0–6–0T No. 38 *Ajax* (1605) built 1918
[6]Ruston Hornsby 4WDM No. 39 *Spitfire* (242868) built 1946
LBSCR nine-compartment third-class coach No. 2416 built 1916
IWR four-compartment second No. 2421 (body only) built c. 1880
LCDR five-compartment brake/third No. 4115 (body only) built 1898
SECR four-compartment brake/third coaches Nos 4145 and 4149 built 1911
LBSCR five-compartment brake/third coach No. 4168 built 1922 on an underframe constructed in 1905
IWR three-compartment composite No. 6335 (body only) built 1882
SR to LBSCR design eight-compartment composite coach No. 6349 built 1924
SECR composite saloon coach No. 6375 built 1911
LSWR 'Road Van' No. 56046 built 1898
LBSCR 10-ton open wagons Nos 27834 and 64396 built c. 1924
LBSCR 10-ton rebuilt BR dropside open wagons Nos 27766 and 28345 built c. 1924 and rebuilt to ballast wagons in 1966
SR 13-ton high-sided open wagons Nos 27910, 27926, 27936 and 27937 built 1927 (acquired from Messrs Corralls in 1975 and some to be rebuilt for Engineering Department use)
LBSCR 10-ton machinery wagon No. 60579 built 1923
SBSCR single-bolster wagons Nos 59030, 59049 and 59050 built c. 1909
IWCR (originally Midland Railway) six-wheeled crane No. 429S built c. 1860
IWCR (originally LSWR) four-wheeled match wagon No. DS3139
IWCR eight-ton goods van (body only) built c. 1880 at Newport, Isle of Wight
SR PMV parcels van No. 1052 built 1943
BR single bolster wagons Nos DB450157, DB451289, DB451924, DB452018, DB452715, DB453374 built 1950–59
BR Wickham petrol trolley No. DS3320
BR Matisa tamping unit No. DS72
Underframe of Drewry Railcar No. 2 (Ryde Pier Tramway) built 1927

A number of the above passenger and goods vehicles are privately owned and are on loan to the Wight Locomotive Society.

Just a few months ago this engine was Britain's biggest pub sign! Thanks to Whitbread's brewery, this little Brighton Terrier No. 8 *Freshwater* has been returned to the Isle of Wight and was quickly back in her Southern livery at Haven Street. Cheers!

[1]Stroudley 'Terrier' sold to the LSWR in 1903 as their No. 734. Resold to Freshwater, Yarmouth and Newport Railway, becoming their No. 2 in 1913. Became SR No. W8 *Freshwater* and returned to the mainland in 1949 as BR No. 32646. Sold to Sadler Rail Coach Ltd in 1964 and resold to Brickwoods Ltd, who restored it to LBSCR yellow livery for use as a 'pub' sign in 1966. Returned to the Isle of Wight in 1979.
[2]Originally LBSCR No. 40 *Brighton*, sold to Isle of Wight Central Railway in 1902, becoming their No. 11, later SR No. W11 *Newport*. Returned to mainland in 1947 as SR No. 2640. Withdrawn as BR No. 32640 in 1963 and restored to LBSCR livery at Eastleigh Works in 1964 for sale to Butlins Ltd for display at their Pwllheli holiday camp. Placed on loan to the Wight Locomotive Society in 1973 and purchased outright in 1976. Restored externally to IWCR lined black livery with replica Hurst and Wheeler chimney and being restored mechanically by 1978.
[3]Originally LSWR No. 209. Rebuilt with enlarged bunker and Westinghouse brake and transferred to the Isle of Wight in 1925 as SR No. W24. Withdrawn in 1967 and purchased for preservation. Moved to Haven Street with remainder of WLS stock in 1971. Now the sole survivor of this once numerous class.
[4]Built for use at Woolwich Arsenal during World War I. Transferred in 1959 to the RAE, Farnborough, to haul coal and stores from the BR goods yard through the streets of the town to the RAE some miles away. Purchased by a Southampton businessman in 1968 and placed on loan to the WLS in 1971. This locomotive has been fitted with Westinghouse brake equipment at Haven Street for the operation of passenger trains. Now owned by the WLS.
[5]Latterly worked at British Steel Corporation works at Harlaxton, near Grantham. Purchased by a private owner and placed on loan to the WLS in 1972. *Ajax* is believed to have

been the heaviest single load to cross the Solent on the Portsmouth–Fishbourne car ferry.
[6]This locomotive entered service with the Gas Light and Coke Co. at Southall Gas Works in 1946. Made redundant in 1965, it was purchased privately for possible use in the Meon Valley when attempts were being made to reopen this line. Placed on loan to the WLS and transferred to Haven Street in June 1972.

### Wight Locomotive Society

*Full details from:* The Secretary, Wight Locomotive Society, Haven Street Station, Ryde, Isle of Wight PO33 4DS
*Membership rates:* £3 ordinary; £1.50 junior (under 16), associate or Isle of Wight railway staff; £75 life.


## 57  Hollycombe Woodland Railway            A

Hollycombe Woodland Garden, Steam Fair and Steam Railway, Hollycombe House, near Liphook, Hampshire

*Operated by:* Mr J. M. Baldock

A 2 ft gauge passenger-carrying line, 1½ miles long plus a short standard-gauge line and other steam attractions in the grounds of Hollycombe House.

*Access:* A3 and Liphook BR station 1½ miles.
OS Ref: SU B52295

The Woodland Railway and Steam Fairground are open every Sunday and Bank Holiday from Easter to October from 2 pm onwards. Car park and gardens open at noon.
In an attractive wooded setting of azaleas, rhododendrons and trees planted at the turn of the century, a unique collection of steam-driven equipment has been assembled. It includes a 2 ft gauge and a standard gauge railway, a roundabout with its own steam organ, the steam swing yacht 'Neptune', road locomotive 'Princess Mary', the only 'Razzle-Dazzle' still in existence, and other items. Traction engine rides are available.
Facilities for visitors include car parking, museum, souvenir shop, refreshments and toilets.

### Stock
[1]Barclay 0–4–0WT No. 1 *Caledonia* (1995) built 1931
[2]Hunslet 0–4–0ST *Jerry M* (638) built 1895
[3]Motor rail 4WDM 8979 built 1946
Ruston Hornsby 4WDM 203016 (44/48HP Class) built 1941
Three ex-Ramsgate Tunnel Railway bogie coaches built 1936
Open-sided bogie coach
The railway runs up to a quarry where there is a vantage point from which extensive views of the South Downs are commanded.
Also a 300-yard standard gauge line on which the following locomotive hauls 2 flat wagons and an LNER Brake Van adapted for passenger-carrying:
[4]Aveling Porter 0–4–0TG *Sir Vincent* (8800) built 1917)

[1]Formerly at Dinorwic Slate Quarries, Llanberis, Caernarfonshire, until 1962 when it was preserved by the Hampshire Narrow Gauge Railway Society (Group No. 80)
Re-sold to John Baldock in 1967.

[2]Ex Dinorwic Slate Quarries Co. Ltd., Llanberis, Caernarfonshire, 1967.
[3]Ex Sir Robert McAlpine and Sons Ltd., Hayes, Middlesex, 1968.
[4]Ex BOCM Ltd., Erith, Kent, 1966. *Sir Vincent* is a standard gauge tramway or shunting locomotive built by Aveling and Porter, the famous makers of steam rollers, in 1917. There are only six of these strange locomotives with flywheels left. They are a cross between a ploughing engine (top half) and a railway locomotive (below). They are slow but very powerful. All Aveling and Porter engines carried the Kent horse Invicta on their smoke-box doors as they were built at Rochester.

*Standard gauge static exhibits*
Hawthorn Leslie 0–4–0ST *Albert* (2450) built 1899
SR steam crane
Ex J. W. Hardwick, Sons and Co. Ltd., dealers, West Ewell, Surrey

*Stone handling and crushing.* At the railheads of the quarry railway and the tramway a Grafton crane can be seen grabbing stone from a bank formed by the tipping trucks, representing the transfer from narrow to standard gauge line. The crane is especially interesting as it was probably the last steam-propelled vehicle to operate on British Rail track in London, where it was working as a shunting engine at Nine Elms in 1967. The stone crusher is driven by a large Marshall 12 nhp portable engine, No. 72531, new to Henry Sykes Ltd of London in 1920 for pumping service.


## 58  Dreamland Park Railway            A

Dreamland Park, Margate, Kent

OS Ref: TR 352706
*Access:* Margate BR Station

Passenger carrying 15 in. gauge railway, ¾ mile in length, laid out in the form of a balloon loop.
The line operates at Easter and then from Spring Bank Holiday until mid-September.
The Dreamland Railway is one of the oldest established miniature railways in Great Britain. The present line was opened in 1924, but was laid on the site of an earlier line dating from 1913. Trains start from, and finish at Park Station, which has two platform roads with a centre run round loop. The line has recently been restored to good order and features include gradients as steep as 1 in 40.

### Stock
Barnes 4–4–2 No. 1 *Billie* 104 built in 1928
Ford Bo-BoPM *Roadrunner* rebuilt A. Lynch 1959
Pepper 0–4–0PM built 1975
Six articulated open bogie coaches
Goods brake van
Steam locomotive obtained secondhand from the Rhyl Marine Lake Miniature Railway


## 59  Littlehampton Miniature Railway            A

Mewsbrook Park, Littlehampton, Sussex

Passenger carrying 12¼ in. gauge railway 900 yards in length. The railway operates at Easter, then at weekends until Spring Bank Holiday, after which operation is daily until the middle of September.

The railway was opened in 1948 from the eastern end of the Common at Littlehampton, close to the junction of Norfolk and Sea Roads, to Mewsbrook Park, on the eastern fringe of town. The track is single throughout, with two roads at each terminus serving an island platform. The journey time, outwards and return is about 12 minutes.

**Stock**

Cookson/Bullock 4–6–4 No. 1005 built *c.* 1933 re-built 1939

Cookson/Bullock 4–6–4 No. 2010 built *c.* 1933 re-built 1939

Bognor Pier Railway 0–4–2P No. 3015 built *c.* 1966 (steam outline)

Bognor Pier Railway 2–4–2P No. 4020 built 1969 (steam outline)

Ten vacuum-braked bogie open coaches

Both steam locomotives converted from 10¼ in. gauge tank engines designed by H. C. S. Bullock for the Surrey Border and Camberley Railway and can each haul eight coaches up the maximum gradient of 1 in 70.

## 60  Canterbury                                     E

Dane John Gardens, Canterbury, Kent

Standard gauge steam locomotive on static display

**Stock**

Canterbury & Whitstable Railway 0–4–0 *Invicta* (Robert Stephenson 24 built 1830)

Withdrawn 1839 and presented for preservation in Darlington in 1850. Later removed and displayed at various exhibitions until presented to the City of Canterbury and placed on display in 1906. Restored by the Transport Trust in association with the National Railway Museum, York 1978-79.

## 61  Great Cockrow Railway                     A

Hardwick Lane, Lyne, Chertsey, Surrey

*Access:* Alder Valley bus from Chertsey or Woking to Holloway Hill (½ mile walk). Chertsey BR station
OS Ref: TQ 025666

Passenger carrying 7¼ in. gauge railway offering a run of ⅞ mile in total.

The railway operates on Sundays from the first Sunday in May to the last Sunday of British Summer time, between 3 pm and 6 pm. Much of the system of the Great Cockrow

Railway was material from the former Greywood Central Railway, established by the late Sir John Samuel in Burwood Park, Weybridge. This was bought by Ian Allan in 1965 and services began at Great Cockrow in 1968. The railway consists of a double track main line with single track loop lines, affording a total run of ⅞ mile. Intensive operation is a feature of this railway; an extremely comprehensive signalling installation allowing as many as six trains to run on the circuit at once. The line is fully signalled with semaphores and colour lights controlled from two signal boxes which are linked by block instruments and bells as in full size practice. Further interest is added by the varied gradients, some of them as steep as 1 in 50. A branch line, 306 yards in length, engineering works for which include a 45 ft viaduct, should be open fully for the 1980 season. A friendly welcome awaits all steam enthusiasts on this fascinating little railway.

**Stock**

Freelance GCR 4–6–2 No. 1947 *Eureka* built *c.* 1934

LMS 4–6–0 No. 5157 *The Glasgow Highlander* (Class 5MT) built Penfold 1972

SR 4–6–0 No. 837 (Class S15)

LNER 2–6–0 No. 206 (Class K5)

LNER 2–6–0 No. 1935 (Class K3)

GWR 4–6–0 No. 7915 *Mere Hall*

[1]SR 2–6–0 No. 1803 *River Itchen*

LMS 4–6–0 No. 6100 *The Royal Scot*

Marsh 0–4–2T 'Tinkerbell' class built 1978

Freelance 0–6–0TT *Wendy*

LMS 0–6–0DM No. 11 *Winifred*

Shepperton 4WDM *Thunderbolt 1*

Cromar White Bo-BoPM No. D7025 built 1978

Sixteen bogie coaches

Eighteen wagons of various kinds

Visiting locomotives are often to be seen on the railway, whose resident locomotive stock is steadily growing each year.

[1]Rebuilt from GWR-type 2–6–0 *Maid of Kent*, formerly owned by Mr Alex Schwab of the Saltwood Miniature Railway (Group No. 88).

The railway is operated by a consortium of enthusiasts on behalf of Ian Allan Ltd.
*Details from:* The Secretary, Terminal House, Shepperton, Middlesex TW17 8AS.

## 62  Stonecot Miniature Railway             A

Queen Mary's Hospital for Children, Carshalton, Surrey

Passenger-carrying 10¼ in. gauge railway. This line is on private property, but opens to the public quite frequently.

**Stock**

LMS 4–6–0 No. 6100 *The Royal Scot* built Wilmot

Cromar White Bo-BoDM No. D7022

Four open bogie coaches

## 63  Birchley Railway                                              A

Birchley House, Biddenden, Kent

*Access:* Nearest Stations, Headcorn BR or Tenterden Town
K&ESR
Tel: 0580 291413
OS Ref: TQ 845372

Passenger-carrying 10¼ in. gauge railway, 700 feet in length
in the private grounds of Mr D. M. Randall at Birchley House.
The railway may be visited by prior arrangement only. Please
write or telephone beforehand to make firm arrangements.
Casual visitors will not be well received.
The Birchley Railway was opened as recently as 1976 and
will ultimately offer a ¾-mile run over a figure of eight track.
To date, over 700 ft of track has been laid, a bridge and
tunnel are to be built, and another 500 feet of track laid to
complete the first loop. Trains are operated over this part
of the layout whilst construction work is in progress. Regular
operation of the railway has not yet commenced, though
operating days are held from time to time.

### Stock
LBSCR 0-6-0T No. 84 *Crowborough* (A1X Class)
Two battery electric locomotives
Petrol hydraulic locomotive under construction
Four sit astride coaches
Two open wagons

## 64  Medina Valley Railway                                         F

Newport–Cowes, Isle of Wight

Passenger-carrying 15 in. gauge railway to be laid on the
trackbed of the former IWCR Newport–Cowes line.
Planning permission for the construction of three miles of
this line has been obtained. The railway will have as a
nucleus of its rolling stock, all the locomotives and stock
formerly operated by Mr T. E. Tate at Haswell Lodge, County
Durham

### Stock
Bassett Lowke 4-4-2 *Little Giant* built 1905
Younger 4-4-0 *Yvette* (LNER D49 Class)
Bassett Lowke 4-4-4PM *Blacolvesley* built 1909 (steam
outline)
LMS 4-6-0 No. 6100 *Royal Scot* built Carland
Barlow 4-6-2DM *Princess*
Barlow 4-6-2DM
Two 24-seat articulated bogie coaches
Cowans Sheldon steam crane built Cheeseman 1974

## 65  Wey Valley Light Railway                                      B

Old Pumping Station, Guildford Road, Farnham, Surrey

OS Ref: SU 848473

Operated by Farnham District Scouts Service Team. This
passenger-carrying 2 ft gauge line is at present confined to
a ¼-mile run, but the final track plan envisages both 'out
and back' and 'continuous run' arrangements around the

Scouts' HQ, totalling over half a mile.
The Wey Valley Railway also operates as a 'portable' line,
visiting fairs, fetes and exhibitions in the locality. On these
occasions full advantage is taken of the light weight nature
of the 2 ft equipment; locomotives, rolling stock and 'Jubilee'
track all being readily transportable by this enterprising
Scout Group.

*Details from:* Michael Hayer, 1 Heather View Cottages,
Shortfield Common, Frensham, Farnham, Surrey.

### Stock
Jung 4WDM 5869
Hibberd 4WDM No. 395 2528
Hunslet 4WDM 1974 built 1939
Thakeham 4WPM *Thakeham* built 1950
Ruston Hornsby 4WDM 189972 built 1938
Hibberd 4WDM 1767 built 1931
Bredonvale 4WPM *Bredonvale* built 1950
Wickham/Petters 4WDM No. 4 3031 built 1941
Three open four-wheeled coaches
Fifteen four-wheeled skip wagons
Tank wagon
Two roofed 4-wheel coaches

## 66  Hythe Pier Electric Railway                                   B

Hythe, near Southampton, Hampshire

*Access:* By ferryboat from Southampton
OS Ref: SU 423081

Passenger-carrying 2 ft gauge electric railway, 700 yards
in length operated by the General Estates Co. Ltd, Hot-
spur House, Hythe, Hampshire, in conjunction with the
Hythe–Southampton ferry.
The ferry service and pier railway operate each weekday
throughout the year and on Sunday afternoons, June to
September inclusive from 2 pm to 8 pm. The train fare is
now included in the ferry fare. The railway was operated in
the early 1900s and converted to electrical operation in July
1922 using a raised outside third rail energised at 240 volts
80 amps. The pier itself dates back to 1880. Trains run in
connection with the ferry boat service which generally
operates half hourly.

### Stock
Brush 4WE 16302 built 1917
Brush 4WE 16307 built 1917
Four bogie saloon passenger coaches
Tank wagon
Baggage wagon

## 67  Drusilla's Zoo Park                                           B

Alfriston, East Sussex

*Access:* Berwick BR Station or Southdown Bus 126. Just
off the B1208 between Berwick and Alfriston
Tel: 0323-870234
OS Ref: TQ 524050

Passenger-carrying 2 ft gauge railway, ¼ mile in length.

Open from 1 April to 20 September on a daily basis and at weekends in March and October.

Facilities for visitors include car parking, refreshments, toilets, souvenir shop, pottery and woodworking craftsmen, antique shop, art gallery, garden centre and zoo.

The present railway at Drusilla's was opened in 1948 and reconstructed on a circular route in 1951. However, in pre-war years, a 9½ in. gauge steam-operated line conveyed passengers for about a mile from Drusilla's to the River Cuckmere on which boats could be hired. Motive power was provided by a Stroudley LBSCR steam locomotive built by R. H. Morse, of Henfield. Unfortunately, this early line became a war victim, being used by the Canadian Army as a target for tanks. Nowadays, the ride takes passengers past several paddocks and skirts the playground before passing through part of the zoo park. Here the animal paddocks adjoin the track and wallabies and flamingoes, llamas and monkeys may be seen before arriving back at the station. In 1979, both zoo and railway celebrated their Golden Jubilee.

**Stock**

Hibberd 4WPM Y type 3116 built 1946 (now static exhibit)
Ruston Hornsby 4WDM *Emily* 226294 (steam outline)
Five 4-seat, 4-wheeled open coaches

## 68   Volks Electric Railway                     B

Madeira Drive, Brighton, Sussex

*Access:* All buses to Pool Valley and Old Steine pass the Aquarium terminus of the railway, 100 yards off Palace Pier
Tel: Brighton 681061

Passenger-carrying 2 ft 8½ in. gauge electric railway, 1¼ miles in length operated by the Borough of Brighton, Royal York Buildings, Brighton BN1 1NP.

The railway operates from Easter to the end of September between 9.45 am and 6.15 pm approx. Also runs later on Bank Holidays and Sundays.

The Volks Electric Railway was the first electrically-powered railway in Great Britain, being opened in 1883, and is thus fast approaching its operating centenary. The track is single throughout and fenced to keep pedestrians off the 'live' third rail. There are three stations and two passing loops allowing a five minute frequency service to operate. There are warning signals at pedestrian crossings, whilst trains are despatched from the stations by means of a bell signal supported by a flashing light indication controlled from the headquarters at Paston Place. After experiments in 1964, all the cars have now been fitted for multiple working in units of two in order to cope with heavy traffic periods.

**Stock**

Roofed cross-bench cars Nos. 1 and 2
Semi-saloon cars Nos. 3, 4, 5, 6 and 7
Ex Southend Pier Railway crossbench cars Nos. 8 and 9.

## 69   Brighton and Hove Engineerium          E

Hove, Sussex

Miniature gauge steam locomotives on static display.

**Stock**

LNER 4-6-2 No. 4472 *Flying Scotsman* built Stewart 1976 (15 in. gauge)
LSWR 4-6-0 No. 486 H15 class built 1926 (7¼ in. gauge)
Stephenson 0-4-0 Locomotive (7¼ in. gauge)
Netherlands Railway 2-2-2 built 1864 (7¼ in. gauge)

## 70   Brockham Museum                           E

Chalkpit Lane, Brockham, Betchworth, Surrey RH3 7EZ

*Access:* Betchworth BR Station (1 mile), Dorking North BR Station (2 miles), London country bus route 414 to Brockham Lane
OS Ref: TQ 198510

An operational museum which demonstrates the remarkable variety and uses of narrow gauge railways. A large collection of locomotives and rolling stock has been assembled from all over the country and many items can be demonstrated in action on a ½-mile 2 ft gauge line built along the side of the North Downs. Open Days are held on the third Sunday of each month, between 11.30 am and 5.30 pm, from April to September, when all exhibits are available for close inspection. Visitors and prospective members are also welcome to look around most Sundays throughout the year.

The museum is in the natural setting of a chalk quarry, at the foot of Box Hill, Surrey. Access to the site is via a track off the A25 between Dorking and Reigate. The Pilgrim's Way footpath passes right through the museum. Visitors are asked to take great care when coming on to the site, for the lane is a farm track, with a poor surface, although quite passable.

There is a level crossing with the BR tracks. Should the gates be closed, please sound your horn and wait for them to be opened for you. Please do not open them for yourself. There is a large car park on the site, and it would be appreciated if all visitors would come right up to this, rather than parking in the lane or on the main road.

Parties are always welcome, but notification should be given in advance of any party of more than fifteen people planning to visit the site, especially if the visit is not planned to coincide with one of the 'open days'. In such cases it is possible sometimes for special trains to be run, but where parties include children (under 16), there must be at least one adult to every ten children.

**Stock**

Bagnall 0-4-0ST *Peter* (2067) built 1918 (2 ft gauge)
Bagnall 2-4-0T *Polar Bear* (1781) built 1905 (2 ft gauge)
Peckett 0-6-0ST *Scaldwell* (1316) built 1913 (3 ft gauge)
Fletcher Jennings 0-4-0T *Townsend Hook* 172 built 1880 (3 ft 2¼ in. gauge)
Spence 0-4-0T No. 23 built 1920 (1 ft 10 in. gauge)
Ransomes & Rapier 2WDM 80 built 1937 (2 ft gauge)
Ruston Hornsby 4WDM No. 2 166024 built 1933 (2 ft gauge) 16HP Class.
Motor rail 4WPM 872 built 1918 (2 ft gauge)
Orenstein and Koppel 4WDM *The Major* 7741 built 1937 (2 ft gauge)
Orenstein and Koppel 4WDM *Monty* 7269 built 1936 (3 ft 2¼ in. gauge)

Orenstein and Koppel 4WDM 6193 built 1937 (2 ft gauge)
Hunslet 4WDM 3097 built 1944 (2 ft gauge)
Fowler 4WDM *Peldon* 21295 built 1936 (2 ft gauge)
Wickham 4WPMR No. WD 904 3403 1943 (2 ft gauge)
Motor Rail 4WDM No. LR3041 1320 built 1918 (2 ft gauge)
Lister 4WPM 29890 built 1946 (2 ft gauge)
Wingrove & Rogers 4WBE No. 2 5031 built 1953 (2 ft gauge)
Wickham 4-wheeled 12-seat trailer coach No. 3404 (2 ft gauge)
Rye and Camber Tramway bogie coach built 1895 (3 ft gauge)
RAF Fauld Railway Hudson bogie coach No. 275 built 1940 (2 ft gauge)
Groudle Glen Railway coach (2 ft gauge)
Oakeley incline man-rider car
Colne Valley/Hudson man-rider car
Spence Converter bogie No. 4 built 1919 (5 ft 3 in. gauge)
Dorking Greystone Lime side tipping wagon No. 3 built 1930 (3 ft 2¼ in. gauge)
Dorking Greystone Lime end tipping wagon No. 10 (3 ft 2¼ in. gauge)
Staveley Minerals Wooden side tipping wagon (3 ft gauge)
Sussex & Dorking United Brick cable-hauled side tipping wagon No. 19 (2 ft 6 in. gauge)
Two Alpha Cement side-tipping wagons built by Allens of Tipton (2 ft gauge)
Robert Brett side discharge wagon (2 ft gauge)
Robert Hudson braked 'V' hopper wagon built 1940 (2 ft gauge)
South Durham Iron & Steel Incline 'Breakaway' wagon (2 ft gauge)
London Brick Co. Cable-hauled side-tipping wagon No. 167E (2 ft 6 in. gauge)
Dinorwic Quarries coal wagon (1 ft 10¾ in. gauge)
Dinorwic Quarries Incline Slab wagon No. 115 (1 ft 10¾ in. gauge)
Oakeley Quarries Slate rubbish wagon (1 ft 11½ in. gauge)
Llechwedd 2-ton slate wagon built LNWR in 1887 (1 ft 11½ in. gauge)
Maen Offeren 2-ton slate wagon built GWR in 1889 (1 ft 11½ in. gauge)
Ball Clay Mine Wagon (1 ft 10 in. gauge)
Fireclay Mining tub No. 12 (1 ft 10 in. gauge)
Penrhyn Quarries Slate Wagon No. 205 (1 ft 10¾ in. gauge)
Penrhyn Quarries Fullersite wagon No. 46 (1 ft 10¾ in. gauge)
Penrhyn Quarries Coal wagon No. 2 (1 ft 10¾ in. gauge)
Chain-hauled clay tub (Flangeless Plateway Type) (1 ft 6 in. gauge)
London Brick Co. Side-discharge clay wagon No. 26 (2 ft 11 in. gauge)
Robert Hudson end-tipping 'V'-hopper wagon (2 ft gauge)
Colne Valley inside-framed flat wagon (2 ft gauge)
Alpha Cement outside-framed flat wagon (2 ft gauge)
Cornish China Clay metal-framed rotary tipping wagon (2 ft gauge)
Cornish China Clay wooden-framed rotary tipping wagon (2 ft gauge)
Nine Robert Hudson 'V'-hopper wagons.

The museum is administered by the Brockham Museum Trust, which is registered as an Educational Charity (No. L247044). The Brockham Museum Association was formed to enable interested persons to contribute towards the construction of this museum, by working on the site, helping with the organisation, or by just paying a modest annual subscription and maintaining an interest. Our members come from all trades and professions, and work together on an entirely voluntary basis.

*Membership:* 90.
*Annual Subscription:* £2.50; Introductory 20p. (1979 rate).
All visitors must become a member at present.
*Details from:* David H. Smith, 'The Mount', 14 Sydney Road, Haywards Heath, West Sussex RH16 1PZ.

## 71    Island Narrow Gauge Railway Group    C

Complete 2 ft gauge portable light railway for hire.
The Group take their rolling stock to fairs, fetes, exhibitions and other narrow gauge railways during the course of the year. During the winter season, the stock is generally housed on the Great Bush Railway (Group No. 81).

**Stock**
¹Kerr Stuart 0-4-0ST No. 13 *Peter Pan* 4256 built 1922
Lister 4WDM No. 3 *Goat* 8022 built 1921

¹The *Wren* was one of the smallest types of steam locomotive built for industrial use and was once common on road building contracts, in sandpits and quarries, etc., at home and overseas. A total of 167 locomotives were built between 1905 and 1941, the last four being built by the Hunslet Engine Company Ltd in Leeds after the closure of Kerr, Stuart in 1930. Of the 167, 58 had inside Stephenson valve motion and were known as the 'old type', whilst the rest, including *Peter Pan*, were of the 'new type' with outside Hackworth valve gear. Our locomotive is now one of only four survivors in this country, all of which are of the 'new type'. *Peter Pan* was one of 27 *Wrens* sold to R. H. Neal & Co. Ltd during 1922/3. It is believed to have been used on a sewer construction scheme at Barkingside, Essex, and was afterwards bought by T. W. Ward Ltd (Plant Dealers), Grays, Essex. In 1929 it was sold to Devon County Council and sent to Wilminstone Roadstone Quarry near Tavistock. By the 1950s it had been transferred to Beacon Down Quarry, Parracombe, and lay derelict there until purchased by L. Lamb of Bromsgrove. It was later transferred to J. Hardy, also of Bromsgrove, and then to Trevor Coburn, who stored the locomotive on the Leighton Buzzard Narrow Gauge Railway. During this time the boiler was sent for repairs to the Midland Rolling and Haulage Co. Ltd of Birmingham, and some other restoration work was done before being sold to the INGRG in July 1975.

## 72    Chalk Pits Museum    G

Southern Industrial History Centre Trust, Amberley, near Arundel, West Sussex

This new industrial museum site covers more than 30 acres of disused chalk pits complete with lime burning kilns formerly owned by Messrs Pepper & Sons of Amberley. The nucleus of the collection of historic industrial plant and equipment is now being gathered on the site, and this already includes a number of railway items. The site is not yet open to the public.

**Stock**
Hibberd 4WDM 1980 built 1936 (2 ft gauge)
Orenstein and Koppel 4WDM 5926 built 1935 (2 ft 6 in. gauge)
Skip wagons (2 ft gauge)
Half a mile of 2 ft gauge 'Jubilee' track

## 73   Alderney Railway Society            F

Grosnez Fort, Alderney, Channel Islands

A standard-gauge railway preservation scheme aimed at the operation of a short line running inland from Grosnez Fort.

**Stock**
Wickham 4WPMR 7091
Wickham 4WPMR 7095
Wickham 4WPMR No. PWM 394 6939 built 1955

## 74   Reed Paper and Board (UK) Ltd       I

Imperial Paper Mills, Gravesend, Kent

OS Ref: TQ 640743

Industrial steam location with locomotives stored out of use. Rail traffic has ceased and locomotives are for disposal. No public admittance.

**Stock**
Barclay 0-4-0F No. 2 1471 built 1916
Barclay 0-4-0F No. 3 1496 built 1917

## 75   National Coal Board                 I

Snowdown Colliery, Normington, Kent

OS Ref: TR 246512

Industrial steam location featuring regular steam working. No public admittance.

**Stock**
Avonside 0-6-0ST St Thomas 1971 built 1927
Avonside 0-6-0ST St Dunstan 2004 built 1927
Hunslet 0-6-0ST No. 9 3825 built 1954
Fowler 0-4-0DM 4160002 built 1952

## 76   Best Brothers                       C

D., W. & S. Best, 'The Warren', Swinton Street, Bredgar, near Sittingbourne, Kent
Tel: Wormshill (062 784) 245

OS Ref: TQ 873585

Short private 2 ft gauge railway and collection of narrow gauge locomotives.

**Stock**
²Schwartzkopf 0-4-0WT Bronhilde 9124 built 1927
¹Hunslet 4WDM No. 15 Olde 2176 built 1940 (For sale)
Ruston Hornsby 4WDM No. 3 172892 built 1934
Ruston Hornsby 4WDM No. 177604 built 1936
Orenstein and Koppel 4WDM 7728 built 1935 (For sale)
Wingrove & Rogers 4WBE F7116 built 1966
Wingrove & Rogers 4WBE F7117 built 1966
Riorden 4WBE T6664 built 1967

¹Ex Great Bush Railway, 1979.
²Ex Bressingham Steam Museum, 1979.

## 77   Ministry of Defence                 I

Navy Department, Chatham Dockyard, Kent

OS Ref: TQ 764703

Industrial steam location featuring occasional steam working. No public admittance.

**Stock**
RSH 0-4-0ST No. 361 Ajax 7042 built 1941
Hibberd 4WDM No. 562 Rochester Castle 3738 built 1955
Hibberd 4WDM No. 570 Upnor Castle 3742 built 1955
Hibberd 4WDM No. 5219 Leeds Castle 3745 built 1955
Hibberd 4WDM No. 18 Dover Castle 3770 built 1955
Hibberd 4WDM No. 533 Cooling Castle 3771 built 1955
Hibberd 4WDM No. 218 Deal Castle 3772 built 1955
Hunslet 0-4-0DH No. 12228 Allington Castle 6975 built 1968

## 78   CEGB, Croydon 'B' Power Station     I

Waddon Marsh, Croydon, Surrey

OS Ref: TQ 305665

Industrial steam location with locomotive stored out of use.
No public admittance.

**Stock**
Peckett 0-4-0ST (Class R4 special) 2103 built 1950
RSH 0-4-0DH Hengist 8367 built 1962
English Electric 0-4-0DH No. 2 D1122 built 1966

## 79   Ministry of Defence                 I

Army Department, Marchwood, Hampshire

OS Ref: SU 395103

Industrial steam location. Locomotive used on internal railway system.
No public admittance.

**Stock**
Hunslet 0-6-0ST No. 92 Waggoner 3792 built 1953
North British 0-4-0DH No. 413 27648 built 1959
Ruston Hornsby 0-6-0DH No. 425 459519 built 1961
Ruston Hornsby 0-6-0DH No. 432 466623 built 1962

## 80 Hampshire Narrow Gauge Railway Society    C

'Four Winds', Durley, Hants

OS Ref: SU 512167

A short 2 ft gauge passenger-carrying private line.
The Hampshire Narrow Gauge Railway Society was formed in 1961 to promote the construction of a public narrow gauge railway in Hampshire following the precedent set by the Welsh lines, but over the years has modified these original aims and has now become a group of people building and operating a railway simply for their own pleasure without regard to maintaining a regular public service.
*Details from:* Paul Hitchcock, 44 St Thomas Avenue, Hayling Island, Hants.

### Stock
Hanomag 0-8-0T No. 6 8310 built 1918
[1]Hunslet 0-4-2ST No. 2 *Lady Morrison* 1842 built 1936
[2]Hunslet 0-4-0ST *Cloister'* 542 built 1891
[3]Bagnall 0-4-0ST *Wendy* 2091 built 1919
Motor Rail 4WDM *Agwi Pet* 4724 built 1929
Motor Rail 4WPM *Brambridge Hall* 5226 built 1935
Motor Rail 4WDM No. 2 *Lord George* 8998 built 1946
Orenstein and Koppel 0-4-0DM 20777 built 1936
Orenstein and Koppel 0-4-0DM 21160 built 1938
Orenstein and Koppel 4WDM 4013 built 1930
Orenstein and Koppel 4WDM 5125 built 1935
Ruston Hornsby 4WDM 392117 48DL Class built 1956
Two bogie coaches (ex Cotswold Light Railway)
Two bogie toastrack semi-open coaches built by English Electric in 1936 (ex Ramsgate Tunnel Railway)
Three hopper wagons

[1]Ex British Aluminium Co. Ltd, Locaber Works, Fort William, Inverness-shire, 1969. Rebuilt from 3 ft gauge.
[2]Ex Dinorwic Slate Quarries Co. Ltd, Llanberis, Caernarfonshire, 1962
[3]Ex Dorothea Slate Quarry Co. Ltd, Nantlle, Caernarfonshire, 1962.

Mention should also be made of one of the Society's more unlikely possessions – the carriage portion of Dugald Drummond's 1899 LSWR 4-2-4T inspection saloon (originally No. 733, Class F9, and nicknamed *The Bug*). Latterly this saw service as a hut at Eastleigh Carriage Works but has now been mounted on a concrete plinth at Durley and restored in LSWR colours.

## 81 Great Bush Railway    C

J. C. Jessett, Tinkers Park, Hadlow Down, near Uckfield, Sussex

OS Ref: TQ 538241

Private 2 ft gauge passenger-carrying line.

### Stock
Motor Rail 4WDM No. 1 *Animal* built 1931

Avonside 0-4-0T *Sezela No. 2* 1720 built 1915
Motor Rail 4WDM No. 4 *Mild* 8687 built 1941
Ruston Hornsby 4WDM No. 5 *Alpha* 183744 built 1937
Avonside 0-4-0T *Sezela No. 6* 1928 built 1923
Hibberd 4WDM No. 8 *Fido* 2586 built 1941
Hibberd 4WDM No. 12 2535 built 1942
Ruston Hornsby 4WDM No. 14 *Albany* 213840 built 1941
Hibberd 4WDM No. 1 2163 built 1938

The Great Bush Railway also acts as host to the Island Narrow Gauge Group (see Group No. 71), accommodating their stock for winter storage.

## 82 Portsmouth City Museum    G

Standard gauge locomotive in store at British Gas Corporation Works, Easterney, Southsea, Hampshire. No public admittance.

OS Ref: SU 663027.

### Stock
Peckett 0-4-0ST No. 2 2100 built 1949
Ex Southern Gas Board, Hilsea, Portsmouth.

## 83 Collection 'X'    G

A private collection of narrow gauge locomotives and rolling stock owned by P. J. Rampton and others kept in locked storage and not available for public inspection. All are 600 mm gauge unless otherwise stated.

### Stock
[1]Couillet 0-6-0T No. 1 *Sabero* 1140 built 1895
[1]Couillet 0-6-0T No. 2 *Sahelices* 1209 built 1898
[1]Couillet 0-6-0T No. 3 *Olleros* 1318 built 1900
[1]Sabero 0-6-0T No. 6 *La Herrera* built 1937
[1]Borsig 0-6-2T No. 7 *Sotillos* 6022 built 1906
[1]Henschel 0-4-2T No. 101 16073 built 1918
[1]Henschel 0-4-2T No. 102 16043 built 1918
[1]Henschel 0-4-2T No. 103 16045 built 1918
Avonside 0-4-4-0TG *Renishaw 4* 2057 built 1931
Bagnall 0-4-4-0T *Renishaw 5* 2545 built 1936
Hanomag 2-6-2 + 2-6-2T No. 82 (SAR Class NGG13 Garratt) 10634 built 1928
[3]Hunslet 0-4-0ST *Lillian* 317 built 1883
Bagnall 0-4-2T 2895 built 1948
[2]Dick Kerr 4WDE No. 18 built *c.* 1918
Motor Rail 4WDM No. 16 4709 built 1936 (2 ft gauge)
Motor Rail 4WDM No. 38 8540 built 1940 (2 ft gauge)
Motor Rail 4WDM 8994 built 1946 (2 ft gauge).
Motor Rail 4WDM 7153 built 1937 (2 ft gauge).
[1]Sabero Colliery Railway 4-wheeled 'Presidents Coach'.
Isle of Man Railway bogie coaches Nos. F6, F37, F38 & F68 (3 ft gauge).

[1]Ex Hulleras de Sabero y Anexas SA, Sabero, near Cistierna, Leon, Spain, 1968.

[2]Ex Compagnie Industrielle des Sables de Nemours, Seine et Marne, France, 1968.
[3]Ex Penrhyn Quarries, Bethesda, Caernarfonshire, 1966.

## 84   Ripley, Surrey                                    G

J. Butler and Frank Jux, 5 Heath Rise, Grove Heath, Surrey
OS Ref: TQ 046557

Private collection of narrow gauge locomotives. The site is on private property and casual visitors are most actively discouraged.

### Stock
[1]Hunslet 0-4-0ST *Covertcoat* 679 built 1898 (1 ft 10¾ in. gauge).
Deutz 0-4-0DM 19531 (600 mm gauge).
Motor Rail 4WDM 5646 built 1933 (600 mm gauge).
Motor Rail 4WDM No. 16 4709 built 1936
Motor Rail 4WDM No. 38 8540 built 1940
Motor Rail 4WDM 8994 built 1946
Motor Rail 4WDM 7153 built 1937

[1]Ex Dinorwic Slate Quarries Co. Ltd, Llanberis, Caernarfonshire, 1964.

## 85   Woking, Surrey                                    G

J. B. Latham, 'Channings', Kettlewell Hill, Woking, Surrey
OS Ref: TQ 003598

3 ft 2¼ in. gauge privately preserved static steam locomotive exhibit.

### Stock
Fletcher Jennings 0-4-0T No. 5 *William Finlay* 173 built 1880
Ex Dorking Greystone Lime Co. Ltd, Betchworth, Surrey, 1960.

## 86   Chessington Zoo Miniature Railway     B

Chessington Zoo, Surrey

*Access:* Chessington South BR Station

Passenger-carrying 12 in gauge line, 925 yards in length.
The railway operates as required by demand throughout the year, when the Zoo is open.
The line was opened in 1937 and still operates with its original equipment.
The locomotives are vacuum-braked and drum brakes are fitted to the rolling stock.

### Stock
Barnard 4-4-0PM No. 1 *Princess Margaret* built 1937
Barnard 4-4-0PM No. 2 *Queen Elizabeth* built 1937
Six open bogie carriages

The locomotives are both steam outline, based on GWR 'Dukedogs'.

## 87   Hastings Miniature Railway               B

Rock-a-Nore Road, Hastings, Sussex

*Access:* Hastings BR Station

Passenger-carrying 10¼ in. gauge line, 600 yards in length running from Marine Parade to Rock-a-Nore.
The railway operates during Easter week, then at Spring Bank Holiday daily until the end of September.
The railway has operated on this site since 1948 with equipment from Lord Downshire's line at Easthampstead Park. The line at first consisted of 250 yards of straight track but was extended to its present length in 1959. One by one the steam locomotives were withdrawn and sold, being replaced by today's more mundane power units. The railway is single track throughout with a midway passing loop.

### Stock
Shepperton 2-4-2D *Meteor V* built 1970
Shepperton Bo-BoD built 1968
Seven open bogie coaches
Air compressor wagon

## 88   Saltwood Miniature Railway               B

Brockhill Road, Saltwood, Hythe, Kent

Passenger-carrying 7¼ in. gauge miniature railway, 610 yards in length situated in the private grounds of Mr Alex Schwab.
The railway was first opened in 1925 as a private line, but in 1975 it opened regularly to the public after extensive track relaying. The line is laid out as a continuous oval and a ride consists of three circuits of the track.

### Stock
Smith BoBoBE No. 5060 *Earl of Berkeley* built 1974
Smith BoBoBE No. 7007 *Great Western* built 1976
Smith enclosed saloon bogie coach (former battery electric rail car)
Smith GWR 'Centenary'-style bogie coach
4-car articulated bogie open set
Two 6-seat 'children's' carriages.

## 89   Kent County Nurseries Ltd               B

Challock, near Ashford, Kent

Passenger-carrying 10¼ in gauge railway laid out round a garden centre. This attractive little line includes a timber viaduct over a lake and a tunnel.

### Stock
American Freelance 4-4-0D *General Shirley* built 1970 (steam outline)
American Freelance Bo-BoP *Trailblazer*

## 90   J. Lemmon Burton                            C

'Paynesfield', Aldbourn Green, Sussex

Private passenger-carrying 15 in. gauge railway situated in the grounds of Mr J. Lemmon Burton.

**Stock**
Lister 4WPM 51721 built 1960
Morse 0-4-0 No. 212 built 1939
Burton 0-6-0

## 91   Surrey Light Railway   C

Private 2 ft gauge light railway operating at an undisclosed location.
Casual visitors are strictly not allowed.

**Stock**
Wickham 4WPMR No. 16 1309 built 1933
Hunslet 4WDM No. 22 3621 built 1947
Motor Rail 4WDM 20073 built 1950
Ruston Hornsby 4WDM 174535 built 1936
Ruston Hornsby 4WDM 264252 built 1952
Ruston Hornsby 4WDM 277265 built 1949
Ruston Hornsby 4WDM 177642 built 1936
Ruston Hornsby 4WDM 226302 built 1944
Passenger coach No. H305B rebuilt from Vallins 4WPM loco
Dick Kerr side-tipping skip wagons

## 92   Chippens Bank Railway

Drive Cottage, Chippens Bank, Hever, near Edenbridge, Kent

*Access:* 3 miles from Edenbridge. 10 minutes walk from Hever BR station
Tel: Edenbridge (0732) 863411

Private, passenger-carrying 7¼ in gauge railway running for ¼-mile through the grounds of Mr John Topham's residence. The line is not open to the general public and visitors can only be accommodated by postal application (please send sae). A charge is made for the facilities offered and invitations cannot be issued to more than three persons per day.
The Chippens Bank Railway is a private line with a difference. Upon invitation, and paying an advance booking fee, the visitor has the opportunity to undergo steam locomotive driving instruction and experience – with expert tuition – and be served with a meal! The railway is laid out as a dumb-bell-shaped circuit and features cuttings and embankment. There is a raised maintenance bay and a train shed. It is not intended that the railway should be open to the general public and is therefore strictly private. Please respect the owner's wishes.

**Stock**
LSWR 0-4-0T Class B4
Swann 0-4-0 *Jessie* under construction 1979
Freelance 0-4-0BE
Usual riding carriages

## 93   Sandham Castle Mini-Railway   B

Sandham Grounds, Culver Parade, Sandown, Isle of Wight

Passenger-carrying 10¼ in gauge line 300 yards in length, arranged as a continuous circuit.

**Stock**
Shepperton 2-4-2DM *Sandham Castle* built 1969 (Meteor class)

A young man's steam dream comes to life on an old time engine, South Eastern Railway No. 65 in sojourn at Ashford

Photo: John Gardner

Southern Min. Railways Co-BoPM No. D108 *Vanguard*
Southern Min. Railways Bo-BoPM No. 608
Six open bogie coaches

## 94   South Eastern Steam Centre   G

Ashford, Kent

This centre has been closed and its collection is being dispersed. A few items remain on a temporary basis, but no public access is available.

OS Ref: TR 022416

**Stock**
¹SECR 0-6-0 No. 65 (Stirling 01 Class) built 1896
RSH 0-6-0F *Northmet* 7056 built 1942
Greenwood and Batley 4WBE 1210 built 1930
SECR Birdcage family saloon coach
SECR Pullman car *Sapphire* built 1910
SR Bulleid three-coach double-deck electric train No. 4002 built 1949
SECR six-wheeled carriage van

SR four-wheeled box vans Nos. 081969 and DS44551 built 1931
SR Grafton four-wheeled two-ton steam crane *Horace* 2671 built 1928
[2]LPTB 'Q35' stock underground trailer car No. 08063 built 1935

[1]Withdrawn from Dover shed in 1961 as BR No. 31065. The original 'O' Class locomotive designed by James Stirling dates from 1878, and when new was typical of the Stirling domeless round-cab locomotives so familiar on the Great Northern Railway. Between 1903 and 1917 a number of the class were rebuilt by Harry Wainwright along the lines of his larger 'C' Class (see Group No. 53), the 01s being distinguished by their older-style tenders with springs above running plate level, giving them an appearance of great antiquity. No. 65 was intercepted at the last moment after being prepared for its final journey to the scrapyard in 1965 and saved for preservation.
[2]Owned by the London Underground Railway Society.

## 95   Brooklands Miniature Railway          B

Brooklands Pleasure Park, East Worthing, Sussex

Passenger carrying 10¼ in. gauge line, ¾-mile in length built on the site of an earlier 9½ in. gauge, steam-operated line. The railway operates daily during the holiday season

**Stock**
Severn-Lamb Co–CoPH *Western Comet* built 1967

## 96   Payton Heights Railway          C

Mr A. Pay, Green Lane, East Northdown, Margate, Kent

Private passenger-carrying 10¼ in. gauge railway, 600 ft in length, running round the private grounds of Mr Pay. Despite its short length, the railway features a 20 ft tunnel, a level crossing and a 2-road loco shed.

**Stock**
Minimum Gauge Railways 0-6-0 *Marie* 69 built 1977
Curwen & Newbury Bo–BoDM *Lady Sonia*
Six ex-Margate Pier Railway coaches

## 97   Southsea Miniature Railway          B

Southsea, Hampshire

OS Ref: SZ 641982

Passenger-carrying 1 ft 6½ in. gauge railway built on the site of the former Southern Miniature Railways 10¼ in. gauge line. Opened in 1977, this new line has a unique gauge for an operating railway in the British Isles.
It is a simple 'out-and-back' layout, so trains are hauled in one direction and propelled back.

**Stock**
Belgian Bo–BoBE built 1976 (steam outline)
Three toastrack open bogie coaches

The driver operates the controls from the front seat of the leading coach, so one fortunate passenger can sit in the locomotive!

# AREA C

# Eastern Counties

Norfolk
Suffolk
Essex
Cambridgeshire
Lincolnshire
South Humberside

---

## 101   Bressingham Steam Museum and Gardens

A

Bressingham Hall, Diss, Norfolk

*Access:* Two miles west of Diss on the A1066 road
Tel: Bressingham 386
OS Ref: TM 080806

Museum open Thursdays, Sundays and Bank Holidays, May–September, also at Easter and on Wednesdays during August only. Opening time 1.30 pm. The site incorporates the 1 ft 11½ in. gauge Nursery Railway (2 miles in length), the 15 in. gauge Waveney Line (2½ miles in length), a short 9½ in. gauge line, as well as a museum of steam road and rail locomotives and a 500-yard standard gauge demonstration line.

Facilities for visitors include car parking museum of over forty railway, road and stationary steam engines, model railway, souvenir shop, steam roundabouts and organs, six acres of gardens, refreshments and toilets.

The Bressingham Steam Museum is the result of the enthusiasm of one man, Alan Bloom, and his love for steam engines, great and small. The collection is housed on the 450-acre nursery surrounding Bressingham Hall and grew steadily from a nucleus of traction engines and steam agricultural machinery to embrace first a 9½ in. gauge garden line, then a 2 ft line using former Welsh slate quarry locomotives. Major expansion occurred in 1968 when standard gauge locomotives from the official BR collection began to arrive. These are housed in the specially constructed museum building and have now been joined by others formerly on display at Butlins holiday camps. A 500-yard demonstration line has been built for the use of these engines, one or more of which may be seen in steam and giving footplate rides on Bressingham open days. With some justification, Bressingham claims to be the most comprehensive live steam museum in the British Isles. Its extensive collection is safely housed under cover in a purpose-built Exhibition Hall.

*Details from:* Alan Bloom, Bressingham Hall, Bressingham, Diss, Norfolk IP22 2AB.

### Stock

*Bressingham Hall Miniature Railway* (750 yards long, opened in 1965) 9½ in. gauge
4-6-2 *Princess* built by Motor Gear and Engineering Co., 1947
4 open bogie coaches

*Waveney Valley Railway* (two-and-a-half miles in length, opened in 1973) 15 in. gauge
Krupp 4-6-2 *Rosenkavalier* 1662 built 1937
Krupp 4-6-2 *Mannertreu* 1663 built 1937
Nineteen Toastrack bogie coaches built 1937

*Nursery Railway* (two miles long, opened in 1966) 1 ft 11½ in. gauge
Hunslet 0-4-0ST *Gwynedd* 316 built 1883
Hunslet 0-4-0ST *George Sholto* 994 built 1909
Hudswell Clarke 0-6-0WT *Bronllwyd* 1643 built 1930
Orenstein and Koppel 0-4-0WT *Eigiau* 5668 built 1912
Ruston Hornsby 4WDM 437367 built 1959

*Standard Gauge*
[1][2]BR 4-6-2 No. 70013 *Oliver Cromwell* (Riddles Class 7MT) built 1951
[3]LMS 4-6-2 No. 6233 *Duchess of Sutherland* built 1938
[4]LMS 4-6-0 No. 6100 *Royal Scot* built 1927
[6]LMS 2-6-4T No. 2500 Class 4MT built 1934 BR No. 42500
[1]LTSR 4-4-2T No. 80 *Thundersley* built 1909 BR No. 41966
[5]LBSCR 0-6-0T No. 62 *Martello* (Class AIX) built 1875
[7]LSWR 0-4-0T No. 102 (Class B4) built 1893
NSB 2-10-0 No. 5865 (Class 52) (Schichau, built 1941)
SNCF 2-8-2 No. 141R73 (Class 141R) (Lima, built 1945)
[1]GER 0-6-0 No. 1217E (Class G58) built 1905 BR No. 65567
Beyer Peacock 0-4-0 + 0-4-0 *William Francis* 6841 built 1937

Manning Wardle 0-6-0ST No. 4 *Solomon* 641 built 1877
Neilson 0-4-0WT No. 1 4444 built 1892
Neilson 0-4-0ST No. 25 5087 built 1896
RSH 0-4-0CT *Millfield* 7070 built 1942
Sentinel 4WVBTG *Joyce* 7109 built 1927
Barclay 0-4-0F 1472 built 1916
[1]ECJS Royal Saloon Coach No. 396 built 1908
[1]Eastern Counties Railway four-wheeled coach built 1851

[1]On loan from British Railways Board.
[2]Built at Crewe in May 1951. Withdrawn from Carnforth shed on 11 August 1968 after hauling the Manchester–Carlisle section of the last BR steam train. No. 70013 was the final steam locomotive to be overhauled by British Railways and as such was selected as the official representative of the 'Britannia' pacifics for preservation. Appropriately, for an engine that spent much of its life in East Anglia, it was sent to Bressingham immediately on withdrawal.
[3]LMS 'Coronation' class Pacific withdrawn from Liverpool (Edge Hill) in February 1964 as BR No. 46233. One of a batch of five engines (Nos 6230–34) built without streamlined casings for performance comparisons with the streamlined members of the class. *Duchess of Sutherland* was purchased by Butlins Ltd and restored to LMS maroon livery for display at Ayr holiday camp in Scotland. It was transferred to Bressingham in 1971.
[4]Three-cylinder 'Royal Scot' class locomotive built by the North British Locomotive Co. Ltd (Works No. 23595) in August 1927. Completely rebuilt with new frames and boiler at Crewe in 1950 and withdrawn from Nottingham shed in 1962 as BR No. 46100. When new the 'Royal Scots' were the largest passenger engines on the LMS. The design was based on the Southern 'Lord Nelson' class and 50 were built in 1927 as a matter of great urgency to cope with the Anglo-Scottish expresses. Twenty more were delivered in 1930, whilst in 1935 the experimental high-pressure engine *Fury* was rebuilt with a Stanier taper boiler and formed the prototype for the eventual rebuilding of all the 'Royal Scots'. Rebuilding commenced in 1943 at a time when, owing to wartime conditions, materials were in short supply. Unrebuilt engines in sound condition were overhauled where possible, and it was 1955 before the whole class had been rebuilt. Displaced from their normal work by diesels, many of the class migrated to the old Great Central line and to the southern sections of the Midland. Here they were gradually relegated to goods and parcels traffic, finally being withdrawn as they became due for major repairs. As befitted such a famous locomotive, *Royal Scot* was selected for preservation by Butlins Ltd and was displayed at Skegness holiday camp until moved to Bressingham in 1971.
[5]Withdrawn from Eastleigh shed in November 1963 as BR No. 32662. *Martello* led a fairly commonplace existence compared with most Stroudley 'Terriers', spending its entire working life on the former LBSCR system. It was restored to original yellow livery when bought by Butlins for display at their Ayr holiday camp and was moved to Bressingham in 1971.
[6]Three-cylinder passenger tank locomotive built at Derby for the London, Tilbury and Southend line services. Withdrawn from Shoeburyness shed as BR No. 42500 in July 1962.

Pacing its short length of standard gauge track at Bressingham like a caged tiger, Britannia Pacific No. 70013 *Oliver Cromwell* looms large in Alan Bloom's parkland surroundings

Whilst identical in outward appearance to the other Stanier 2-6-4 tanks, the small batch numbered 2500–36 were built with three cylinders. The whole class spent virtually all its working life on the LT & S line, replacing the older 'Tilbury' 4-4-2 tanks. On the last day of steam haulage on the LT & S, all the remaining Stanier engines were written off without ceremony, many being sent to Doncaster for cutting-up. Selected as typical of a modern suburban passenger tank engine for official preservation, No. 2500 spent several years in store before going to Bressingham in 1968.
[7]Withdrawn from Eastleigh shed in September 1963 as BR No. 30102. For many years locomotives of this class were a familiar sight at Southampton Docks, where their only readily visible identity was a name painted on their tanksides, numbers being only in evidence on the motion or a small plate at the back of the cab. No. 102 sported the name *Granville*. These names were painted out when the engines moved away from the docks in 1946 on being replaced by the larger USA 0-6-0 tanks. No. 102 was restored to LSWR

Yes, *William Francis* is the only standard gauge Beyer Garratt to be preserved in Britain. So steam along to Bressingham and see it!

Photo: Geoff King

livery at Eastleigh when purchased by Butlins Ltd for display at their Skegness holiday camp. It was moved to Bressingham in 1971.

## 102   North Norfolk Railway                               A

Sheringham Station, Sheringham, Norfolk NR26 8RA

*Access:* BR trains from Norwich and Wroxham. Eastern Countries buses from Norwich, Yarmouth and Kings Lynn (change at Cromer)
Tel: Sheringham (0263) 822045
OS Ref: TG 156430

Passenger-carrying standard gauge railway from Sheringham to Weybourne, 3 miles in length.

Sheringham Station is open daily from April to October between 10 am and 5 pm. Steam train services operate from June to the end of September on Saturdays, on Sundays from April to October and on selected weekdays from April to September.

Facilities for visitors include car parking (adjacent to Sheringham Station), museum, souvenir shop, refreshments and the engine shed at Weybourne. The North Norfolk Railway is part of the former Midland and Great Northern Joint Railway and runs for three miles along unspoilt coastline in an area designated as being of outstanding natural beauty. Despite the general impression that East Anglia is largely flat, the line is steeply graded and the run to Weybourne is largely 'uphill' along two gradients of 1 in 97 and 1 in 80. Although this is, at present, perhaps the shortest of the preserved standard gauge lines, we intend to eventually extend over the delightful Kelling Heath and perhaps on to

Photo: Brian Fisher

the market town of Holt. The railway project can perhaps be seen in some perspective when it is realised that when the line was acquired from British Rail it had already been reduced to a very basic railway with only one single line at Sheringham and no railway at all at Weybourne! Many years of endeavour by our volunteer members have restored the railway to operating condition and after a gap of over ten years the line is again echoing to the sound of steam as trains pound the gradients to Weybourne.

## Stock

[9]LNER 4-6-0 No. 61572 (Class B12) Beyer Peacock 6488 built 1928
[10]GER 0-6-0 No. 564 (Class J15) BR No. 65462 built 1912
[1]RSH 0-6-0T No. 12 7845 built 1955
[2]Kitson 0-6-0ST No. 45 *Colwyn* 5470 built 1933
[3]Peckett 0-6-0ST No. 5 *John D. Hammer* 1970 built 1939
[4]Hunslet 0-6-0ST *Ring Haw* 1982 built 1940
[5]Hawthorn Leslie 0-4-0ST *Pony* 2918 built 1912
Hudswell Clarke 0-6-0ST *Wissington* 1700 built 1938
[6]Barclay 0-6-0T *Harlaxton* 2107 built 1941
[7]Bagnall 0-6-0ST *Birchenwood* 2680 built 1944
[8]Fowler 0-4-0DM *Doctor Harry* 4100001 built 1945
Fowler 0-4-0DM No. 3 4210080 built 1953
English Electric 0-4-0DH No. 108431 built 1963
BR four-wheeled diesel railbuses Nos 79960 and 79963 built 1958
LNER quad-art set No. 74 built 1924
LNWR directors saloon No. 5318 built 1913
L & YR directors saloon No. 1 built 1906
GER brake/third coach No. 295 built 1907
BR tourist open second bogie coach No. E3868 built 1953
LNER passenger brake van No. E040923 built 1929
BR CL bogie coaches Nos E43034 and E43041 built 1954

It took a £10,000 rebuild to get Great Eastern Railway J15 No. 564 back on the rails again. But, as you can see, she looks worth every penny of it. Restoration on the North Norfolk Railway was under the supervision of that grand stalwart of steam, Bill Harvey

BR SLO bogie coach No. E48026 built 1954
LNER Gresley TK bogie coach No. 3395 built 1930
LNWR Saloon bogie coach No. 5318 built 1913
LNER Gresley Buffet car No. 51760 built 1937
LNER Bogie Passenger brake van No. 70621 built 1945
BR SLSTP Van No. 624 built 1951
BR Brake 2nd compartment coach No. 43357 built 1954
BR Compartment 2nd class coach No. 46147 built 1954
BR Brake 2nd compartment coach No. 43359 built 1955
BR Brake Composite coach No. 21103 built 1956
SR 'Brighton Belle' Pullman cars Nos 87 and 91 built 1932
Two GER six-wheeled coach bodies
GER flat wagon (converted from a Colman's mustard van) built 1901
SR 25-ton brake van No. S55169 built 1949
GWR five-plank wagon No. 124148 built 1936
BR 'Vanfit' covered van No. 756939 built 1949
SR 12-ton crane and match truck No. DS1749 built 1943
LMS covered van No. 755094 built 1950
Shell Mex and BP oil tank wagon No. 164686 built 1944
M & GNRJ petrol trolley No. 1
Six GER box vans
Two NER drop-floor hoppa wagons
Two Wickham 4WPM rail trolleys
GER 'Colman's Mustard' van No. 4807 built 1908
GWR 'Pasfruit' van No. W92097 built 1936
L & YR Flat wagon built 1890

Carrick & Wardale steam crane No. 12 built 1919
Esso tank wagon No. 163058 built 1942
BR Lowmac Wagon No. 904093 built 1953

[1]Ex Hams Hall Power Station, Birmingham, 1974.
[2]Ex Stewarts and Lloyds Minerals Ltd, Gretton Brook, Corby, Northants, 1971.
[3]Ex NCB Ashington Colliery, Northumberland, 1969.
[4]Ex Nassington Barrowden Mining Co, Nassington, Peterborough, Cambs, 1971.
[5]Ex Blyth Harbour Commission, Blyth Docks, 1971. After a short stay on the Yorkshire Dales Railway, arrived at Sheringham, 1972.
[6]Ex Stewarts and Lloyds Minerals Ltd, Harlaxton Quarry, Northants, 1969. On Keighley & Worth Valley Railway until 1973 when sold to Buckminster Trust Estate, Sewstern, Lincs. In 1974 re-sold and arrived at Sheringham in same year.
[7]Ex Market Overton (High Dyke), Northants, 1976.
[8]Ex West Norfolk Fertilizer Co. Ltd (later Fisons Ltd), 1973. First diesel to be built by Fowlers after the war. Built to a 1930's design and delivered new to WNF at King's Lynn, Norfolk. WNF had extensive sidings off the M & GNJR at South Lynn. Possibly the first diesel ever to work on the 'Joint'. Restored by the West Norfolk Area and moved to Sheringham in 1974.
[9]Built as LNER No. 8572 and withdrawn from Norwich shed in 1961, this locomotive is the only inside-cylinder 4-6-0 in existence in Great Britain, sole survivor of a once-numerous collection of such classes.
[10]GER Class Y14 locomotive (LNER Class J15) withdrawn from Stratford shed in 1962 as BR No. 65462. At the time of the 1923 grouping, the 289 J15s were the most numerous class of LNER locomotives and accounted for over 20 per cent of the former GER locomotive stock. Whilst primarily

freight engines, many worked passenger services on branch lines at various times. No. 930 of this class made history in 1891 by being erected at Stratford works in just 9¾ hours! Forty-two of them served overseas during World War 1.

**Midland and Great Northern Joint Railway Society**

Sheringham Station, Sheringham, Norfolk NR26 8RA
Tel: Sheringham 2045
Membership: 4,000 plus
Secretary: Paul J. Cooper, 11 Blenheim Close, Sprowston, Norwich, Norfolk NR7 8AN.

The Society was formed in 1959 to preserve part of the former M & GN Joint Railway. This truly Norfolk Railway was an independant system with its own rural main line from the Norfolk coast to the Midlands. Although only three miles (so far!) have been saved, the emphasis is on recreating the spirit of the old days. The M & GNJRS supports the railway (which is operated by the North Norfolk Railway Company Ltd) in many varied ways: for example it owns nearly half the rolling stock assembled on the line, including the J15 and B12 locomotives, and operates an extensive programme of rail tours to raise funds (it is, in fact, the largest operator of rail tours engaged in railway preservation). New members are always welcome to join the ever-increasing ranks at any of the preservation sites.

## 103   Nene Valley Railway                        A

Wansford Station, Stibbington, near Peterborough, Cambs

*Access:* Adjacent to Main A1 road
Tel: Stamford 782854
OS Ref: TL 903979

Passenger-carrying standard gauge steam railway from Wansford to Orton Mere, a distance of 5½ miles.
The railway is in operation at weekends and Bank Holidays

On just one of those lazy, hazy summer days, Kitson 0-6-0ST *Colwyn* tiptoes through the cowslips with a train bound for Weybourne on the North Norfolk Railway

Photo: Brian Fisher

Oil burning Swedish 2–6–4T No. 1928 displays its elegant lines at the head of the inaugural through freight
working from British Railways on to the Nene Valley
Railway

from April to October, and on Tuesdays, Wednesdays and Thursdays in June, July and August. Facilities for visitors include car parking, museum, souvenir shop, refreshments and toilets.

The first passenger train ran on the Nene Valley Railway line on 2 June 1845. After a tremendous amount of hard work, the Peterborough Railway Society were able to reopen the line for all traffic on 1 June 1977. Since then, it has established itself in a unique position amongst preserved railways in Great Britain by specialising in operating locomotives and rolling stock from all over Europe and Scandinavia.

### Stock

[4]BR 4-6-0 No. 73050 *City of Peterborough* (Class 5MT) built 1954
Swedish State Railways 2-6-4T No. 1928 (Class S1) Nohab 2229 built 1953
Swedish State Railways 2-6-2T No. 1178 (Class S) built Motala 1914
Swedish State Railways 4-6-0 No. 1697 (Class B) built 1943
Danish State Railways 2-6-4T No. 740 (Class S) built 1925
Danish State Railways 0-6-0T No. 656 (Class F) built Fricks 1949
[1]Nord 4-6-0 No. 3628 (SNCF Class 230D) Henschel 10745 built 1911
DB 2-6-2T No. 64-305 (Class 64) built Krupp-Essen 1934
[2]SR 4-6-2 No. 34081 *92 Squadron* (Bulleid 'BB' Class) built 1948
Hawthorn Leslie 0-6-0ST No. 16 3835 built 1934
Hudswell Clarke 0-6-0ST *Derek Crouch* 1539 built 1924
Hudswell Clarke 0-6-0ST 1604 built 1928
Hudswell Clarke 0-6-0T No. 2 *Thomas* 1800 built 1947, rebuilt NVR incorporating boiler and other parts from Hudswell Clarke 1844 *Whitwood No. 4*
Hunslet 0-6-0ST No. 75006 2855 built 1943
Peckett 0-6-0ST 2000 built 1942
Hunslet 0-6-0ST *Jacks Green* 1953 built 1939
[5]Avonside 0-6-0ST *Pitsford* 1917 built 1924
Avonside 0-4-0ST No. RS16 *Fred* 1908 built 1925
Avonside 0-6-0ST 1945 built 1926
Barclay 0-4-0ST No. 90432 2248 built 1948
Hibberd 4WPM *Percy* 2894 built 1944
Hibberd 4WDM No. 2896 *Frank* built 1944, rebuilt Perkins 1976
Ruston Hornsby 4WDM 294268 built 1951
Ruston Hornsby 4WDM 88DS class 321734 built 1952
Smith Rodley five-ton steam shunting crane No. 11756 built 1934
[3]SR S10096S: '4 COR' corridor third from unit 3142
[3]SR S11161S: '4 RES' motor brake third saloon originally in unit 3065, but transferred to '4 COR' 3142 in 1945
[3]SR S11201S: '4 COR' motor brake third saloon, identical to S11161S from the passengers' point of view, from unit 3142
[3]SR S11773S: '4 PUL' corridor composite, built for the Brighton line electrification 1933. Transferred to '4 COR' 3159 in 1965
[3]SR S11825S: '4 COR' corridor composite from unit 3135

[3]SR Pullman car No. 278 *Bertha* (a '6 PUL' composite kitchen car built 1933)
Wagons-Lits Dining Car No. 2975 built 1927
NSB balcony-end suburban bogie coach
Four DSB bogie coaches built 1948 and 1961
GNR six-wheeled parcels van No. D940400
LNWR six-wheeled parcels van
BR CK coach No. E15296 (built Craven 1952)
BR CK coach No. E15514 built Metro-Cammell 1954
BR SK coach No. E24656 built BC & W Co. 1953
BR BSK coach No. M35239 built Wolverton 1958
LMS six-wheeled van No. M40284 built Wolverton 1949
BR 20-ton brake van No. B953944
SR Bogie van No. 1990 built 1951
LMS 20-ton hopper wagon built 1938
Two LNWR wooden-bodied open wagons built 1920
LNWR four wheeled box van built 1910
MR five-plank wooden-bodied wagon
One Wickham petrol-driven permanent way trolley
One GER pump trolley rebuilt 1975
LMS 20-ton goods brake van No. DM730302 built 1938

[1]Owned by the Nord Locomotive Preservation Group.
[2]Owned by the Battle of Britain Locomotive Preservation Society (*q.v.*).
[3]Owned by the Southern Electric Group (*q.v.*).
[4]Withdrawn from Patricroft shed in 1968 and purchased for preservation. One of a class of 172 locomotives built between 1951 and 1957 to a design that was basically a modified LMS Stanier Class 5.
[5]Ex-Byfield Ironstone Co. Ltd, Pitsford Quarries, Northants, 1966. Worked on Mr W. H. McAlpine's Fawley Hill Railway (see Group No. 468) until 1973.

### Battle of Britain Locomotive Preservation Society   H

Wansford Station, Nene Valley Railway, near Peterborough, Cambs

No. 34081 *92 Squadron* was built at Brighton Works in 1948 to the design of Mr O. V. S. Bulleid, last chief mechanical engineer of the Southern Railway. For the first ten years of her working life she was based at Ramsgate and worked Kent coast expresses and continental boat trains, including such trains as the 'Golden Arrow' and 'Night Ferry'. In 1958, following electrification of the South Eastern area, the locomotive was transferred to Exmouth Junction shed at Exeter, from where she worked all over the West Country on such trains as the 'Atlantic Coast Express'. Withdrawal came in 1964 and *92 Squadron* was sold for scrap to Woodham Brothers of Barry, South Wales, where she joined over 200 other locomotives awaiting the breaker's torch. However, fate, in the form of the Battle of Britain Locomotive Society, intervened. In 1973 BBLS purchased *92 Squadron* and since then have concentrated on raising funds to cover the costs of restoration to working order. Following discussions with several organisations it was decided that *92 Squadron* should come to the Nene Valley Railway and the move took place during the first week of November 1976.

During its sojourn in the scrapyard all of the non-ferrous parts of the locomotive and many of the easily accessible high quality steel components were removed, including the main axle bearings, couplings rods and valve gear. These removals, plus the deterioration following 12 years lying in a scrapyard, have meant that it was impossible to move *92 Squadron* by rail and the move was, therefore, carried out by road. This move marked the commencement of a restoration programme which is likely to take five years and cost several thousands of pounds. Peterborough Railway Society Limited is pleased and proud to be associated with this project and looks forward to the time when *92 Squadron* will be seen again in steam, hauling trains on the Nene Valley Railway.

## Southern Electric Group                                    H

*Aims:* To promote and further interest in the electric railway system of the former Southern Railway Company, its predecessors and its successors.
*Membership:* 450.
*Details from:* SEG Membership Secretary, 38 Reddons Road, Beckenham, Kent BR3 1LZ.
*Subscription:* £2 per year. Life membership also available.
*Other activities:* The Group organises regular meetings in London, Croydon and Worthing, and at least one visit to a railway installation each month. Special events, such as rail tours, are also promoted. Group members receive a bimonthly magazine, 'Live Rail', which includes Group news, Southern Region news and historical articles.
Formed in 1970 by a group of enthusiasts in Surrey to preserve an example of the first generation Southern Railway mainline stock. After the withdrawal of the 4-LAV units and the BR decision to retain a 2-BIL, the rapidly expanding group made the decision to concentrate on the second generation, and with the aid of a bank loan and two private purchases, 4-COR No. 3142 was secured at the end of 1972. It is currently in use, steam-hauled on the Nene Valley Railway while work continues on full restoration of the electrical equipment.

## Peterborough Railway Society Limited

Wansford Station, Old North Road, Stibbington, Wansford, near Peterborough, Cambs

*Subscription:* £2.50 per annum single, £3.00 joint, £1.00 OAP and Junior.
*Membership:* 1,100
*Membership details from:* J. H. Maddocks, 36 Sallows Road, Peterborough, Cambs.

## 104   Stour Valley Railway             A
Preservation Society

Chappel and Wakes Colne Station, Essex

*Access:* Chappel and Wakes Colne BR Station. 7 miles North West of Colchester, off A604
OS Ref: TL 898289
Tel: Earls Colne 2903

Standard gauge railway preservation centre offering short steam-hauled rides on periodic open days throughout the year.

The Society proposes to purchase all or part of the Marks Tey to Sudbury branch lines (11½ miles), which will close unless it continues to be grant-aided by local authorities. It would then be their intention to operate a diesel service on weekdays and steam-hauled trains at weekends. The Society is also considering restoring the Stour Valley line between Sudbury and Long Melford, subject to local authority consent, as an alternative to the Marks Tey–Sudbury section if this remains open under BR ownership.
Steaming takes place on selected days from Easter to October. See railway press for details. The site will be open from 11 am to 6 pm each day. Refreshments, car park, model shop, bookshop available.
At least one locomotive will be in steam each day and coach rides will be available within the steam centre.
*Note:* The Society reserves the right to alter or cancel this programme at short notice if circumstances beyond their control cause such action.

*Details from:* R. G. Booth, 20 Wainfleet Avenue, Romford, Essex.
*Subscription:* Adults £1.25; under 16s, students and OAPs 50p; husband and wife £2; family £2.50.
*Membership:* 900.

### Stock
[4]BR 2–6–4T No. 80151 (4MT Class) built 1956
[1]LNER 0–6–2T No. 69621 GER No. 999 (N7 Class) built 1924
[2]Peckett 0–4–0ST 2039 built 1943
[3]RSH 0–6–0ST No. 54 7031 built 1941
Hunslet 0–6–0ST No. 68067 *Gunby* 2413 built 1941
RSH 0–6–0ST *Jupiter* 7671 built 1950
Barclay 0–6–0ST *Belvoir* 2350 built 1954
Barclay 0–4–0ST *Storefield* 1047 built 1905
Bagnall 0–4 0ST *Jubilee* 2542 built 1936
[7]Robert Stephenson & Hawthorn 0–6–0T 7597 built Newcastle 1949
[7]Robert Stephenson & Hawthorn 0–6–0T No. 13 7846 built Darlington 1955
Hibberd 4WDM *Barking Power* 3294 built 1948
Barclay 0–4–0DM AMW No. 144 *Paxman* 333 built 1938
Metrovick 0–4–0E No. 2 built 1912
Motor rail 4WPM 2029 built 1920
GER four-wheeled first-class coach No. 19 built 1878
MSLR six-wheeled coach No. 373 built 1889
GER four-wheeled *Pooley* van No. 3 built 1911
GER ten-ton ventilated van No. 32518 built 1920
[6] [7]BR 2nd class lavatory open coach No. E48001 built 1955
[6] [7]BR lavatory composite coach No. E43043 built 1955
[7]BR bogie suburban coach No. E46139 built Wolverton 1954
[7]LNER 61 ft bogie brake (pigeon) van No. E70427E built York 1941
[7]LNER 61 ft. bogie buffet car No. E9122E built York 1937
[7]LNER 60 ft. bogie Post Office sorter No. E70294E built York 1937
[7]LNER 51 ft. bogie Post Office tender No. E70268E built Dukinfield 1931
[7]LNER 52 ft. bogie brake third corridor No. E62565E built York 1927

Photo: Geoff King

**Blue skies ahead for Great Eastern Railway N7 Class 0–6–2T No. 999, the last to be built by the GER at Stratford works, and now being restored by the Stour Valley RPS at Chappel and Wakes Colne**

[7]LNER 61 ft. bogie composite coach No. E18033E built York 1924

[5] [7]LSWR four-wheeled passenger luggage van No. 5025 built Eastleigh 1917

[7]GER four-wheeled ventilated van No. 32518 built Bristol Carriage and Wagon Co. 1921

[7]PO (Wm. Cory & Son) four-wheeled coal wagon No. 18973 built Midland Carriage and Wagon Co. 1923

[8]GER six-wheeled passenger brake van No. 553 built 1890

[8]LNER fish van No. 15139 built 1925

GER four-wheeled gas tank wagon No. 055 built *c* 1902 underframe only

BR bogie suburban coach No. 43147 built 1954

Grafton four-ton steam crane

BR ten-ton covered goods van

Three Wickham petrol rail trolleys

SR 'Southern Belle' motor/brake third Pullman coach No. 288 built 1931

Two SR four-wheeled PMV vehicles Nos 1218 and 1152

[1]Hill Class L77 locomotive which was the last of a batch ordered just prior to the grouping by the GER. Withdrawn from Stratford shed in 1962 and purchased for preservation. The engine was stored at Neville Hill shed, Leeds, for eleven years prior to moving to Chappel and Wakes Colne. The Class N7 (LNER designation) was highly successful on the tightly-timed Liverpool Street suburban 'Jazz' service and 134 examples were built. No. 999 was in fact the last GER locomotive ever built at Stratford Works.

[2]Owned jointly with the Bishop's Stortford Railway Society.

[3]Ex Stewarts and Lloyds Minerals Ltd, Gretton Brook, Corby, Northants, 1969.
[4]Owned by the Anglian Locomotive Group.
[5]At Quainton Road.
[6]At Nene Valley Railway.
[7]Owned by Railway Vehicle Preservations (*q.v.*)
[8]Owned by the Great Eastern Railway Group (*q.v.*)

### Railway Vehicle Preservations                              H

Chappel and Wakes Colne Station, Essex

*Details from:* D. Pearce, 77 Gosling House, Sutton Street, London E1

RVP is an energetic group of enthusiasts who since they started in 1968 have amassed an interesting collection of locomotives and rolling stock, much of it with a GER/LNER/BR(ER) bias. The majority of the collection has been gathered at Chappel and Wakes Colne for use at the Stour Valley Steam Centre, though two coaches are on the Nene Valley Railway and a van at Quainton Road. Thus it can be seen that RVP's role is to support operating pre-servation centres by providing rolling stock of practical use. *Membership:* 75.
*Annual Subscription:* Associate Member £2.50, OAPs and under-16s £1.00.

### Great Eastern Railway Group                               H

Chappel and Wakes Colne Station, Essex

*Details from:* J. Watling, 22 Manor Way, Chingford, London E4 6NW
A small group of enthusiasts dedicated to saving items of GER interest, including the two vehicles maintained at Chappel and Wakes Colne.

## 105   Colne Valley Railway                               A

Castle Hedingham Station, near Halstead, Essex

*Access:* On the A604, ½ mile North of Castle Hedingham
Tel: Hedingham 61174
OS Ref: TL 774362

Standard gauge steam railway one mile in length on the site of the former Colne Valley and Halstead Railway.
The site is open daily for static display. Operation takes place on selected days from Easter to October when short steam-hauled rides are available.
Facilities for visitors include car parking, railway shop, refreshments and toilets.
The late and much-lamented Colne Valley and Halstead Railway was closed by BR on 1 January 1962. Ten years later, the idea was born to recreate a small portion of the railway on its former site, incorporating as much original material as possible. Since then, what has been achieved on a 'greenfield' trackbed by sheer determination and hard work is little short of amazing. Richard Hymas and his fellow enthusiasts have re-erected the former Sible and Castle Hedingham station brick-by-brick, including 200 ft platforms as well as relaying all the necessary track and pointwork. The goods shed from Great Yeldham now lives again as the Loco shed, whilst the old crossing-keeper's hut from White

Photo: Geoff King

Helping the Colne Valley Railway back to life again is this demobbed Austerity 0–6–0ST No. 90, now to be found at Castle Hedingham station

Colne has taken on a new lease of life as the signal box. More tracklaying is planned to extend the line and discussions are taking place with the nearby Stour Valley society with a view to future co-operation. Very definitely a little line with a big future.

### Stock
Hunslet 0–6–0ST *Castle Hedingham* 3790 built 1952
Vulcan Foundry 0–6–0ST No. 72 5309 built 1945
RSH 0–6–0T No. 40 7765 built 1954
[1]Hawthorn Leslie 0–4–0ST No. 1 3715 built 1928
Barclay 0–4–0ST *Victory* 2199 built 1945
Ruston Hornsby 4 WDM (48DS class) 221639 built 1943
[2]Avonside 0–4–0ST *Barrington* 1875 built 1921
BR Mk.1 open 2nd class coach built 1954
NSB Balcony-end coach No. 18803
Three bogie wagons
LNWR open-wagon No. DM202440 built 1911
LNER Goods brake van No. 2 (ex Bowes Railway)

[1]This was the first of six similar locomotives supplied to APCM, Swanscombe Works. In her active life she moved 8½ million tons of chalk from the quarry to the cement works. She was withdrawn from service in 1970, presented to the Gravesend Railway Enthusiasts' Society (*q.v.*) in 1972 and stored at the South Eastern Steam Centre until 1976.
[2]Owned by the Avonside Steam Preservation Society (*q.v.*).

### Gravesend Railway Enthusiasts' Society                    H

Colne Valley Railway, Castle Hedingham, Essex

Other Society activities centred on Gravesend include modelling, meetings and tours. For full details please contact the Secretary, R. Shields, 29 Golf Links Avenue, Gravesend, Kent.

**Avonside Steam Preservation Society**　　　H

Colne Valley Railway, Castle Hedingham, Essex
*Details from:* Mr K. Rogers, 58 Castle Street, Cambridge
CB3 OAP

## 106　Lincolnshire Coast Light Railway　　A

North Sea Lane Station, St Anthony's Bank, Humberston,
Grimsby, Humberside

OS Ref: TA326059

A one-mile long 60 cm gauge passenger-carrying line opened
in 1960. Operates during Spring Bank Holiday week, then
daily from mid-July to mid-September from 10 am to 6 pm.
Steam trains by previous arrangement only.
Facilities for visitors include car parking, souvenir shop,
refreshments and toilets.
In April 1960 a group of Lincolnshire railway enthusiasts
formed a company to build and operate a passenger-carrying
railway that would also fill a real transport need. A site at
Humberston, near Grimsby, was chosen and half-a-mile of
2 ft gauge line opened between North Sea Lane and Humberston Beach on 27 August 1960. The line has been relaid
on a new alignment and extended a further half-mile to
South Sea Lane, near the centre of the Humberston Fitties
Holiday Camp. The headquarters of the railway and the
locomotive shed are at North Sea Lane Station, where there
is a run-round loop and sidings. Miniature signals formerly
in use on the GN and L & Y railways have been installed.
The original track and rolling stock, including several goods
vehicles, came from Smith's Potato Estates agricultural
railway at Nocton, Lincolnshire, and had also been used in
France in the 1914–18 war. For passenger traffic there is an
open bogie coach and also two former Ashover Light
Railway coaches, now restored and fitted with leather
upholstered seats from Glasgow, Leeds and Liverpool
tramcars.
This interesting line can be reached via the A16, A18 and
A46 roads. It is also served by Grimsby–Cleethorpes Transport buses from the Bull Ring, near Grimsby Town Station,
and from the Market Place, Cleethorpes.
Further information can be obtained from the General Manager, Lincolnshire Coast Light Railway Company Limited,
North Sea Lane Station, Humberston, Grimsby, Lincs.

**Stock**
Motor Rail 4WDM No. 1 *Paul* 3995 built 1927
Peckett 0–6–0ST No. 2 *Jurassic* 1008 built 1903
Hunslet 0–4–0ST No. 3 *Elin* 705 built 1899
Simplex 4WDM No. 4 *Wilton* 7481 built 1940
Simplex 4WDM No. 5 8622 built 1941
Simplex 4WDM No. 6 *Major* 8874 built 1944
Simplex 4WDM No. 7 *Nocton* 1935 built 1920
Two bogie coaches ex Ashover Light Railway built 1925
One bogie coach ex Sand Hutton Railway built 1924
Bogie open coach
Bogie vans Nos 8 and 9
Six four-wheeled open wagons Nos 10–15
Three bogie open wagons Nos 17–19

## 107　Audley End Miniature Railway　　A

Passenger-carrying 10¼ in. gauge line, 1½ miles in length,
in the grounds of Audley End House, near Saffron Walden,
Essex

*Access:* Off the A11 adjacent to Audley End House. Nearest
station, Audley End
Tel: Saffron Walden 22354
OS Ref: TL 530366

The railway is in operation on Sundays and Bank Holidays
from May to October, plus Tuesdays, Wednesdays, Thursdays and Saturdays in the school summer holidays.
Facilities offered to visitors include car parking, refreshments
and souvenir shop.
The railway was opened in 1964, the ceremony being
performed by Stirling Moss. Originally just under one mile
in length, a half-mile extension was added in 1979. Trains
run through attractive woodlands and cross the River Cam
twice before returning to Audley End station, adjacent to
the coach park. The railway is noteworthy for its attention
to line-side detail, incorporating scale-sized signal boxes,
signals and gradient posts which add considerably to its
overall effect.

**Stock**
Rio Grande 2–8–2 built 1979
Curwen 4–4–2 No. 3548 *Bobbie* built 1948
GNR 4–4–2 No. 4433 *Curwen* built 1965
LMS 4–6–0 No. 6100 *Royal Scot* built Winkler Engineering
Curwen Co-CoDM No. D7011 *Western Thunderer* built 1964
12 articulated open bogie coaches
2 open bogie coaches

**Saffron Walden Model Railway Club**　　　H

Audley End House, Essex (alongside Audley End Miniature
Railway)

Static exhibit used as club headquarters

**Stock**
GER four-wheeled third-class family saloon coach No. 37
built 1897 (formerly six-wheeled).
The coach also houses the Club's '00' gauge model railway
layout and is open to visitors on Bank Holiday Sundays and
Mondays.

## 108　Southend Miniature Railway　　A

Southend-on-Sea, Essex

OS Ref: TQ 886850

Passenger-carrying 10¼ in. gauge railway, 365 yards in
length operating daily during the holiday season. The line
was opened in 1977.

**Stock**
Viking 2–4–2 No. 100 built 1977 (LNER V2 class style)
Freelance Bo–BoPM No. D3152 (BR Mainline Diesel style)
Freelance 4WBE
Six Cromar White/Viking bogie coaches

## 109 Felixstowe Miniature Railway     A

A 7¼ in. gauge line located between Sea Road and the Promenade and is laid out in the shape of an irregular oval. The railway is equipped with semaphore signals, an engine shed, turntable, sidings and a signalbox. Trains make three circuits of the track, commencing and finishing at Felixstowe Lawn Station.
Open weekends, Easter to Spring Bank Holiday, then daily until mid September.

**Stock**
Freelance 2–6–0 *Rupert* rebuilt 1960 (GWR type)
Cromar White Bo–BoPM built 1974
Articulated open bogie coaches

## 110 Ingoldmells Miniature Railway     A

Ingoldmells Point, Skegness, Lincolnshire

Passenger-carrying 7¼ in. gauge railway, 100 yards in length, arranged in a continuous circuit. Operates daily during the holiday season.

**Stock**
LMS 4–6–2 *Ingoldmells Flyer* ('Princess Royal' type) built 1969
Cromar White Bo–BoPM No. D7017 built 1969
'Sit-astride' bogie coaches

## 111 Somerleyton Hall     A

Near Lowestoft, Suffolk

*Access:* 5 miles North West of Lowestoft, off B1074
Tel: Blundeston 224

Passenger-carrying 7¼ in. gauge railway, 300 yards in length, arranged in a U-shaped layout round the estate of Lord and Lady Somerleyton.
Facilities for visitors include car parking, refreshments, 16th-century mansion and grounds, with a famous maze and gardens.
The railway operates on Thursday and Sunday afternoons and Bank Holidays. Also on Tuesdays in July and August.

**Stock**
Wright 0–4–0T *Lulu* built c 1972 ('Hercules' type)
Cromar White Bo–BoPM No. D7026 *Somerleyton* built c 1971
Open bogie coaches

## 112 Cushing's Thursford Collection of Steam Engines and Organs     A

Laurel Farm, Thursford Green, near Fakenham, Norfolk

*Access:* Off the A148 Fakenham-Cromer road
OS Ref: TF 983342

George Cushing has brought together at Laurel Farm a unique collection of steam traction engines and fairground organs. These are displayed in modern exhibition buildings and steaming demonstrations and organ concerts are regular features.
On 20 August 1978, a ¾-mile, passenger-carrying, 1 ft 10¾ in. gauge steam railway was opened running through Norfolk farmland from a terminal station behind the organ museum.

**Stock**
Hunslet 0–4–0ST *Cackler* 671 built 1898
Two covered bogie coaches

## 113 Wells Harbour Railway     A

Beach Road, Wells-next-the-Sea, Norfolk

*Access:* Eastern Counties bus to Wells-next-the-Sea
Tel: Fakenham 710439

Passenger-carrying 10¼ in. gauge railway, ⁷⁄₁₀ mile in length, connecting Wells Town with the beach and Pinewoods Caravan Site. This little line claims a major distinction in that it supplies a local transport need previously performed by a now-discontinued bus service.
The railway operates during Easter week, then on weekends only until Spring Bank Holiday when a timetable service is run daily until 30 September.
Timetable services commence at 10.30 am and operate at 40 minute intervals until 8.10 pm – surely one of the longest operating days of any miniature railway in the British Isles.
The Wells Harbour Railway was built during 1975 and 1976, finally opening for public traffic on 1 July of that year. During its first two seasons it carried the dramatic total of 80,000 passengers – a major achievement for so small a line. However, disaster struck on 11 January 1978, when severe storms washed away ½-mile of track and ballast when waves swept over the sea defence banks and the sea-front road. But an energetic rebuilding campaign allowed services to be restored on 1 July 1978.

**Stock**
King 0–4–2WT *Edmund Hannay* built 1971
Five 12-seat open coaches

The locomotive was built in Norwich and has much of the eccentric charm of that other Norfolk-built 0–4–2WT, *Gazelle*, to which it has an overall resemblance.
The railway is operated by Lt-Cmdr R. W. Francis on behalf of Hannay Hill Railway Ltd.

## 114 Belton House Miniature Railway     A

Belton House, Grantham, Lincolnshire

Passenger-carrying 7¼ in. gauge railway, 300 yards in length at present, but due to be extended to ¾ mile.
The Belton House railway opened on 7 April 1979, using stock and track from the former line at Wyndham Park, Grantham.

**Stock**
LNER 4-6-2 No. 4472 *Flying Scotsman* built Broadfield 1949
Barnes & Thomas 2-6-2 built 1974
5 bogie coaches
Another 'Pacific' locomotive is under construction.

## 115   Barton House Railway                          AE

Barton House, Hartwell Road, The Avenue, Wroxham, Norfolk

*Access:* by road – off A1151; by rail – 15 minutes from BR Wroxham station; by river – adjacent to the River Bure
Tel: Wroxham 2470
OS Ref: TG 302178

Passenger-carrying 3½ in. gauge line laid out as an 80-yard oval. Most of the railway's other equipment comprises full-size railway items. There is a complete M & GNJR signal box with 26-lever frame and instruments, M & GN signals from Guestwick and Melton Constable, a gradient post, two Tyers No. 1 tablet instruments and other items mainly from the M & GNJR.
The railway is open on the third Sunday of each month from April to October between 2.30 pm and 5.30 pm.
Facilities for visitors include refreshments, toilets, railway shop and car parking nearby.
Work on the Barton House Railway began in 1960 and continued steadily until the official opening on 28 April 1963. Until 1970, all money raised was in aid of Wroxham Church Restoration Fund, a total of £600 having been reached. From 1971 receipts have been in aid of charities.

**Stock**
GNR 4-4-2 No. 251 built *c* 1920, rebuilt 1960
GNR 4-4-2 No. 1442 built Elsden *c* 1939, rebuilt 1964
Way 0-4-0BE (used as standby loco only)
'Sit-astride' bogie trolleys

## 116   East Suffolk Light Railway                    B

East Anglia Transport Museum, Chapel Road, Carlton Colville, Lowestoft, Suffolk

*Details from:* the Secretary at the above address
OS Ref: TM 505903

A 2 ft gauge line of about 200 yards length commenced operation early in 1973, running along the northern side of the museum site between two stations, Chapel Road and Woodside.
The rails and rolling stock have all served in East Anglian sites or quarries at some time and there is even a short section of original Southwold Railway track now being used in Chapel Road Station.
The signalbox at Chapel Road was formerly on the Norfolk and Suffolk Joint Railway line between Lowestoft and Yar-mouth dating back to 1903; the associated signals and equipment are primarily of Great Eastern Railway parentage. Many other railway relics are in store and will be restored for use in the station buildings, which it is hoped to erect at a future date.
Near the signal box is the body of the only remaining item of Southwold Railway rolling stock, a passenger luggage van, believed to be No. 14 built in 1885 and rebuilt by English Bros. of Wisbech about 1918.
Future work will entail building a locomotive shed and developing the station areas and facilities, connecting signals and points to the box and the provision of telephone communication between stations. Locomotives are being rebuilt and closed coaches may later be provided for wet weather use. A battery-powered tramcar is also under construction and will later run on the line supplementing the train service.

**Stock**
Motor Rail 4WPM No. 1 5902 built 1934
Motor Rail 4WPM No. 2 5912 built 1934
Hibberd 4WDM No. 3 3307 built 1948
Hudson 24-seat open bogie coach No. 10 (rebuilt 1973)
Penrhyn Railway quarrymen's coaches Nos 11 and 12

*Standard gauge static exhibit*
Wickham 4WPM railcar, Army No. 9035 8195 built 1958

The Museum grew from small beginnings as a result of the purchase in 1961 of a former Lowestoft tramcar which had been in retirement for many years as a summerhouse. Work started in earnest in 1966 on land kindly provided by the founder, Mr A. V. Bird. Since then buildings have been erected, track and overhead wiring constructed, and generating plant for powering the trams and trolleybuses installed. The Museum has one of the widest ranges of preserved vehicles of any museum in the country.

## 117   Wolferton Station Museum                       E

Wolferton, Kings Lynn, Norfolk

*Access:* 9 miles North East of Kings Lynn, on B1440

The former railway station at Wolferton, which was the disembarking point for the Royal Family's journeys to Sandringham House, Norfolk, has been restored as a museum commemorating its many years of royal service.
The museum is open from April to the end of September on weekdays from 11 am to 6 pm (except Saturdays) and on Sundays from 2 pm to 6 pm.
The museum exhibits are housed in the former down side Royal building which was once used by Kings and Queens and their distinguished guests visiting Sandringham House. Built in 1898, it contains fine old panelling, original fittings (some gold plated), unusual small railway relics and Edwardian curios, including some from Royal trains and Queen Victoria's travelling bed made for her in 1828.
It is the only museum in the country whose theme is Edwardian Royal travel.

**Stock**
Wickham 4WPMR No. 960220 built 1933

## 118   Museum of Lincolnshire Life                E

Burton Road, Lincoln

OS Ref: SK 972723

Static locomotive exhibits in a museum of crafts, tools and machinery evoking life in Lincolnshire in bygone times. Museum operated by The Lincolnshire Association.

**Stock**
Ruston Hornsby 4WDM 192888 11/13HP Class built 1939 2 ft 3 in. gauge
[1]Ruston Proctor 4WPM 52124 built 1918 2 ft 6 in. gauge

[1]This locomotive was discovered in April 1974 after being buried under a pile of scrap Army tanks in a breaker's yard for seventeen years.

## 119   Scunthorpe Corporation                E

Jubilee Playing Fields, Ashby, Scunthorpe, Humberside

OS Ref: SE 893088

Standard gauge steam locomotive exhibit on static display.

**Stock**
RSH 0–6–0ST *Lysaght's* 7035 built 1940
Presented by John Lysaghts, Scunthorpe Works Ltd, 1964.

## 120   Caister Castle Motor Museum             E

Caister Castle, Caister-on-Sea, Norfolk

*Access:* Four miles north of Great Yarmouth off A1064
Tel: 057-284-251
OS Ref: TG 504123

Standard gauge steam locomotive on static display in motor museum.
The Museum is open from mid-May to the end of September from 10.30 am to 5 pm daily except Saturdays.
Facilities for visitors include car parking, museum shop, refreshments, toilets, woodland walk and moated castle ruins.
The Museum specialises in unique vehicles of all types, principally steam cars, having examples of Locomobile, White, Stanley and Doble on display. An added attraction is the original Festival of Britain Battersea Park Tree Walk!

**Stock**
Manning Wardle 0–6–0ST No. 42 *Rhondda* 2010 built 1921

Ex BSC Harlaxton Ironstone Quarry, Lincolnshire, 1973.

## 121   Harlow Development Corporation          E

Lower Meadow Play Centre, off Paringdon Road, Southern Way, Harlow, Essex

OS Ref: TL 452078
Standard gauge static locomotive exhibit.

**Stock**
Planet 4WDM 3596 built 1953

## 122   Strumpshaw Hall Steam Museum      AE

Strumpshaw Hall, near Brundall, Norwich, Norfolk

OS Ref: TF 345065

Passenger-carrying 15 in. gauge railway in the grounds of Strumpshaw Hall.
When not in operation, the locomotive is on static display. The museum is open from 2 pm to 5 pm daily except Saturdays from Easter until 30 September.

**Stock**
McGarigle Machine Co. 4–4–0 *Brookes Railroad No. 2* built 1902

This historic American-built 4–4–0 is of the classic Cagney type and formerly worked on the Blakesley Hall Railway.

## 123   Rayleigh, Essex                          E

Sharpe Brothers, Gables Service Station, Rayleigh Spur Road, Rayleigh, Essex

OS Ref: TQ 784920

Standard gauge steam locomotive on static display.

**Stock**
Hawthorn Leslie 0–4–0ST No. 139 *Beatty* 3240 built 1917

Ex Dorman Long (Steel) Ltd, Dock Street Foundry, Middlesbrough, Yorkshire, 1972.

## 124   Proctor & Gamble Ltd                     I

West Thurrock, Essex

OS Ref: TQ 595773

Industrial steam location with locomotive stored pending preservation. No public admittance.

**Stock**
Bagnall 0–6–0F 2370 built 1929

## 125   Courtaulds Ltd                           I

Courtelle Division, P.O. Box 24, Great Coates, Grimsby, Humberside

OS Ref: TA 238124

Industrial steam location with locomotives in store. No public admittance.

**Stock**
Sentinel 4WVBTG *William* 9599 built 1956
Sentinel 4WVBTG *George* 9596 built 1955
Hibberd 4WDM 3817 built 1956

## 126 Swaffham Light Railway A

Cockley Cley Hall, near Swaffham, Norfolk

Passenger-carrying 7¼ in. gauge railway under construction at the time of going to press.
This ambitious 1-mile miniature line will feature steam operation when it opens to the public. The line runs through gardens and woodland and incorporates two bridges over streams and a 165 ft tunnel – claimed to be the longest in the world on 7¼ in. gauge.

## 127 The Crofts Collection G

A collection of 10¼ in. gauge equipment for which an East Anglian site is being sought where a public railway can be operated.

**Stock**
Jennings 4-4-2 No. 1430 *Lake Shore*
LNER 2-6-2 No. 4771 *Green Arrow* (V2 Class) built Scrimshaw
Broome Bo-BoPE No. 300 *Santa Fe*
Crofts 2-2-0PM built 1972

## 128 Ickleton, Cambridgeshire C

Mr A. B. H. Braithwaite, Caldress Manor, Ickleton, Cambs

*Access:* BR Great Chesterford Station

OS Ref: TL 493438

Short private 1 ft 6 in. gauge line in the grounds of Caldress Manor.

**Stock**
Regent Street Polytechnic 4-2-2 built 1898.

This locomotive was constructed from a set of castings and forgings supplied by W. G. Bagnall of Stafford to give instruction on fitting and engine work to students. Amongst those who worked on the engine was Henry Greenly. The locomotive was formerly used on the Jaywick Railway.

## 129 Romford, Essex G

Mr P. Elms, 73 Crow Lane, Romford, Essex

OS Ref: TQ 500878

3 ft 6½ in. gauge locomotives in store.

**Stock**
Bagnall 0-4-0ST *Sir Tom* 2135 built 1925
Bagnall 0-4-0ST *Woto* 2133 built 1924

Both ex BICC Ltd., Belvedere, Kent, 1969.

## 130 Burnham Market Garage G

Mr A. B. Mason, Burnham Market Station, near Wells, Norfolk

OS Ref: TF 835419

Rolling stock in store

**Stock**
[1]Hudswell Clarke 0-6-0ST No. 39 *Rhos* 1308 built 1918 standard gauge
[2]Curwen 4-4-2 No. 1865 built 1965 10¼ in. gauge
[2]Four open articulated bogie coaches 10¼ in. gauge

[1]Ex Stewarts & Lloyds Minerals Ltd, Corby, Northants, 1968.
[2]Ex Lowestoft Miniature Railway, 1974.

## 131 Wimpole, Cambridgeshire G

Mr C. Roads, Hillside, Wimpole, Cambs

OS Ref: TL 364510

Standard gauge locomotive in store.

**Stock**
Hudswell Clarke 0-6-0ST 1208 built 1916

## 132 South Cams Rural and C
## Industrial Steam Museum

New Buildings Farm, Heydon, near Royston, Cambs

OS Ref: TL 419409

Short private standard gauge light railway. Planning permission for this site specifically excludes public access, therefore, written permission is required before entry will be permitted. Casual visitors ignoring this stipulation have found themselves turned away at shotgun point. You have been warned!

**Stock**
[1]Kitson 0-6-0ST No. 44 *Conway* 5469 built 1933
[2]Manning Wardle 0-6-0ST *Newcastle* 1532 built 1901
Barclay 0-4-0ST 1219 built 1910
Wickham 4WPMR 1519 built 1934
GNR six-wheeled passenger brake van built 1888
MS & LR six-wheeled coach
Two GER six-wheeled coach bodies

[1]Ex Stewarts & Lloyds Minerals Ltd, Gretton Brook, Corby, Northants, 1969
[2]Ex Wissington Light Railway, Norfolk, 1973

## 133 Kirton in Lindsey Railway E
## Museum and Windmill

The Mill, North Cliff Road, Kirton Lindsey, Gainsborough, Lincolnshire DN21 4NH

*Owner:* Mr Alan Turner

*Access:* The Mill and Museum are adjacent to the B1398 road from Lincoln to Scunthorpe, just to the north of Kirton

Lindsey. Lincoln is 19 miles away, Scunthorpe 8 and Gainsborough 12

Standard gauge steam locomotive and equipment plus smaller exhibits on display in a newly-opened railway museum in the grounds of Kirton Lindsey Windmill.

Efforts are now being made to acquire equipment for a 2 ft gauge railway in the grounds.

In 1980, the museum will be open on the first and third weekends in each month plus extra openings on public holidays and special occasions, which will be announced. Entry will be, adults 25p and children 15p. Entry to the mill is free unless it is working, when there may be a small charge. At present the mill is driven occasionally, using a tractor and belts to an outside wheel

Light refreshments are available but we cannot offer toilet facilities. The nearest public toilets may be found ¼ mile away in Kirton market place. There is limited parking space in the mill yard and ample parking in Kirton.

A temporary sales counter is situated in the museum until a separate shop is ready.

Children unaccompanied by an adult are not permitted within the grounds. No dogs allowed on the premises.

Visitors will please refrain from smoking.

The collection herein represents a lifelong interest in the old railways, especially those of Lincolnshire (mainly the London and North Eastern, the Great Northern and the Great Central). Other companies are however represented.

Entry is by a ticket bought at the genuine ticket window in the Booking Office. The first display area contains mainly small items ranging from station lamps down to tickets and buttons. Many facets of the railways are in evidence here and the visitor may take a nostalgic look at labels and printed ephemera from long closed Lincolnshire stations. Various locomotive, wagon, bridge and notice plates line the walls, whilst rail chairs and block instruments represent the heavier side. All furniture in the museum is from local railways. Some 4 mm scale EM gauge models, many scratch built, may be seen in the large showcase along with a model of a typical country branch station. Although far from complete, the interior of the Booking Office and Station Master's Office may be seen through the windows.

On entering the platform area, the visitor will see the larger exhibits, including the fully fitted signal box and GNR and GCR signals. A GCR coach side awaits restoration along with numerous large items.

**Stock**
Peckett 0-4-0ST *Annie* 1159 built 1908

## 134   Collection 'Z'                                     G

Mr Clarke, Cleethorpes, Humberside

A private collection of standard gauge industrial steam locomotives.

**Stock**
RSH 0-6-0ST 7680 built 1950
Peckett 0-4-0ST *Ffione Jane* 1749 built 1928

## 135   Bacton, Suffolk                                    G

Mr R. Finbow, 'Caithness', Bacton, Suffolk

OS Ref: TM 064682

Standard gauge locomotive in store.

**Stock**
Sentinel 4WVBTG *Fry* 7492 built 1928

Ex J. S. Fry & Sons Ltd., Somerdale, Bristol, 1964. Presented to Mr Alfred Lewis by the company in 1968 and subsequently resold to Mr Finbow.

## 136 Aveling-Barford Ltd                                  G

Grantham, Lincolnshire

OS Ref: SK 923346

3 ft gauge locomotive in store.

**Stock**
Aveling Porter 2-2-0WTG *Excelsior* 1607 built 1880

Ex James Whittaker & Son, Ramsbottom, Lancashire, 1961.

## 137   Malcolm W. Knight                                  G

A 2 ft 6 in. gauge locomotive in store.
Very limited access by prior arrangement only.

OS Ref: TF 393079

*Details and correspondence:* M. W. Knight, 'The Limes', Hollycroft Road, Emneth, Wisbech, Cambs PE14 8BD

**Stock**
Tubize 2-6-2T 2369 built 1948 (ex Jokiosten Railway, Finland)

This locomotive is now for sale.

## 138   Carless, Cape & Leonard Ltd                        E

Harwich Refinery, Parkeston, Essex

OS Ref: TM 232323

Standard gauge steam locomotive on static display.

**Stock**
RSH 0-4-0F 7803 built 1954

## 139   Holbeach St Johns                                  G

Mr J. H. P. Wright, Fenland Airfield, Holbeach St Johns, Lincolnshire

OS Ref: TF 333179

1 ft 9 in. gauge locomotives in store, though it has been proposed to build a short line on the airfield for them to run on. At present, both locomotives are dumped in a compound with piles of scrap cars.

**Stock**
Hudswell Clarke 4–6–2DM D611 built 1938 (steam outline)
Hudswell Clarke 4–6–2DM No. 6203 *Queen Elizabeth* D612 built 1938 (steam outline)

## 140    Yaxham Park                                  C

Yaxham, Dereham, Norfolk
OS Ref: TG 003101

Short 2 ft gauge, private line owned by Mr D. C. Potter. No visitors on Sundays, please.

**Stock:**
Potter 2–2–0VBT *The Coffee Pot* built 1970
Lister 4WPM *Gnat* 40011 built 1954
Lister 4WPM 32801 built 1948
Orenstein and Koppel 4WDM 7688 built 1936
One open bogie coach
Two four-wheeled open coaches
Hudson bogie flat wagon
Two four-wheeled flat wagons

## 141    Maldon Miniature Railway                    B

The Promenade, Maldon, Essex

Passenger-carrying 10¼ in. gauge line, 250 yards in length.

This railway was originally steam-worked, but when its boiler wore out, the locomotive was converted to electric power by fitting a motor in the tender. The line is straight and the train is hauled in one direction and propelled in the other

**Stock**
LMS 4–6–0E No. 4716 built Carland 1948 ('Royal Scot' type)
Three bogie open coaches

## 142    Cleethorpes Miniature Railway               B

Marine Embankment, Cleethorpes, Humberside

A 14½ in. gauge double-track railway located at the south end of the town. The line is four-fifths of a mile long, passing along the length of the boating lake and miniature golf course with a panoramic view of the Humber estuary and shipping. Opened as a steam railway in 1948, it changed hands and became electrically powered in 1954 and was purchased by Cleethorpes Corporation five years later. The system was remodelled and extended in 1972 and now operates with two terminal stations at the bathing pool and zoo, with one intermediate halt at Thrunscoe.
The gauge of the line is unusual, as is the choice of fuel for the locomotives, for the engines have large propane gas tanks mounted in their tenders. Further unusual features are to be found in the operation of the line, which is double track throughout, as two parallel single independent tracks. The railway operates at Easter, then on Sundays only until

Spring Bank Holiday, thence daily until the second half of September.

**Stock**
Severn-Lamb 2–8–0GasH No. 278 built 1972 (Steam outline)
Severn-Lamb 2–8–0GasH No. 800 built 1978 (Steam outline)
Ten bogie coaches, some of them roofed

## 143    Butlins, Clacton                            B

Clacton Holiday Camp
OS Ref: TM 164136

Passenger-carrying 2 ft gauge railway running round the camp.

**Stock**
Baguley 0–4–0DM 3232 built 1947 (steam outline)

## 144    Skegness Rail Services                      B

Tower Esplanade, Skegness, Lincolnshire
OS Ref: TF 570627

Passenger-carrying 10¼ in. gauge railway running from Tower Esplanade to Prince's Parade.
The line operates daily in the holiday season.

**Stock**
Cable Bo-BoBE *Duplex 2*
Yorkshire EV Bo-BoBE No. 15577 *The Fisherman*
Cromar White 4WBE No. E7052
Two articulated 4-car sets of coaches

## 145    Peewit Caravan Park                         B

Walton Avenue, Felixstowe, Suffolk

Passenger-carrying 10¼ in. gauge railway, 190 yards in length. This little line opened in 1974 and manages to include a 31 ft span bridge in its run alongside the caravan park.

**Stock**
Ward 4WPM *Peewit Flyer* built 1970 (steam outline)

The locomotive was rebuilt from a battery electric loco and resembles a Hunslet Quarry tank in appearance.

## 146    Mablethorpe Miniature Railway               B

Queens Park, Mablethorpe, Lincs

Passenger-carrying 7¼ in. gauge railway operating on a continuous circuit. This short line was regauged from 10¼ in. in 1971 and for a short while was steam-operated.

**Stock**
Mawsby Bo-BoPM No. 1958 *Nottingham-Derby* built 1971

## 147 Basildon Zoo Miniature Railway     B

Basildon Zoo, Essex

Passenger-carrying 10¼ in. gauge railway, 200 yards in length.

**Stock**
Severn-Lamb Co-CoPM built 1969
Four open bogie coaches

## 148 Butlins, Skegness     B

Skegness Holiday Camp, Ingoldmells, Lincolnshire

A 2 ft gauge passenger-carrying line running round the camp

**Stock**
Chance 4–2–4DH No. 30 *C. P. Huntingdon* 64–5030–24 built 1964 (steam outline)

## 149 Ferry Meadows Miniature Railway     A

Nene Valley Park, Peterborough

*Access:* Orton Mere Station, Nene Valley Railway

Passenger-carrying 10¼ in. gauge railway, ¾-mile in length under construction at the time of going to press. It is expected to be open by 1980.

**Stock**
Dove 4–6–4 built 1950
Mills 0–4–0ST *Alice* built 1977

## 150 Suffolk Country and Wildlife Park     B

Kessingland, near Lowestoft, Suffolk

Passenger-carrying 10¼ in. gauge railway, 1½ miles in length under construction at the time of going to press. It is expected to be open by 1980.

**Stock**
Fenlow Bo-BoDH No. 10 *Conway Castle* built *c* 1972
Fenlow Bo-BoDH No. 11 *Rhuddlan Castle* built *c* 1972
Two seven-coach sets of articulated bogie coaches

Locomotives, coaches and track were all obtained from the former Prestatyn Miniature Railway in 1979.

# AREA D

## North East

**Yorkshire**
**Durham**
**Northumberland**
**Cleveland**
**Tyne & Wear**
**North Humberside**

---

### 151 Keighley and Worth Valley Railway A

Haworth Station, Keighley, West Yorkshire BD22 8NJ

*Access:* By BRITISH RAIL, Keighley Station is served by local trains from Leeds, Bradford, Skipton, Morecambe, etc. Some Leeds–Carlisle expresses also stop at Keighley.
By BUS, Services from Bradford and Leeds pass Keighley Station. Other bus services operate to Keighley from Halifax, Hebden Bridge and Todmorden (for Manchester trains), Ilkley, Skipton, Colne, Nelson, Burnley, Preston, Accrington, Blackburn and Blackpool.
By ROAD, A650 road from Bradford and Leeds, A629 road from Halifax and M62, A629 road from Skipton, A6033 road from Hebden Bridge.

Tel: Haworth 43629 (Timetable enquiries)
Haworth 45214 (All other enquiries)

OS Ref: SE 034371

The Keighley and Worth Valley Railway packs more into its five-mile run than practically any other preserved railway in the British Isles. For a start, it's a complete working branch line with a main line junction with BR, several small country stations, two tunnels, two level-crossings, a viaduct and a rural terminus in the shelter of Oxenhope Moor. Its scenery varies from the industrial townscape of Keighley to pleasant West Riding countryside, whilst its collection of over 30 steam locomotives is one of the largest and most varied in the country. It was built in 1867 by the Midland Railway and operated in unspectacular fashion until closed by British Railways in 1962. The K & WVRPS was formed in that year and progressed steadily until it was able to reopen the railway in 1968.

A regular steam service has operated every weekend since then with additional services midweek in summer. Diesel railbuses operate the morning services on Saturdays and Sundays. All these trains are operated by unpaid Society Member volunteers. The Society has built up a fine collection of over thirty locomotives and a similar number of carriages, which are on display at Haworth and Oxenhope.

The railway operates on every weekend throughout the year, also on Bank Holidays and every day in July and August.

Facilities for visitors include car parking, museum, railway shops, refreshments, toilet and picnic area at Oxenhope.

Keighley and Worth Valley Railway Preservation Society Membership details from: Steve Dickens, 12 Rossefield Close, Bramley, Leeds LS13 3RT.

Members are entitled to Concessionary fares (up to 3 days free). They also have the chance to help in the operation of the Railway and receive a free copy of the Society's quarterly magazine 'Push and Pull'. Subscription Rates: Life Member £50, Annual (Adult) £4, (Under 16) £2, (Member's Wife) £2, Senior Members (60 and over) £2, Family £6.

*Hire a Train*

Our ordinary trains can be arranged to seat up to 450 for special visits, but we can also offer a steam-hauled Pullman train (incorporating the Jubilee Bar Car) for up to 150 persons. Another speciality is a conducted tour by diesel railbus (seating 56) which can be arranged for summer evenings.

**Stock**
BR 4-6-2 No. 34092 *City of Wells* (West Country Class) built 1949
BR 2-6-2T No. 41241 (Class 2MT) built 1949
BR 2-6-4T No. 80002 (Class 4MT) built 1952
[6]BR 4-6-0 No. 75078 (Riddles Class 4MT) built 1956
[6]BR 2-6-0 No. 78022 (Riddles Class 2MT) built 1953
[1]L & YR 'Pug' 0-4-0ST No. 19 bullt 1910
[1]L & YR 'Pug' 0-4-0ST No. 51218 built 1901
[1]L & YR 0-6-0ST No. 752 (Beyer Peacock 1989) built 1881
[3]MR 0-6-0 No. 3924 (Class 4F) built 1920
LMS 0-6-0T No. 47279 (Class 3F) built 1924
LMS 2-6-0 No. 42765 (Class 6P5F) built 1927
LMS 4-6-0 No. 45212 (Class 5MT) built 1935
LMS 2-8-0 No. 8431 (Class 8F) built 1944

Photo: John Gardner

Haydock Foundry 0–6–0WT *Bellerophon* (C) built 1874
[4]Manning Wardle 0–6–0ST *Sir Berkeley* (1210) built 1890
Hudswell Clarke 0–6–0ST *Lord Mayor* (402) built 1893
Hudswell Clarke 0–6–0T *Hamburg* (31) (697) built 1903
Hudswell Clarke 0–6–0T No. 67 (1379) built 1919
Hudswell Clarke 0–6–0ST No. 118 *Brussells* (1782) built 1945
Barclay 0–6–0ST No. 68077 (2215) built 1947
Peckett 0–4–0DM *Austins No. 1* (5003) built 1961
Hunslet 0–6–0DM MDHB No. 32 (2699) built 1944
English Electric 0–6–0DE No. D0226 (2345) built 1956
Hudswell Clarke 0–6–0D No. D2511 D1202 built 1961
Hudswell Clarke 0–4–0DM ESC No. 32 D816 built 1954
Diesel railbuses Nos 62 and 64 (Waggon and Maschinenbau) built 1958
LMS compartment bogie coach No. M12066M built 1938 (KWVR No. 6)
BR open bogie coach No. E4555 (KWVR No. 31)
BR open bogie coach No. E4588 (KWVR No. 25) (bar car)
BR compartment brake bogie coach No. E43345 built 1955 (KWVR No. 10)
[1]L & YR Hughes brake/third coach No. M23964M built 1910 (KWVR No. 102)
[2] [7]GNR six-wheeled brake/third coach No. DE940281E
[2] [8]MSLR four-wheeled coach No. 103
[2] [9]MR six-wheeled coach No. DM284677
[2] [10]SR Bulleid SO bogie coach No. S1469
[2] [11]SR BSK bogie coach No. 3554
[2] [12]Metropolitan Railway brake/third bogie coach No. 427
[2] [12]Metropolitan Railway third-class bogie coach No. 465
[2] [13]Metropolitan Railway first-class bogie coach No. 509
[2] [14]LNER Gresley brake/third coach No. E16520E
[5]LNER bogie saloon No. 21661 built 1871, rebuilt 1904
BR open bogie coach No. E4280 built 1956 (KWVR No. 13)
BR open bogie coach No. E3825 built 1954 (KWVR No. 14)
BR compartment bogie coach No. E46145 built 1954 (KWVR No. 15)
BR compartment bogie coach No. E46157 built 1954 (KWVR No. 16)
BR open bogie coach No. E48011 built 1955 (KWVR No. 17)
BR open bogie coach No. E48018 built 1955 (KWVR No. 19)
BR compartment brake coach No. E43128 built 1954 (KWVR No. 20)
BR trailer buffet coach No. E59575 built 1960 (KWVR No. 24)
LNER bogie passenger brake van No. E100E built 1948 as tool van (KWVR No. 100)
LNER Thompson sleeping car No. W1770E built 1951 (KWVR No. 103)
LNER Thompson sleeping car No. W1769E built 1951 (KWVR No. 104)
LNER bogie passenger brake van No. E70442E built 1940 (KWVR No. 105)
LNER bogie passenger brake van No. E70470E built 1939 (KWVR No. 106)

Swedish State Railways 2–8–0 No. 1931 (WD Class) (Vulcan Foundry 5200) built 1945
Polish State Railways 2–8–0 No. 203–474 Lima 8758 built 1945
SR 0–6–0T No. 72 (BR No. 30072) (USA Class) (Vulcan Iron Works 4446) built 1943
GWR 0–6–0PT No. L89 (Class 57XX) built 1929
L & YR 0–6–0 No. 52044 (Class 2F) built 1887
TVR 0–6–2T No. 85 (Class 02) built 1899
RSH 0–6–0ST *Fred* (7289) built 1945
RSH 0–6–0ST No. 57 (7668) built 1950
RSH 0–6–0ST No. 62 (7673) built 1950
RSH 0–6–0ST No. 63 (7761) built 1954
Barclay 0–4–0ST No. 2226 (2226) built 1946

SR parcels and miscellaneous van No. S1125S built 1936 (KWVR No. 107)
BR 'Weltrol' wagon No. B900802
BR plate wagon No. B931692 built 1952
BR 'Shark' brake van No. DB993889 built 1957
GWR 'Toad' brake van No. 17898 built 1914
LMS open VB No. M401155
SR 'Walrus' ballast hopper No. DS62041
Shell BP oil tankers Nos. A5066, A5281 and A5081 built 1938
Pullman car No. 84 built 1930
LYR inspection saloon No. 2 (Sc45038M) built 1878
NER inspection saloon No. 1173 built 1870
Rail-mounted diesel crane (5 ton)
Rail-mounted steam crane (10 ton)
LNER 'Dolphin' rail/sleeper wagon No. DE150667
[2]Mineral wagon No. AB18 (to be restored to the livery of a local coal merchant)

[1]Owned by L & Y Saddletanks Fund (q.v.).
[2]Owned by Vintage Carriages Trust (q.v.).
[3]Withdrawn as BR No. 43924 in 1965 and sold to Woodham Brothers, Barry, for scrap. Purchased for preservation in 1968. This locomotive was the first of the many rescued from Barry scrapyard to be restored to working order and run again under its own steam. Apart from the solitary 0-10-0 Lickey banker, this class was the largest and most powerful goods engine constructed by the Midland. They can only be described as of medium size, but throughout their long and active life worked hard on all forms of freight duties. Owned by the Midland 4F Preservation Society (q.v.).
[4]Built in 1890 to the order of Logan and Hemingway, contractors for the MS & LR Derbyshire lines and London Extension construction, this little engine went on to a second career in the ironstone quarrying industry before being honourably retired in 1964.
[5]Built 1871 as a six-wheeled saloon for the Stockton and Darlington Railway. Became NER No. 1661 and used as Locomotive Superintendent's saloon hauled by locomotive No. 66 Aerolite. Rebuilt 1904 as a bogie saloon and altered to present restored condition by LNER in 1934. Owned by North Eastern Railway 1661 Coach Partnership (q.v.).
[6]Owned by Standard 4 Locomotive Preservation Society Ltd (q.v.).
[7]This is a six-wheeled brake/third built by the GNR at Doncaster in 1888. It is restored externally to its original varnished teak finish.
[8]This four-wheeled tri-composite has one first-class, one second-class, two third-class and a central luggage compartment. It was built at Dukinfield by the Manchester, Sheffield and Lincolnshire Railway in 1876. Restoration of this carriage began in 1973.
[9]A Midland Railway six-wheeled composite having two first-class, two third-class and a central baggage compartment. This carriage was built at Derby in 1886.
[10]Built by British Railways in 1951 to a Southern Railway design by O. V. Bulleid, this carriage is a gangwayed open second. It ended its BR days in 1969 on the Eastern Region. It is restored to the livery of British Railways Southern Region.
[11]An ex-Southern Railway third-class/brake end, side corridor coach, this is the last surviving example of the distinctive South Eastern and Chatham Railway designed 'Matchboards', so called because of the unusual vertical panelling below the waist. It was built by the Metropolitan Carriage, Wagon and Finance Co. at Birmingham in 1924 for use on the 'continental' trains between London, Dover and Folkestone. Withdrawn from service in 1962, it was acquired by the VCT in 1972, and has since been extensively renovated and restored to its Southern Railway livery.
[12]Two of the Metropolitan Railway's high-capacity suburban coaches of the 'Dreadnought' type, familiar to commuters from Aylesbury and the north-west London suburbs until the mid-1960s, when they were withdrawn from service by London Transport. Acquired in 1975, they are to be restored to their London Transport livery. No. 427 is a seven-compartment brake/third, built by the Metropolitan Carriage, Wagon and Finance Company in 1910, and No. 465 is a nine-compartment third built by the same company in 1919.
[13]Similar to Nos 427 and 465, this is a seven-compartment first-class carriage built in 1923 by the Metropolitan Carriage Wagon and Finance Company.
[14]The VCT are the curators of this vehicle, which is owned by the Gresley Society. This is a third-class six-compartment side corridor coach with brake end, built at York in 1939 by the LNER. It is the last survivor of a type very familiar on the Eastern Region of BR as late as the mid-1960s, when the decision to withdraw from service all wooden-bodies stock began to take effect. It is to be restored to its LNER appearance of varnished teak.

**Vintage Carriages Trust**                                  H

Keighley and Worth Valley Railway

*Details from:* Secretary, Vintage Carriages Trust, c/o Haworth Station, Haworth, Keighley, West Yorkshire BD22 8NJ

**L & Y Saddletanks Fund**                                   H

Keighley and Worth Valley Railway

*Secretary:* G. Hallos, 9 Fairfield Close, Ossett, Yorkshire

**Midland 4F Preservation Society**                          H

Keighley and Worth Valley Railway

*Details from:* Ian Johnson, 3 Meldon Avenue, Chase Park, Sherburn, Durham DH6 1JX

---

When the Worth Valley bought an American S160 class 2-8-0 built by Alco at Schenectady, NY State in 1945, from the Polish State Railways in 1977 (it was their Tr203-474) the engine soon went back into USA Transportation Corps livery of battleship grey and black for film work in *Yanks*. Here (above left) it's seen in the BR goods yard at Keighley with some of the 1,500 extras used during the making of the film

Freight trains worked for civil engineering purposes are a frequent sight in the morning or on non-operating days on the Worth Valley Railway. Here (below left) Midland 4F No 43924 gets away from Oakworth with freight for Oxenhope

**Standard 4 Locomotive Preservation Society Ltd**  H

Keighley and Worth Valley Railway

*Details from:* T. R. England, 105 Laudsdale Road, Rotherham, South Yorkshire S65 3NT

*Subscriptions:* Life £15; annual adult £1; annual junior 50p

This society owns two locomotives, both of which were rescued from that well-known establishment at Barry. Both locomotives were withdrawn in 1966 and were bought for preservation in 1972 and 1975 respectively.

**North Eastern Railway 1661 Coach Partnership**  H

*Details from:* J. B. Dawson, 20 Towton Avenue, York YO2 2DW

## 152  Middleton Railway  A

Tunstall Road/Moor Road, Leeds 11, West Yorkshire

*Access:* (to Tunstall Road Halt).
By car via M1 motorway from the south to Exit 45 (Beeston, Hunslet), then turn right along Tunstall Road, then right at the roundabout. The halt is on the right. Or via the A653 to Tunstall Road traffic lights, approximately one mile past the city boundary, then turn down Tunstall Road to the roundabout and proceed as above.
By public transport: bus No. 74 or 76 from Park Row (across City Square from BR City Station) to Tunstall Road roundabout, then proceed as above.
Tel: Leeds 645424
OS Ref: SE 302309

Passenger-carrying standard gauge steam railway, 2 miles in length. The Middleton Railway, which can claim to be the direct descendant of Branding's Railway, authorised by Act of Parliament in 1758 (the first railway legislation), which subsequently saw the first successful commercial use of steam locomotives in 1812, was also the first standard gauge railway to be taken over by a preservation society in 1960. The undertaking is now a registered charity and a limited company, and has acquired a selection of industrial locomotives and stock in keeping with its long history of service. All work is carried out by volunteers.

*All enquiries to:* Mrs E. M. Lee, 71 Knightsway, Whitkirk, Leeds LS15 7BL. (Please enclose stamped addressed envelope)
*Subscription:* £2.50 adult. Membership details on application.
*Membership:* 200
Facilities for visitors include free car parking, a small museum, railway shop, refreshments and toilets a short distance away.
The Middleton Railway is run by Rail-fans as a working museum. It is the only line of its kind that carries goods for local firms during the week, and on weekends and Bank holidays a steam-hauled visitors service. Trains leave Hunslet Moor (Tunstall Road) for Middleton (Park Gates) half hourly, from 2 pm to 4.30 pm. This service runs from Easter to the end of October. It is an inexpensive and popular way of

Photo: Tom Heavyside

*Windle* wends her way down 'The Old Run' at Middleton. The Borrows well tanks were a unique design that hailed from St Helens in Lancashire

reaching one of the largest parks in Leeds. Special trains can be arranged for parties.
Train services may be altered in accordance with demand.

**Stock**
[1]Peckett 0–4–0ST 2003 built 1941
Hudswell Clarke 0–4–0ST *Henry de Lacy II* (1309) built 1917
Borrows 0–4–0WT *Windle* (53) built 1909
Bagnall 0–4–0ST *Matthew Murray* (2702) built 1943
Hawthorn Leslie 0–4–0ST No. 6 (3860) built 1935
Hudswell Clarke 0–4–0DM *Carroll* (D631) built 1946
Sentinel 4WVBTG No. 59 (BR 68153) (8839) built 1933
[4] [5]NER 0–4–0 No. 1310 (LNER Class Y7) built 1891
[5]DSB 0–4–0WT No. 385 (Class HS) (Hartmann 2110) built 1895
[2]Hudson–Hunslet 4WDM *Courage* (1786) built 1935
Fowler 4WDM 3900002 built 1945
LMS goods brake van
LMS covered wagon
LMS and GWR open wagons
[3]Middleton colliery wagon No. 350 built 1890
LNER ballast brake/riding van built 1940
GWR four-wheeled steam crane built Thomas Booth, *c.* 1880
MR hand crane and match trucks built 1880
Several industrial wagons in original state or converted for use on the Middleton Railway

[1]Owned jointly by the MRT and one of its members.
[2]Owned by Leeds University Union Railway and Transport Society.
[3]Static exhibit.
[4]Worsdell Class H withdrawn as LNER No. 1310 in 1931 and sold to Pelaw Main Collieries Ltd. Purchased for preservation from NCB Watergate Colliery in 1965.
[5]Owned by Steam Power Trust '65 (*q.v.*).

*Details from:* A. Bowman, 'Evergreen', Durham Road, Stockton-on-Tees, Cleveland

## 153 North Yorkshire Moors Railway    A

Pickering Station, Pickering, North Yorkshire

*Access:* By British Rail from Darlington, Middlesbrough and Newcastle to Grosmont Station, near Whitby; by United Bus from York and Scarborough, to Pickering, from Whitby to Goathland or Pickering; by car on the A169 from York towards Whitby, on the A171 from Middlesbrough towards Whitby, turning off at Egton for Grosmont Station.
Tel: Pickering 72508
OS Ref: SE 797842

Passenger-carrying standard gauge steam railway, 18 miles in length, from Pickering to Grosmont.
The railway is open from Easter to the end of October, with reduced services in early and late season. Please consult full timetable.
*Facilities:* Catering. Private trains can be booked or coaches reserved on normal trains. Bar and light refreshments available on most trains from Goathland to Pickering and return. Car parks at Grosmont and Pickering Stations. Shops at Grosmont, Goathland and Pickering Stations. Locomotive shed with inspection gallery at Grosmont.
The North Yorkshire Moors Railway is of considerable historic merit. It was constructed as long ago as 1836 by George Stephenson as a horse-worked line incorporating a 1,500-yard incline on a gradient of 1 in 10 between Grosmont and Beckhole over which trains were rope-hauled. Between Ellerbeck and Pickering the line threaded its way through sinuous Newtondale, a classic Ice-Age gorge cutting through the heart of the Moors. The line was reconstructed to make it suitable for locomotive haulage and in 1865 a four-and-a-half mile deviation route on a 1 in 49 gradient replaced the old rope-hauled incline.
The railway was closed by British Railways as part of the implementations of the iniquitous Beeching Plan in 1965. But two years later, a preservation society was formed which entered into an agreement to purchase the railway, initially with the intention of operating the Grosmont-Goathland section. Subsequently the remainder of the line was also bid for and, following the issuing of a Light Railway Order, the railway was re-opened by HRH The Duchess of Kent on 1 May 1973.
From Grosmont Station to Goathland trains are steam-hauled up a 1 in 49 average gradient and from Goathland through the North Yorkshire Moors National Park to Pickering, diesel-hauled scenic trains are used to give better viewing and to protect the forest environment. Passengers can change from steam to diesel at Goathland for no extra charge.

### Stock

[4]SR 4-6-0 No. 841 *Greene King* (BR No. 30841) (S15 Class) built 1936
[2] [6]LNER 2-6-0 No. 2005 (Class K1) built 1949
[1] [6]NER 0-8-0 No. 2238 (Class T2) built 1918
[7] [10]NER 0-8-0 No. 901 (Class Q7) built 1919
[5] [9]LMS 4-6-0 No. 5428 *Eric Treacy* (Class 5MT) built 1937
[7]LMS 4-6-0 No. 4767 *George Stephenson* (Class 5MT) built 1947
[7]Lambton Railway 0-6-2T No. 5 (Robert Stephenson 3377) built 1909
[8]Lambton Railway 0-6-2T No. 29 (Kitson 4263) built 1904
S & DJR 2-8-0 No. 53809 (S & D No. 89) (Stephenson 3895) built 1925
BR 2-6-4T No. 80135 (Riddles Class 4MT) built 1956
GWR 0-6-2T No. 6619 (Class 56XX) built 1928
[3]GNR 0-6-0ST No. 1247 (J52 Class) built 1899
RSH 0-6-0T No. 31 *Meteor* 7604 built 1956
RSH 0-6-0ST No. 47 *Moorbarrow* (7849) built 1955
Hudswell Clarke 0-6-0T No. 20 *Jennifer* (1731) built 1942
Hudswell Clarke 0-4-0ST No. 1 *Mirvale* (1882) built 1955
Barclay 0-6-0ST No. 2 *Salmon* (2139) built 1942
Borrows 0-4-0WT No. 3 (37) built 1898
[10]BR AIA-AIADE No. D5500 built Brush 1957
BR Bo-BoDE No. D5032 (Class 24) built 1959
BR Co-CoDH No. D1048 *Western Lady* built 1963
BR Co-CoDH No. D1041 *Western Prince* built 1963
BR Bo-BoDH No. D823 *Onslaught* built 1958
BR/Drewry 0-6-0DM No. D2207 (2482) built 1953
Sentinel 4WVBTG *Teesside No. 5* (9629) built 1957
Yorkshire Engine Company 0-4-0DE *Stanton No. 44* (2622) built 1956
Fowler 0-4-0DH No. 21 (4210034) built 1954
AC cars 4WDM railbus No. E79978 *Premier* built 1958
BR/Gloucester DMU E50341/E56099 (two-car set, motor brake second and trailer composite) built 1957
BR/Gloucester DMU E51118/56097 (two-car set, motor brake second and trailer composite) built 1957
BR corridor first-class coach No. E13102 built 1957
BR Mk I bogie coaches Nos. E13043, E24804 and E21100 (ex Derwent Valley Railway)
BR open second-class saloon coach No. E4481 built 1957
BR second-class coach No. E46142 built 1953
BR second-class coach No. E24808 built 1953
BR tourist open second coach No. E3798 built 1953
BR brake/second corridor coach No. E35089
BR corridor composite coach No. E15709
BR brake/second-class open saloon coaches Nos E9235 and E9267 built 1955
BR tourist open second-class coach No. E3860 built 1953
BR tourist open second-class coach No. E4597 built 1956
BR first-class buffet car No. SC79443 built 1956
BR second-class coach No. E25142 built 1954
[11]H & BR semi-corridor bogie brake third No. 5 built Birmingham RC & W 1912
[11]H & BR bogie brake third No. 40 (R. Y. Pickering & Co.) built 1907
GWR officers inspection saloon No. 80974 built 1947
[12]NER clerestory bogie Autocoach No. 3453 built 1904
[12]NER Main line open 3rd coach No. 945 built 1924
[12]NER 6-wheel luggage composite coach No. 1111 built 1890
LNER Gresley BSO bogie coach No. E16547E built 1934
LNER first-class sleeping coach No. E1259E built 1949
LNER buffet car No. E9134S built 1937

Photo: Valerie Burns

Jubilee day on the North Yorkshire Moors Railway as flags herald the arrival of Lambton tank No. 29 at Grosmont. Nice one, Valerie!

LNER corridor composite coach No. 18477 built 1950
LNER composite coach No. 88329 built 1947
LNER Gresley Mess and Tool coach
GCR 'Barnum' brake/third-class coach No. 695 built 1911
GNR bogie brake/composite coach No. 2856 built 1898
NER 20-ton hopper wagons Nos. 4503, 4551 and 4561
GNR eight-wheeled 20-ton goods brake van No. 23791 built 1914
NER LWB ballast brake van No. DE58033 built 1914
LMS 20-ton goods brake van No. M732170 built 1946
NER 12-ton goods van No. 101707 built 1911
LNER 10-ton goods van No. 632802 built 1923
GWR 10-ton open wagons Nos 77306 and A893 built 1908
Shell-Mex Ltd tank wagon No. 7285 built 1943
[11]H & BR 18 ft 6 in. open wagon No. 3697 (C. Roberts & Co.) built 1905
[11]H & BR 15 ft 6 in. open wagon (believed to be No. 577)

(Ashbury RCW) built 1886
[11]H & BR four-wheeled engineer's van No. 2 (Metropolitan RC & W) built 1885
British Molasses tank wagon
NER 10-ton wagon No. 104
LNER BZ van (used as PW tool van)
10-ton open wagon No. 117 (used by C & W Department)
[6]GWR long-wheelbase Fruit Van No. 642432
NER Steam crane No. CME 13
[13]LNER vacuum-fitted goods brake van No. 246710 built 1941
[13]GCR single bolster wagon No. 14 (NYMR No. 110) built 1920
[13]NER 26-ton six-wheeled snowplough No. DE900572 built 1909
[13]GNR double bolster wagon No. 1352 (NYMR No. 111) built 1920
[13]LSWR Lowmac SB wagon No. DS63024 built 1921
[13]NER covered goods van No. 75544 built 1915
[6]LNER 10-ton tool van No. 53929 built 1923
LNER BG No. E110E built 1947

Photo: Maurice Burns

Here's a sight to stir every steam enthusiast's imagination. Black Five No. 4767 *George Stephenson* with Stephenson valve gear, blackens the sky over the North Yorkshire Moors

BR dmu buffet cars Nos SC59098 and SC59099 converted to camping coaches built 1960
Seven Wickham petrol rail trolleys
Seven five-plank open wagons
Pullman brake/third coach No. 79 built 1928
Five-ton diesel mobile crane
Three-ton Coles diesel electric mobile road crane
Dumper, air compressor and Chaseside loader for coal

[1]Withdrawn from Sunderland in 1967 as BR No. 63395 (LNER Class Q6), 2238 was one of 120 0-8-0s built by the North Eastern Railway for working heavy coal traffic. Powerful engines built with superheated boilers and steam reversing gear, they were popular with drivers all over the region. After withdrawal was sold by BR to a scrap dealer in Blyth, but a determined effort by Group members raised the purchase price of £2,300 within the incredible time of only five months, enabling the engine to be purchased on 1 April 1968. The engine has now been vacuum-fitted and entered traffic on the NYMR in June 1970.
[2]Thompson Class K1 locomotive withdrawn in 1967 as BR 62005. Built by the North British Locomotive Co. Ltd,

Glasgow, the K1 worked its full life in the north-east and gained fame by working several 'royal' trains and enthusiast specials. No. 62005 was donated to the Group by the 5428 Stanier Black Five Preservation Society Ltd in 1972. A restoration appeal raised £1,200, which enabled a major overhaul and retubing to be undertaken, including repainting in LNER apple green livery and numbered 2005. The engine entered NYMR service in June 1974.
[3]Built by Sharp Stewart & Co. of Glasgow (Works No. 4492) in 1899. After 60 years railway service, finally as shed pilot at King's Cross MPD, the locomotive was acquired and restored to its original livery in April 1959. Believed to be the first privately owned locomotive permitted to work passenger trains over BR metals, No. 1247 was donated to work specials for SLS, RCTS and other societies. It worked

Photo: Geoff King

Far from its native sunny south, S15 4–6–0 No. 841 *Greene King* now adds a touch of malachite green to the North Yorkshire Moors Railway

the first 'Bluebell' from London Bridge to Sheffield Park in April 1962. The locomotive is currently on loan to and operated by the North Yorkshire Moors Railway. In both the 1975 and 1976 seasons No. 1247 worked the highest locomotive mileage on the Moors line, totalling in all approximately 5,600 miles.

During the 1976–77 winter No. 1247 underwent major repairs to its running gear at Grosmont MPD, this being the first 'shop' attention received since 1958 at BR Doncaster works.

Believed to be the oldest standard gauge steam locomotive continuing regularly to work time-tabled passenger trains. Owned by the 1247 Society (*q.v.*).

[4]Withdrawn as BR No. 30841 in 1964 and sold to Woodham Brothers, Barry, for scrap. Purchased for preservation in 1972. Owned by the Essex Locomotive Society Ltd.

[5]No. 5428 was built by Armstrong Whitworth & Co. (Works No. 1483) and was a standard member of the class with Walschaert's valve gear; withdrawn from Leeds (Holbeck) in 1967 as BR No. 45428.

[6]Owned by the North Eastern Locomotive Preservation Group (*q.v.*).

[7]In the care of the North Eastern Locomotive Preservation Group (*q.v.*).

[8]Owned by the Lambton No. 29 Locomotive Syndicate (*q.v.*).

[9]Owned by the 45428 Stanier Black 5 Preservation Society Ltd. (*q.v.*).

[10]On loan from National Railway Museum, York.

[11]Owned by the Hull and Barnsley Railway Stock Fund (*q.v.*).

[12]Owned by the North Eastern Railway Coach Group (*q.v.*).

[13]Owned by the Hexham Rolling Stock Group (*q.v.*).

**45428 Stanier Black Five Preservation Society Ltd**  H

North Yorkshire Moors Railway

*Details from:* J. B. Hollingsworth, 'Creua', Llanfrothen, Penrhyndeudraeth, Gwynedd LL48 6SH
Tel: 0766-770-534

*Membership:* 10

**North Eastern Locomotive Preservation Group**  H

North Yorkshire Moors Railway

Registered Charity No. 261122

Group members receive six technical and informative newsletters each year about NYMR locomotive news and have the opportunity to attend regular meetings in Newcastle upon Tyne to hear first-class speakers. There is a very active sales service and special opportunities to participate in the

North Yorkshire Moors Railway Locomotive Department, and reduced fares to travel on the picturesque Grosmont to Pickering line.

Membership of the Group is £20 life (payable in four annual instalments of £5); £1.50 per annum ordinary; £2 husband and wife; £1 young people under 18

*Details from:* Peter Robinson, 53 West Dene Drive, North Shields, Tyne and Wear.

*Membership:* 300

The Group's particular claim to fame is that it is the only voluntary organisation to purchase and restore a locomotive which is on view in the National Railway Museum, this being NER P3 class 0-6-0 No. 2392

### Hull and Barnsley Railway Stock Fund H

North Yorkshire Moors Railway

Apart from its preservation activities, the Group specialises in collecting tools, equipment and historical data appertaining to the H & BR.

*Facilities:* Sales stand at Goathland and at various exhibitions; also regular meetings for members in the Hull area.

*Annual subscription:* Minimum donation of £1 a year (50p a year for full-time students and pensioners)

*Details from:* A. Halman, 6 Chequerfield Court, Chequerfield Avenue, Pontefract, Yorkshire WF8 2TQ

*Membership:* 50

The Group's principal claim to fame is that its coach No. 5, hauled by Borrows Well Tank No. 3, formed the very first passenger train to run on the NYMR after closure of the line in 1965.

### Lambton No. 29 Locomotive Syndicate H

North Yorkshire Moors Railway

*Secretary:* J. M. Richardson, c/o Midland Bank Ltd, 7 Prospect Crescent, Harrogate, Yorkshire HG1 1RN

### North Eastern Railway Coach Group H

*Secretary:* P. J. Brumby, 48 Laburnum Walk, Gilberdyke, Brough, North Humberside HU15 2TU

Life membership of the Group by purchase of one or more shares in any of the Group's vehicles

### Hexham Rolling Stock Group H

North Yorkshire Moors Railway

*Details from:* G. Hall, 24 Welton Close, Stocksfield, Northumberland

Formed in 1972 as a temporary arrangement to raise funds and purchase a much needed fitted goods brake van for the NYMR. On completion of this project the Group became permanent and has since purchased further essential goods vehicles for the railway. The Group has also preserved two small industrial locomotives (RSH 0-4-0ST *Eustace Forth* and Armstrong Whitworth 0-4-0DE *Hexhamshire*), both on loan to the National Railway Museum at York.

Many items have been purchased and restored for a small museum at Wylam, Northumberland, the village now known as the 'Cradle of railways'. This museum of local history has

special reference to George Stephenson, Hedley and Hackworth and the Newcastle–Carlisle line. The Museum is located at Falcon Terrace, Wylam, Northumberland and is open at weekends and most weekdays during the summer season.

Tel: Wylam 2174

### 1247 Society H

North Yorkshire Moors Railway

*Details from:* Captain W. G. Smith, VRD, RNR, c/o Pickering Station, NYMR

## 154 Tanfield Railway A

*Headquarters:* Marley Hill Engine Shed, Marley Hill, Tyne and Wear

*Access:* One mile south of Sunniside, off the A6076 Sunniside–Stanley road, 5 miles south-west of Gateshead. Buses Nos. 701/704 connect from Marlborough Crescent Bus Station, Newcastle, alighting at Andrews House.

Tel: Newcastle 742002
OS Ref: NZ 207573

Passenger-carrying standard gauge steam railway, currently ½-mile in length but being extended.

The railway is in operation from Easter Sunday to the last Sunday in September, plus Bank Holiday Mondays during this period. Marley Hill shed is open every Sunday throughout the year.

Facilities for visitors include railway shop, refreshments, car parking and toilets.

The Tanfield Waggonway, the most famous of the wooden waggonways, was opened in 1725, replacing earlier lines used by the owners, the Grand Allies. Its advanced engineering features, such as the Causey Arch and Embankment, still stand today and some will be used by the Tanfield Railway. The railway is being built on a three-mile section of the waggonway between Sunniside and East Tanfield.

Thus the Tanfield Railway lays claim to being the oldest existing railway in the world. The longstanding industrial character is being retained in the railway with its resemblance to the self-contained minor and colliery railways of former years. These lines used locos from the private manufacturers and most had small, non-bogie coaches. A large collection of steam locomotives has been acquired for use on the Tanfield Railway, many of them built in Newcastle, whilst the railway is constructing its own coaches, typical of those used on the minor railways.

### Stock
Black Hawthorn 0-4-0ST *Wellington* 266 built 1873
R. W. Hawthorn 0-4-0ST No. 3 2009 built 1884
[1]Andrew Barclay 0-6-0ST *Horden* (1015) built 1906
Hawthorn Leslie 0-4-0ST *Cyclops* (2711) built 1907
Barclay 0-4-2ST No. 6 (1193) built 1910
Hawthorn Leslie 0-4-0ST No. 2 (2859) built 1911
Andrew Barclay 0-4-0ST No. 32 (1659) built 1920
Hawthorn Leslie 0-6-0ST *Stagshaw* (3513) built 1923
Hawthorn Leslie 0-6-0ST No. 3 (3575) built 1923

Hudswell Clarke 0-4-0ST *Coronation* (1672) built 1937
R. Stephenson & Hawthorn 0-4-0CT *Hendon* (7007) built 1940
R. Stephenson & Hawthorn 0-4-0ST *Sir Cecil A. Cochrane* (7408) built 1948
Hudswell Clarke 0-6-0T No. 38 (1823) built 1949
[1]R. Stephenson & Hawthorn 0-6-0ST No. 49 (7089) built 1943
[1]R. Stephenson & Hawthorn 0-6-0ST No. 16 (7944) built 1957
Sentinel 4WVBT No. 4 (9559) built 1953
[1]R. Stephenson & Hawthorn 0-6-0ST No. 44 (7760) built 1953
R. Stephenson & Hawthorn 0-6-0ST No. 38 (7763) built 1954
R. Stephenson & Hawthorn 0-4-0ST No. 21 (7796) built 1954
Armstrong Whitworth 0-4-0DE No. 2 (D22) built 1933
Joshua Wilson 10-ton steam crane *Joshua*
Darlington W&E Co. 4-wheel saloon 'Glass Carriage' built c. 1880
Tanfield Rly 4-wheel saloon coach No. 1 built 1976
GNR 6-wheel compartment coach No. 2 built c. 1890
NER 4-wheel composite coach No. 3 built c. 1870
Tanfield Rly 4-wheel saloon coach No. 4 built 1977
NER 4-wheel passenger brake van No. 5 built 1882
NER 4-wheel compartment coach No. 6 built 1882
Ashington Colliery Goods Brake Van No. 665
Bowes Railway 10-ton Hopper Wagon No. 608
CEGB 20-ton Hopper Wagons Nos 16, 25 and 33 built 1921
Heworth Colliery 10-ton Hopper Wagon No. 210
LH & JC 10-ton Hopper Wagon
Pelaw Main Colliery 10-ton Hopper wagon No. 1207
P & JR 10-ton Hopper wagon No. 359

[1]Locomotives stored elsewhere.

Tanfield Railway Co. details may be obtained from Mr E. Maxwell, 33 Stocksfield Avenue, Newcastle upon Tyne 5.

## 155   Derwent Valley Railway                              B

Derwent Valley Railway Company, Layerthorpe Station, York YO3 7XS

*General Manager:* Mr J. Acklam

*Access:* ½ mile from City centre in Hall Field Road, off Layerthorpe Road.
Buses run to within 200 yards of Layerthorpe Station
Tel: York 58981
OS Ref: SE 612521

A 4½-mile goods-only line from Layerthorpe to Dunnington opened in 1912. Operates throughout the year using two diesel shunters, although the company has owned at various times an ex-WD petrol shunting locomotive, a Sentinel steam locomotive and a Ford railcar set. Originally an agricultural line, there have been extensive commercial developments since the war. These include a grain drier, a pre-mix concrete plant and warehouses. A fully mechanised coal depot at Layerthorpe is the only such installation on a light railway. Unique amongst standard gauge light railways in this country, the DLVR has remained in independent ownership throughout its three-score years, escaping both the 1923 grouping and the 1948 nationalisation. This, coupled with its resilience and adaptability to modern operating conditions, plus a personal connection with the preservation of two of its ancient coaches, ensures it a place in any book of mine. The line originated in May 1899 as a project by local rural district councils, who were granted a Light Railway Order in 1902. These powers were not taken up for financial reasons, and in 1907 a new Order was granted to a fresh company. The section from Cliff Common to Wheldrake was opened on 29 October 1912, and the whole formally by Lady Deramore, wife of the company's chairman, on 19 July of the following year. North Eastern Railway No. 1679 hauled the first passenger train, but passenger services succumbed to omnibus competition in 1926.

Fifty years later, passenger excursions reappeared on the DVR, hauled by *Hardwicke* from the National Railway Museum. Encouraged by their success, the Derwent Valley purchased J72 class 0-6-0T *Joem* and three coaches and ran a regular passenger service themselves, commencing in 1977. Sadly, the venture was not an economic success and the service was discontinued at the end of August 1979. Thereafter the DVR has reverted to its more profitable role as a freight-carrying line.

**Stock**
BR/Drewry 0-6-0DM No. 1 *Lord Wenlock* (2679) built 1960 (BR No. D2298)
Fowler 0-4-0DM No. 2 *Claude Thompson* 4210142 built 1955

## 156   Yorkshire Dales Railway                              A

Embsay Station, Embsay, Skipton, North Yorkshire

*Access:* 2 miles from Skipton off the A59 Harrogate Road. On bus routes 75 & 76 from Skipton
Tel: Skipton 4727
OS Ref: SE 007533

Passenger-carrying standard gauge steam railway, currently ½ mile in length but being extended towards Bolton Abbey. Embsay station is open every weekend throughout the year. Steam trains operate on certain Sundays and Bank Holidays. Facilities for visitors include car parking, museum (open when steaming), railway shop, refreshments (summer weekends), chemical toilets, miniature steam railway (summer Sundays) and a 2 ft gauge line under construction.
Founded in 1968, the YDR is based on a 1¼-mile stretch of the former Midland Railway Skipton–Ilkley line. Initial plans to operate the Grassington branch were thwarted in the early seventies, so the aim now is to relay and run the 3½ miles to Bolton Abbey. Considerable progress has been made in this direction and at the time of going to press, the Light Railway Order was awaited. Once this is granted, services may commence during the 1980 season.

The Yorkshire Dales now echo to the sound of steam again as Hunslet saddle tank *Primrose No. 2* meanders in a Midland setting at Embsay

Emphasis has been laid on establishing a collection of industrial tank locomotives, these being the most suitable for the line. However, ex-BR locomotives are being obtained to work the heavier trains of the future.

The railway is now administered by the 'Museum Trust' and is entirely run by volunteers.

*Details from:* Mr J. R. Ellis, Publicity Officer, c/o Embsay Station

*Membership:* 300

*Annual Subscription:* Adults £2, Children & OAPs £1, Life £20

**Stock**
Hudswell Clarke 0-6-0ST *Dorothy* (1450) built 1922
Hudswell Clarke 0-6-0ST *Slough Estates Ltd No. 5* (1709) built 1939
Hunslet 0-6-0ST *Primrose No. 2* (3715) built 1951
Peckett 0-4-0ST *Foleshill* (2085) built 1948
Sentinel 4WVBTG *Ann* (7232) built 1927
Hunslet 0-6-0ST *Airedale* (1440) built 1923
Hunslet 0-6-0ST *Darfield No. 1* (3783) built 1953
Yorkshire Engine Co. 0-4-0ST *City Link* (2474) built 1949
Hudswell Clarke 0-6-0ST No. S140 (1821) built 1948
¹Hunslet 0-6-0ST No. 7 *Spitfire* (2414) built 1941
Hunslet 0-6-0ST *Beatrice* (2705) built 1945
Hunslet 0-6-0ST No. 69 (3785) built 1953
¹Barclay 0-4-0ST No. 22 *Defiant* (2320) built 1952
RSH 0-4-0ST *BEA No. 2* (7661) built 1950
LMS 2-8-0 No. 48151 (Stainer Class 8F) built 1942
Baguley/Drewry 4WDM No. MDE15 (2136) built 1938

Fowler 0-4-0DM *H. W. Robinson* 4100003 built 1946
Ruston Hornsby 4WDM No. 887 394009 built 1955
Wickham 4WPMR No. DB965095 7610 built 1957
MSJ & AR compartment composite coaches Nos 29666 & 29670 (117 & 121)
NER 6-wheel Directors' Saloon No. 41 built 1896
BR Compartment bogie coach built *c.* 1954
LNER Fruit Van
SR 'BY' 4-wheel Parcels/Brake van
Fuel tanker wagon

**9½ in. gauge Stock**
Freelance 2-4-2 *King Tut* built in 1922 by Stephen Smith
One Pullman car
Three open bogie coaches built *c.* 1926
One bogie wagon

**2 ft gauge Stock**
Lister 4WPM 9993 built 1938
Lister 4WPM 10225 built 1938
Skip wagons

¹Locomotives owned by Steam Enterprises Ltd (see Group No. 254).

## 157  Bowes Railway                           ABE

Tyne and Wear Industrial Monuments Trust, Springwell, near Gateshead, Tyne and Wear

*Access:* From A1 (M), along B1288 road from Gateshead (Wrekenton) to Washington, through Springwell village. Northern bus routes Nos 188 and 189 from Newcastle. Blackham's Hill – road traffic via Galloping Green Road, Wrekenton; buses 726 from Newcastle to Houghton-le-Spring and 727 from Newcastle to Sacriston, alighting at the Mount Level Crossing, Eighton Banks.
Tel: Washington 461847
OS Ref: NZ 298606

Standard gauge operating industrial railway 1½ miles in length offering short steam-hauled rides, demonstrations of rope-worked inclines, historic workshops and static exhibits. Operating weekends are advertised during April, May, July, August and September – see advertisements for specific dates. The railway is open on non-operating weekends from 10.45 am to 4.30 pm. Operating days open from 12 noon to 5.30 pm.

Facilities for visitors include car parking, museum, refreshments, toilets, souvenir shop, exhibitions of documents, etc and historic wagons, guided tours round workshops. There are no admission or car park charges.

The Bowes Railway (called the Pontop and Jarrow Railway until 1932) was one of a number of large colliery railways developed to carry coal to the rivers of North-East England for shipment. Its oldest section, from Mount Moor Colliery via Springwell to Jarrow, was designed by George Stephenson and opened in 1826. At its fullest extent the railway, owned by John Bowes & Partners Ltd, was 15 miles long, and during its life it served 13 collieries, with another three on a section of the Pelaw Main Railway, which was linked to it in 1955. It had seven rope-worked inclines and three locomotive-worked sections, and for a time ran its own passenger service. For nearly 150 years it fulfilled its purpose without any radical alteration, but colliery closures have meant that from 1974 only the section from Monkton to Jarrow has remained in use by the NCB.

As the Railway was not only a direct link to George Stephenson but an almost unique early relic of the Industrial Revolution, Tyne and Wear County Council decided to preserve part of the line, and in March 1976 it purchased the main line between Black Fell Bank Head (near the former Mount Moor Colliery) and Springwell Bank Head, together with two electric winding engines, the lineside buildings and a large number of wagons. This section, part of the 1826 line, consists of two inclines (750 yards at 1 in 15 approx and 1170 yards at 1 in 70 approx) operated by the Blackham's Hill Engine, which are thus the only preserved rope inclines in the world. This was followed in September 1977 by the purchase of the Railway's Engineering and Wagon Shops at Springwell with much of their machinery, at the eastern end of the preserved section. The whole Railway, its buildings and machinery, is now a scheduled Ancient Monument protected by the Department of the Environment. The Tyne and Wear Industrial Monuments Trust, a registered charity set up in 1975 and run by volunteers, is the Council's agent in restoration work and in operating the Railway for the public. Public passenger operation commenced on 1 July 1979.

**Stock**
[1]Barclay 0-4-0ST No. 22 (2274) built 1949
Hibberd 4WDM No. 101 (3922) built 1959
Smith 4-wheeled crane (18773) built 1948
*Wagons* - 10-ton hopper wagons
Darlington Wagon & Engineering 1887 (No. 122)
Darlington Wagon & Engineering 1897 (Nos 197, 202, 210)
Springwell Shops (Nos 6, 80, 289, 308, 364, 406, 511, 525, 572, 573, 605, 649, 701, 717, 775, 782, 788, 790, 842, 939, 971)
ex NER (Nos 1104, 1107, 1111, 1160, 1212, 1220, 1254, 1255, 1289)
Watts Hardy (Nos 1611, 1615)
3-plank wagons Nos B24 and B39
Flat wagons Nos B3 and B51
Loco coal wagon No. 1424
Kibblesworth Drift Bogie (used in rope haulage shunting of sidings)
Reel Wagon (used for unwinding new rope on inclines)
[2]Brake Van No. 1
Tool Van (ex GER)
MR Goods Brake Van No. 1872 built 1920

[1]The only steam locomotive purchased new for the Railway still surviving; acquired on loan from Thomas Ness Ltd in June 1976
[2]Built by Lambton, Hetton & Joicey Collieries Ltd at their Philadelphia Shops in 1933 to run over LNER between Penshaw and Sunderland; acquired in March 1977.

*Details can be obtained from:* Tyne and Wear Industrial Monuments Trust, Sandyford House, Archbold Terrace, Newcastle-upon-Tyne NE2 1ED. Tel: Newcastle (0632) 816144
*Annual Subscription:* Adults £1.50, Juniors 50p

## 158 Whorlton Lido Railway A

Whorlton Lido, Whorlton Bridge, Barnard Castle, County Durham

*Access:* Near to A66 and A1(M) roads
Tel: Whorlton 397
OS Ref: NZ 106146

A 15 in. gauge line opened in 1971 in attractive surroundings in a popular beauty spot on the Yorkshire bank of the River Tees, offering a ride of over ½ mile in length. The railway operates from Easter until the end of September every weekend. The line is also in operation on most days during the school holiday periods, subject to demand and weather conditions.
Facilities for visitors include car parking, refreshments, toilets, souvenir shop, swimming, fishing, etc.
Future developments will include signalling, other lineside equipment and possible extension of the line itself.

**Stock**
Bassett-Lowke 4-4-2 *King George* 21 built 1912
Coleby-Simkins Bo-BoDM *Wendy* built 1972
Four 12-seater bogie coaches

It is proposed to add further items of rolling stock in due course. The management meanwhile offers facilities to any 15 in. gauge locomotive owner who would like to try out his locomotive on the railway.

## 159 Newby Hall Miniature Railway A

Newby Hall, Skelton-on-Ure, Ripon, Yorkshire

*Access:* 4 miles South-East of Ripon, off B6265 road

A 10¼ in. gauge line running for nearly half a mile along the wooded banks of one of the most secluded stretches of the River Ure. The railway, with two stations, crosses a lifting steel bridge over the old ferry boat shipway, runs through a deep cutting and a tunnel. Newby Hall and gardens are open to the public on Wednesdays, Thursdays, Saturdays, Sundays and Bank Holidays from Easter Saturday to the second Sunday in October from 2 pm to 6.30 pm. Teas and light refreshments are served in The Old Orangery.
Other facilities for visitors include car parking, 18th Century House and gardens and river cruises.

**Stock**
LMS 4-6-0 No. 6100 *Royal Scot* built Battison 1950
Severn-Lamb Bo-BoPH *Countess de Grey* built 1973
Six open bogie coaches

## 160 National Tractor and Farm Museum B

John Moffitt, Peepy Farm, Bywell, Stocksfield-upon-Tyne, Northumberland

Passenger-carrying 2 ft 6 in. gauge railway, 1½ miles in length under construction at the time of going to press

The rolling stock, equipment and rails being used here are

all from the former Dalmunzie Hotel Light Railway in Scotland, which was bought in its entirety by Mr Moffitt following its closure in 1978.

**Stock**
Motor Rail 4WPM *Dalmunzie* 20HP Class 2014 built 1920
Two open carriages
Two enclosed carriages

## 161  Howdenclough Light Railway  C

J. Buckler, 123 Howdenclough Road, Bruntcliffe, Leeds

OS Ref: SE 244272

Passenger-carrying 1 ft 10¾ in. gauge private line, 230 yards long.

**Stock**
[1]Hunslet 0–4–0ST *Alan George* 606 built 1894
Hunslet 4WDM *Sholto* 2433 built 1941

[1]Ex Penrhyn Quarries Ltd, Bethesda, Caernarfonshire, 1965

## 162  Lake Shore Railroad  A

South Marine Park, South Shields, Tyne and Wear

Passenger-carrying 9½ in. gauge railway, 500 yards in length, running round the boating lake in the park

**Stock**
Jennings 4–6–2 No. 3440 *Mountaineer* built *c.*1950 (American Type)
FFCC Magdalena-Colombia 2–6–2 built 1979 (South American Type)
Wabash RR 4–6–4 under construction
Open bogie coaches

## 163  Shipley Glen Cable Tramway  B

Shipley Glen, Middle Airedale, Yorkshire

Quarter-mile, 1 ft 8 in. gauge double-track, cable-operated line running between Easter and 31 October each year from 11 am to dusk. Maximum gradient 1 in 12; maximum speed 10 mph; journey time two minutes

The trains consist of two double-cars (one on each track) capable of seating thirty passengers each. Power is provided by a 35 hp electric motor installed in the power-house near the upper station where the 'motorman' controls the operation by observing the speed of the ascending car.

## 164  North Bay Railway, Scarborough  B

Northstead Manor Gardens, Scarborough, Yorkshire
OS Ref: TA 035898

This is the largest municipally-owned miniature railway in the country. The gauge line was opened in 1931 and runs for seven-eighths-of-a-mile through the Northstead Manor Gardens from Peasholm to Scalby Mills. The railway is single track throughout with terminal and midway loops, and though unsignalled, has a tablet control system to ensure safety of operation.
The railway operates daily from Easter until early October. A service approximately every 20 minutes operates in the early and late season, but a ten minute interval applies in the height of the season.

**Stock**
Hudswell Clarke 4–6–2DH No. 1931 *Neptune* D565 built 1931
Hudswell Clarke 4–6–2DH No. 1932 *Triton* D573 built 1932
Ten open toastrack bogie coaches, each seating 20 passengers
Both locomotives are of the LNER 'Pacific' steam outline.

## 165  North of England  ABE
## Open Air Museum

Beamish, near Stanley, County Durham
*Access:* A1(M) to Chester-le-Street turnoff, A693 towards Stanley. Beamish is permanently signposted on all major surrounding roads
Tel: Stanley (0207) 31811
OS Ref: NZ 217547

Beamish is a 200-acre site housing a comprehensive reconstruction of all aspects of life in the North of England. Particular emphasis is placed on the significant industrial history of the region and so railways figure largely in the museum. There is a ¼ mile standard gauge track on which visitors can ride behind a full-scale working replica of George Stephenson's *Locomotion No. 1*. Also a half-mile electric tramway operated by Gateshead tramcar No. 10.
The Museum is open every day April to August inclusive from 10 am to 6 pm. Closed on Mondays during the rest of the year.
Facilities for visitors include car parking, museum shop, colliery with furnished pit cottages, farm transport collection, refreshments and toilets.
The Museum shows the past way of life in the North East around the early 1900s. Collecting commenced in 1958 and there was a preliminary opening in 1971 followed by an official opening in 1972. Since then a railway area with station, footbridges, goods shed, signal box and weighbridge house has been rebuilt on the site. At Home Farm visitors can see traditional northern farm animals, exhibitions and a large collection of farm implements and carts. A complete Northern colliery has been rebuilt on the site and here visitors can see an old pit cage, an 1855 steam winding engine in operation and furnished pit cottages. Demonstrations of pottery throwing, hand printing, bread baking and 'proggy' mat making.
A society has been formed of those interested in the project, known as 'Friends of the North of England Open-Air Museum', and currently has a membership of 800.

*Details from:* The Museum Secretary.

If cameras had been invented in 1825, steam rail travel would have looked like this. Visitors to Beamish museum in 1980 can ride behind this full scale working replica of *Locomotion No. 1*

Smith/Rodley steam crane No. 8371 built 1913
NER express bogie brake van
NER 'Birdcage' goods brake van No. 44824 built 1895
Ruston Hornsby 4WDM 256285 built 1937 (2 ft gauge)

**Stock**
[1]NER 0-6-0 No. 876 (BR No. 65033) (LNER Class J21) built 1889
Stephenson 0-4-0 *Locomotion* (Replica) built 1975
Stephenson 0-4-0 Hetton Colliery loco built 1822
Stephenson 0-6-0T No. 3 *Twizell* (2730) built 1891
Hawthorn Leslie 0-4-0ST No. 14 (3056) built 1914
[2]Stockton Ironworks 0-4-0ST *South Durham Malleable No. 5* built 1900
Head Wrightson 0-4-0VBT built 1871
Lewin 0-4-0T No. 18 built 1863
[3]Stephenson 2-4-0VBCT E No. 9 (2854) built 1898
Simplex 4WDM 1364 built 1918
Ruston Hornsby 4WDM 476140 built 1963
Forcett Railway four-wheeled coach built 1850
NER luggage composite coach No. 818 built c.1900
NER luggage composite coach No. 1149 built 1900
NER third-class bogie coach No. 1972 built 1911
NER third-class bogie coach No. 118 built 1913
NER snowplough
Chaldron wagons Nos 1912, 1219 and 434

[1]Two-hundred-and-one of these useful locomotives were acquired by the LNER at the grouping. Most of the class were built as Worsdell-Von Borries two-cylinder compounds, but all had been rebuilt as simple-expansion locomotives before 1923. The class were equally at home on passenger or freight trains and No. 876 must certainly be the luckiest engine to be preserved, since it survived to become the last member of its class, having been withdrawn at the outbreak of World War II but reinstated a month later. It was set aside for possible preservation by BR, but the decision was later reversed and the engine sold to a scrap merchant. In the nick of time it was purchased for the Beamish Hall collection, a fitting end for a machine that saw 73 years hard work in its native north-east.
[2]Origin not recorded, but most likely built by Stockton Ironworks.
[3]Ex Consett Iron Co. Ltd.

Also on display is a large collection of horse-drawn vehicles including trader's vans, fire engine, gypsy caravans, tram, sleigh and fine collection of Northumbrian carts.
Visitors can also see buses, trolley bus, trams, fire engines and coal wagons.

Leeman Road, York YO2 4XJ

*Access:* Short walk from York BR station
Tel. York (0904) 21261
OS Ref: SE 594519

*Opening times:* Weekdays 10 am–6 pm; Sundays
2.30 pm–6 pm; closed on some public holidays
Admission free
There are limited parking facilities, a museum shop and
refreshment room.
Comprehensive education facilities, including an 80-seat
lecture theatre, are available for school parties *by prior
arrangement.*
The Museum's collection is an extensive one, and there are
three or four times as many items as can be exhibited in the
Museum at one time. Various items are loaned to other
museums and preservation societies, while others are
'rotated' between the Museum and the reserve collection in
the annexe. Within the currency of Steam Year Book 1980,
therefore, it is not possible to indicate exactly which locomotives, carriages and wagons will be on display in the
Museum, but List 1 indicates those items which form the
first choice for public exhibition. For completeness the other
items expected to be located at York are given in List 2, but
it is unlikely that any of these will be on public display in the
immediate future.

*Keeper:* Dr J. A. Coiley

The National Railway Museum, which is part of the Science
Museum, London, was opened by the Duke of Edinburgh on
27 September 1975.
The building is based on the old York North motive power
depot, and two of the turntables, with their radial tracks,
are used to house the full-size exhibits in the two-acre main
hall. Two tracks connect the building with British Railways
main lines, permitting locomotives and rolling stock to be
exchanged with other museums and preservation societies,
as well as the operation of steam specials using those of the
Museum's locomotives which are passed for steaming. A
balcony along one side of the hall enables visitors to view
the exhibits below, as well as housing the display cases
which depict the social and economic aspects of the development of the railways. Other show cases around the walls
of the main hall house models showing technical features of
locomotives, as well as the development of locomotives,
rolling stock, signalling and permanent way.
A supporting organisation, the 'Friends of the NRM', exists
and details may be obtained from the Museum.

**The venerable Furness Railway 0–4–0 *Coppernob*
stands surrounded by a mouth watering display of steam
power inside the National Railway Museum**

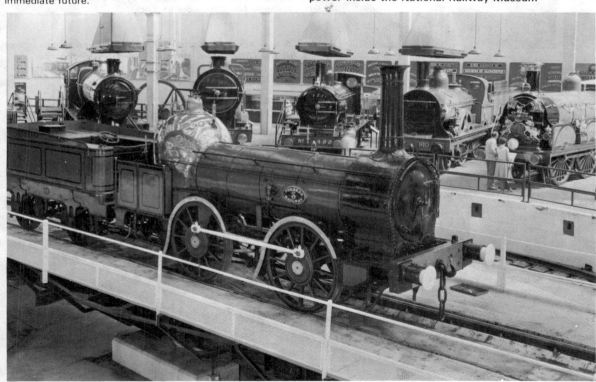

Photo: National Railway Museum

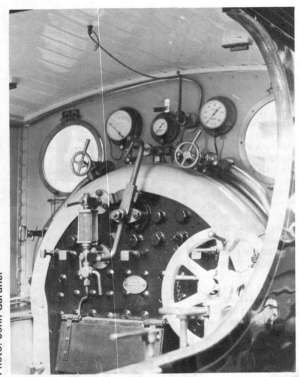

Photo: John Gardner

## Exhibits

*Locomotives* (List 1)
Shutt End Railway 0-4-0 *Agenoria* (Foster, Raistrick, built 1829)
Grand Junction Railway 2-2-2 *Columbine* built 1845
Furness Railway 0-4-0 No. 3 *Coppernob* (Bury, Curtis and Kennedy, built 1846)
NER 2-2-4T No. 66 *Aerolite* built 1869
GNR 4-2-2 No. 1 built 1870
NER 2-4-0 No. 910 built 1875
[1,2]De Winton 0-4-0VBT *Chaloner* built 1877 (2 ft gauge)
LB & SCR 0-6-0T No. 82 *Boxhill* (Class A1) built 1880
LB & SCR 0-4-2 No. 214 *Gladstone* built 1882
L & YR 0-4-0ST *Wren* (Beyer Peacock 2825) built 1887 (1 ft 6 in. gauge)
[1]LNWR 2-4-0 No. 790 *Hardwicke* built 1892
NER 4-4-0 No. 1621 (Class M) built 1893
LSWR 4-4-0 No. 563 (Class T3) built 1893
[2]S & MR 0-4-2WT No. 1 *Gazelle* (Dodman) built 1893
GER 2-4-0 No. 490 (BR No. 62785) (Class T26) built 1894
Waterloo & City 4W electric No. 75S built 1898

How's this for Great Eastern interior decorating? Every day working surroundings for the crew of Great Eastern Railway No. 490, now at York

A new addition to the ranks of preserved steam power at the NRM is tiny Hunslet 0-4-0ST *Hodbarrow*

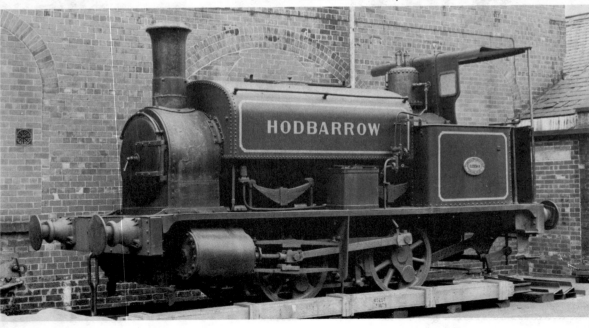

Photo: Tom Heavyside

GNR 4-4-2 No. 990 *Henry Oakley* built 1898
SECR 4-4-0 No. 737 (BR No. 31737) (Class D) built 1901
GNR 4-4-2 No. 251 built 1902
MR 4-4-0 No. 1000 (BR No. 41000) built 1902
GER 0-6-0T No. 87 (BR No. 68633) (Class P57) built 1904
L & YR 2-4-2T No. 1008 (BR No. 50621) built 1889
LSWR 4-4-0 No. 120 (Class T9) (Br No. 30120) built 1899
[13]Beyer Peacock 0-6-0T *The Earl* 3496 built 1903 (2 ft 6 in. gauge)
[3]NER Bo-Bo E No. 1 (BR No. 26500) built 1904
[4]GWR 2-8-0 No. 2818 (28XX Class) built 1905
[14]LMS 0-6-0DM No. 7401 Hunslet 1697 built 1932
[11]LNER 2-6-2 No. 4771 *Green Arrow* built 1936
LNER 4-6-2 No. 4468 *Mallard* (BR No. 60022) (Class A4) built 1938
[5]LMS 4-6-2 No. 6229 *Duchess of Hamilton* (BR No. 46229) built 1938
[6]SR 4-6-2 No. 35029 *Ellerman Lines* built 1948 (sectioned)
BR 2-10-0 No. 92220 *Evening Star* (Class 9F) built 1960
BR 0-6-0 DM No. 03 090 built Doncaster 1960
[15]Tasmanian Railways 0-4-0+0-4-0T No. K1 (built Beyer Peacock 1909) (2 ft gauge)
[7]NER 0-6-0 No. 2392 (Class P3) built 1923
[10]LMS 2-6-0 No. 2700 (Class 5MT) built 1926
BR Bo-Bo Electric No. 26020 built Gorton 1951
BR Bo-Bo Electric No. E5001 built 1958
BR 0-4-0DH No. D2860 built 1960
BR Co-Co DH No. 1023 *Western Fusilier* built Swindon 1963
BR advanced passenger train APT-E built 1972 (two power cars plus two intermediate trailers)
[16]Armstrong Whitworth 0-4-0DE No. 14 (21) built 1933
BR Bo-Bo E No. 84001 25 kV. electric (built 1960)

*Locomotives* (List 2)
LSWR 0-4-4T 245 (Class M7) (BR No. 30245) built 1897
SR 4-4-0 No. 925 *Cheltenham* (V class) built 1934
Ruston Hornsby 4w DM built 1937 (2 ft gauge)
[8]Hunslet 0-4-0ST *Hodbarrow* (299) (built 1882)
[16]RSH 0-4-0ST No. 15 *Eustace Forth* (7063) built 1942
Barclay 0-4-0F *Imperial No. 1* 2372 built 1956

*Rolling stock* (List 1)
Peak Forest Canal quarry truck built 1797
Belvoir Castle Railway truck built 1816
Cramlington Colliery chaldron wagon built 1825
Stockton & Darlington Railway horse dandy built 1828
South Hetton Colliery chaldron wagon No. 1155 built c.1850
Londonderry Railway chaldron wagon No. 31 built c.1870
Bodmin and Wadebridge Railway Third Class Coach built 1834
Bodmin and Wadebridge Railway Composite Coach
London & Birmingham Railway Queen Adelaide's Saloon built 1842
Stockton & Darlington Railway Composite coach No. 59 built 1845
NBR Port Carlisle Horse Dandy No. 1 built 1861
LNWR Queen Victoria's saloon built 1869 as two six-wheel coaches
NLR Directors' Saloon No. 1032 built 1872

MR six-wheel composite coach No. 901 built 1885
WCJS Dining Saloon LMS No. 76 built 1900
NER Dynamometer Car LNER No. 902502 built 1906
ECJS Royal Saloon No. 395 built 1908
Pullman Car *Topaz* built 1913
LNWR 'Oerlikon' electric motor coach LMS No. 28249 built 1915
SR '3-SUB' electric motor coach No. 8143 built 1925
LMS Third class sleeping car No. 14241 built 1928
LNER Buffet Car No. 650 built 1937
SR '4Cor' electric motor coach No. 11179 built 1938
LMS Royal Saloons Nos. 798 and 799 built 1941
BR Griddle Car No. Sc1100 built 1960
BR Pullman Cars *Eagle* and *Emerald* built 1960
Shell Mex tank wagon No. 512 built 1889
ICI Nitric Acid tank wagon No. 14 built 1928
LMS 3 plank open wagon No. 472867 built 1936
BR Flatrol No. B900402 built 1949
BR Weltrol No. B900805 built 1950
BR Cattle Wagon No. B892156 built 1950
BR Cattle Wagon No. B893343 built 1951
ICI Liquid Chlorine tank wagon No. 47484 built 1951
National Benzole tank wagon No. 2022 built 1954
BR Iron ore tippler wagon No. B383560 built 1954
BR Banana Van No. B882583 built 1960

*Rolling Stock* (List 2)
Liverpool & Manchester Rly. First class coach (reproduction built 1930)
Liverpool & Manchester Rly. Third class coach (reproduction built 1930)
Bodmin & Wadebridge Rly. Second class coach built 1834
Great Northern Railway hand crane built 1850
WCJS Travelling Post Office No. 186 built 1885
Great Northern Railway six-wheel brake van No. 948 built 1887
NER Snow Plough No. DE900566 built 1891
ECJS third class corridor coach No. 12 built 1898
LSWR Goods brake van No. 99 built 1894
LSWR Open Carriage truck No. 5830 built 1895
Duke of Sutherland's saloon No. 57A built 1899
LNWR King Edward's saloon built 1903
LNWR Queen Alexandra's saloon built 1903
LSWR Tri-Composite Coach No. 3598 built 1903
Great Northern Railway goods van No. E432764
Midland Rly Officers' Saloon No. 2234 built 1904
ECJS Passenger brake van LNER No. 109 built 1908
LBSC Open Wagon No. 3537 built 1912
GWR Shunter's truck No. 94988 built 1914
GWR Goods brake van No. 56518 built 1916
LMS Vestibule third class coach No. 8207 built 1927
LNER Tube wagon No. 181358
GWR 'Mink-G' goods van No. 112884 built 1931
LMS Ballast plough brake van No. 197266 built 1932
GWR 'Mogo' motor car van No. 126438 built 1935
LNER Wickham petrol trolley No. 960209 built 1932
GWR Diesel Rail Car No. 4 built 1934
LNER Goods brake van No. 187774 built 1936
LMS Corridor Third Brake No. 5987 built 1937

LMS Tube wagon No. 499254 built 1936
WD 'Warflat' BR No. 161042 built 1940
LMS 'Lowmac' No. 700728 built 1944
LNER Hopper Coal wagon No. 270919 built 1946
LMS Mobile Test Unit No. 45053 built 1947
LMS/BR Dynamometer Car No. 45049 built 1949
LMS/BR Travelling Post Office No. 30272 built 1949
BR Iron Ore Hopper wagon No. 436275 built 1950
BR Show Cattle Van No. S3733S built 1951
BR Bogie Bolster C No. 943139 built 1952
BR Horse box No. S96369 built 1957


*Other exhibits include*
Weatherhill winding engine built 1833 (in operating order)
Leicester & Swannington winding engine built 1833 (in operating order)
KESR horse bus
Gaunless Bridge
Euston turntable
LNER Gresley articulated carriage bogie built 1930
LNER sleeping car section (four-berth, third-class) built 1931
BR standard stock compartments built 1951
BR standard locomotive cab
Midland Railway Heavy Horse Dray


[1]This locomotive took part in the Railway Race to the North in 1895, covering the section from Crewe to Carlisle at an average speed of 70 mph. The 'Precedents' were the only really reliable express engines that the LNWR possessed until the advent of Whale's 'Precursors' in 1904. It was not until later years that the sterling worth of these remarkable locomotives came to be realised, and some of their prodigious feats of haulage, considering their small size, have probably seldom been equalled elsewhere. *Hardwicke* was withdrawn in 1932 and stored in Crewe paintshop until transferred to Clapham Museum.

[2]*Gazelle* was originally built as a 2-2-2WT for Mr W. Burkitt who had private running powers over the GER and M & GNJR. Sold to the Shropshire and Montgomeryshire Railway in 1911 and rebuilt into its present form. Taken into BR stock in 1950 and immediately placed on permanent loan to the Army. It is the smallest standard gauge engine in the country, and is even more unusual in combining inside cylinders with a well tank.

[3]Originally NER No. 1. Withdrawn as BR No. 26500 in 1964 and stored until presented by the British Railways Board in 1968.

[4]Withdrawn from Severn Tunnel Junction as BR No. 2818 in 1963 and stored until restored at Eastleigh Works in 1966-67. Presented by BRB and moved to Bristol in 1967. At the time of their introduction, Churchward's 2-8-0 mineral engines were in many ways well in advance of their time and remained the standard GWR heavy goods type for the rest of the Company's existence. They were the first 2-8-0 locomotives to be introduced in this country.

[5]Withdrawn from Liverpool (Edge Hill) as BR No. 46229 in 1964 and restored to LMS livery at Crewe. Put on display later that year. The appearance of this class of locomotive in 1937 brought with it the climax of development of steam express passenger locomotives on the LMS. When new, this locomotive was fitted with streamlined casing which was removed in 1948 to ease access to the moving parts. No. 6229 was sent to America in 1938 after having exchanged numbers with No. 6220 *Coronation*, but resumed its correct identity on return. On long-term loan from Butlins Limited. Exhibited as BR No. 46229 in BR crimson lake livery.

[6]Built by BR at Eastleigh in 1949 to a design of O. V. S. Bulleid. Rebuilt without air-smoothed casing and with conventional Walschaert's valve gear in 1959. Withdrawn from service in 1966 and recovered from Woodham Brothers of Barry in 1973. Section by Flying Scotsman Enterprises Limited.

[7]Withdrawn from Sunderland in 1967 as BR No. 65894 (LNER Class J27), 2392 was the final engine of a batch of ten ordered by the NER prior to the grouping, but was completed by the LNER in 1923. With 5 ft 6 in. diameter boilers the J27s were the largest of the NER 0-6-0s and were powerful hardworking engines which, like the Q6s, lasted until the end of steam traction in the north-east. The engine was purchased from BR on 1 December 1967 at a cost of £1,400.

[8]Ex Millom Hematite Ore and Iron Co., Hodbarrow Mines, 1968. Preserved by the Hunslet Engine Co., it is the oldest of their make in existence.

[10]Class 5 mixed traffic locomotive built at Horwich Works in May 1926. Withdrawn from Birkenhead shed as BR No. 42700 in March 1966. The first locomotive to be built to an LMS design (though admittedly following Hughes L & YR concepts) and forerunner of a useful class of 245 engines all of which gave at least 30 years service. Nicknamed 'Crabs' because of their high running plates, prominent cylinders and rolling gait, their main employment was on fast freight and parcels trains, especially in Scotland. Constructed as No. 13000, this locomotive was renumbered 2700 in 1934 and 42700 by BR. Selected as an official museum piece, it was stored at Hellifield for some months before being loaned to the K & WVR. It was moved to the museum in 1978.

[11]Withdrawn from King's Cross shed in 1962 as BR No. 60800 and stored until moved to Carnforth via Norwich and Tyseley in 1973. One-hundred-and-eighty-four of these highly successful locomotives were constructed principally for hauling express freight and parcels trains. However, they could often be found working alongside the LNER 'Pacifics' on express passenger turns. They were the first 2-6-2 tender engines built for use in Great Britain (with the exception of the Paget Midland Railway experimental locomotive of 1908).

[12]On loan from the Leighton Buzzard Narrow Gauge Railway (see Group No. 451)

[13]On loan from the Welshpool & Llanfair Light Railway (see Group No. 302)

[14]On loan from the Middleton Railway. Named *John Alcock* (see Group No. 152)

[15]On loan from the Festiniog Railway (see Group No. 301)

[16]On loan from the Hexham Rolling Stock Group (see Group No. 153)

## 167 Darlington North Road Museum   E

North Road Station, Darlington, County Durham

*Access:* By rail direct from Darlington Main Line Station. By road, turn off A167 into Station Road, ½ mile from town centre
Tel: Darlington 60532
OS Ref: NZ 289157

The terminus of the pioneer Stockton and Darlington Railway has become the fitting home for a splendid collection of locomotives and other railway relics with strong associations with the North-East. Darlington North Road is now probably the oldest station in Britain still in use. The building, with its long facade and entrance portico, dates from 1842 and was restored as a museum in 1975 as a contribution to the 150th Anniversary of the opening of the Stockton & Darlington Railway. Apart from the principal locomotive exhibits, the collection of small exhibits and models illustrates the history of the S & D and NER companies. The surrounding area still contains several buildings of railway history significance and DMUs still pass through the station.
The museum is open from Mondays to Saturdays 10 am–5 pm and on Sundays 2 pm–4 pm from Easter to the end of October.
Facilities for visitors include car parking, museum shop, refreshments and toilets.

**Stock**
[1]Stephenson 0–4–0 S & DR No. 1 *Locomotion* built 1825
[2]Kitching 0–6–0 S & DR No. 25 *Derwent* built 1845
Head Wrightson 0–4–0VBT No. 1733 built 1873
NER 0–6–0 No. 1275 Dubs 708 built 1874
NER 2–4–0 No. 1463 built 1885
Hawthorn Leslie 0–4–0ST *Met* 2800 built 1909
S & DR Composite carriage
NER open wagon

[1]Hauled the first train on the Stockton and Darlington Railway. Withdrawn from regular service in 1846 but worked occasionally thereafter. Sold for scrap in 1850 but reinstated as pumping engine at Lucy Pit, Crook. Returned to the NER and restored for display in 1857. Placed on present site in 1890.
[2]Withdrawn and sold to Joseph Peace & Co., *c.* 1865. Presented to the NER in 1898 and placed on display.

The activities of the museum are supported by 'The Friends of the Museum'. Details may be obtained from the curator at the above address.

## 168 Tyne and Wear County Council   E

Tyne and Wear County Museums and Art Galleries Service, Museum of Science and Engineering, Exhibition Park, Great North Road, Newcastle upon Tyne NE2 4PZ.

Tel: 0632–815129
OS Ref: NZ 247658

Standard gauge steam locomotive on static display
Open daily throughout the year
*Admission:* Free

**Stock**
Killingworth Colliery 0–4–0 *Billy* A4 built 1826
Presented to the Corporation of Newcastle upon Tyne in 1881 to commemorate the centenary of the birth of George Stephenson. Placed on display beside the High Level Bridge until 1896, then at Newcastle Central Station until 1945, when it was put on display at the museum.

## 169 Preston Park and Museum   E

Yarm Road, Eaglescliffe, Stockton, Teesside, Cleveland

*Access:* Eaglescliffe BR station
OS Ref: NZ 430158

Standard gauge steam locomotive on static display included in the Transport Museum collection. The Park is open from Monday to Saturday 10 am–6 pm throughout the year.

**Stock**
Head Wrightson 0–4–0VBTG 21 built 1870
Ex-Seaham Harbour Dock Co. Ltd, Seaham, Co. Durham, 1959

Also exhibited are bicycles, veteran and vintage cars, carriages, commercial vehicles and motor-cycles.

## 170 Leeds City Museum of Science and Industry   E

Armley Mills, Leeds, West Yorkshire
OS Ref: SE 275342

Static narrow gauge locomotive exhibits in the newly-opened Transport Gallery at Armley Mills.

**Stock**
[1]Hunslet 0–4–0WT *Jack* 684 built 1898 (1 ft 6 in. gauge)
[2]T. Green 0–6–2ST *Barber* 441 built 1908 (2 ft gauge)
[3]Hudswell Clarke 0–4–0ST *Lord Granby* 633 built 1902 (3 ft gauge)
Lister 4WDM 29890 (2 ft gauge)
Lister 4WDM 34521 (2 ft gauge)
Ruston Hornsby 4WDM 172901 (2 ft gauge)
Motor Rail 4WDM (2 ft gauge)
Orenstein & Koppel 4WDM (2 ft gauge)
Steam locomotives preserved by the Narrow Gauge Railway Society

[1]Presented by John Knowles (Wooden Box) Ltd, Woodville, Leicestershire, 1958
[2]Presented by North Eastern Gas Board, Harrogate, Yorkshire, 1957
[3]Presented by Staveley Minerals Ltd, Eastwell Quarries, Leicestershire, 1961

## 171 Cusworth Hall Museum     E

Doncaster Rural District Council
OS Ref: SE 547039

2 ft gauge static locomotive exhibit

**Stock**
Hunslet 0-4-0DM 2008 built 1939

## 172 Eccleshill Industrial Museum     E

Bradford Metropolitan Corporation, Moorside Mill, Eccleshill, Bradford

*Access:* BR Bradford Exchange Station, thence by bus to Museum Interchange
Tel: Bradford 631756

OS Ref: SE 184353

The Museum is open daily except Good Fridays, Christmas and Boxing Days from 10 am to 5 pm
Facilities for visitors include car parking, a museum shop, refreshments and toilets

The Industrial Museum in the four-storey former spinning mill at Moorside Road, Eccleshill, has proved itself to be Bradford's premier museum attraction since it opened to the public in 1974.
Part of its success is due to the genuine mill atmosphere. The machines are almost all in working order and may be seen in operation from time to time. Another reason is the museum's variety. The transport gallery contains a colourful array of vehicles including several of the famous Bradford-made Jowett cars and the now equally famous tank engine *Nellie*.
The entrance hall presents both a permanent history of Bradford, emphasising the development of its woollen industry and a series of temporary displays.
A little museum on its own is the mill manager's house, set apart off the cobbled drive. Each room has been furnished in genuine Victorian or Edwardian style and the curious bath-shower always draws surprised comments.
Those who have wondered what happened to the façade of the old Kirkgate Market will have their answer as they leave the museum. The carved masonry from the entrance to the Market is set into a grassy bank in the mill yard.

**Stock**
Hudswell Clarke 0-4-0ST *Nellie* 1435 built 1922
Smith Rodley four-ton steam crane No. 10302 built 1924
Other items of interest include a Sentinel steam wagon, a Bradford tram and trolleybus, several stationary steam engines and a 10¼ in. gauge model of an NER 4-4-0.

## 173 Kingston-upon-Hull Corporation     E
##        Transport Museum

36 High Street, Kingston-upon-Hull, North Humberside
OS Ref: TA 102284

Static exhibits

Open weekdays 10 am–5 pm; Sundays 2.30 pm–4.30 pm
Closed Good Friday, Christmas Day and Boxing Day
Admission free

**Stock**
[1]Portstewart Tramway 0-4-0 Tram Loco. No. 1 (Kitson T56) built 1882 (3 ft gauge)
Ryde Pier Tramway horse tram

[1]Withdrawn 1926 on the closure of the Tramway and stored at York Road Works, Belfast. Presented for display by the LMS (NCC) in 1939.

## 174 Monkwearmouth Station Museum     E

Tyne and Wear Metropolitan County Council, North Bridge Street, Sunderland SR5 1AP
Tel: 0783 77075
OS Ref: NZ 396576

Standard gauge rolling stock exhibits on static display at restored historic railway station of considerable architectural note
Open daily throughout the year
Admission free

**Stock**
Kitson 0-6-0PT No. 41 2509 built 1883
Consett 0-6-0DM No. 10 built 1958
NER Electric Parcels Van No. 3267 (on loan from National Railway Museum)
NER Goods Brake Van built 1916
River Wear Commissioners side-tipping wagon

## 175 Durham County Council     E

Dinsdale Park Residential School, near Darlington
OS Ref: NZ 341121

Standard gauge static locomotive exhibit.

**Stock**
Fowler 0-4-0DM No. 4 4210087 built 1953

## 176 National Coal Board     G

Model Colliery Museum Project, Thorne Colliery, near Barnsley, Yorkshire

A collection of railway and mining industry exhibits being gathered at Thorne Colliery. No public access at present.

**Stock**
Barclay 0-4-0ST *Henry Ellison* 2217 built 1947
Hudswell Clarke 0-6-0T No. S102 *Cathryn* 1884 built 1955
Both locomotives are currently stored at S. Harrison & Sons, (Transport) Ltd. (See Group No. 179)

## 177 Burton Constable Miniature Railway A

Burton Constable Hall, Sproatley, Humberside

*Access:* 8 miles North-East of Hull, off B1238 road

Passenger-carrying 9½ in. gauge railway, 100 yards in length operating on Sunday afternoons until the end of September

Facilities for visitors include Burton Constable Hall itself, which is an Elizabethan manor house built in 1570, 200 acres of parkland, children's zoo, aviaries, lakes, vintage motor museum, refreshments, toilets, picnic grounds and camping. A traction engine rally is held each Spring Bank Holiday.

**Stock**
LMS (NCC) 4-4-2 *Gloria*
Cromar White Bo-BoPM No. D7043

## 178 South Tynedale Railway      F
##      Preservation Society

The Railway Station, Alston, Cumbria CA9 3JB (all enquiries to this address please).

*Access:* A686, A689 & B6277 roads.
Nearest B.R. station – Haltwhistle (13 miles)
Buses – Ribble 681 (Haltwhistle–Alston). Wright Bros. 888 (Newcastle–Alston–Keswick). Alston Station is just off the A686 (Hexham) road; five minutes walk from the town centre.
OS Ref: NY 717467
Tel: Alston 696 (STD 04983)

*Aims:* Construction of a 2 ft gauge railway along part of the trackbed of the former Haltwhistle–Alston branch line; also the promotion of interest in the history of the branch. It is hoped to begin work on the first 1½ mile section (Alston to Gilderdale Burn) during 1980.

*Facilities at Alston Station:* Visitor Centre–displays and exhibits on the history of the Haltwhistle–Alston branch line and other aspects of the Alston Moor area.
Admission free (donations welcome). Open most afternoons during summer season and other times by arrangement.
Bookshop and Tourist Information Centre – Railway and local interest books, maps, gifts, tourist board publications, local information and accommodation booking service. Open daily May to September; limited service for remainder of year.

*Membership:* Approx. 175 (September 1979). Local groups in Sunderland, Newcastle, Carlisle and London.

*Subscriptions:* Annual £2. Life £30. Special rates for members' wives, senior citizens and under 18's.

*Newsletter* Published six times per year; free to members.

*Railtours:* Programme of railtours organised each year, from Carlisle, Tyne Valley, Newcastle, Sunderland and Durham areas.

**Stock**
Hibberd 4WDM built *c* 1941
Skip Wagon
Four Wagon Frames
A member also owns the following standard gauge stock, housed at Slaggyford Station, Northumberland.

**Stock**
Hawthorn Leslie 0-4-0ST No. 13 *The Barra* 3732 built 1928
Fowler 0-4-0DM 22900 built 1941

## 179 S. Harrison & Sons      F
##      (Transport) Ltd

310 Sheffield Road, Tinsley, Sheffield, South Yorkshire
OS Ref: SK 399910

Standard gauge locomotives undergoing restoration

**Stock**
Barclay 0-4-0ST *Henry Ellison* 2217 built 1947
Hudswell Clarke 0-6-0T No. S102 *Cathryn* 1884 built 1955
Barclay 0-4-0ST *Wee Yorkie* 2360 built 1954

## 180 Hallamshire Railway      F
##      Preservation Society

A scheme to establish an operating standard gauge railway in the Sheffield area

**Stock**
Hudswell Clarke 0-4-0ST No.7 1689 built 1937
Locomotive in store at Brown Bayley Steels Ltd, Attercliffe, Sheffield

## 181 Humberside Locomotive      G
##      Preservation Group

Dairycoates Depot, Hull, North Humberside

Locomotive in store undergoing restoration

**Stock**
¹SR 4-6-0 No. 30777 *Sir Lamiel* Class N15 N.B. Locomotive Co 23223 built 1925

¹Maunsell 'King Arthur' Class locomotive originally SR No. 777 and finally withdrawn from Basingstoke shed in 1961. The Maunsell N15s, or 'Scotch Arthurs' as they were known, had their beginnings in R. W. Urie's LSWR N15 Class and quickly became one of the most popular Southern express engine designs. They worked over all sections of the SR, being progressively displaced due to electrification schemes. Towards the end of their career many of the class were stored during the winter, only being put into traffic to assist with mixed traffic duties at busy periods in the summer. It was originally intended to put the Urie N15 *King Arthur* aside for preservation, but plans were revised at the last minute and *Sir Lamiel* was retained by BR as the official museum piece.

## 182 Patons & Baldwins Ltd      I

Worsted Spinners, Darlington, County Durham
OS Ref: NZ 317151

Industrial steam location with locomotive in store.

**Stock**
Bagnall 0-4-0F *Patons* 2898 built 1948

## 183   Crossley Bros (Shipley) Ltd                    I

Shipley Station, West Yorkshire
OS Ref: SE 148372

Industrial steam location with locomotive in very occasional use.

**Stock**
Barclay 0-4-0ST *Chemicals* 1823 built 1924
Ruston Hornsby 4WDM No. 9 *Beth* 425483 built 1958
Ruston Hornsby 4WDM No. 602 417892 built 1959

## 184   Yorkshire Water Authority                     I

Esholt Purification Works, Bradford, West Yorkshire
OS Ref: SE 185394

Industrial steam location with locomotive as spare to the diesel fleet.

**Stock**
Hudswell Clarke 0-4-0ST *Elizabeth* 1888 built 1958
Hudswell Clarke 0-4-0DM No. 398 D989 built 1957
Hunslet 0-4-0DH *Prince of Wales* 7159 built 1969

## 185   National Coal Board                            I

North East, Barnsley, North Yorkshire and South Yorkshire Areas

Industrial steam locations. No public admittance.

**Stock**
RSH 0-6-0ST No. 77 7412 built 1948 Norwood Coke Ovens, Dunston-on-Tyne
Bagnall 0-6-0ST 2779 built 1945 Vane Tempest Colliery, Seaham Harbour
Barclay 0-6-0ST No. L2 2212 built 1946 Widdrington Disposal Point
Hunslet 0-6-0ST *Monckton No. 1* 3788 built 1953 North Gawber Colliery, Mapplewell, Yorks
Hunslet 0-6-0ST No. 8 3183 built 1944 Woolley Colliery, Darton, Yorks
Bagnall 0-6-0ST 2746 built 1944 Ackton Hall Colliery, Featherstone, Yorks
Hunslet 0-6-0ST No. 134 3168 built 1944 Allerton Bywater Colliery
Hunslet 0-6-0ST No. S115 *Antwerp* 3180 built 1944 Wheldale Colliery, Castleford
RSH 0-6-0F *Carbonisation No. 1* 7847 built 1955 Manvers Main Coking Plant, Wath
Hunslet 0-6-0ST *SWCP No. 1* 3193 built 1944 Smithywood Coking Plant, Chapeltown, Yorks

## 186   Lightwater Railroad                            B

Lightwater Valley Leisure Ltd, Ripon, North Yorkshire

Passenger-carrying 15 in. gauge railway opened in 1979. The line is in the form of a continuous loop just over a mile in length.

**Stock**
Severn-Lamb 2-8-0DH built 1979
Two semi-open covered bogie coaches
Two open bogie coaches

## 187   W. Elliott & Son (York) Ltd                    G

Rufforth Airfield, near York
OS Ref: SE 529507

2ft gauge locomotive in store.

**Stock**
Motor Rail 4WPM No. LR 2832 1111 built 1918

## 188   Sedgefield District Council                    G

Public Works Department Yard, Burke Street, Shildon, Co. Durham
OS Ref: NZ 226263

Standard gauge locomotive in store.

**Stock**
[1]Hackworth 0-6-0 *Braddyll* built 1835

[1]Withdrawn 1875 and used as a snowplough at South Hetton Colliery until remains preserved 1951. It is hoped to move *Braddyll* into the Timothy Hackworth Museum workshop when this is re-roofed.

## 189   Arthington                                     G

Mr R. N. Redman, Arthington Station, Yorkshire
OS Ref: SE 257445

2 ft 11 in. gauge locomotive in store.

**Stock**
Hudswell Clarke 4WDM D571 built 1932

## 190   Slaggyford Light Railway                       C

Mr W. F. Horseman, The Island, Slaggyford, near Alston, Northumberland
Tel: Alston (049-83) 422

Private passenger-carrying 2 ft gauge line, 360 yards in length, running round a caravan park. The railway was opened in May 1978.

**Stock**
Baguley 0-4-0DM 29HP type 3236 built 1947 (steam outline)

Baguley open bogie coaches Nos 3237 and 3239.

Mr Horseman also offers bed and breakfast accommodation.

## 191    Ocean Park Railroad                     B

Seaburn, Sunderland, Tyne and Wear

Passenger-carrying 15 in. gauge railway, 300 yards in length.
The line is laid out in a horseshoe shape and operates daily
during the holiday season.

**Stock**
Collins 4WPM built *c.* 1971
Two articulated open bogie coaches

## 192    Saville Bros Ltd                         B

Garden Centre, Garforth Cliff, Leeds, West Yorkshire

Passenger-carrying 10¼ in. gauge railway.
The line was opened on 20 May 1978 and is an ambitious
project in an attractive setting. The track is laid out as a pair
of joined balloon loops and incorporates an impressive girder
bridge over an ornamental pond. As befits a railway located
in a Garden Centre, the main station, Cactus Junction, is to
be found *inside* a large greenhouse!

**Stock**
Severn-Lamb 2-8-0PH built 1978 (steam outline)
'Wild West'-style toastrack bogie coaches

## 193    Olicana Miniature Railway                B

Riverside, Newbridge, Ilkley, West Yorkshire

Passenger-carrying 10¼ in. gauge railway, ¼ mile in length.
This line originally opened in 1967 using 12 in. gauge track
but was extended and converted to its present gauge in
1975. Operation is at weekends only by members of the
Yorkshire Dales Railway Society.

**Stock**
Coleby-Simkins / Stanhope 0-6-0PM built 1972 (steam
outline)
Stanhope 6WBE built 1976
Clitheroe 4-6-4BE built 1954 ⎫
Clitheroe 4-6-4BE built 1954 ⎬ Ex Cleethorpes Miniature
Clitheroe 4-6-4BE built 1954 ⎭ Railway
Open bogie coaches ex Cleethorpes Miniature Railway

## 194    Lambton Pleasure Park                    B

Chester-le-Street, County Durham
OS Ref: NZ 298518

Passenger-carrying 15 in. gauge railway.

**Stock**
Severn-Lamb 2-8-0DH No. 278 R9 built 1976 (steam outline)

## 195    Westcliff Miniature Railway              B

Westcliff Sports Ground, Whitby, North Yorkshire

Passenger-carrying 10¼ in. gauge railway, 300 yards in
length, laid in an irregular circle. The line operates daily in
the holiday season.

**Stock**
Shepperton 2-4-2DM *Meteor II* built 1969
5 articulated bogie coaches

## 196    Flamingo Park Railroad                   B

'Flamingoland' Park and Zoo, Kirby Misperton, Pickering,
North Yorkshire

Passenger-carrying 10¼ in. gauge railway, 350 yards in
length, linking the car park to the fairground.
This is a simple continuous loop with no spurs or sidings,
running for most of its length between two rows of trees.

**Stock**
LNER 4-6-2 Gas, No. 4472 *Flying Scotsman* built Dex
Recreational Products 1979
Potter Engineering Bo-BoDM
Gwrych Castle 4-6WD *Hiawatha* built 1968 (out of use)
Four articulated bogie coaches

## 197    Saltburn Miniature Railway               B

Italian Gardens, Saltburn-by-the-Sea, Cleveland
OS Ref: NZ 666215

Passenger-carrying 15 in. gauge railway, ½ mile in length
running from Cat Nab to Valley Gardens Station
After many seasons out of use, during which time it suffered
heavily at the hands of vandals, the Saltburn Miniature
Railway is being reconstructed by Mr Brian Leonard in time
for the 1980 season.

**Stock**
Barlow 4-6-2DE *Prince of Wales* built 1953 (steam outline)
Four open bogie coaches

# AREA E

## Scotland

most important collections of historical rolling stock north of the border.

The decision of the Scottish Tourist Board to offer a substantial grant to assist in the construction of a tourist steam railway at Bo'ness, West Lothian, has given the SRPS its long awaited chance to set up a permanent home for its Falkirk stock. It will enable work on the project to start immediately.

With a well established reputation for running successful railtours, the SRPS has been building up its reserves and has negotiated the lease from Falkirk District Council of the land required for the laying of 1¼ miles of track along the foreshore of the River Forth.

Falkirk depot is open to the public virtually every Saturday and Sunday in the year between 11 am and 4 pm when visitors are very welcome, subject to a nominal admission charge. A sales stand and other facilities are provided. Special open days are held as advertised, when engines may be steamed and other attractions provided. Visitors are asked to note that the depot is not open at other times, except by prior special arrangement. Large party groups are especially welcome at weekends, but organisers are asked to give adequate prior notice when tours are planned to call at Falkirk in order that special arrangements can be made.

The Society has gained wide recognition for the comprehensive and balanced collection of locomotives, rolling stock and other equipment which it has built up to illustrate the history and development of Scottish railways and the Scottish railway industry. Many items have been restored to full working order by the Society's volunteer members and an extensive and ambitious work programme is in hand at Falkirk depot, which is best described as a workshop rather than just a museum. Several of the Society's passenger coaches have been plated by British Rail for operating over BR lines and some of the Society's steam engines have seen occasional outings onto main line, notably to Rail 150 at Shildon in 1975.

The Society, which is incorporated as a company limited by guarantee, and is recognised as a charity, has a flourishing membership. Annual subscription is £2 (persons under 18, 75p; wife or husband of ordinary member, £1; life membership, £20; groups £6; family membership £3.50). A bi-monthly magazine *Blastpipe* is issued free to members.

The Society runs an enterprising sales department and an extensive programme of special excursion trains from stations in central Scotland to places of scenic or other interest, many of them composed partly or wholly of SRPS preserved coaches.

*Registered Office*: 57 Queen Street, Edinburgh (for formal correspondence only; no callers)
*Publicity Officer*: Andrew J. Harper, 16 Livingstone Place, Edinburgh EH9 1PE
*Membership Secretary*: Mrs I. M. Gollan, 16 West Relugas Road, Edinburgh EH9 2PL

**Stock**
¹BR 2-6-4T No. 80105 Class 4MT built 1955
²LNER 4-4-0 No. 246 *Morayshire* Class D49 built 1928
³CR 0-4-4T No. 419 built 1907
⁴NBR 0-6-0 No. 673 *Maude* built 1891

---

## 201    The Scottish Railway          DF
          Preservation Society

SRPS Depot, Soringfield Yard, Falkirk, Central Region, Scotland

Stock is now gradually being concentrated at Bo'ness, West Lothian, where the SRPS is constructing a 1¼ mile standard gauge branch line to Kinneil, along the foreshore of the River Forth.

*Access*: Falkirk; ½ mile north of town centre along Grahams Road. Near BR Falkirk Grahamston Station
Bo'ness; Immediately east of the dock on the river frontage
Tel: Falkirk 20790
OS Ref: NS 891805 (Falkirk)

The SRPS owns a large and varied collection of locomotives and rolling stock, principally of Scottish origin. To date, these have been housed at Falkirk depot, which is open to the public every weekend. However, the Society has been striving for a number of years to acquire a branch line of its own on which to operate what has now become one of the

[5]Neilson-Reid 0-6-0T No. 1 5710 built 1902
[6]Neilson 0-4-0ST No. 13 *Kelton Fell* 2203 built 1876
[7]Hawthorn (Leith) 0-4-0WT *Ellesmere* 224 built 1861
Barclay 0-6-0ST No. 3 1458 built 1916
Barclay 0-4-0CT No. 6 2127 built 1942
Black Hawthorn 0-4-0ST *City of Aberdeen* 912 built 1887
[8]Barclay 0-6-0T No. 20 2068 built 1939
[9]Barclay 0-4-0ST No. 3 1937 built 1928
Barclay 0-4-0T *The Fair Maid of Foyers* 840 built 1899 3 ft
gauge
Barclay 0-6-0DM 343 built 1941
Ruston Hornsby 4WDM 262998 built 1949
Ruston Hornsby 4WDM No. D7 *Pioneer* 275883 built 1949
Ruston Hornsby 4WDM 506500 built 1965
Ruston Hornsby 0-4-0DE No. 3 Class 165DE 423658 built
1958
Ruston Hornsby 0-4-0DE *C.I.W. No. 1* 42139 built 1958
[10]English Electric 4WE 1131 built 1940
Two LMS open second coaches Nos 27389 and 27407 built
1946 and 1948
LMS design composite coach No. 24725 built 1950
CR Brake composite bogie coach No. 7369 464 built 1921
CR Corridor third bogie coach No. 1375 built 1921
CR non-corridor bogie third coach No. 426 built 1914
HR six-wheeled coupe composite coach No. 17 89 built
1909
GNSR non-corridor bogie saloon No. 1 built 1898
LNER Gresley Buffet car No. 644 built 1937

*Kelton Fell* is alive and well and all set to steam along
the Scottish RPS's new line at Bo'ness beside the Firth
of Forth

---

LNER Thompson TO No. SC13883E built 1949
LMS 2nd class sleeping car No. M622M built 1951
LNER Gresley corridor third coach No. DE320874 built 1924
LNER-type non-corridor brake composite coach No.
SC80417E built 1951
GSWR corridor bogie third class coach No. 731 built 1914
GSWR six-wheeled passenger brake No. 122 built 1901
NBR bogie invalid saloon No. 461 built 1919
LNER Gresley bogie pigeon van No. E70494E built 1940
CR six-wheeled goods brake van No. 437 built *c.* 1920
Two CR covered goods vans Nos 73004 and 73007 built
*c.* 1920
Carron Iron Co. dumb-buffered mineral wagon No. 755 built
*c.* 1890
GNSR single-plank wagon No. 1329 built *c.* 1880
William Baird & Co. three-plank wagon No. 7 built 1903
Shell-BP oil tank wagon No. A43 built 1897
Two Briggs of Dundee tank wagons Nos 17 and 20 built
1927 and 1918
Scottish Tar Distillers tank wagon No. 78 built 1877; rebuilt
Leith General Warehouse covered grain hopper No. 120 built
1903
Robert Hutchison & Son (Kirkcaldy) covered grain hopper
No. 6 built 1903

Two NCB mineral wagons Nos 4898 and 5362 built c. 1930
GNR high-sided mineral wagon No. 31 built c. 1880
LMS six-wheeled fish van No. M40226 built 1946
Clyde Iron Works eight-ton hopper wagon (rebuilt)
GWR bogie bolster wagon No. 84762
GWR bogie bolster wagon
Matisa ballast tamping machine No. 48626 built 1957
Wickham Type 'B' 4WPM rail trolley No. 6049 and trailer No. 6050
In addition, the Society owns numerous items of plant and machinery, including the former wheel lathe from Heaton MPD, Newcastle.

[1]Withdrawn as BR No. 80105 and sold to Woodham Brothers, Barry, for scrap. Purchased for preservation in 1973 by Locomotive Owners Group (Scotland) Limited, who now own the Locomotive.

[2]Withdrawn as BR No. 62712 in 1961 and purchased by Mr I. N. Fraser for private preservation. Externally restored at Inverurie Works in 1964 and presented to the Royal Scottish Museum, Edinburgh, in 1966. Restored to working order by SRPS in 1975, under loan agreement with RSM.

[3]McIntosh Class 439 locomotive withdrawn by BR from Carstairs shed in 1962 as No. 55189. Purchased by Society for preservation and restored to CR livery at Cowlairs Works, 1965. Restored to working order by Society.

[4]North British Railway Class C (LNER Class J36) withdrawn by BR from Bathgate shed in 1966 as No. 65243. This locomotive was one of 25 of its class shipped to France during World War I and named on their return. One hundred and sixty-eight engines of this class were built and two of of the class survived to become the final steam engines in traffic with BR Scottish Region in 1967. Presently being extensively overhauled.

[5]Outshopped as Lord Roberts by Neilson-Reid and Company of Glasgow in 1902 for the Coltness Iron Company Limited at Newmains, Lanarkshire, where the engine stayed until 1955. Bought by the NCB in that year upon closure of the works and sent to Bedlay Colliery, near Coatbridge. Retired in 1968 following the breakage of a cross-head. Donated to the Society by NCB.

[6]Built for William Baird and Son (Iron-founders) by Neilson of Glasgow in 1876, this engine saw service at the company's hematite mine at Lamplugh in West Cumberland, bearing the name Kelton Fell, the hill from which the ore was extracted. The engine returned to Scotland in 1914 to work in the Twechar area, passing into NCB stock as No. 13 in 1947. Its external appearance altered little through the years, and it received its final overhaul in 1965 at Shotts Workshops. No. 13 was withdrawn from Gartshore Colliery in 1968 and donated to the Society by the NCB. Restored to full working order and original livery by the Society in 1974, and celebrated its centenary in 1976 with a special re-naming ceremony at Falkirk.

[7]The oldest Scottish-built locomotive known to be in existence. Spent all her working life at Howe Bridge Colliery, near Wigan, and withdrawn by the NCB in 1957. Privately preserved and brought to Falkirk in 1966, this engine is now owned by the Royal Scottish Museum and is intended for eventual display in Edinburgh.

[8]The largest locomotive owned by the Society, the last of five such engines delivered to the Wemyss Coal Company Limited at Fife in the 1930s. The company's own railway, the Wemyss Private Railway, escaped nationalisation, and No. 20 worked on the line until its closure in 1970 following the Michael Colliery disaster. The engine was overhauled and reboilered by the builders in 1968 and was purchased by the Society in 1970.

[9]Standard 14 in. Barclay 0-4-0ST. Built in 1928 for the Clyde Valley Electric Power Company, Clydesmill Power Station. Donated to the Society by the SSEB and brought to Falkirk under its own steam in January 1970.

[10]Ex Fairfield Shipyard, Glasgow.

**Progress 1979**
In July 1978 Falkirk District Council granted planning permission for 'the formation of a railway system and the erection of an engine shed and station platform at the Foreshore, Bo'ness'. This means that the Scottish Railway Preservation Society will now have a permanent home and a line for their rolling stock. At present, the stock of over 60 locomotives, carriages and wagons is housed in a converted goods shed at Wallace Street, Falkirk.

Bo'ness, an old Firth of Forth port about 15 miles west of Edinburgh, was once the scene of considerable railway activity with a rail link along the foreshore from Kinneil in the west to Carriden in the east, a passenger service to Polmont, and a complex network of some 7 miles of sidings around the harbour and dock. Few traces now remain of this once extensive system.

The railway centre will be located immediately to the east of the dock and the rail link along the foreshore will be reinstated for about 1¼ miles to Kinneil, the present terminus of the British Railways branch from Bo'ness Junction. The first building to be put up will be the engine shed and it will be a two road steel-framed structure with a 'traditional' external appearance. It will be about 120 ft long, sufficient for two coaches and four locomotives, and will also provide accommodation for machines and tools for use in restoration and maintenance.

When the line is completed, steam trains will be operated and it is likely that Bo'ness will become a tourist centre of considerable importance.

The future of the BR line from Kinneil to Manuel (on the Edinburgh–Glasgow line) appears uncertain. In the event of its closure it is hoped that it will be incorporated into the scheme giving a 4½ mile stretch of railway, most of it in a fairly secluded and scenic location.

## 202   Strathspey Railway                                            A

*Headquarters:* The Station, Boat of Garten, Highlands, PH24 3BH

*Access:* BR main line trains serve Aviemore Station from North and South. By road, off A9, take A95 Grantown road, then first right to Boat of Garten (signposted). Highland Aviemore–Grantown bus service passes Boat of Garten. Aviemore (Speyside) station is off the A951 to Cairngorm.
Tel: Boat of Garten 692
OS Ref: NH 9419

**Summer on the Strathspey Railway. LMS type 2–6–0 locomotive No. 46464 leaves Boat of Garten for Aviemore (Speyside)**

Passenger-carrying standard gauge steam railway, 5½ miles in length running from Aviemore (Speyside) to Boat of Garten. The railway operates at weekends from mid-May to the end of September and daily (not Mondays or Fridays) in July and August.

Facilities for visitors include car parking, railway shop, museum and toilets.

The line from Aviemore to Boat of Garten is part of the former main line between Perth and Inverness, opened 1863 as the Inverness and Perth Junction Railway. The section between Aviemore and Forres was closed to passenger traffic in 1965, leaving the shorter route to Inverness via Carr Bridge, opened 1898, for all trains. The tracks north of Boat of Garten were lifted in 1969, but what now forms the Strathspey line was left, although stripped of sidings and signalling.

The line runs through typical Scottish moorland country and provides fine views of the Cairngorm and Monadhliath mountains, scenes which have changed little since the line was built. Aviemore is well known as an all-year-round holiday centre and is well served by main line trains from as far away as London. Strathspey trains operate from a new station on their own line, which is about ten minutes walk from the main line station and car parks. Boat of Garten retains its rural station appearance and nameboard proclaiming 'Change for Speyside Line', a reference to its role as exchange point between Highland (LMS) and Great North (LNER) trains, an atmosphere which is retained by the sight of stock of the former companies sitting side by side. The station has a small museum and railway shop.

The Strathspey railway reopened in July 1978 following six years of restoration by the Company and Strathspey Railway Association.

*Membership:* Details of membership are available from the Secretary of the Association.

In addition to providing a workforce on the line the members are responsible for publishing newsletters and the journal, manning stands at exhibitions, and all the one-hundred-and-one other jobs which can be done away from Speyside. Area groups meet regularly in Edinburgh, Glasgow, Aberdeen, Inverness, Dundee and Speyside.

*Secretary, Strathspey Railway Co. Ltd:* D. B. Barclay, C.A., 111 Union Street, Glasgow G1 (registered office)

*Secretary, Strathspey Railway Association:* W. Brownlie, 44 Knocklea, Biggar, Lanarkshire ML12 6EQ

*Press and Publicity Officer:* R. Black, 37 Castle Avenue, Balloch, Alexandria, Dunbartonshire G83 8HU

*Annual subscription:* Adult £3, Junior & OAP £1.50, Family £5, Group £15

## Stock

[1]LMS 4-6-0 No. 5025 (Stanier Class 5MT) built 1934
[2]LMS 2-6-0 No. 46464 (Ivatt Class 2MT) built 1950
[3] [4]LMS 2-6-0 No. 46512 (Ivatt Class 2MT) built 1952
LMS 2-6-0 No. 46428 (Ivatt Class 2MT) built 1948
[4]Barclay 0-6-0T WPR No. 17 2017 built 1935
[4]Barclay 0-4-0ST No. 3 *Clyde* 2315 built 1951
[5]Hunslet 0-6-0ST No. 48 (2864) built 1943
[5]RSH 0-6-0ST No. 9 *Cairngorm* (7097) built 1943
[6]Hunslet 0-6-0ST No. 60 (3686) built 1948
Barclay 0-4-0ST No. 4 2047 built 1937
Barclay 0-6-0ST No. 20 1833 built 1924
[7]Barclay 0-4-0ST No. 10 *Forth* (1890) built 1926
[8]Barclay 0-4-0ST No. 1 *Dailuaine* (2073) built 1939
[9]Barclay 0-4-0ST No. 2 *Balmenach* (2020) built 1936
[10]Hudswell Clarke 0-4-0DM No. 13 *Inverkeith* (D613) built 1939
[10]Ruston Hornsby 0-4-0DM No. 14 *Inveresk* (165DS Class) (260756) built 1950
[11]Simplex 4WDM No. 15 *Inverdon* 5763 built 1957
[12]North British 0-4-0DH 27549 built 1956
BR Mk I Corridor Composite coach No. 101 (formerly E15401) built 1954
BR Mk I Non-gangwayed corridor composite No. 102 (formerly E43024) built 1954
BR Mk I Corridor open 3rd coach No. 103 (formerly W4127) built 1955
BR Mk I Brake/3rd coach No. 104 (formerly E43349) built 1955
BR Mk I Buffet Car *Glenfiddich* No. 105 (formerly SC79441) built 1956
BR Mk I Corridor open brake/3rd coach No. 106 (formerly SC9362) built 1959
LMS 6-wheel Full Brake Coach No. 153 (formerly M32988M) built 1938
BR Pullman Car *Amethyst* (formerly E325E) built 1960
LMS 3rd class sleeping car No. 621 built 1952
LMS corridor brake third No. 27043 built 1951
LMS corridor open third No. 27234 built *c.* 1945
LMS 'Stove R' six-wheeled full brake No. 33003 built 1939
LMS 12-wheeled first-class sleeping car No. 394 built 1952
LMS third-class sleeping car No. 14452 (latterly No. DM395778) built 1928
LMS engineer's inspection saloon No. M45021 built 1944 (not at Aviemore)
LNER first-class sleeping car No. 1211 built 1935
HR four-wheeled full brake No. 5 built *c.* 1870
NBR dormitory coach No. DE970012 built 1905
GNSR six-wheeled luggage van No. 68 (latterly No. DE320010) built 1898
GNSR six-wheeled composite No. 34 (latterly No. DE970204) built 1896
BR Bogie bolster wagon (latterly B944445)
Three-ton diesel crane built 1951
CR five-ton hand crane built 1905
LMS crane runner built 1935
LNER bolster wagon
Two flat wagons
'SMD' Tank wagons Nos 1 and 4
'SGB' Mineral wagons Nos 13, 16, 22 and 24
Box Van
Wickham 4WPMR 1288 built 1933
AC Cars Railbus body SC79979 built 1958
Esso tank wagon No. 731 built 1908

[1]One of the first batch of the famous 'Black Fives', built at Newton-le-Willows by the Vulcan Foundry (Works No. 4570). Entered service on 2 August 1934 and allocated to Perth shed for work on the Highland line to Inverness and the Caledonian route to Aberdeen. Withdrawn from Carnforth shed in August 1968 after hauling what was at that time thought to be one of the last steam trains on BR. Overhauled, first by Hunslet's at Leeds and then by Barclay at Kilmarnock, she travelled to the Strathspey Railway under her own steam on 29 May 1975.
[2]Owned by the '46464 Preservation Trust'. Purchased by the Trust for preservation following withdrawal from Dundee shed. For many years the locomotive worked the Carmyllie Branch and was known locally as 'The Carmyllie Pilot'. Stored at Dundee until moved to the Strathspey Railway in March 1975
[3]Withdrawn in November 1966 and sold to Woodham Brothers, Barry, for scrap. Purchased by the Strathspey Railway, moved to Bewdley on the Severn Valley Railway in June 1973 and subsequently on to Bulmers, Hereford, where it is undergoing restoration
[4]Owned by the Highland Locomotive Company Ltd (*q.v.*).
[5]Purchased from the National Coal Board (ex Backworth Colliery).
[6]Purchased from the National Coal Board (ex Dawdon Colliery, Seaham Harbour).
[7]Donated by the (Scottish) Gas Board (ex Granton Gas Works, Edinburgh).
[8]Donated by Scottish Malt Distillers. Formerly used on the branch from Carron Station to Dialuaine Distillery. Latterly this locomotive swopped duties with *Balmenach* and before the line from Cromdale was lifted it was moved to Aviemore.
[9]Donated by Scottish Malt Distillers. Formerly used on the branch from Cromdale to Balmenach Distillery.
[10]On loan from the Inveresk Paper Group.
[11]Donated by the Scottish Gas Board, Aberdeen Gas Works.
[12]Purchased from the South of Scotland Electricity Board. Formerly used at Barony Power Station, Ayrshire.

## The Highland Locomotive Company Limited    H

*Registered office:* The Station, Boat of Garten, Inverness-shire PH24 3BH

*Secretary:* D. B. Barclay CA at the above address.
Tel: Bridge of Allan 3013
*Subscription:* Minimum shareholding £5

Company formed in 1975 to represent the original supporters of an appeal to purchase Ivatt Class 2, 46512, in 1973. Its function is to purchase, restore, maintain and supply locomotives for use on the Strathspey Railway. The Company is a subsidiary of the Strathspey Railway Co. Ltd and shareholders also include the Strathspey Railway Association. In 1976 Barclay 0–4–0ST (SR No. 3) and 0–6–0T (SR No. 7) were transferred to the Company.
The restored locomotives carry the Strathspey colours – an adaptation of the Highland Railway scheme, Dark green with 'Strathspey Railway' – in full on the tanks or tender sides.
Enquiries regarding purchase of shares are welcome.

## 203   Lochty Private Railway    A

One mile passenger-carrying line near Anstruther, Fife
*Access:* By own transport (1½ miles from nearest bus route)
OS Ref: No. 522080

The railway operates on Sundays from mid-June to early September between 2 pm and 5 pm.
Facilities for visitors include car parking and souvenir shop.

The Lochty Private Railway forms part of the former East Fife Central Railway, closed in 1965. The Lochty-Knightsward section lies bordered by farmland owned by John B. Cameron and thus no statutory authority was necessary for services to commence in 1967. It was the first standard gauge preserved line to operate in Scotland. Operation of the railway is now undertaken by members of the Fife Railway Preservation Group. Membership of the Group is open to railway enthusiasts who are interested in helping with the operation, maintenance and development of the LRP as a working steam railway museum. The Group is engaged in acquiring items of railway equipment previously used in and around Fife for use or display at Lochty.

### Stock
[1]LNER 4–6–2 No. 60009 *Union of South Africa* Class A4 built 1937
[2]Peckett 0–4–0ST No. 1 1376 built 1915
[3]Bagnall 0–6–0ST WPR No. 16 2759 built 1944
Ruston Hornsby 4WDM 88DS Class 421415 built 1958
LNER bogie observation coach No. 1719 built 1937
BR brake/second open bogie coach No. E9315E built 1956
Five RCH Mineral Wagons
Two 3-plank dropside wagons ex Tullis Russell of Markinch
NBR 8-ton box van built 1901
Briggs of Dundee bitumen tank wagon

[1]Withdrawn from Aberdeen (Ferryhill) shed as BR No. 60009 in 1966. Purchased for preservation in 1967 and moved to

**Hoots mon, it's a wee Peckett propelling its coach load of passengers along the Lochty Railway**

Photo: Peter M. Westwater

the Lochty Private Railway, where it was for several seasons the sole motive power. During 1973, however, the locomotive was returned to BR tracks to work a number of steam-hauled excursions in Scotland. Consequently, additional motive power has been acquired at Lochty.

[2]Ex British Aluminium Co., Burntisland, 1972.
[3]Ex Wemyss Private Railway, 1973.

Details of the FRPG may be obtained from P. M. Westwater, 48 Hendry Road, Kircaldy, Fife. Tel: 0592-4587.

Cameron's Machine No. 60009 *Union of South Africa* blows away the cobwebs at Markinch in preparation for an Edinburgh to Aberdeen rail tour on Easter Sunday, 1978

## 204   Alford Valley Railway                        A

Alford, Murray Park, Grampian
Tel: Alford 2326

Passenger-carrying 2 ft gauge railway under construction
from the former GN of SR Alford Station to Bridge of Alford,
a distance of 3 miles. At the time of going to press, 1 mile
of track had been laid and services commenced in 1979.
Operation from 1 June to the end of September.
Facilities for visitors include car parking, railway shop,
refreshments and toilets.
Work commenced on constructing the railway in February
1979 and the first section, from Haughton Country Park to
Murray Park, was brought into use at the end of June 1979.
The total length of the line will be three miles and will be
worked by steam and diesel traction. The company owns
a Lister diesel locomotive and a selection of rolling stock
and has already laid half a mile of line from Bridge of Alford
Station through the Murray Park. The Project would be
complementary to the proposed Grampian Region Museum
of Transport which is proposed to be sited in the area of the
old station at Alford. The railway will have eight stations
and passes through a recognised tourist area with popular
picnic areas and caravan/camping sites. The railway trav-
erses nature trails, woodland and a historic battlefield. The
company is being closely assisted by the Alford Valley
Railway Association.
Help and finance are required to assist the company in its
aims and membership of the Association is open to all
interested parties. Members will be entitled to free travel on
the line and a regular newsletter on progress. Volunteer help
is always required with track laying and train operation. The
Association will be shareholders of the railway company.

### Stock
Fowler 0–4–2T *Saccharine*
Lister 4WDM 3298 built 1930
Two open 4-wheel coaches
Two closed 4-wheel coaches
Six 4-wheeled peat wagons

There is also to be a display of GN of SR standard gauge
exhibits at Alford Station.
Details of the AVRA may be obtained from 9 Blackcraig
Road, Cruden Bay, Aberdeenshire.

*Annual subscription:* £1.50, Life £10, Family Life Membership
£15.


## 205   Royal Scottish Museum                        E

Chambers Street, Edinburgh EH1 1JF
Tel: 031-225-7534
OS Ref: NT 258734

Locomotives on static display in transport gallery.
The museum is open on weekdays from 10 am to 5 pm and
on Sundays from 2 pm to 5 pm.
Facilities for visitors include a museum shop, refreshments
and toilets.

The Royal Scottish Museum is the most comprehensive
display in Britain under one roof comprising the decorative
arts, natural history, geology and technology. Transport is
represented, including a colliery locomotive of 1813, many
scale model locomotives and models of ships. There are
galleries covering aeronautics, space flight, science and there
is a Radiation Corridor.
Further details from The Keeper, Mr J. D. Storer, at the
above address.

### Stock
[1]William Hedley 4WVCG *Wylam Dilly* built 1813 (5 ft gauge)
[2]Baldwin 4WE *Oakbank No. 2* 20587 built 1902 (2 ft 6 in.
gauge)

[1]Withdrawn in 1864 and acquired from Wylam Colliery,
Northumberland, by the sons of the builder. Loaned by them
for display in 1882.
[2]Ex Scottish Oils Ltd, Winchburgh Shale Mine, Midlothian,
1961. In store at present.

The following standard gauge locomotives are on loan to
the Scottish RPS at Falkirk (see Group No. 201):
LNER 4–4–0 No. 246 *Morayshire* Class D49 built 1928
Hawthorn (Leith) 0–4–0WT *Ellesmere* 224 built 1861

The following locomotive is in store at Biggar Gas Works
(see Group No. 208):
Barclay 0–4–0T No. 5 988 built 1903 (2 ft gauge)


## 206   Glasgow Museum of Transport                  E

25 Albert Drive, Glasgow G41 2PE
*Access:* In easy reach of the M8 Motorway, near Eglinton
Toll. Albert Drive connects with Pollokshaws Road, the A77
signposted to Kilmarnock. The nearest Subway station is
West Street. By bus, going South from Renfield Street (City
Centre). By train, Pollokshields East Station is adjacent to
the museum with frequent electric trains from Glasgow
Central Station
Tel: 041-423-8000
OS Ref: NS 581632

Standard gauge steam locomotives on static display in a
large museum devoted to all aspects of Scottish, and par-
ticularly Glaswegian, transport.
The Museum is open daily from 10 am to 5 pm and on
Sundays from 2 pm to 5 pm. Closed on Christmas Day and
New Year's Day.
Admission Free.
Facilities for visitors include car parking, museum shop,
refreshments and toilets.
Many aspects of Transport History are represented in the
Museum. The horse-drawn vehicles display includes private
passenger carriages, public coaches and wagons, including
a Royal Mail Coach of the 1840s.
The bicycle and motor cycle collections, like other sections,
include important exhibits.
The most notable is perhaps the oldest surviving pedal cycle
in the world, a contemporary copy of MacMillan's of 1839.
The car collection traces the fascinating history of the motor
car. Amongst others can be seen an important group of

Scottish built vehicles, including Argylls, Albions and Arrol-Johnstons, as well as more modern cars.

Trams are by no means forgotten – the Glaswegians' love of the 'caurs' is legendary – from the original horse-drawn tram of 1894, to the Cunarder, the story of the trams can be seen, and times-past recalled.

The development of the various Scottish railway companies can be seen with the aid of models and full-size exhibits.

The model railway is an attraction for railway enthusiasts of all ages.

Also to be seen are commercial vehicles, ranging from a steam-powered traction engine to road rollers.

Further details may be obtained from Mr A. S. E. Browning, The Keeper, at the above address. (SAE with your enquiry appreciated.)

**Stock**
[1]CR 4-2-2 No. 123 (Neilson 3553) built 1886
[2]CR 0-6-0 No. 828 built 1899
[3]GSWR 0-6-0T No. 9 (NB Loco. 21521) built 1917
[4]GNSR 4-4-0 No. 49 *Gordon Highlander* (NB Loco. 22563) built 1920
[5]HR 4-6-0 No. 103 (Sharp Stewart 4022) built 1894
[6]NBR 4-4-0 No. 256 *Glen Douglas* built 1913
[7]Barclay 0-6-0F No. 1 1571 built 1917

[1]Built for display at the International Exhibition of Industry, Science and Art, held at Edinburgh in 1886. Taken into Caledonian Railway stock at the closure of the exhibition and worked as the Chief Mechanical Engineer's saloon engine and royal train pilot. Withdrawn as LMS No. 14010 in 1935 and restored to CR blue livery. Stored at St Rollox Works until returned to traffic to work special excursion trains in 1958. Taken out of traffic in 1965 and moved to the Museum in 1966.
[2]McIntosh 812 Class withdrawn from Ardrossan shed in 1963 as BR No. 57566. Purchased by the Scottish Locomotive Preservation Trust Fund in 1964 and stored until restored to CR livery at Cowlairs in 1966. At the time of their construction, the 812 Class were the largest CR goods engines; a freight counterpart of the famous 'Dunalastair' 4-4-0s. This locomotive is to be moved to the Strathspey Railway in due course.
[3]Smellie Class 5 withdrawn as LMS No. 16379 in 1934 and sold to Ruabon Coal and Coke Co. Ltd. Withdrawn in 1962 and presented by the NCB for display. Stored until moved to the Museum in 1966.
[4]A member of the Heywood 'F' Class (LNER Class D40), this graceful 4-4-0 was withdrawn from Keith shed in 1958 as BR No. 62277. Restored to GNSR livery and returned to traffic in 1959 to work special trains. Withdrawn in 1965 and moved to the Museum in 1966.
[5]'Jones Goods' Class withdrawn as LMS No. 17916 in 1934. Restored to Highland Railway green livery in 1935 and stored at St Rollox Works until repainted in HR yellow livery and returned to traffic in 1959. Taken out of traffic in 1965 and moved to the Museum in 1966. The 'Jones Goods' was the first 4-6-0 design to enter service in the United Kingdom.
[6]Reid 'K' Class (LNER Class D34), became BR No. 62469 and was restored to NBR livery in 1959 whilst still in service. Officially withdrawn in 1962, it was retained to work special

trains along with the other preserved Scottish locomotives. Taken out of traffic in 1965 and moved to the Museum in 1966.
[7]Presented by the South of Scotland Electricity Board, Dalmarnock Power Station, Glasgow, in 1969. Originally built for the Ministry of Munitions.

Other railway items include a collection of exhibition models of locomotives built by the North British Locomotive Co. and an important collection of material illustrating the development of permanent way. There is a large '00' gauge model railway of Carlisle Station which is operated regularly.

Representing other forms of transport, there are seven Glasgow tramcars ranging from 1894 to 1952, numerous cars, horse-drawn vehicles, bicycles and motor-cycles, several fire engines (including two steamers) and two aeroplanes.

## 207    Carnegie Dunfermline Trust                 E

Pittencrieff Park, Dunfermline, Fife
OS Ref: NT 086872

Standard gauge static locomotive exhibit.

**Stock**
Gibb & Hogg 0-4-0ST No. 11 (16) built 1898
Presented by National Coal Board, Cardowan Colliery, 1968.

## 208    Gladstone Court Museum                       G

Bigger Gasworks (Branch of Royal Scottish Museum)

2 ft gauge steam locomotive in store pending the construction of this long-term museum project.

**Stock**
Barclay 0-4-0T No. 5 988 built 1903

## 209    Ayrshire Railway                             G
         Preservation Group

Near Kilmarnock, Strathclyde. Site not open to the public
*Details from:* J. Davidson, 31 Moorfield Avenue, Kilmarnock, Strathclyde

Collection of locomotives undergoing restoration by the Group.

**Stock**
Barclay 0-4-0ST 1889 built 1926 (standard gauge)
Ruston Hornsby 4WDM *Blinkin Bess* Class 88DS 284839 built 1950 (standard gauge)
Ruston Hornsby 4WDM 183749 built 1937 (2 ft 6 in. gauge)
Ruston Hornsby 4WDM 211681 built 1942 (2 ft 6 in. gauge)
Ruston Hornsby 4WDM 210959 built 1941 (2 ft 6 in. gauge)

## 210    Lochranza Transport Museum                   E

The Piggery, Corriegills, Isle of Arran, Strathclyde

Static 4 ft gauge coach exhibit.

**Stock**

Glasgow Underground Railway Coach No. 10 built 1896 rebuilt 1935

## 211  Scottish Society for the Preservation   G of Industrial Machinery

Prestongrange, Midlothian
OS Ref: NT 374737

Standard gauge rolling stock in store.

**Stock**

Barclay 0–4–0ST No. 17 2219 built 1946
Grant Richie 0–4–2ST No. 7 *Prestongrange* 536 built 1914
Motor Rail 4WDM 9925 built 1963
Several ex-NCB mineral wagons

## 212  Aberdeen, Duthie Park   G

Aberdeen City Council
OS Ref: NJ 940044

Locomotives stored in Duthie Park, adjacent to BR Ferryhill Motive Power Depot.

**Stock**

[1]Barclay 0–4–0ST *Mr. Therm* 2239 built 1947
[2]Barclay 0–4–0ST *Bon Accord* 807 built 1897

[1]Ex Scottish Gas Board, Aberdeen, 1972. Depot, Aberdeen. It is intended that this locomotive will form a static display item at a children's playground in Aberdeen.
[2]Ex Scottish Gas Board, Aberdeen, 1972. Owned by the Aberdeen Gas Works Locomotive Preservation Trust Fund.

*Details from:* Alan Greig, Broomfold Cottage, Tornaveen, Torphins, Kincardine and Deeside.

## 213  Brechin Railway   F Preservation Society

Brechin Goods Shed, Brechin Station site

A standard gauge railway preservation scheme aimed at re-opening the line from Brechin to Bridge of Dun, then possibly on to Dubton, a total distance of 7 miles. Locomotives undergoing restoration.

**Stock**

Bagnall 0–6–0ST No. 6 2749 built 1944
Hunslet 0–6–0ST *Diana* 2879 built 1943

*Society details from:* Mrs Claire Maxwell, 17 Grampian View, Ferryden, Montrose.

## 214  Shell UK Ltd   I

North Crescent, Ardrossan, Strathclyde
OS Ref: NS 230428

Industrial steam location featuring regular steam working. No public access.

**Stock**

Barclay 0–4–0F 1952 built 1928

## 215  R. B. Tennent Ltd   I

Steel and Iron Roll Manufacturers, Whifflet Foundry, Coatbridge, Strathclyde
OS Ref: NS 738643

Industrial steam location featuring regular steam working. No public access.

**Stock**

Sentinel 4WVBTG *John* 9561 built 1953
Sentinel 4WVBTG *Ranald* 9627 built 1957
Sentinel 4WVBTG *Robin* 9628 built 1957
Sentinel 4WVBTG *Denis* 9631 built 1958

## 216  British Aluminium Co. Ltd   I

Burntisland, Fife
OS Ref: NT 225862

Industrial steam location with locomotive stored out of use, nominally spare to the diesels. No public access.

**Stock**

Barclay 0–4–0ST *BA Co No. 3* 2046 built 1937
Fowler 0–4–0DM No. 1 4210004 built 1949
Fowler 0–4–0DM No. 2 4210045 built 1951

## 217  National Coal Board   I

Scottish Area

Industrial steam locations, many of them featuring regular steam working.

**Stock**

Barclay 0–4–0ST No. 6 2043 built 1937 out of use at Kinneil Colliery, Bo'ness
Barclay 0–6–0T No. 8 1296 built 1912. Polkemmet Colliery, Whitburn, West Lothian
Barclay 0–4–0ST No. 29 1142 built 1908. Arniston Stores
Barclay 0–6–0ST No. 12 1829 built 1924. Polkemmet Colliery, Whitburn, West Lothian
Hunslet 0–6–0ST No. 17 2880 built 1943. Polkemmet Colliery, Whitburn, West Lothian
[1]Barclay 0–6–0ST No. 8 1175 built 1909. Polkemmet Colliery, Whitburn, West Lothian
Barclay 0–6–0ST No. 25 2358 built 1954. Polkemmet Colliery, Whitburn, West Lothian
Barclay 0–4–0ST No. 17 2292 built 1951. Frances Colliery, Dysart
Barclay 0–4–0ST No. 17 2296 built 1950. Bedlay Colliery, Glenboig
Hudswell Clarke 0–6–0T No. 9 895 built 1909. Bedlay Colliery, Glenboig

Hunslet 0-6-0ST No. 19 3818 built 1954. Comrie Colliery, Saline, Fife
Hunslet 0-6-0ST No. 5 3837 built 1955. Comrie Colliery, Saline, Fife
Bagnall 0-6-0ST No. 7 2777 built 1945. Comrie Colliery, Saline, Fife
Barclay 0-4-0ST No. 5 2260 built 1949. Cardowan Colliery, Stepps, Lanarkshire
Barclay 0-4-0ST No. 29 1996 built 1934. Bilston Glen Colliery, Loanhead
Barclay 0-4-0ST No. 8 2369 built 1955. Barony Colliery, Auchinleck
Barclay 0-4-0ST No. 16 1116 built 1910. Barony Colliery, Auchinleck
Barclay 0-4-0ST No. 21 2284 built 1949. Arniston Stores
Barclay 0-4-0ST No. 10 2244 built 1947 Dunaskin, Waterside, Strathclyde
Barclay 0-6-0T No. 17 1338 built 1913. Arniston Stores
Barclay 0-4-0ST No. 19 1614 built 1918. Waterside Washery, Dalmellington
Barclay 0-6-0T No. 24 2335 built 1953. Waterside Washery, Dalmellington
Barclay 0-4-0ST No. 1 2368 built 1955. Waterside Washery, Dalmellington

[1]Restored as a static exhibit by the gateway to Polkemmet Colliery, Whitburn, West Lothian.


## 218   Babcock & Wilcox (Operations) Ltd   I

Dumbuck Works, Dumbarton, Strathclyde
OS Ref: NS 411746

Industrial steam location with locomotive being restored by apprentices.

### Stock
Hawthorn Leslie 0-4-0ST 3640 built 1926
Ruston Hornsby 4WDM 262995 built 1948


## 219   Cupar Industrial Estate   I

Cupar, Fife
OS Ref: No. 388149

Industrial steam location with locomotive stored out of use.

### Stock
Barclay 0-4-0ST No. 17 1863 built 1926


## 220   Shipbreaking Industries Ltd.   I

Faslane, Strathclyde
OS Ref: NS 243897

Industrial steam location with locomotive stored, partially dismantled.

### Stock
Sentinel 4WVBGT 9593 built 1954
Barclay 0-4-0DM *ROF Drigg No. 3* 350 built 1941

Fowler 0-4-0DM *ROF No. 7 No. 8* 22993 built 1942
Ruston Hornsby 4WDM 312430 built 1951


## 221   Ritchie & Young   G

Haddington, Lothian

A private collection of narrow gauge locomotives in store

### Stock
Ruston Hornsby 4WDM 249530 built 1947 (2 ft gauge)
Ruston Hornsby 4WDM 242916 built 1946 (2 ft 6 in gauge)
Ruston Hornsby 4WDM 273843 built 1949 (3 ft gauge)


## 222   Hardbridge Grouse Railway   C

Private 2 ft gauge passenger-carrying grouse railway operated by Sir William Lithgow at Hardridge, Kilmacolm, Strathclyde
OS Ref: NS 313675

### Stock
Motor Rail 4WDM No. 2 8700 built 1941
Motor Rail 4WPM 2097 built 1922
Motor Rail 4WPM 2171 built 1922


## 223   Fraserburgh Mini-Railway   B

Fraserburgh Town Council, Fraserburgh, Grampian

2 ft gauge passenger-carrying line.
OS Ref: NK001659.

### Stock
Lister Blackstone 4WDM No. 677 *Kessock Knight* 53541 built 1963


## 224   Butlins Ltd   B

Heads of Ayr Holiday Camp
OS Ref: NS 299187

A 2 ft gauge passenger-carrying line.

### Stock
Ruston Hornsby 4WDM *Sue* (LF Class) 476106 Built 1964 (steam outline)


## 225   Kerrs Miniature Railway   B

West Links Park, Arbroath, Angus

A 10¼ in. gauge line 400 yards long running from West Links Station, alongside the BR East Coast main line, to Burnside. The railway was originally opened in 1935 as 7¼ in. gauge, but converted to 10¼ in. in 1938. Operation is daily throughout the summer.

**Stock**
Jennings 4–4–2PM No. 9872 *Auld Reekie* built *c.* 1934
(steam outline)
Kerr 4–6–4BE *Prince Andrew* built 1961
Croall 4–4–0 CR No. 769 built 1898 (11 in. gauge)
Six open bogie coaches

## 226   Craigtown Miniature Railway                    B

Craigtown Park, near St Andrews, Fife
OS Ref: NO 481139

Passenger-carrying 15 in. gauge railway, operating from
11 am onwards on Saturdays.

**Stock**
Severn-Lamb 2–8–0PH R8 built 1976
Two open bogie coaches
Closed bogie coach

## 227   Strathan Miniature Railway                    B

George Allan Park, Strathaven, Larkhall, Lanarkshire

Passenger-carrying 7¼ in. gauge railway, 50 yards in length
laid out as a continuous circuit. In operation daily during the
holiday season.

**Stock**
Curwen Bo-BoPH built *c.* 1960
Three open bogie coaches

## 228   Ayr Miniature Railway                    B

The Promenade, Ayr

Passenger-carrying 10¼ in. gauge railway forming a short
circuit in the seafront children's playground. In operation
daily during the holiday season.

**Stock**
Severn-Lamb Co-CoPH *Ayr Princess* built 1968

## 229   Thomas Muir                    G

Scrap Metal Contractor, Easter Balbeggie, near Thornton,
Fife
OS Ref: NT 291962

This is the 'Woodhams of the North'!
A collection of industrial steam locomotives retained pending
scrapping.

**Stock**
Barclay 0–4–0ST No. 47 2157 built 1943
Barclay 0–4–0ST No. 3 946 built 1902
Barclay 0–4–0ST No. 22 1069 built 1906
Barclay 0–6–0T No. 10 1245 built 1911
Hunslet 0–6–0ST No. 18 3809 built 1954
Barclay 0–4–0ST No. 7 2262 built 1949
Barclay 0–4–0ST No. 53 1807 built 1923
Barclay 0–6–0ST No. 15 2183 built 1945
Barclay 0–4–0ST No. 6 2261 built 1949
[1]Grant Ritchie 0–4–0ST No. 61 272 built 1894

[1]Reserved for Glenrothes Council for some considerable time,
though this scheme is now thought doubtful.

# AREA F

# North West

Cumbria
Lancashire
Cheshire
Isle of Man
Merseyside

## 251   Ravenglass and Eskdale Railway      A

Ravenglass Station, Ravenglass, Cumbria

*Access:* Ravenglass BR station. Cumberland Motor Services buses serve Ravenglass and Muncaster Mill. By road, along the A595
Tel: Ravenglass (06577) 226
OS Ref: NY 086967

Passenger-carrying 15 in. gauge steam railway, 7 miles in length, running from Ravenglass to Eskdale (Dalegarth).
The railway is in operation from the end of March to the end of October and trains run from 7.45 am to 7.20 pm in high season.
Facilities for visitors include car parking, refreshments, toilets, a museum devoted to 15 in. gauge railways, souvenir

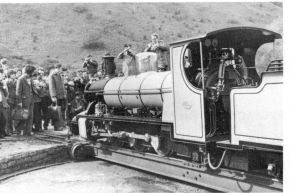

All eyes around *Northern Rock*, the Ravenglass and Eskdale Railway's latest steam locomotive, seen here on the turntable at Dalegarth

Photo: Graham Scott-Lowe

shops, a restored watermill at Muncaster and a picnic area at Dalegath. The RER owns a pub at Ravenglass called the 'Ratty Arms' in the former station house of the BR main line station.
It also owns two Pullman camping coaches which are let to visitors. The Pullmans are kitchen/firsts *Elmira* and *Maid of Kent*, both built 1914 and converted 1921.
The Ravenglass and Eskdale Railway, 'T'laal Ratty' to Cumbrians, was originally opened in 1875 to bring iron ore, and later passengers, from Eskdale. A very chequered existence during which it almost died twice has brought it to the present day, when the line has to depend almost entirely on passenger traffic. Always a private company, the railway is to-day supported by a Preservation Society.
It is England's oldest Narrow Gauge Railway, but features train control by VHF FM radio telephone, a system unique in the United Kingdom.

R&ER Preservation Society details from: Mr J. D. Stanbra, 5 Sheriff Bank, Greenodd, Ulverston, Cumbria LA12 7RF. *Membership:* 1700

**Stock**
*The Preservation Society owns:*
Clarkson 2–8–2 *River Mite* (4669) built 1966
*The Ravenglass and Eskdale Railway Company owns:*
Heywood 0–8–2 *River Irt* (built 1894 as 0–8–0T *Muriel* and rebuilt at Ravenglass in 1927)
R&ER 2–6–2 *Northern Rock* built 1976
Davey Paxman 2–8–2 *River Esk* (21104) built 1923
Curwen/Severn-Lamb 4–6–4DH *Shelagh of Eskdale* built 1969
Kerr Stuart 0–4–0T No. 15 *Bonnie Dundee* (720) built 1901 (2 ft gauge, being rebuilt as 15 in. gauge 0–4–2T)
Muir-Hill 4WPM *Quarryman* built 1926
Muir-Hill 0–4–4 DM *Pretender*, converted in 1929 from 1925 Muir-Hill 0–4–0

R&ER 3-car bogie diesel railcar multiple unit *Silver Jubilee* built 1977
Eighteen open bogie coaches built 1928–73
Eighteen saloon coaches built 1972–74
Six semi-open coaches built 1972–74
Six steel drop-side granite wagons
Twelve wood-framed flat wagons
One steel tank wagon
One weed-killing wagon

The society owns LMS brake/third coach No. M20165M (built 1927) to accommodate members wishing to work on the line.

## 252   Lakeside and Haverthwaite Railway   A

Haverthwaite Station, near Newby Bridge, Ulverston, Cumbria
Tel: 04483–594
OS Ref: SD 349843

Passenger-carrying standard gauge steam railway from Haverthwaite to Lakeside, a distance of 3¼ miles.

Operated by the Lakeside and Haverthwaite Railway Co. Ltd supported by the Lakeside Railway Society

*Details from:* A. Middleton, at Haverthwaite Station.
Facilities for visitors include car parking, souvenir shop, refreshments and toilets.

The Lakeside Railway was opened by the Furness Railway Co. on 1 June 1869 and after almost 100 years of operation was closed at the end of 1965. The Lakeside Railway Society was founded in 1967 as the supporting enthusiasts body of the company, who were then proposing to purchase and reopen the Plumpton Junction to Lakeside branch in its entirety. This original proposal had to be abandoned and the

**Steam to spare as the *Boat Express* blasts its way out of Haverthwaite Station on the Lakeside Railway**

Photo: Lakeside Railway Trust

Society and company subsequently gave their attention to the eventual reopening of the three-and-a-quarter mile Haverthwaite to Lakeside section. Services commenced over Easter 1973 and the railway was officially opened by the Bishop of Wakefield on 2 May 1973.

**Stock**

[1]LMS (Fairburn) 2–6–4T No. 2073 (Class 4MT) built 1950
[1]LMS (Fairburn) 2–6–4T No. 2085 (Class 4MT) built 1951
Hudswell Clarke 0–6–0ST LHR No. 5 (1631) built 1929
Hudswell Clarke 0–6–0ST LHR No. 6 (1366) built 1919
Bagnall 0–6–0ST LHR No. 14 *Princess* (2682) built 1947
[2]Hunslet 0–6–0ST No. 94 *Cumbria* (3794) built 1953
Hunslet 0–6–0ST *Repulse* (3698) built 1950
Peckett 0–4–0ST LHR No. 1 *Caliban* (1925) built 1937
Barclay 0–4–0ST No. 1 *David* (2333) built 1953
Barclay 0–4–0ST No. 12 *Alexandra* (929) built 1902
Avonside 0–4–0ST *Askham Hall* (1772) built 1917
Fowler 0–4–0DM LHR No. 2 *Fluff* (21999) built 1937
BR/Gardner 0–6–0DM LHR No. 8 (BR Class 03 No. 2117) built 1959
Motor rail 4WPM *Rachel* (2098) built 1924
BR Mk 1 SK carriages Nos. E24248, 24377, 24381, 24449, 24731 and 24799 built 1953/54
BR Mk 1 BSO carriage No. E9218 built 1953
BR Mk 1 BSK carriage No. E34181 built 1951
LNER BG No. E70361 built 1936
MR clerestory third-class coach built 1913
LMS 20-ton goods brake van No. M731874 built 1947
LMS bogie bolster wagon No. 319192 built 1925
GWR 12-ton box van No. 142096 built 1941
SR 12-ton box van No. 515142 built 1940

BR Conflat 'A' wagon No. B706063 built 1958
Esso oil tank wagon No. 2375 built 1942
Five-plank coal wagon (ex Vickers Ltd, Barrow)
Wickham petrol rail trolley and trailer

[1]Withdrawn from Normanton shed as BR Nos 42073 and 42085 in October 1967. The LMS 2–6–4 tanks, which were developed over a number of years from the original Fowler design of 1927, proved highly successful on suburban and cross-country passenger work. As an interim measure, pending the appearance of a BR standard type, the Fairburn version of the LMS design was constructed in reasonably small numbers to replace the remaining LBSCR 4–4–2 and 4–6–2 tanks. Both engines were built at Brighton Works and worked on the Southern Region until displaced by electrification schemes.
[2]Ex MODAD, Shoeburyness Military Railway, Essex, 1973.

## 253    Isle of Man Railway      A

PO Box 30, Station Buildings, Douglas, Isle of Man

*Access:* Short Walk from Douglas Bus Station, Harbour and Town Centre
Tel: Douglas 4646
OS Ref: SC 374754

Turning back the years on the Isle of Man railway with the simultaneous 10 am departures from Douglas. No. 11 *Maitland* is in charge of the Port Erin train on the right, and No. 12 *Hutchinson* heads for the now rail-less Ramsey on the left. Stirring stuff!

Passenger-carrying, 3 ft gauge steam railway, 15½ miles in length, running from Douglas to Port Erin.

The IMR, with absorbed companies, was opened in stages between 1873 and 1886. Services were maintained on all lines until World War II when the two-and-a-half mile Foxdale branch was closed. Complete closure of the rest of the system took place in 1965. The railway was leased in 1967, but at the end of the 1968 season the Peel and Ramsey lines were closed and have now been lifted. Eventually, the railway, now reduced to the present 15½ mile section, was purchased by the Manx Government at the end of 1977.

**Stock**

[2]Beyer Peacock 2-4-0T IMR No. 3 *Pender* 1255 built 1873
[1]Beyer Peacock 2-4-0T IMR No. 4 *Loch* 1416 built 1874
[2]Beyer Peacock 2-4-0T IMR No. 5 *Mona* 1417 built 1874
[2]Beyer Peacock 2-4-0T IMR No. 6 *Peveril* 1524 built 1875
[2]Beyer Peacock 2-4-0T IMR No. 9 *Douglas* 3815 built 1896
[1]Beyer Peacock 2-4-0T IMR No. 10 *G. H. Wood* 4662 built 1905
[1]Beyer Peacock 2-4-0T IMR No. 11 *Maitland* 4663 built 1905
[1]Beyer Peacock 2-4-0T IMR No. 12 *Hutchinson* 5126 built 1908
[1]Beyer Peacock 2-4-0T IMR No. 13 *Kissack* 5382 built 1910
[3]Walker Brothers bogie diesel railcar No. 19 built 1950
[3]Walker Brothers bogie diesel railcar No. 20 built 1951
Thirty-eight bogie carriages (about 12 in regular use)
Eighteen wagons
Wickham 4WPMR 7442 built 1956
Wickham 4WPMR 5763 built 1950

[1]Still operational.
[2]Stored out of use and not on display.
[3]Ex County Donegal Railways Joint Committee, 1961.

## 254   Steamtown Railway Museum           AD

Warton Road, Carnforth, Lancashire

*Access:* Short walk from BR Carnforth Station. By road via the M6 Junctions 35 and 35A and the A6
Tel: Carnforth (052473) 4220 and 2625
OS Ref: SD 496708

Major standard gauge railway preservation centre housing a large collection of main line and industrial locomotives from Great Britain and the continent. Steam-hauled rides are available in vintage vehicles over nearly a mile of track within the boundaries of the centre. There is also a passenger-carrying 15 in. gauge railway, 1,000 yards in length.

Steamtown is open daily (except Christmas Day) between 9 am and 4 pm in winter and 9 am and 5 pm the remainder of the year. Facilities for visitors include car parking, souvenir shop, refreshments, toilets, picnic area, Collectors Corner for Railway relics and model railway. Cairnforth Motive Power Depot (10A in British Railways shed classification) was one of the last in the country to retain steam locomotives. After the final withdrawal of steam motive power in 1968, a private company promoted by some steam enthusiasts leased the depot in order to house various locomotives which had been bought for preservation. The leased area covers about 20 acres and in addition to the shed, offices and workshops contains a coaling tower, ash disposal plant, water columns, a 70 ft turntable and a carriage and wagon shop. From end to end the site is about a mile long and has about five miles of track. The southern end lies on the west side of the main line from London to Glasgow, now electrified. A rail connection at the northern end allows access to and from the Furness line of British Railways.

There are between 25 and 30 British and Continental main line and Industrial locomotives on view. Further locomotives will be added to the collection as they become available. Occasionally exchanges are made with locomotives of the National Railway Museum and private owners.

Main line steam specials are run by arrangement to Leeds, York, Scarborough and Ravenglass. We are not allowed to give timings of steam specials other than for passengers.

In addition to restoring steam locomotives, Steamtown can undertake engineering contracts within the scope of its well-equipped workshop, which includes a 7 ft wheel lathe.

Further locomotives will be added to the collection as they become available from home and abroad.

Steamtown is the operating base for many main line locomotives, principal amongst them, *Flying Scotsman*.

**Stock**

[4]SR 4-6-2 No. 35005 *Canadian Pacific* (Bulleid MN Class) built 1941
[1]LNER 4-6-2 No. 4472 *Flying Scotsman* (Gresley A3 Class) built 1923
[4]GWR 0-6-2T No. 5643 (Class 56XX) built 1925
[2]SNCF 4-6-2 No. 231K22 *La France* built 1914, rebuilt 1937
SR 4-6-0 No. 30850 *Lord Nelson* (LN Class) built 1926
LMS 4-6-0 No. 44871 *Sovereign* (Class 5MT) built 1945
LMS 4-6-0 No. 44932 (Class 5MT) built 1945
LMS 4-6-0 No. 45407 (Class 5MT) built 1937
LMS 2-6-0 No. 6441 (BR No. 46441) (Class 2MT) built 1950
DB 4-6-2 No. 01.1104 (Schwartzkopf) built 1940
DR 0-6-0T No. 80.014 (Class 80) (Wolf 1228) built 1927
[9]LNER 4-6-2 No. 4498 *Sir Nigel Gresley* (Class A4) built 1935
LMS 4-6-0 No. 5690 *Leander* (Class 5XP) built 1936
[3]L&YR 0-6-0 No. 1122 (BR No. 52322) built 1896
Hudswell Clarke 0-6-0T *Whitwood No. 6* (1864) built 1952
Barclay 0-4-0ST No. 5 *John Howe* (1147) built 1908
Barclay 0-4-0ST No. 2 *Jane Darbyshire* (1969) built 1929
Barclay 0-4-0ST No. 3 *Coronation* (2134) built 1942
Barclay 0-4-0CT No. 1 *Glenfield* (880) built 1902
Peckett 0-4-0ST *May* (1370) built 1915
Bagnall 0-6-0F *Trimpell* (3019) built 1953
Bagnall 0-6-0ST *Cranford No. 2* (2668) built 1942
[5] [6]Barclay 0-4-0ST No. 1 *Douglas* (2230) built 1947
[5] [7]Barclay 0-4-0ST No. 4 *British Gypsum* (2343) built 1953
[5] [8]Hunslet 0-6-0ST No. 6 *Courageous* (3855) built 1954
Sentinel 4WBTG *Gas Bag* (8024) built 1929
General Electric Bo-BoDE *New Jersey* 30483 built 1949
BR 0-6-0DM No. D2381 (Class 03) built 1960
Hunslet 0-6-0DM No. 7049 *Tom Rolt* (2697) built 1944
Ruston Hornsby 4WDM No. 5 *Flying Flea* (48DS Class) 294266 built 1951

Photo: John Gardner

Here's a Jubilee class sporting an appropriate headboard. LMS No. 5690 *Leander* has been leading an active life on rail tours based at Carnforth

LNWR steam breakdown crane (30 ton capacity) built 1908
NER clerestory bogie saloon No. 305 built 1903
GER saloon bogie coach No. 1 built 1920
CR saloon bogie coach No. 41 built 1897
GER royal saloon bogie coach No. 5 built 1898
GER directors saloon No. 63 built 1912
LMS 12-wheeled sleeping car No. M395 built 1951
GER six-wheeled coach No. 14 built 1889
GWR saloon No. 9004 built 1930
BR Mk 1 BSK bogie coach No. E34612 built 1955
GNR saloon No. 397 built 1912
GNR invalid saloon No. 3087 built 1909
LNER Gresley buffet car No. 24287 built 1938
Pullman car *Zena* built 1928
SECR 12-wheeled Pullman cars *Rosalind* and *Padua* built 1921

Pullman car No. 301 *Perseus*
Pullman car No. 308 *Cygnus*
BP tank wagon built 1932
GWR 'Toad' 20-ton brake van No. 35234 (Neath and District)
Four BR 16-ton mineral wagons
LMS open wagon
Shell/BP tank wagons Nos A56 and A350 built 1902
Two flat wagons
Twelve-wheeled heavy machinery wagon
Wickham 4WPMR No. 4153
Smith Rodley steam crane
Bogie bolster wagon

[1]Withdrawn as BR No. 60103 in 1963 and purchased for preservation by Mr Alan Pegler. Restored to LNER livery with two tenders at Doncaster Works in 1963. Toured in the United States from 1969 to 1972. Bought by Mr W. H. McAlpine and returned to this country early in 1973. *Flying Scotsman* completed over two million miles in regular

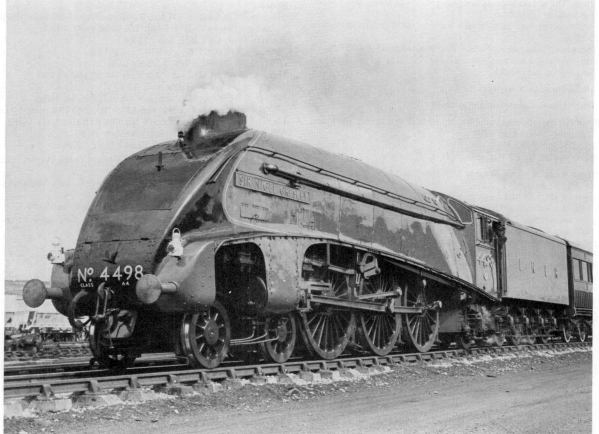

Photo: John Gardner

**The distinctive sound of a Gresley chime whistle heralds the approach of garter blue A4 No. 4498,** *Sir Nigel Gresley*

---

express passenger service and since then has become the most famous preserved steam locomotive in the world.

[2]French National Railways four-cylinder compound 'Pacific' built by the Paris–Lyons–Mediterranean Railway and rebuilt in 1937. Used on the Calais to Amiens section of the 'Golden Arrow' service. The locomotive arrived at Steamtown in 1970.

[3]Withdrawn from Lees, Oldham, as BR No. 52322 in 1960. The correct L&YR number should be 1300. One of a class of 385 engines for working medium-range freight traffic throughout the L&Y system.

[4]Withdrawn and sold for scrap to Woodham Brothers, Barry. Purchased for preservation and moved to Carnforth in 1973.

[5]Owned by Steam Enterprises Ltd (*q.v.*).

[6]Ex Cook and Nuttall Ltd, Vale Paper Works, Horwich, Lancashire, 1972

[7]Ex British Gypsum Ltd, Thistle Plaster Works, Kirkby Thore, Westmorland, 1971.

[8]Ex NCB, Glasshoughton Colliery, Castleford, Yorkshire, 1973.

[9]Owned by the A4 Locomotive Society Ltd (*q.v.*).

*15 in. gauge Stock*
Bassett-Lowke 4-4-2 *George the Fifth* 18 built 1911
Lane Bo-Bo DH *Royal Anchor* built 1956

## Steam Enterprises Ltd                                     H

Locomotives located at Steamtown, Carnforth, Lancashire

*Details from:* Mr M. Hanson, 130 Brookhouse Road, Brookhouse, Lancaster, Lancashire
Tel: Lancaster 770256

The organisation was formed in 1972 by the owners of a number of industrial steam locomotives in order to cooperate in the supply of spare parts and equipment to ensure the continued operation of steam locomotives on private rail-

ways. The group's locos are being, or have been, overhauled and vacuum-fitted.
Locomotives may be available for loan, sale or hire from time to time.
This group also owns the Hunslet 'Austerity' 0-6-0ST No. 7 and Andrew Barclay 0-4-0ST No. 22 located at Embsay. (See Group No. 156.)

## A4 Locomotive Society Ltd                                    H

Steamtown, Carnforth, Lancashire

*Membership Secretary:* Mrs Heather Burton, 50 Parkland Crescent, Leeds LS6 4PR
Tel: 0532 681923
Membership at £2 per annum or £15 for life

The A4 Locomotive Society Ltd owns ex LNER Pacific 4498 *Sir Nigel Gresley.*
Some £15,000 has been spent in 1967 on a major overhaul at BR workshops at Crewe, where restoration to LNER garter blue took place. The aims of the Society are to continue to maintain this locomotive in main line working order and to organise whenever possible steam-hauled excursions over the main lines of British Railways with this famous engine. New members are always welcome and receive certain concessions on railtours organised by the Society.
A newsletter, *Chime,* is sent out quarterly to the members and this reports on the activities of the Society so that members can take an active interest in the progress of the Society. The locomotive is also available for charter to reputable organisations and societies.

## 255   Bury Transport Museum                              DE

Castlecroft Road, Bury, Greater Manchester BL9 0LN

*Access:* Off Bolton Street, Bury. By road, via A56 and A58. Short walk from BR Bury Station
Tel: 061-764-7790
OS Ref: SD 803109

A Museum of standard gauge steam locomotives and rolling stock and commercial road vehicles. On special open days, steam-hauled trains are demonstrated over ¼ mile of track. The Museum is open every Saturday and Sunday, Easter Monday, Spring and Late Summer Bank Holidays. Loco in steam on the last Sunday in each month from March to September and on Bank Holidays.
Facilities for visitors include car parking, museum shop, model railway, refreshments (steam days only) and toilets.
The East Lancashire Railway Preservation Society moved to Bury in 1972. Its home is a former East Lancashire Railway Goods Shed built in the mid 1840s and converted by the Society into Bury Transport Museum.
The Museum is adjacent to the Bury–Rawtenstall line on which BR still operate coal trains but the ultimate aim is to operate steam hauled passenger services.
In the meantime a ¼ mile of track has been laid alongside the BR line and vacuum braking equipment has been fitted to a brake van and one loco. Permission has not yet been given to carry passengers.

## Stock
[1]Hudswell Clarke 0-6-0T No. 32 *Gothenburg* 680 built 1903
[1]Hudswell Clarke 0-6-0T No. 70 1464 built 1921
Barclay 0-4-0ST 945 built 1904
[2]Barclay 0-4-0ST No. 1 1927 built 1927
[3]RSH 0-6-0T MEA No. 1 7683 built 1951
Hibberd 4WDM No. 1 *Mr Mercury* 3438 built 1950
Motor Rail 4WDM 9009 built 1948
BR Mk 1 TSO bogie coach No. NE 4350 built 1956
L&YR four-wheeled goods van LMS No. 149196 built 1914
L&YR Brake/3rd bogie coach No. DB 975154 built 1910
MR hand crane and match truck built 1880
BR Goods brake van No. B953942 built 1958

[1]Ex Manchester Ship Canal Co., Mode Wheel Works, Old Trafford, Manchester, 1973.
[2]Ex North Western Gas Board, Oswald Street Gasworks, Burnley, Lancashire, 1970.
[3]Ex CEGB, Meaford Power Station, Staffordshire, 1971.

ELRPS details may be obtained from The Secretary at the Museum.
*Membership:* 180.

## 256   Southport Locomotive and                      DE
##        Transport Museum (Steamport)

Steamport Southport Ltd., Derby Road, Southport, Merseyside PR9 0TY
OS Ref: SD 341161
Tel: Southport 30693

A live steam museum housing a collection of standard gauge steam locomotives based in the former LMS Southport Derby Road loco shed. Regular steam open days held throughout the year when short brake van rides are available over ¼ mile of track.
The depot is open every weekend afternoon, at Easter, and daily from the end of May to mid-September.
*Details from:* C. M. Lee, 35 Balfour Road, Southport, Sefton, Merseyside PR8 6LE.

## Stock
LMS 4-6-0 No. 44806 *Magpie* (Stanier Class 5MT) built 1944
BR 2-6-0 No. 76079 (Riddles Class 4MT) built 1957
[1]GWR 2-6-2T No. 5193 (51XX Class) built 1934
[2]Mersey Railway 0-6-0T No. 5 *Cecil Raikes* (Beyer Peacock 2605) built 1885
[1]LMS 0-6-0T No. 47298 (Class 3F) built 1924
[1]Avonside 0-6-0ST *Lucy* 1568 built 1909
[1]Barclay 0-4-0ST *Efficient* 1598 built 1918
Peckett 0-6-0ST No. 5 2153 built 1954
Peckett 0-4-0ST *North Western Gas Board* 1999 built 1941
Hudswell Clarke 0-4-0ST *Waleswood* 750 built 1906
[1]Sentinel 4WVBTG *St Monans* 9372 built 1947
Fowler 0-4-0DM *Persil* 4160001 built 1952
LOR trailer coach No. 7 built 1895, rebuilt 1947
LMS vestibuled third-class saloon coach No. 8200 built 1927
Smith-Rodley diesel crane No. X63486 (Type 75 Super)
Open wagon UGB 'Cullet' No. 10
BR Mk 1 BCK brake/composite corridor coach

Photo: Tom Heavyside

**No, it's not just another little Peckett, it's a mighty monster in the shape of No. 5 *Birchenwood* at Steamport, Southport**

LMS 13-ton open wagon No. 130397
LMS goods brake No. 731733
LMS goods brake No. 732386
[1]M.R. four-wheeled goods van
[1]LMS 20-ton goods brake van
2 ft gauge 'Silver Belle' train which formerly operated on Southport Pier, comprising Barlow 4-6-0DE locomotive and bogie coach No. 5 built 1953

[1]Owned by the Liverpool Locomotive Preservation Group (*q.v.*).
[2]Locomotive in store at present. Withdrawn in 1903 and sold to Coppice Colliery, Derbyshire. Presented by NCB to BTC in 1956. Stored until presented by BRB in 1964 and moved to Liverpool in 1967.

**Liverpool Locomotive Preservation Group**          H

Steamport, Southport, Merseyside

*Hon. Secretary:* E. Wheelwright, 25 Glendevon Road, Childwall, Liverpool L16 6AE
*Membership:* 60
*Subscription:* 50p per annum

*Facilities:* Working parties are held each weekend. A bimonthly newsletter is produced. Bi-monthly meetings and film shows are held on alternative months to the newsletter

## 257  Manx Electric Railway          B

Manx Electric Railway Board, 1 Strathallan Crescent, Douglas, Isle of Man
Tel: Douglas 4549

3 ft gauge electric light railway, 18 miles long, running from Derby Castle, Douglas (connects with Douglas Horse Tramway, see Group No. 259) to Ramsey. Change at Laxey for the Snaefell Mountain Railway (Group No. 258)

This railway has no parallel within the British Isles, being a genuine electrically-worked light railway which formerly carried a large quantity of goods traffic but now relies mainly on tourists. It runs through magnificent scenery and no visitor should miss the opportunity of a ride on one of its trains. It was opened in stages between 1893 and 1899 and passed through the ownership of several companies before being nationalised by the Manx Parliament at the end of 1956. The line is double-track throughout and electrified at 500 volts dc, current collection from the overhead wire being by trolley pole.

**Stock**
Ten saloon motor cars
Three saloon trailer cars
Fourteen semi-open motor cars
Twenty-two semi-open trailer cars
Five four-wheeled wagons
Five four-wheeled vans
Wickham 4WPMR 8849 built 1961

## 258 Snaefell Mountain Railway                B

Laxey, Isle of Man

Operated by the Manx Electric Railway Board 3 ft 6 in. gauge electric mountain railway opened in 1895, running four-and-three-quarter miles to the summit of Snaefell (2,034 ft). Operates May–September.
With a riding gradient of 1 in 12 it is the steepest line in the British Isles worked by adhesion only; but a centre rail, using the Fell system, is also installed, being used only for braking purposes on the descent.

**Stock**
Rolling stock consists of six 48-seat bogie electric passenger cars built by G. F. Milnes of Birkenhead for the opening of the line.
There are also two four-wheeled service wagons and a double-cab works car incorporating a six-ton wagon body. This latter vehicle borrows power bogies from one of the passenger cars when its services are required.
Wickham 4WPMR 5864 built 1951

## 259 Douglas Horse Tramway                B

The only example of a horse tramway still operating in the British Isles is at Douglas in the Isle of Man. The Douglas Horse Tramway has survived changes of ownership, closure and electrification proposals and omnibus competition to remain extremely popular and carry well over a million passengers during a summer season.
Built originally by Thomas Lightfoot and Sons, services began on 7 August 1876 and have continued ever since, apart from a period during World War II when part of the Promenade became a prisoner of war camp. Douglas Corporation Transport Department acquired the tramway in 1902 and run cars daily from May to September.
The line, of 3 ft gauge and now double-track throughout, runs for 1⅝ miles along the sea front, from Victoria Pier in the south to a northern terminus near the Manx Electric Railway station, and uses 31 cars of various types seating 30–40 passengers. The 60 horses, mostly from Ireland, are fine animals and are well cared for.
The tramway operates daily from 9 am to 11 pm approximately with cars every one-and-a-half minutes when traffic is heavy.

## 260 West Lancashire Light Railway                B

Station Road, Hesketh Bank, near Preston, Lancashire
OS Ref: SD 448229

A 2 ft gauge passenger-carrying line, 380 yards long and being extended

*Details from:* N. McMurdy, 4 Devonshire Road, Southport, Lancashire PR9 7BX

**Stock**
¹Hunslet 0–4–0ST No. 3 *Irish Mail* (823) built 1903
Kerr Stuart 0–6–0T No. 9 (2405) built 1915
Motor Rail 4WDM No. 7 (8992) built 1946
Hunslet 4WDM No. 8 (4478) built 1953
Ruston Hornsby 4WDM No. 18 283507 built 1949
Ruston Hornsby 4WDM 202036 built 1941
Ruston Hornsby 4WDM No. 2 *Tawd* (20DL Class) (222074) built 1943
Ruston Hornsby 4WDM No. 1 *Clwyd* (13DL Class) (264251) built 1951
Hibberd 4WPM No. 4 (1777) built 1931
Ruston Hornsby 4WDM No. 5 (25/30 HP Class) (200478) built 1940
Motor Rail 4WDM 5851 built 1933
Motor Rail 4WDM 9263 built 1947
Motor Rail 4WDM No. 17 11142 built 1960
Motor Rail 4WDM 5906 built 1934
Hibberd 4WDM No. 10 (2555) (type 39) built 1946
Three 20-seat coaches, ex Southport Pier Railway built 1953
Six-seat open coach

¹Ex Dinorwic Slate Quarries Co. Ltd, Llanberis, Caernarfonshire, 1969. Not in service at present.

The railway was constructed in 1967 by a local group of narrow gauge railway enthusiasts and runs from Becconsall (off Station Road, Hesketh Bank) via Willow Tree Halt to Asland terminus. At present, passengers travel at their own risk – no fares are charged and no tickets issued.

## 261 Blackpool Coastal Tramway                B

Standard gauge electric tramway operated by Blackpool Corporation Transport Department, Blundell Street, Blackpool, Lancashire.
Tel: Blackpool 23931

The tramway extends just over 11 miles from South Shore, Blackpool, to Fleetwood Ferry. Frequent services are operated on the coastal tramway during the summer season with short journey cars increasing the frequency of the through service over parts of the route.
Stock includes single-deck railcars of several types, double-deck cars and single-deck cars hauling a trailer, all of modern design. During the summer season open 'boat' cars run on part of the system at the Blackpool end.
Special coastal, promenade and illuminations tours and tours using illuminated cars are also run.

## 262 Moseley Industrial Tramway Museum   B

Moseley Boys School, Northdowns Road, Cheadle, near Stockport, Greater Manchester

*Access:* Short walk from BR Cheadle Hulme Station
OS Ref: SJ 864871
Tel: 485-4372 (School)

Passenger-carrying 2 ft gauge railway, ⅓ mile in length, running round the side of the school playing field.
The railway operates on the second Sunday of every month from 10.30 am to 4 pm, or by appointment at any other time.
Facilities for visitors include car parking, museum and toilets. The project began as a school activity in 1969 under the direction of Mr Colin Saxton. For two years a horse tram was operated, originally single deck but later converted to double deck. This was novel, but expensive and inconvenient to operate, so a move to new premises in 1971 coincided with a change to 1 ft 8 in. gauge after the purchase of a railway system from a brickworks at Crowle in Lincolnshire. In 1974 the system was converted back to 2 ft gauge to enable more stock to be added. The railway has been extended and developed ever since.

**Stock**
Motor Rail 4WPM 4565 built 1928
Motor Rail 4WDM 7333 built 1938
Motor Rail 4WDM 7522 built 1948
Kent Construction Co. 4WDM built *c.* 1926
Ruston Hornsby 4WDM 462365 built 1960
Ruston Hornsby 4WDM 229647 built 1943
Ruston Hornsby 4WDM 223667 built 1943
Motor Rail 4WDM 8934 built 1944
Motor Rail 4WDM 7191 built 1937
Lister 4WPM 4404 built 1932
Motor Rail 4WDM 8663 built 1941
Motor Rail 4WDM 8878 built 1944
Motor Rail 4WDM 8937 built 1944
Two open bogie coaches ex Southport Pier Railway built 1953
4-seat open coach
9-seat open coach
Approx. 20 wagons, from 10¼ in. gauge static chain haulage tubs to skips and peat wagons, etc

## 263 Queens Pier Tramway   B

Ramsey, Isle of Man
OS Ref: SC 449947

A 3 ft gauge passenger-carrying line, almost half-a-mile long, operating during the summer months

*Owners:* Isle of Man Harbour Board, PO Box 11, Douglas, Isle of Man. Tel. Douglas 4336

*Operators:* Manx Electric Railway Society

*Fares:* Adults 3p; children 1p

**Stock**
Wickham 4WDM 20-seat railcar 5763 built 1947

Planet 4WPM 2027 built 1937
Bogie 'Toastrack' passenger coach built 1937
Covered baggage van
Six open wagons

The tramway runs the length of the pier and is single track throughout with a mid-way passing loop. At the seaward end it divides into two sidings of about 10 yards each. At the landward end, the tramway extends through the pierhead buildings and out into the street to enable baggage to be unloaded into road vehicles. At the shore end there is also a siding in which rolling stock not in use is stored.
The service in summer is from approximately 9 am until the pier closes at 10 pm, and this frequency is rather 'as and when required'. In practice this works out about every 15 minutes, except when a steamer berths – both vehicles then run a continuous shuttle service until all passengers and luggage are cleared. Queens Pier was opened in 1887 and is 2,245 ft long. The railway was originally intended to convey luggage only, but passenger stock was provided in 1937 and the railcar was added in 1950.

## 264 Pleasure Beach Railway, Blackpool   B

South Shore, Blackpool, Lancashire
OS Ref: SD 305332

Passenger-carrying, 1 ft 9 in. gauge line two-thirds-of-a-mile long, opened in 1934. The engineering works include four tunnels and a scale model of the Forth Bridge spanning the boating pool. The layout of the railway is similar in shape to a letter 'A' with the bar joining each leg of the 'A' in a triangle junction, enabling trains to be sent in either direction. Each leg of the 'A' ends in a turning loop. All points and signals are electrically operated and it is possible for three trains to operate at once, but only two are normally in service.
In 1970 the original station was replaced by another built in the LMS style of the 1920s. The elaborately-decorated steelwork originally formed the structure of the Pavilion on Southport Pier, whilst the booking office, ticket collectors' box and other station furniture are copies of items to be found on LMS stations in the Fylde area. The LMS colour scheme is used throughout.
The railway is in operation throughout the summer season from 10 am on weekdays and 2 pm on Sundays until approximately 11 pm at night.

**Stock**
Hudswell Clarke 4-6-4T No. 4473 *Carol Jean* (D579) built 1933
Hudswell Clarke 4-6-2 No. 6200 *Princess Royal* (D586) built 1935
Hudswell Clarke 4-6-2 No. 4472 *Mary Louise* (D578) built 1933
Twelve open six-seater bogie coaches
Pullman dining car
Two fuel-oil tank wagons
Two bogie flat wagons
Two four-wheel box vans
Six tipping skips

All three locomotives are steam outline, powered by diesel engines.

## 265 Morecambe Pleasure Park Railway    B

West End Promenade, Morecambe, Lancashire
OS Ref: SD 428639

Passenger-carrying 1 ft 8 in. gauge line, one-third-of-a-mile long, opened in April 1953 under the same management as the Blackpool Pleasure Beach Railway. This single-track railway has a circular loop at the eastern end, a turntable at the Promenade Station end and runs alongside the famous 'Cyclone Coaster'.
The line operates from Easter until October 10 am to approximately 10 pm.

**Stock**
Hudswell Clarke 4-6-4T No. 1932 *Robin Hood* (D570) built 1932
Hudswell Clarke 4-6-2 *May Thompson* (D582) built 1933
Four bogie open coaches
Fuel-oil tank wagon
Several goods wagons

Both locomotives are steam outline, powered by diesel engines.


## 266 Southport Pier Railway    B

Southport, Merseyside
OS Ref: SD 335176

A 900-yard, 60 cm gauge passenger-carrying line on Southport Pier operated by the County Borough of Southport, Town Hall, Southport, Lancashire PR8 1DA

**Stock**
Five-coach train built by Severn-Lamb Ltd in 1973 comprising a Bo-Bo DH locomotive, *English Rose*, permanently coupled to three open and one saloon bogie coaches. Seating capacity approximately 100.
Southport Pier is noteworthy as the first pier in this country to be constructed of iron, and it is also one of the longest in Great Britain, having a length of 1,211 yards. Work on the present pier commenced in August 1859 and the official opening took place in 1860.
There have been several railways and tramways on the pier during its history. The first was a cable tramway operated by a stationary engine opened as long ago as 1863. The 60 cm gauge line dates from 1954 and was operated by an eight-car train, *The Silver Belle*, consisting of a diesel-powered car at each end with four open and two closed coaches between. This train was retired in 1973 and replaced by the Severn-Lamb train described above.
The railway operates daily from Easter to October between 9 am and 10.45 pm. During the winter months an hourly service is operated from 10 am to dusk.


## 267 Port Erin Railway Museum    E

Strand Road, Port Erin, Isle of Man
*Access:* Adjacent to Port Erin Station, Isle of Man Railway

OS Ref: SC 198689
Museum of 3 ft gauge locomotives and rolling stock and smaller exhibits associated with the steam railways in the Isle of Man.
The Museum is open from May to September inclusive, 6 or 7 days a week. Operated by Isle of Man Railways assisted by members of the Isle of Man Railway Society (*q.v.*).
The Museum has a small souvenir shop. Refreshments and toilets are available at Port Erin Station.
The Museum was opened in 1975 in the former bus garage at Port Erin.

**Stock**
Beyer Peacock 2-4-0T IMR No. 1 *Sutherland* 1253 built 1873
Dulas 0-6-0T MNR No. 4 *Caledonia* 2178 built 1885
Beyer Peacock 2-4-0T IMR No. 16 *Mannin* 6296 built 1926
Isle of Man Railway coach No. F36 in which HM Queen Elizabeth II travelled in 1972
Isle of Man Railway coach No. F75 used in 1873 by the Duke of Sutherland.
[1]Manx Northern Railway 6-wheel Cleminson coach No. 3 built 1879.
There are numerous other small exhibits, ranging from documents, posters and photographs to signal windlasses, lamps and signals.

[1]Owned by the Isle of Man Railway Society.

### Isle of Man Railway Society    H

*Patron:* The Most Hon. the Marquess of Ailsa
*President:* J. J. Christian, Esq., MHK, Chairman Manx Electric Railway Board
*Details from:* R. P. Hendry, 4 Clifton Road, Rugby, Warwickshire
*Annual subscription:* Adults £2, Juniors & OAPs £1.25

The Society works in conjunction with IOM Railways to promote the Island's steam and electric railways, and is actively engaged in preservation. The Society has provided many exhibits for the two railway museums on the Island, the Port Erin Steam Museum, opened in 1975, and the Electric Railway Museum at Ramsey which opened on 31 May 1979. (See Group No. 271.)
With UK and Manx based officers, the Society is ideally placed to stimulate interest in the Island's railways, and members have the satisfaction of being involved with an ambitious preservation programme embracing steam, electric and even horse drawn vehicles. Funds are raised by subscriptions and a vigorous sales campaign of Manx railwayana. The Society owns a number of items of rolling stock which are not yet on display at either of the Museums. These are listed hereunder.

**Stock**
[1]Frames of Beyer Peacock 2-4-0T IMR No. 7 *Tynwald* 2038 built 1880
[2]Beyer Peacock 2-4-0T IMR No. 8 *Fenella* 3610 built 1894
Isle of Man Railway 4-wheel Gibbins accident crane built 1893

[1]No. 7 *Tynwald* was dismantled some thirty years ago and the superstructure has been scrapped. The frame has been preserved for use as an instructional exhibit in due course.

[2]No. 8 *Fenella* of 1894 was the last small boilered IMR engine to remain in service. She was withdrawn in 1968 and is to be restored by the Society.

## 268 Lytham Motive Power Museum and Lytham Creek Railway  BE

*Operator:* J. M. Morris, Helical Springs Ltd, Dock Road, Lytham, Lancashire
Tel. Lytham 7971

OS Ref: SD 381276

*Opening hours:* Mid-May to mid-October daily, except Monday and Friday, 11 am to 5 pm.

The collection embraces railway locomotives, cars and road engines, gas lamps, aircraft exhibits and a vintage model railway.

**Stock**
[1]NBR 0–4–0ST No. 42 (BR No. 68095) built 1887
[2]NB Locomotive Co. 0–4–0ST No. 20 (18386) built 1908
[3]Peckett 0–4–0ST *Miranda* (2087) built 1948
Peckett 0–4–0ST *Lytham No. 1* (2111) built 1949
[4]Neilson 0–4–0CT *Snipey* (4004) built 1890
[5]Vulcan Foundry 0–4–0ST *Vulcan* (3272) built 1918
[6]Hawthorn Leslie 0–4–0ST No. 3 *Penicuik* (3799) built 1935
[7]Hudswell Clarke 0–4–0ST *Ribble Cement No. 3* (1661) built 1936
[8]Sentinel 4WVBTG No. 7 *Susan* (9537) built 1951
Howard 4WPM *Hotto* (965) built 1930
LNER Pullman coach *Minerva* 1928
MR 12-ton locomotive coal wagon

[1]North British Railway 'G' Class (LNER Class Y9) withdrawn as BR No. 68095 from St Margarets shed, Edinburgh, in 1962.
[2]Owned by Bairds and Scottish Steel Ltd, Gartsherie, near Glasgow. It has been steamed occasionally since arrival and has received a temporary repaint.
[3]A 42-ton Peckett. Previously used at Courtaulds, Preston, and was last used for hauling coal to their power station. Formerly at Wolverhampton, where she was named *Daffyd*.

---

Yes, it is another little Peckett! This one, appropriately named *Lytham No. 1*, stands round the turntable at Lytham motive power museum with *Gartsherrie No. 20*

Photo: Roger Crombleholme

The livery is that of the Lancashire and Yorkshire Railway.
[4]Formerly Hodbarrow Mining Co. No. 6 *Snipey*, where it was until moved to Lytham in 1968. Since its arrival it has been used more than any of the other locomotives. The livery is that of the North Eastern Railway.
[5]Former works shunter at Vulcan Foundry, Newton-le-Willows. Originally intended as a narrow gauge locomotive. She was built in 1918 and named *Pax*. In later years a larger tank and a new chimney were added.
[6]Oil-fired locomotive used by the paper manufacturing firm of Alex Cowan Ltd, at Penicuik, near Edinburgh. Its present livery is that of the London, Brighton and South Coast Railway.
[7]Previously owned by Ribble Cement Co., at Clitheroe, Lancashire. She has been steamed on a number of occasions at Lytham. The livery is after the style of the LNWR as used on the locomotive *Greater Britain*.
[8]A Sentinal steam locomotive with a vertical boiler inside the cab. It has been steamed several times and has received no alterations since arrival from the Chesterfield Tube Co., apart from the addition of a number and a whistle from a BR Stanier 8F.

## Lytham Creek Railway

The 1 ft 10¾ in. gauge Lytham Creek Railway runs through the Motive Power Museum and is operated on Sundays. The railway is approximately one-third-of-a-mile in length and derives its name from its proximity to Lytham Creek, offering panoramic views of the Ribble estuary from the Pennines to the Fylde coast.

### Stock

Hudson-Hunslet 4WDM LOD758049 (2198) built 1940
Groudle Glen railway coach
Dinorwic Quarry slate wagons
NCB open coaches

### Road vehicle exhibits

The largest and most impressive of these is TB2847, a Burrell single-crank compound traction engine (2513) built in 1902. The veteran car is a 1933 Austin Saloon. The Leyland engines on display were supplied by the British Leyland Motor Corporation.

### Aircraft exhibits

These include a Cheetah engine; cylinders from a Hercules engine; propellers from a Britannia, Viscount and Flying Flea; wheels from a Junkers JU52; an ejector seat and an aircraft radar unit. Several models are on display, including one of the TSR2. The fullsize glider is a Slingsby Tutor and the cockpit is from a Spitfire. Parts of the first seaplane to fly from Lytham Creek are also on view. Outside are two operational aircraft, a Provost powered by an Alvis Leonides petrol engine and a T11 Vampire powered by a DH Goblin jet engine.

## 269   City of Liverpool Museum                       E

Merseyside County Museums
Lane Transport Gallery, William Brown Street, Liverpool
L3 8EN
OS Ref: SJ 349908

Standard gauge locomotives and rolling stock on static display.
*Open:* Weekdays 10 am-5 pm; Sundays 2 pm-5 pm. Admission free

The collection includes locomotives, steam tractors, a road-roller and a steam fire-pump

### Stock

LOR Bo-Bo electric coach No. 3
[1]L & MR 0-4-2 *Lion* (Todd, Kitson and Laird) built 1838
[2]Avonside 0-6-0ST *MD & HB No. 1* (1465) built 1904

[1]Originally Liverpool and Manchester Railway No. 57, becoming Grand Junction Railway No. 116 in 1845. Withdrawn as LNWR No. 116 in 1859 and sold to the Mersey Docks and Harbour Board for use as a pumping engine at Princes Dock. Taken out of service in 1928 and presented to the Liverpool Engineering Society in 1929. Restored by the LMS and put on display at Liverpool (Lime Street) Station in 1931. Removed to Crewe for storage in 1939 until returned to Liverpool in 1967. The locomotive has appeared in several films, principally as the 'star' of *The Titfield Thunderbolt*.
[2]Ex Mersey Docks and Harbour Board, 1969, after restoration at Brunswick Dock.

## 270   Hadlow Road Station Museum               E

Willaston-in-Wirral, Cheshire

This station on the former Birkenhead Railway Hooton-West Kirby line has been restored to LMS condition as part of the Wirral Country Park scheme.
The station and park are open all year round between 9 am and 6 pm
Tel: 051-648-4371
*Details from:* The Head Ranger, Wirral Country Park, Station Road, Thurstaston, Merseyside L61 0HW

Facilities for visitors include car parking and toilets as well as the 12-mile Country Park itself.

### The Character of the Park

A railway line once linked the towns of West Kirby and Hooton. It was twelve miles long and for seven of those miles it ran close to the Dee estuary before curving inland to Hooton. For nearly seventy years its cuttings echoed to the rumble of steam engines and carriages but today there are different sounds, for the abandoned railway is the backbone of a country park developed by Cheshire County Council and the Countryside Commission. A country park is a new idea. It is not a park with rose gardens, fountains and football pitches but a stretch of open countryside amid towns and farmland. It is a place to relax or take a closer look at nature. The Wirral Country Park is a place to walk, ride, picnic, camp and fish, too.
Each country park has its own personality. The Wirral Country Park is a place of contrasts. It has embankments open to the wind and sky with views across the Dee to the Welsh hills. It also has cuttings where trees form an arch overhead. It has mud flats and cliffs. This place of contrasts provides for a variety of wild life, from badgers and foxes

to the wading birds of the estuary and the frogs and newts of the ponds.

## 271   Ramsey Electric Railway Museum   E

Ramsey, Isle of Man
*Access:* Near Ramsey Station, Manx Electric Railway

A Museum of electric railway rolling stock and equipment, principally tracing the history of the electrically-worked lines in the Isle of Man.
The Museum is open from May to September inclusive, 6 or 7 days a week. Operated by Isle of Man Railways assisted by members of the Isle of Man Railway Society.

**Stock**
[1]MER BoBoE No. 23 built Derby Castle 1900
[2]MER Bogie freight car No. 26 (ex-passenger car No. 10) built 1895

[1]No. 23 of 1900 is the oldest preserved bogie locomotive in the British Isles. She was built at Derby Castle works, the only locomotive to have been built in the IOM, and is owned by the Isle of Man Railway Society.
[2]Built as a passenger car in 1895 and withdrawn in 1902 for conversion to freight use. In store since 1944 and restored by the Isle of Man Railway Society in 1979.

## 272   Salford Metropolitan District Council E

George Thorns Recreation Centre, Liverpool Road, Irlam, Greater Manchester
OS Ref: SJ 722943

Standard gauge steam locomotive on static display.

**Stock**
Peckett 0-4-0F 2155 built 1955
Presented by CWS Ltd, Irlam Soap Works, 1969.

## 273   Delph Station   E

Mr Alf Hall, Delph Station, Oldham, Greater Manchester
OS Ref: SD 987074

Standard gauge static exhibits on a 75-yard length of track
**Stock**
[1]Hunslet 0-6-0ST *Brookes No. 1* (2387) built 1941
BR Mk 1 bogie coach
Oil tank wagon
Goods brake van

[1]Ex Brookes Ltd, Chemical Works, Lightcliffe, Yorkshire, 1972.

## 274   Skelmersdale New Town   E
## Development Corporation

Skelmersdale, Lancashire

Standard gauge steam locomotives on static display.

**Stock**
[1]Peckett 0-4-0ST *Daphne* (737) built 1899
[2]Avonside 0-6-0ST MDHB No. 26 (1810) built 1918

[1]Presented by Pilkington Brothers Ltd, St Helens, 1966. At New Church Farm Play Area (OS Ref: SD 477061)
[2]Presented by Mersey Docks and Harbour Board, Liverpool, 1969. At Digmoor Shopping Parade Play Area (OS Ref: SD 497048)

## 275   Ulverston   E

Cumbria Education Committee, Stone Cross Special School, Ulverston, Cumbria
OS Ref: SD 283783

Standard gauge steam locomotive on static display.

**Stock**
Furness Railway 0-4-0ST No. 17 (Sharp Stewart 1585) built 1865
Presented by Barrow Hematite Steel Works Ltd, 1960. Originally a Furness Railway 0-4-0 tender loco No. 25

## 276   Barrow-in-Furness   E

Cumbria Education Committee, George Hastwell Training Centre, Abbey Road, Barrow-in-Furness, Cumbria.
OS Ref: SD 208711

Standard gauge steam locomotive on static display.

**Stock**
Furness Railway 0-4-0ST No. 7 *Chloe* (Sharp Stewart 1435) built 1863
Presented by Barrow Hematite Steel Works Ltd, 1960. Originally a Furness Railway 0-4-0 tender loco No. 18

## 277   Red Rose Live Steam Group   G

Standard gauge locomotives in store at present
**Stock**
[1]Avonside 0-4-0ST 1563 built 1908
[2]Ruston Hornsby 4WDM 244580 built 1946 (48DS Class)
[3]Wigan Coal and Iron 0-6-0ST *Lindsay* built 1887

[1]Ex Millom Hermatite Ore and Iron Co Ltd, Hodbarrow Mine, Cumberland, 1968. Located at a farm near Newton-le-Willows, Greater Manchester.
[2]Ex Park Webb Ltd, Ince Forge, Wigan 1974. Located at 'The Willows' Children's Home, Skelmersdale, Lancs.
[3]Ex Maudland Metals Ltd, Preston 1976. Located at Quaker House Colliery, Orrell, Lancs.

The Group was formed in 1972 with the aim of establishing in Wigan a museum of industrial steam engines and a short light railway. Until the 1950s, Wigan was one of the main centres of coalmining and heavy industry, as well as being a major cotton town. Now there are few remains of this era when the steam engine was the chief source of power and the Group hopes to assemble a representative selection of engines and exhibits.

## 278   Liverpool Light Railway Society          G

Two-foot gauge locomotive in store near Southport, Merseyside

**Stock**
Lister 4WPM 27411 built 1945

## 279   CEGB North Western Area                   I

Standard gauge Industrial steam locations, some featuring regular steam working.

**Stock**
Barclay 0-6-0F No. 1 *Lancaster* (1572) built 1917 Heysham Power Station
Barclay 0-4-0F No. 2 1950 built 1928 Heysham Power Station
Barclay 0-6-0F *Sir James* (1550) built 1917 Fleetwood Power Station
Barclay 0-6-0F *Lord Ashfield* (1989) built 1930 Fleetwood Power Station
Bagnall 0-4-0F *Huncoat No. 1* (2989) built 1951 Huncoat Power Station
Bagnall 0-4-0F *Huncoat No. 2* (3022) built 1951 Huncoat Power Station
Hawthorn Leslie 0-6-0F *Huncoat No. 3* (3746) built 1929 Huncoat Power Station
RSH 0-4-0ST *Agecroft No. 1* (7416) built 1948 Agecroft Power Station
RSH 0-4-0ST *Agecroft No. 2* (7485) built 1948 Agecroft Power Station
RSH 0-4-0ST *Agecroft No. 3* (7681) built 1951 Agecroft Power Station

## 280   Cheshire Transport Society                G

Runcorn, Cheshire
Standard gauge steam locomotive in store

**Stock**
Barclay 0-4-0ST 1964 built 1929
Ex CPC (UK) Ltd, Cornflour Manufacturers, Trafford Park, Manchester 1979

## 281   National Coal Board                        I

North Western Area
Industrial steam locations featuring regular steam working.

**Stock**
Hunslet 0-6-0ST *Whiston* 3694 built 1950 (Bold Colliery, St Helens)

Hunslet 0-6-0ST *Alison* 3885 built 1970 (Bold Colliery, St Helens)
Hunslet 0-6-0ST *Hurricane* 3830 built 1955 (Walkden Area Central Workshops, Worsley)
Hunslet 0-6-0ST *Warrior* 3823 built 1954 (Bickershaw Colliery, Leigh)
RSH 0-6-0ST *Gwyneth* 7135 built 1944 (Bickershaw Colliery, Leigh)
Hunslet 0-6-0ST *Respite* 3696 built 1950 (Bickershaw Colliery, Leigh)
Hunslet 0-6-0ST No. 8 *Bickershaw* 3776 built 1952 (Bickershaw Colliery, Leigh)
Hudswell Clarke 0-6-0ST No. 7 *Robert* 1752 built 1943 (Bold Colliery, St Helens)

## 282   British Nuclear Fuels Ltd                  I

Windscale Research Centre, Cumbria
OS Ref: NY 025034

Standard gauge industrial steam location with steam locomotive spare to the diesels.

**Stock**
Peckett 0-4-0ST No. 1 (Class W7) 2027 built 1942
Hill 0-4-0DH 108c built 1961
Fowler 0-4-0DM 22919 built 1940

## 283   Glaxo Laboratories Ltd                     I

Ulverston, Cumbria
OS Ref: SO 30677

Standard gauge industrial steam location featuring regular steam working.

**Stock**
Barclay 0-4-0F *Glaxo* 2268 built 1949

## 284   Halton Miniature Railway                   B

Runcorn, Cheshire

A passenger-carrying 7¼ in. gauge miniature railway under construction.

*Details from:* Mr J. Goulden, 55 Victoria Road, Runcorn, Cheshire.

**Stock**
Goulden 0-4-0PM *Pixie* built 1976

## 285   J. K. Holt & Gordon Ltd                    G

Scrap Merchants, Chequerbent, Westhoughton, Greater Manchester
OS Ref: SD 674062

Standard gauge steam locomotives in store pending scrapping.

**Stock**
[1]Hudswell Clarke 0-6-0ST *Harry* 1776 built 1944
[2]Avonside 0-6-0ST 1600 built 1912

[1]Ex NCB Walkden 1976.
[2]Ex NCB Cronton Colliery 1965.


## 286   British Gypsum Ltd                    I

Cocklakes Works, Cumwhinton, Cumbria
OS Ref: NY 457512

Standard gauge industrial steam location with locomotive stored out of use.

**Stock**
Barclay 0-4-0ST WST 2361 built 1954
Barclay 0-4-0DH *B.G.* 559 built 1970


## 287   Carrex Metals                         G

Scrap Merchants, Regent Street, Rochdale, Greater Manchester
OS Ref: SD 900140

Standard gauge steam locomotive in store pending scrapping.

**Stock**
Hawthorn Leslie 0-6-0F *Hartshead* 3805 built 1932
Ex CEGB, Hartshead Power Station, 1976.


## 288   Stockport                             G

Mr P. Blackham, Stockport, Greater Manchester

Private 15 in. gauge steam locomotive in store

**Stock**
K. L. Guinness 4-6-2 *Blue Pacific* built c 1935

Mr Blackham proposes to build a 15 in. gauge railway between Stockport Sewage Works and the BR line at Cheadle Heath.


## 289   R. J. Harrison                        G

Border Poultry Farms Ltd, Harraby Green Road, Harraby Green, near Carlisle, Cumbria

OS Ref: NY 413543

2 ft gauge locomotives in store.

**Stock**
Deutz 4WDM 181299 built 1932
Hunslet 4WDM 2577 built 1942


## 290   Knowsley Hall Safari Park             B

Knowsley Hall, Prescott, Merseyside
*Access:* 7 miles east of Liverpool, off the A580

Passenger-carrying 15 in. gauge miniature railway, ¼ mile in length.
The park is open daily from 10.30 am to 6.30 pm (in winter 10 am to sunset).

The railway at Knowsley Hall formerly operated at Alexandra Palace, London, until 1970. It runs from the Amusement Park in a balloon loop, passing through a wood alongside the sealion pool.

**Stock**
Barlow 4-6-2DM *Duke of Edinburgh* built 1950
Five open bogie coaches


## 291   Blackpool Zoo Miniature Railway       B

'World of Animals' Zoological Gardens, Stanley Park, Great Marton, Blackpool, Lancs
OS Ref: SD 335362

Passenger-carrying 15 in. gauge miniature railway, nearly 1 mile in length.

**Stock**
Severn-Lamb 2-8-0PM No. 279 7219 built 1972
Open bogie coaches


## 292   Lakeside Miniature Railway            B

Marine Lake, Southport, Merseyside
OS Ref: SD 331174

A 15 in. gauge line dating from May 1911 and now extending to approximately three-quarters-of-a-mile in length. The line opened under the auspices of the Bassett-Lowke associate company, Narrow Gauge Railways Limited, but in 1913 passed to G. V. Llewelyn and in the early 1930s was re-sold to H. N. Barlow. A disastrous fire in 1938 damaged the two original steam locomotives and much of the line's rolling stock.
Normally, three trains are in operation simultaneously, a 'staff' system being employed to ensure that only one occupies each single line section at a time. Operation commences at Easter, then each weekend until Spring Bank Holiday, then daily until mid-September, thereafter at weekends until the end of October, weather permitting.

**Stock**
Barlow 4-6-2DE *Duke of Edinburgh* built 1948 (steam outline).
Severn-Lamb Co-Co DM *Princess Anne* built 1971
Barlow 4-6-2DE *Golden Jubilee 1911-61* built 1963 (steam outline)
Barlow 4-6-2DE *Prince Charles* (steam outline)
Eighteen bogie open coaches including vehicles from the Far Tottering & Oyster Creek Railway built 1951.

### 293    Fleetwood Miniature Railway                    B

The Promenade, Fleetwood, Lancashire
OS Ref: SD 319481

A one mile long, 15 in. gauge passenger-carrying line running from the promenade car park at Mount Road along the sea front to the west side of the boating lake at Laidleys Walk. Opened in July 1975.

**Stock**
Severn-Lamb 2-8-0PH No. 278 *Rio Grande* (7218) built 1972
Five 16-seat bogie coaches

### 294    The 'Brighton Belle' Inn                        E

Winsford, Cheshire

Coach in use as a restaurant

**Stock**
SR Pullman car No. S2835 (ex 'Brighton Belle' set No. 3053) built 1932

### 295    The 'Yew Tree' Inn                              E

Rochdale, Lancashire

Coach in use as a restaurant

**Stock**
Pullman car *Aries* built c.1923
Bought in 1969 and installed on site.

### 296    Heaton Park Tramway                             B

Heaton Park, off Middleton Road, Manchester
*Access:* Frequent buses from City Centre

A passenger-carrying standard gauge electric tramway, 300 yards in length consisting of double track laid on a reservation alongside the carriage drive leading into Heaton Park from Middleton Road.
Operation is on Sunday afternoons throughout the year.
The tramway is operated by Manchester Transport Museum Society and its construction was supported by grants from Greater Manchester County Council. The Heaton Park route of the Manchester Tramway system was closed in 1934, but instead of the track being lifted, it was covered in tarmac for use as a bus terminal. The tarmac covering has now been stripped away to reveal the track in good order and poles and overhead wiring replaced. Society members have laid a new siding into a storage building and restored electrical power to the system. The tramway opened for public operation on 2 September 1979.

**Stock**
Manchester single-deck semi-saloon bogie tramcar No. 765

Also on display are a Manchester horse bus (built c 1890), a Thorneycroft Tower Wagon and a Lacre 3-wheeled road sweeper.

### 297    Ramsey, Isle of Man                             G

Mr J. Edwards, Ballakillingan Farm, Churchtown, near Ramsey, Isle of Man

Privately-preserved 3 ft gauge steam locomotive undergoing restoration.

**Stock**
Beyer Peacock 2-4-0T MNR No. 3 *Thornhill* 2028 built 1880.
Purchased from the Isle of Man Railway as IMR No. 14 in 1979.

# AREA G

## Wales

Gwynedd
Clwyd
Powys
Dyfed
Gwent
Glamorgan
Anglesey

---

### 301    Festiniog Railway                                          A

Porthmadog Harbour Station, Porthmadog, Gwynedd

*Access:* BR Stations at Porthmadog, Minffordd and Blaenau Ffestiniog
Crosville bus services operate to Porthmadog or Tanygrisiau from Blaenau Ffestiniog, Dolgellau, Caernarfon, Pwllheli and Criccieth
Tel: Porthmadog 2384
OS Ref: SH 584379

Passenger-carrying 1 ft 11½ in. gauge railway, 12¼ miles in length, from Porthmadog to Tanygrisiau.
Trains run daily from April to October inclusive.

Photo: Norman Gurley

A scene that spells Festiniog. Essential ingredients, a double Fairlie, some louvred-window coaches, and a mountain backdrop

*Facilities offered* – Museum at Porthmadog. Shops at Porthmadog, Tan-y-Bwlch and Tanygrisiau. Refreshments on trains, and at Porthmadog, Tan-y-Bwlch. Car parks at Porthmadog, Tan-y-Bwlch and Tanygrisiau. Toilets at Porthmadog, Tan-y-Bwlch and Tanygrisiau. Information bureaux at Porthmadog (Railway and Wales Tourist Board). Nature trail at Tan-y-Bwlch.
The historic Festiniog Railway was built to the plans of James Spooner, to convey slate from the mountains around Blaenau Ffestiniog to the new harbour at Porthmadog. It was opened in 1836.
The line was constructed on a continuously falling gradient from Blaenau Ffestiniog so that the laden trains of slate could run by gravity. The returning empties were hauled up the hill by horses. The Festiniog Railway pioneered the use of steam traction on the 2 ft gauge in 1863. Three out of the four locomotives built at that time are still extant. The first double Fairlie locomotive was introduced in 1869; the outcome of ever increasing traffic. The first bogie carriages to be used in the UK were introduced on the Festiniog Railway in 1872. In the twentieth century the slate trade went into a decline and tourists and holiday makers began to provide the railway with an increasing amount of traffic. By the end of the last war the line was in such a delapidated condition that the Company was unable to restore services. With the exception of a small amount of track in Blaenau Ffestiniog, used by the slate quarries, the line closed in 1946. A new administration obtained control of the Company in 1954 and the Festiniog Railway Society Ltd was formed to assist it in the formidable task of restoring and reopening the derelict railway. Passenger services between Porthmadog and Boston Lodge were resumed on 23 July 1955 and they have been progressively extended to their new (1978) limit at Tanygrisiau.

The Company and the Society have never wavered in their determination to reopen the whole railway to Blaenau Ffestiniog. The completion of the deviation route from Dduallt to Tanygrisiau means that the end is in sight.

## Festiniog Railway Society
*Details from:* J. C. Locke, 23 Faraday Avenue, Sidcup, Kent DA14 4JB
*Subscription:* Full £4; Junior £2; Life £100. Members receive a quarterly magazine and three free 3rd class return journeys (Life members – unlimited free 1st class travel)
*No. of Members:* 5,600

With so many notable 'firsts' to its credit, it's difficult to sum up the Festiniog Railway's special claims to fame in just a few words. However, it does operate the only spiral on a passenger carrying railway in the UK (at Dduallt); the first bogie coaches in the UK (1872) still in service; the only known double Fairlie locomotives still in service in the world.

The Festiniog Railway Society Limited is the supporting organisation to the Railway Company. The principal means of this support have so far been by raising funds and providing voluntary labour. Originally simply called the Festiniog Railway Society, at the end of 1954 a similar organisation was registered as a company limited by guarantee and incorporated as a non-profit-distributing company. For most practical purposes the two are synonymous, but the Festiniog Railway Society (not limited) had to remain in existence to provide status for members under the age of 21 (now 18) and to umbrella the formation of regional Groups. The term 'Society' is normally used to cover both bodies indiscriminately, whilst the term 'Company' is normally applied to refer to the Railway Company, rather than the Society Limited. The Groups mentioned have been formed to organise and co-ordinate practical support on a local basis; over the years their number had already increased until one existed in almost every area of high population in England and Wales, and now endeavours are in hand to form additional ones on a much more localised basis, to cover a still greater proportion of the Society's membership. It can indeed be said truthfully that much of the present-day success of the Festiniog Railway is due to the financial and practical aid given by the Society and its Groups.

## Stock
[1]George England 0–4–0STT *Princess* built 1863
[2]George England 0–4–0STT *Prince* built 1863
[3]George England 0–4–0STT *Welsh Pony* built 1867
FR 0–4–4–0T *Merddin Emrys* built 1879
[4]FR 0–4–4–0T *Livingston Thompson* built 1886
[5]Hunslet 2–4–0STT *Blanche* 589 built 1893
[5]Hunslet 2–4–0STT *Linda* 590 built 1893
[6]Hunslet 0–4–0ST *Britomart* 707 built 1899
[7]Alco 2–6–2PT *Mountaineer* 57156 built 1916
[8]Peckett 0–6–0ST *Volunteer* 2050 built 1944
[9]FR 0–4–4–0T *Earl of Merioneth/Iarll Meirionnydd* built 1979
Baldwin 2–4–0DM *Moelwyn* 49604 built 1918
Simplex 4WDM *Mary Ann* 596 built 1917
Hibberd 4WDM *Upnor Castle* 3687 built 1954

Ruston Hornsby 4WDM *Andrew* 193984 built 1939
Ruston Hornsby 4WDM *Alistair* 201970 built 1940
Simplex 4WDM *Jane* 8565 built 1940
Hunslet 4WDM *Tyke* 2290 built 1941
Hunslet 0–4–0DM *Moel Hebog* 4113 built 1955
Simplex 4WDM *Diana* 21579 built 1957
Lister 4WDM 41545 built 1954
FR 4 wheeled passenger brake van No. 1 built 1964
FR 4 wheeled goods brake van No. 2
FR 4 wheeled knifeboard coaches Nos 3, 4, 5, 6 and 7 built 1864–67
FR 4 wheeled quarrymen's coach No. 8
GWR 4 wheeled luggage/stores van No. 59 (ex W & LLR, built 1923 for V of RR)
FR brake/third bogie coach No. 10 built 1872
FR brake/first observation coach No. 11 built 1880
FR buffet/3rd saloon No. 12 built 1880
Buffet/3rd saloon No. 14 built 1897 for Lynton & Barnstaple Railway
FR 1st/3rd composite bogie coaches Nos 15 and 16 built 1972
FR 1st/3rd composite bogie coaches Nos 17 and 18 built 1876
FR 1st/3rd composite bogie coaches Nos 19 and 20 built 1879
FR 3rd bogie coach No. 22 built 1896
3rd bogie coaches Nos 23 and 26 built 1894 for North Wales Narrow Gauge Railway
FR brake/1st observation coaches Nos 100 and 101 built 1965 and 1970
FR buffet/3rd saloon No. 103 built 1968
FR 1st/3rd composite bogie coaches Nos 104 and 106 built 1964 and 1968
FR 1st/3rd/lav. composite bogie coach No. 105 built 1966
FR 3rd tourist open bogie coaches Nos 37 and 38 built 1971 and 1972
FR 3rd saloon bogie coach No. 110 built 1975 – push-pull fitted FR 1st/3rd composite bogie coach No. 116 built 1972
FR 3rd saloon bogie coaches Nos 117 and 118 built 1977
FR 3rd saloon/lav. bogie coaches Nos 119 and 120 built 1979 and 1980

[1]On display opposite the BR station at North Western Road, Blaenau Ffestiniog.
[2]Major overhaul and rebuild completed, 1979.
[3]Awaiting restoration.
[4]Until recently known as *Earl of Merioneth/Iarll Meirionnydd*, and previously as *Taliesin*. Awaiting restoration as museum piece.
[5]Built as 0–4–0ST for the Penrhyn Quarry Railway. Purchased 1963. *Linda* previously on loan for Summer, 1962.
[6]Ex Penyorsedd Quarry. Privately owned.
[7]Ex Tramway de Pithiviers a Toury (Central France) and previously War Department tramways (during First World War). Acquired 1967.
[8]Ex Harrogate Gas Works, 1957. Name not carried. Awaiting restoration.
[9]Constructed around a new boiler built by the Hunslet Engine Co. in 1969. Mainly new construction but some parts, primarily power bogie frames, from *Livingston Thompson*.

Llanfair Caereinion Station, Powys

*Access:* Infrequent Crosville bus service from Welshpool BR station; railway runs parallel to A458
Tel: Llanfair Caereinion (0938-82) 441
OS Ref: SJ 107069

A five-and-a-half-mile 2 ft 6 in. gauge passenger-carrying line from Llanfair Caereinion to Sylfaen ultimately to extend as far as Welshpool (Raven Square). The railway operates at weekends from Easter to October, daily from June to September and at Bank Holidays.
*Facilities:* Car parks at Llanfair and Castle Caereinion; refreshments and railway shop at Llanfair.
This line, authorised by a Light Railway Order granted in 1899, was opened for goods traffic on 9 March 1903. Passenger services started a month later on 4 April, when the line was officially opened. Just over nine miles in length and running for a short distance over the site of a tramway built by the then Earl of Powis as early as 1818, the line was operated in turn by the Cambrian Railways, the Great Western Railway and British Railways. Passenger services ceased as long ago as 7 February 1931 but, unlike most narrow-gauge railways, the Welshpool and Llanfair was not built to serve a specific industry and until its closure on 5 November 1956 it carried a considerable tonnage of coal and general agricultural traffic, including both sheep and cattle.

The railway is operated by the Welshpool and Llanfair Light Railway Preservation Co. Ltd.
*Details from:* Publicity Officer at Llanfair Station
*Membership:* 1200

---

A sylvan scene on the banks of the Banwy as *The Countess* hurries along the Welshpool and Llanfair line with an afternoon train to Castle Caereinion

Photo: Allan Stewart

**Stock**
Beyer Peacock 0-6-0T No. 1 *The Earl* 3496 built 1903
Beyer Peacock 0-6-0T No. 2 *The Countess* 3497 built 1903
Bagnall 0-4-4-0T No. 6 *Monarch* 3024 built 1953
Drewry 6WDM No. 7 *Chattenden* 2263 built 1949
Barclay 0-4-0T No. 8 *Dougal* 2207 built 1946
Franco-Belge 0-8-0T No. 10 *Sir Drefaldwyn* 2855 built 1944
Hunslet 4WDM No. 11 *Raven* 2251 built 1940
Kerr Stuart 0-6-2T No. 12 *Joan* 4404 built 1927
Hunslet 2-6-2T No. 14 3815 built 1954
Ruston Hornsby 4WDM (16/20 HP Class) 191680 built 1938
Wickham 4WPMR 2904 built 1940
Bogie coach ex Chattenden and Upnor Railway built 1957
Five four-wheeled coaches ex Zillertalbahn, Austria, built 1900-27
Three ex-W & LIR open wagons
Two ex-W & LIR closed vans
One ex-W & LIR cattle wagon
Two ex-W & LIR brake vans
Seven ex-Chattenden and Upnor Railway bogie wagons
Four Sierra Leone Government Railway bogie coaches Nos 1040, 1048, 1066 and 1207 built 1960
Admiralty four-wheeled brake vans Nos 210 and 211
Also BR/Thompson first-class sleeping car E1260E used for volunteer accommodation

The Welshpool and Llanfair Light Railway is notable nowadays for its international collection of narrow gauge rolling stock. Trains are composed of locomotives and carriages from as far afield as Austria, Antigua and Sierra Leone. At present the company is fully committed to completion of its Welshpool extension project.
The length of the railway involved in the extension is 2 miles 1100 yd. The track is being renewed over the whole of the distance from Welshpool to Sylfaen as it is considered essential that it should conform with current operating standards before services begin. A fresh bed of ballast is being laid throughout as a foundation, and new sleepers will be used. Approximately 1500 tons of stone will be required, and 5000 sleepers. The only materials that will be re-used are the rails, which are still fit to carry many years traffic. The earthworks are generally in sound condition, and considerable work has already been completed on culvert reconstruction.
At Welshpool, the new station is being built at Raven Square, on the western edge of the town. The site is alongside the A458 Welshpool-Dolgellau trunk road and the terminus has been designed specifically to suit the tourist traffic which is the lifeblood of the railway. It is a picturesque area, alongside the Sylfaen Brook and bordered by the Powis Castle Estate. The additional land required has been leased to the Company by Powis Estates. The stream has been diverted to give the maximum usable area, as the station facilities will include a large car and coach park. For passengers, there will be a souvenir shop and booking office, and also an attractive picnic area. As the proposed service will require an engine to be kept at Welshpool, a small engine shed has been incorporated in the plans.

## 303 Rheilffordd Llyn Padarn (Llanberis Lake Railway)  A

Gilfach Ddu, Llanberis, Gwynedd

A two-mile 1 ft 11½ in. gauge passenger-carrying line from Llanberis (Gilfach Ddu) to Penllyn following the trackbed of the former Padarn Railway. Opened in 1971
*Access:* Bangor BR Station, thence by bus to Llanberis. To reach the railway leave the A4086 main road almost opposite the Snowdon Railway Station in Llanberis. Follow the signposts down the private approach road to the station at Padarn Park (Gilfach Ddu).
Tel: Llanberis 549
OS Ref: SH 586603

The railway operates daily from Easter to the first Sunday in October. Facilities for visitors include car parking, souvenir shop, picnic area at Cei Llydan, refreshments and toilets.
The Llanberis Lake Railway was the first of the new generation of 'Great Little Trains of Wales' and was constructed to very high standards of workmanship during the early part of 1971. Motive power comes from former Dinorwic slate quarry locomotives assisted by small diesels from a variety of industrial sources, but the railway had to construct all its own passenger carriages prior to the inauguration of services. Operation of the railway is interesting in that westbound trains do not stop at the intermediate station of Cei Llydan but proceed direct to Penllyn where passengers may not alight due to narrow clearances. On the return journey, the train halts at Cei Llydan where passengers may alight to make use of the lakeside picnic area. The railway runs alongside the very edge of the lake and gives unsurpassed views of the Snowdon mountain range.

### Stock
Hunslet 0–4–0ST No. 1 *Elidir* 493 built 1889
Hunslet 0–4–0ST No. 2 *Wild Aster* 849 built 1904
Hunslet 0–4–0ST No. 3 *Dolbadarn* 1430 built 1922
Henschel 0–4–0T No. 5 *Helen Kathryn* 28035 built 1948
[1]Jung 0–4–0WT No. 6 *Ginnette Marie* 7509 built 1937
Ruston Hornsby 4WDM No. 12 *Mor Leidr* 375315 (Class ODL) built 1954
Ruston Hornsby 4WDM No. 11 *Cernyw* 200748 (Class 33/40 HP) built 1940
Ruston Hornsby 4WDM No. 10 *Yr Enfys* 297030 built 1952
Motor Rail 4WDM No. 14 *Rhydychen* 11177 (Type 60S) built 1961
Motor Rail 4WDM No. 9 *Dolgarrog* 22154 built 1962
Ruston Hornsby 4WDM 441427 built 1961
Ruston Hornsby 4WDM 425796 built 1958
Ruston Hornsby 4WDM No. 8 *Twll Coed* 268878 built 1952
Motor Rail 4WDM 8788 built 1943
Motor Rail 4WDM No. 16 *W. R. Williams* 21513 built 1935
Motor Rail 4WDM No. 17 *Garret* 7902 built 1939
Motor Rail 4WDM No. 18 *Braich* 7927 built 1941
Ruston Hornsby 4WDM No. 19 *Llanelli* 451901 (Class 48DLG) built 1961
13 bogie coaches
8 ballast wagons
7 FR slate wagons
6 tipping and flat trucks
5 FR slab trucks
Passenger brake van rebuilt from Motor Rail 4WDM 5861 built 1934

[1]This locomotive is now for sale.

### North Wales Quarrying Museum

Gilfach Ddu, Llanberis, Gwynedd

*Access:* Alongside Gilfach Ddu terminus of Llanberis Lake Railway

A Museum of equipment, machinery and small exhibits tracing the history of the slate-quarrying industry in North Wales. On display is a 1 ft 11½ in. gauge steam locomotive.

### Stock
Hunslet 0–4–0ST *Una* 873 built 1905

The Museum is housed in the former maintenance workshops for the Dinorwic Slate Quarry – the largest slate quarry in the world. After the quarry closed in 1969, a scheme was prepared to transform the Gilfach Ddu area into a major tourist attraction, and a five-year plan to create a Country Park is now under way. The workshop buildings are now open to the public as a quarrying museum, and we are certain that you will find a visit most rewarding. This museum is operated by the National Museum of Wales, and not by the Lake Railway Company.

## 304 Rheilffordd Llyn Tegid (Bala Lake Railway)  A

Llanuwchllyn Station, Gwynedd

*Access:* Off the A494 from Bala to Dolgellau, 5 miles from Bala. Turn left at garage (signposted)
Tel: Llanuwchllyn (06784) 666
OS Ref: SH 881300

A 4½ mile, 1 ft 11½ in. gauge passenger-carrying line opened on 13 Aug 1972 along the trackbed of the former GWR Morfa Mawddach–Ruabon line between Llanuwchllyn and Bala. The Bala Lake Railway, one of the latest of the 'Great Little Trains of Wales', has been built solely for tourist traffic, though a pleasing development is the growing support from local residents along the lakeside, who use it as a convenient method of transport to and from Bala.
The railway operates from Easter to the end of September daily from 10 am to 6 pm.
Facilities for visitors include railway shop, car parking, refreshments and toilets.
Seven years after BR closed the entire length of the Ruabon–Barmouth Jct. Line (54 miles), the Bala Lake Railway started operating trains from Llanuwchllyn to Pentrepiod (1¼ m), and on to Llangower (2 m) within six months, and extended to Pant-yr-hen-felin (3 m) in 1976, and reached Bala (Llyn Tegid) in 1977 (4½m).
We aim to be in Bala near Loch Café in 1980, distance then 5¼m.

Trains run daily from Easter to late September, with special Steam Gala Days in May and September, when two trains are in service.

The scenery along the route is probably the finest in the North Wales area, and is seen to advantage along the south shore of the Lake.

Steam and Diesel hauled trains run on the line, and provide a service to the many Camping and Caravan Sites alongside the Lake, also to the small Housing Estate at Llangower.

Modern Corridor Coaching stock is used on the line, plus Open and Closed Carriages, providing a choice of comfortable travel.

Historic Wagons and items of equipment are on view at Llanuwchllyn, and the Signalling is mainly ex L&Y, however new signals started being made to the Company's own design in 1978.

Special evening Guided Tour trips are run on summer evenings for local Caravan and Camping Site patrons, and they are well supported.

*General Manager:* G. H. Barnes, 'Yr Orsaf', Llanuwchllyn, Bala, Gwynedd.

The Railway is supported by Cymdeithas Rheilffordd Llyn Tegid (Bala Lake Railway Society).

*Details from:* Mr C. Bie, 24 Chestnut Close, Chester
*Membership:* 160
*Subscriptions:* Life member, £15, family member (husband and wife), £1.75 per annum; adult member, £1.15 per annum; junior member (under 17), 75p per annum.

## Stock

Hunslet 0-4-0ST *Holy War* 779 built 1902
[1]Hunslet 0-4-0ST *Alice* 780 built 1902
[2]Hunslet 0-4-0ST *Maid Marian* 822 built 1903 (1 ft 11½ in. gauge)
[3]Hunslet 0-4-0ST *Jonathan* 678 built 1898
Ruston Hornsby 4WDM No. 2 182137 (20 HP Class) built 1936
Ruston Hornsby 4WDM 189972 built 1938
Hunslet 4WDM 1974 built 1939
Ruston Hornsby 4WDM 209430 built 1942
Ruston Hornsby 4WDM No. 3 *Invicta* 200744 built 1940
Motor Rail 4WDM 5821 built 1934
Ruston Hornsby 4WDM 283512 built 1949
Ruston Hornsby 4WDM 194771 built 1939
Hibberd 4WDM 2544 built 1942
Hudson 4WDM 38384 built *c.* 1930
Lister Blackstone 4WDM No. 2 *Alister* 44052 built 1958
Severn-Lamb/Leyland Bo-BoDH No. 4 *Meirionedd* 7322 built 1973
Two 'toastrack' covered bogie coaches built 1972
Three enclosed bogie saloon coaches built 1978
Three compartment bogie coaches built 1973-75
Eight slate wagons
Two flat wagons converted from slate trucks
FR Gunpowder van

[1]Frames and parts only. To be rebuilt as an 0-4-2 tender locomotive in due course.
[2]Ex Dinorwic Slate Quarries Co. Ltd, Llanberis, Caernarfonshire, 1968. Run on the Bressingham Narrow Gauge Railway until the end of 1971 and on the Llanberis Lake Railway

until 1975. Owned by the Maid Marian Locomotive Fund (*q.v.*).
[3]Built by Hunslet in 1898 and completely restored after its purchase from Dinorwic Quarry, Caernarfonshire, who had been its sole owners and where it was named Bernstein. Ran on the Lytham Creek Railway until 1979.

**Maid Marian Locomotive Fund**
Rheilffordd Llyn Tegid, Bala, Gwynedd

*Details from:* Douglas C. Carrington, 223 Sunnybank Road, Unsworth, Bury, Lancashire BL9 8JU

## 305   Vale of Rheidol Railway   A
## (Lein Fach Cwm Rheidol)

Aberystwyth, Dyfed
British Rail's only narrow gauge passenger line, 11¾ miles long, one class only, operated by steam traction.

*Access:* Aberystwyth BR Station
Tel: Aberystwyth 2377
OS Ref: SN 587812

*Facilities:* Car parks and refreshments at Aberystwyth; car park, refreshments and souvenir shop at Devil's Bridge; railway letter service.
*Details from:* Room 3, Divisional Manager's Office, British Rail, Station Road, Stoke-on-Trent, Staffordshire ST4 2AA

This 1 ft 11½ in. gauge line is the sole surviving narrow gauge section of British Railways.

Opened for goods and mineral traffic in August 1902, passengers were first carried on 22 December of the same year. The Cambrian Railways absorbed the line in August 1913 and they in turn were incorporated within the Great Western Railway from 1 January 1923 under the Railway Act of 1921. On 1 January 1948 the line was taken over by British Railways on nationalisation and placed in the Western Region, being transferred to the London Midland Region in 1963.

The service is maintained by three specially designed locomotives variously overhauled at Swindon, Oswestry and Crewe and each capable of hauling six coaches and a brake van up the heavy gradients to Devil's Bridge, climbing to an altitude of 680 ft above sea level.

Between Aberystwyth and Devil's Bridge the line passes through the magnificent scenery of the Rheidol Valley, George Borrow having described the Devil's Bridge area as 'one of the most remarkable localities in the world'.

In 1966-67 the line was diverted into the main station at Aberystwyth (Carmarthen bay platforms). En route to Devil's Bridge the single line serves seven stations and halts on the way at Llanbadarn, Glanrafon, Capel Bangor, Nantyronen, Aberffrwd, Rheidol Falls and Rhiwfron.

In 1967 engines and coaches were repainted in BR blue with arrow totem, whilst tickets include special bilingual platform tickets at both Devil's Bridge (Pontarfynach) and Aberystwyth, card returns for retention as souvenirs and Edmondson issues from the termini.

Last bastion of British Rail steam can, of course, be found on the Vale of Rheidol Railway. No. 8 *Llewellyn* was built at Swindon in 1923, and even BR blue livery can't disguise its Great Western ancestry

**Vale of Rheidol Railway Supporters Association**
The Association has the use of a camping coach of LNWR origin at Aberystwyth with periodic group and management meetings and newsletters.

**Stock**
GWR 2-6-2T No. 7 *Owain Glyndwr* built Swindon 1923
GWR 2-6-2T No. 8 *Llywelyn* built Swindon 1923
VofR 2-6-2T No. 9 *Prince of Wales* built Davies and Metcalfe of Romiley near Manchester in 1902 for the opening of the line
Sixteen bogie coaches, including seven second-class closed coaches Nos 1 to 6 (M4143–M4148) and 10 (M4994), two brake-seconds Nos 11 and 12 (M4995–M4996) and seven open observation coaches Nos 7 to 9 (M4149–M4151) and Nos 13 to 16 (M4997–M5000)
One four-wheeled passenger brake van No. 19 (M137)
Eleven wagons for maintenance and locomotive needs
Wickham 4WPMR No. PWM 2214 4131 built *c.* 1947 (Outstationed at Nantyronen)

## 306   Snowdon Mountain Railway          A

A four-and-three-quarter miles long, 2 ft 7½ in. gauge, passenger-carrying rack railway climbing to the summit of Snowdon (3560 ft). Operated by Snowdon Mountain Railway Ltd, Llanberis, Gwynedd.

*Facilities:* Modern shop and restaurant, snack bar and craft chalet. Parking facilities at Llanberis. Restaurant, bar and shop at the summit. Parties catered for by arrangement outside mid-summer peak period.
*Access:* Bangor BR Station, thence by bus to Llanberis. By road along the A4086 from Caernarfon or Capel Curig.
Tel: Llanberis 223
OS Ref: SH 582597

The railway operates from the end of March to the first weekend in October.
The railway was first opened in 1896 and the ABT system in use in Switzerland was used in the construction of the line. The system involves the laying of two toothed racks laid side by side in the centre of the track and the teeth of the racks are engaged by two cogged wheels or rack pinions fitted to the locomotives.
The Company has seven steam locomotives, all built by the Swiss locomotive works at Winterthur. A train is made up

**If you want to get to the top, take the Snowdon train! All the little Welsh lines are set amongst the mountains, but it takes a rack railway to scale the peaks**

Photo: Geoff King

of one locomotive with one coach of a passenger capacity of a maximum 80 persons. There are severe gradients on the line and in the interests of safety the speed of the locomotives is restricted to a maximum of 5 mph. It is the only rack railway in the British Isles.

## Stock

0–4–2T No. 2 *Enid* 924 built 1895
0–4–2T No. 3 *Wyddfa* 925 built 1895
0–4–2T No. 4 *Snowdon* 988 built 1896
0–4–2T No. 5 *Moel Siabod* 989 built 1896
0–4–2T No. 6 *Padarn* 2838 built 1922
0–4–2T No. 7 *Ralph Sadler* 2869 built 1923
0–4–2T No. 8 *Eryri* 2870 built 1923
All above built by Swiss Locomotive Works, Winterthur
Seven saloon bogie coaches
Bogie works car
Four-wheeled open wagon

A train will not leave the terminus for the ascent if the Company so determines with less than twenty-five return adult passengers or the equivalent in adult fares.
Snow and ice may prevent progress to the summit early and late in the season, and strong winds at high altitude may at any time result in the summit not being reached. The Company accepts no obligation to refund, in any circumstances whatsoever, the fare paid by a passenger or any part thereof.

All enquiries regarding train services and applications for special party fares to: The General Manager, Snowdon Mountain Railway Ltd, Llanberis, Gwynedd
Tel: Llanberis 223 (STD 028 682)

## 307   Talyllyn Railway                               A

Wharf Station, Tywyn, Gwynedd LL36 9EY

*Access:* Tywyn BR Station, Crosville bus routes S26, S28 and S30. By roads A493 and B4405.

Tel: Tywyn 710472
OS Ref: SH 590008

Passenger-carrying 2 ft 3 in. gauge steam railway, 8 miles in length, running from Tywyn Wharf to Nant Gwernol.

*Facilities:* Car park and restaurant facilities at or near Tywyn Wharf, Dolgoch and Abergynolwyn. Railway shop and museum at Tywyn. Special arrangements for parties of 25 and over, except in July and August.

Trains operate from Easter to the end of October daily except during October.
The Talyllyn Railway was the first in the world to be saved by voluntary activity. In 1950, when the preservation society took over this historic 2 ft 3 in. gauge line, it was nearly derelict after years of struggling to maintain services with insufficient resources. Today, the track has been relaid, locomotives and stock have been rebuilt and new units acquired, and a regular passenger service operates every summer. Like many other minor Welsh lines, the Talyllyn came into being to carry slate traffic, in this case from

quarries at Bryn Eglwys. It was built in 1865 and opened for both goods and passenger traffic in 1866. Though prosperous at first, increasing road competition and declining slate traffic would have brought closure in 1950 if the Society had not taken over after the death of the owner, Sir Henry Haydn Jones.
The railway is supported by the **Talyllyn Railway Preservation Society**

*Subscription rates:*

| | |
|---|---|
| Life | £60.00 |
| Full (over 21) | £4.00 |
| Junior (under 21 on 1 Feb.) | £2.00 |
| Associate Life (Wife of Full or Life Member) | £30.00 |
| Associate (Wife of Full or Life Member) | £2.00 |
| Senior Citizens | £2.00 |

*Details from:* TRPS, Wharf Station, Tywyn, Gwynedd.

---

The Talyllyn Railway was the cradle of railway preservation world-wide. It's hard to believe that this fascinating little line is now entering its 30th operating season in the hands of its preservation society. Their pioneering example has been imitated countless times since, but rarely surpassed

Photo: Rimmer Photography

## Stock

Fletcher Jennings 0–4–2ST No. 1 *Talyllyn* (42) built 1865
Fletcher Jennings 0–4–0WT No. 2 *Dolgoch* (63) built 1866
Hughes 0–4–2ST No. 3 *Sir Haydn* (323) built 1878
Kerr Stuart 0–4–2ST No. 4 *Edward Thomas* (4047) built 1921
Ruston Hornsby 4WDM No. 5 *Midlander* (200792) (44/48 HP Class) built 1940
Barclay 0–4–0WT No. 6 *Douglas* (1431) built 1918
[1]Barclay 0–4–2T No. 7 *Irish Pete* (2263) built 1949
Ruston Hornsby 4WDH No. 8 *Merseysider* (476108) (LF Class) built 1964
Hunslet 0–4–0DM No. 9 *Alf* (4136) built 1950
Brown Marshalls four-wheeled coaches Nos 1 and 2 built 1867
Brown Marshalls four-wheeled coach No. 3 built 1866
Lancaster Wagon Co. four-wheeled coach No. 4 built 1870
Brown Marshalls four-wheeled brake van No. 5 built 1866
Corris Railway four-wheeled brake van No. 6
Penrhyn Railway four-wheeled tea van No. 7 built 1963
Talyllyn Railway four-wheeled coach No. 8 built 1966
TR/W. G. Allen compartment bogie coach No. 9 built 1954
TR/W. G. Allen brake/third bogie coach No. 10 built 1954
TR four-wheeled coach No. 11 built 1955
TR four-wheeled coach No. 12 built 1956
TR four-wheeled coach No. 13 built 1957
Glyn Valley Tramway four-wheeled first-class coach No. 14 built 1892
Glyn Valley Tramway four-wheeled first-class coach No. 15 built 1901
TR/Kerr Stuart brake/third bogie coach No. 16 built 1961
Corris Railway third-class saloon bogie coach No. 17 built 1898
TR compartment bogie coach No. 18 built 1965
TR composite bogie coach No. 19
TR compartment bogie coach No. 20
TR compartment bogie coach No. 21 built 1975
TR compartment/brake bogie coach No. 22 built 1975
TR compartment coach No. 23 built 1975
Forty-four goods wagons

[1]Not yet in service. Locomotive being rebuilt from 3 ft gauge 0–4–0WT.

## 308   Marine Lake Miniature Railway    A

Rhyddlan Borough Council, Marine Lake, Rhyl, Clwyd

OS Ref: SJ 002806

A passenger-carrying 15 in. gauge steam railway laid out as a continuous circuit
*Operator:* Alan Keef

### Stock

[3]Barnes 4–4–2 *Joan* 101 built 1920
Barnes 4–4–2 *Railway Queen* 102 built 1922
Barnes 4–4–2 *Michael* 105 built 1930
[2]Barnes 4–4–2 *Billy* 106 built 1934
[1]Guest 0–4–2TPM *Clara* built 1961 (Steam outline)

[1]On loan from Dudley Zoo Miniature Railway (see Group No. 395).

[2]On display at the Town Hall Museum, Rhyl.
[3]Owned by Mr W. H. McAlpine.

## 309   Fairbourne Railway    A

A two-and-a-quarter mile 15 in. gauge line connecting Fairbourne with Barmouth Ferry
Operated by Fairbourne Railway Ltd, Beach Road, Fairbourne, Gwynedd LL38 2EX
Tel: Fairbourne 362
OS Ref: SH 616128
The line started as a 2 ft gauge horse tramway in 1890 and was rebuilt as a 15 in. gauge miniature railway in 1916 by Narrow Gauge Railways Ltd, a subsidiary of Basset-Lowke Ltd. The railway was closed for the duration of the war in September 1940 and was so severely damaged by the weather and the military that it seemed unlikely to reopen. It was, however, acquired by a new company after the war and reopened in stages from 1947. Since then it has been extensively developed, with new and rebuilt locomotives and rolling stock and an enlarged station and depot at Fairbourne. The railway offers panoramic views of the North Wales mountains and the renowned Mawddach estuary. Trains connect with the Barmouth ferry at Penrhyn Point.
The railway operates Easter week daily – then Sundays until Spring Bank holiday; daily to the end of September.
*Facilities:* Car park, railway shop and refreshments, etc, at Fairbourne. Refreshment and sales coach at Ferry terminus. Special reduced rates for parties of ten or more. Season and weekly tickets available.
*Access:* Fairbourne BR Station; Crosville bus service S28; A493 road
*Sales and publicity:* Hugh Sykes, 3 Bakers Lane, Sutton Coldfield, West Midlands B73 6XA

### Stock

Bassett-Lowke 4–4–2 *Count Louis* (32) built 1924
[1]Guest/Twining 4–6–2 *Ernest W. Twining* (10) built 1949, rebuilt 1966–7
Guest 2–4–2 *Katie* (14) built 1954
Guest 2–4–2 *Sian* (18) built 1963
G & S Light Engineering 0–6–0DH *Rachel* (15) built 1959, rebuilt 1972
[1]G & S Light Engineering Bo-Bo PH *Sylvia* (14A) built 1961
Lister 4WPM *Gwril* (20886) built 1941
Two end glass screen open bogie coaches Nos 16 and 20
Four articulated saloon coaches G & S built 1965
Bogie open coaches Nos 14, 15 and 17
Bogie saloon coaches Nos 18 and 19 G & S built 1960
Two three-car open articulated sets Nos 11 (ABC) and 21 (DEF)
Two bogie bolsters ex No. 12 open coach and No. 13 ex first class closed coach. Both converted to bogie tipper wagons
Twelve-wheeled bogie canteen coach G & S built 1969
Two four-wheeled open wagons
One four-wheeled side-tipping wagon
Six flat wagons
Rail-mounted saw
Rail-bender wagon

[1]Locomotive fitted with air-braking system.

## 310   Gwili Railway                                       A

Bronwydd Arms Station, near Carmarthen, Dyfed

OS Ref: SN 417239

*Access:* Carmarthen (BR); A484 road; Crosville bus No. S44 Carmarthen-Cardigan.

A passenger-carrying standard gauge steam railway, 1¼ miles in length, running from Bronwydd Arms to Cwmdwyfran.

The railway operates at weekends from the end of June to the end of September, also at Easter, May, Spring and Summer Bank Holidays. Timetables are issued from the Company's Office: Great Western Chambers, Angel Street, Neath. Glamorgan SA11 1RS. Facilities for visitors include car parking, refreshments and souvenir shop.

**Gwili Railway Preservation Society/Cymdeithas Gadwraeth Rheilffordd Gwili**

The Society has been set up as the supporting society to the Gwili Railway Company Limited. The Society has over 150 members.

*Secretary:* Mrs H. M. Headon, 16 Church Close, Bryncoch, Neath, West Glamorgan.
*Subscriptions:* Life £5; family £4; adults £2.50; juniors and OAPs £1.

**Stock**
GWR 4-6-0 No. 7820 *Dinmore Manor* built 1950
RSH 0-4-0ST 7058 built 1942
[1]Peckett 0-4-0ST *Merlin/Myrddin* 1967 built 1939
Peckett 0-4-0ST No. 1903 built 1936
[2]Manning Wardle 0-6-0ST *Aldwyth* 865 built 1882
Ruston Hornsby 4WDM 207103 built 1941
[2]L & YR four-wheeled inspection saloon BR dmu trailer coach No. E56317
BP Wooden-bodied open wagons Nos 2, 7, 11 & 16
National Benzole tank wagon No. 2002
Diesel rail crane
Wickham 4WPMR No. A123W 3361 built 1942
[1]Wickham 4WPMR Type 17A No. B154 (PWM 2222) (car No. 4139, built *c.* 1949)
Four-wheeled hand-propelled trolley
Taff Vale Railway Brake/third class coach body No. 220 (GWR No. 3846) built 1891

[1]Owned by the Gwili Railway Company Ltd and at present stored in Carmarthen.
[2]On loan from Mr R. L. Dean, Caerleon, Gwent. Locomotive ex MPBW, Kidbrooke, London, 1967. Restored at Kings Wharf, Cardiff.

## 311   Llangollen Railway Society Ltd              DF

Llangollen Station, Llangollen, Clwyd, North Wales

*Access:* Via A539 Ruabon-Corwen road or via A5 Shrewsbury-Holyhead road
Hourly bus services from Chester
Tel: Llangollen (0978) 860951
OS Ref: SJ 211423

A Standard gauge railway preservation centre at Llangollen Station with track being laid westwards towards Corwen. Llangollen station is open all year round with a locomotive in steam on advertised dates. Opening hours 9.30 am to 5.30 pm.
Facilities for visitors include car parking, souvenir shop, refreshments and toilets.
Originally started in 1972 by a group of enthusiasts in Flint, North Wales, and known as Flint and Deeside Railway Preservation Society. They began protracted negotiations with Clwyd County Council for acquisition of Llangollen Station and track bed of 10 miles of former GW Ruabon-Barmouth branch line. This was closed under Beeching in 1965 and was lifted two years later.
The Society eventually gained a lease on the property and site in 1975, and set about the task of transforming a wilderness into the semblance of a GW station again. Membership increased as people were attracted by the idea of reopening the section of line to public use again. The line runs through an area of outstanding beauty on the edge of the Snowdonia National Park, and is the only preserved standard gauge line in North Wales.
As all track and fittings were removed by BR after closure, it has meant that the Society has had to start to completely re-lay all track, etc., as it became available to them.
In 1978 it was decided that the project was becoming much larger, and it was decided that in order to give financial protection to members, the Society should become a limited company. The assets of the former Flint & Deeside Society were transferred to the new body, Llangollen Railway Society Ltd.
Membership continues to expand, and currently stands at 350.
It is the eventual aim of the Society to reopen at least 5 miles of track and to operate a public service again. A Light Railway Order has been applied for, and it is hoped that we may be allowed to start operating soon on a short length of line.

*Society details from:* Mr D. Williams, Toad Hall, Cefn Bychan Road, Pontymwyn, Mold, Clwyd
*Annual Subscription:* Adult £3; Junior (up to 16) £1; Family £4

**Stock**
[1]Kitson 0-6-0ST *Austin 1* 5459 built 1932
[2]Hudswell Clarke 0-6-0T *Richboro* 1243 built 1917
[7]Peckett 0-6-0ST *Ackton Hall No. 3* 1567 built 1920
[3]Fowler 0-4-0DM *Eliseg* 22753 built 1939
Hudswell Clarke 0-4-0DM No. 14 D1012 built 1956
[4]Fowler 0-4-0DM *Burmah* 4000007 built 1947
[5]GWR 'Toad' goods brake van (20-ton) No. 17407 built 1940
GWR brake third-class coach No. 5539 built 1938
[8]BR non-corridor passenger coach No. E46130 built 1954
BR Mk1 Brad/3rd compartment coach No. E43182
Shell tank wagon No. A6264
GWR 'Siphon G' 6-wheel van No. W1037
SR 'BY' passenger van No. S931
[10]LNER 6-wheel pigeon lift van No. 70250
BSC 20-ton hopper wagon
BSC 7-plank open wagon

Low-sided wagon
[9]GWR steam crane No. RS38 built 1947 with match trucks Nos DW38 & DW39 built 1917
GWR 'Open C' tube wagon built 1922
[6]LMS registered 14-ton rail tank wagon (Castrol livery) No. 164494 built 1944

[1]Ex British Leyland Motor Corporation, Austin-Morris Division, Longbridge, Birmingham, 1973. This locomotive was bought for the Society by Burtonwood Brewery Ltd.
[2]Ex National Coal Board, Gresford Colliery and Ifton Colliery.
[3]Ex Hawker Siddeley Aviation Ltd, Broughton, Clwyd, 1974.
[4]Ex Burmah Castrol Ltd, Ellesmere Port, presented for use at Llangollen in 1975.
[5]Privately owned by the 17407 Group. On loan to the Llangollen Railway.
[6]Ex Burmah Castrol Ltd, Ellesmere Port, presented as a gift to the Llangollen Railway Society in 1976.
[7]Ex Keighley & Worth Valley Railway 1979.
[8]This coach was taken out of passenger carrying service on 23 August 1976 at Finsbury Park and was despatched, along with three others, to York for shop repairs. While at York it was decided that they were excess to requirements and were withdrawn and offered for sale in January 1977.
[9]Ex Severn Valley Railway 1978.
[10]Ex Derwent Valley Railway 1979.

**Llangollen Railway Rolling Stock Group**
The Llangollen Railway Rolling Stock Group was formed with the aim of acquiring suitable items of rolling stock for use on the Llangollen Railway. Membership is open to the general public and is available by purchasing one or more shares in any item of stock subsequently purchased by the Group. A number of suitable locomotives, passenger coaches and goods vehicles have been selected for possible purchase when they become available. Further particulars can be obtained from: Mr Medwyn Roberts, 3 Bryn Dyffryn, Holywell, Clwyd, Wales.

Well, stripe us black and yellow! No, not a refugee from a safari park railway, this little beast is camouflaging its familiar Barclay shape at Ebbw Vale steelworks. *Forester* has since moved to Caerphilly and kept its stripes

Photo: Graham Scott-Lowe

## 312 Caerphilly Railway Society Ltd          D

Harold Wilson Industrial Estate, Van Road, Caerphilly, Mid-Glamorgan

*Access:* 2 miles from Caerphilly BR Station. Via Van Road to estate entrance
OS Ref: ST 163865

Standard gauge railway preservation centre incorporating a ½-mile demonstration line.

Formed in 1973, the Society's activities are centred on the former Rhymney Railway's locomotive works at Caerphilly. The site is now an industrial estate and is only open to the public by arrangement or on Society open days. The Society's main object is the restoration to working order of five locomotives that are either owned by or on loan to the National Museum of Wales. In March 1975 the Society was incorporated as a company limited by guarantee. The Company would like to thank the National Museum of Wales and the local council for their help in allowing the Company to establish itself.

*Company details from:* Mr N. Radley (Publicity Officer), at the above address.

### Stock
[5]Avonside 0-4-0ST *Desmond* 1498 built 1906
Barclay 0-4-0ST *Victory* 2201 built 1945
[4]LMS 2-6-2T No. 41312 (Ivatt Class 2MT) built 1952
[1]TVR 0-6-2T No. 28 (GWR No. 450) (Class 01) built 1897
[2]RSH 0-4-0ST 7705 built 1952
[3]Barclay 0-4-0ST *Forester* 1260 built 1911
GWR 'Toad' 20-ton goods brake van No. 35267
BR Mk1 Brake/2nd corridor coach No. M34460
GWR 4-wheel 6-ton hand crane
GWR Ballast wagon No. 60501
BR Fruit Van No. W92040
BR Mess & Tool Van No. KDS 8

[1]Taff Vale Railway No. 28 was sold by the GWR in 1927 and subsequently passed to the National Coal Board, by whom it was presented to the National Museum of Wales in 1962. After being in store for several years work on restoration is now being undertaken. As far as is known this is the only Welsh-built standard gauge locomotive in preservation.
[2]Ex Wiggins Teape, Cardiff, 1973.
[3]Ex British Steel Corporation, Ebbw Vale Steelworks, 1973.
[4]Built Crewe Works 1952, spent most of its working life on Southern Region of BR. Withdrawn 1967 and sent to Barry scrapyard. Bought by a Society member and arrived Caerphilly 1974.
[5]Ex British Steel Corporation, Orb Works, Newport, 1977.

## 313 9642 Preservation Group          D

NCB Workshops, Maesteg, Glamorgan
OS Ref: SS 848915

*Secretary:* W. T. Jones, 'Bryn-Awelon', 55 Salisbury Road, Maesteg, Glamorgan CF34 9EH

### Stock
[1]GWR 0-6-0T No. 9642 (Class 57XX) built 1946
GWR 'Toad' 20-ton goods brake van converted for passenger use
GWR covered van converted for passenger use

[1]Withdrawn in 1964 as BR No. 9642 and sold to R. S. Hayes Ltd, Bridgend, for scrap but retained for shunting purposes. Purchased for preservation in 1968. The most successful shunting engines ever built, the 5700 type could be seen almost everywhere on the GWR. These engines were equally at home on short-distance passenger trains and many of them worked such turns, especially in South Wales. Speeds up to 60 mph have been achieved at times by these remarkable machines. At the other extreme, they have been recorded working 70-80-wagon goods trains. No less than 862 of these locomotives were constructed between 1929 and 1950. As with all large classes there were variations. The earliest engines were constructed with the older flatter-roofed cab and round spectacles, whilst those built from 1932 onwards had the enlarged cab and sundry improvements. Withdrawal commenced in 1956, but three of the class lasted until November 1966 to become the last GWR engines to work on BR. A number of the earlier locomotives were sold to London Transport on withdrawal and some of these have subsequently been preserved.

## 314 Fort Belan Miniature Railway          A

Fort Belan, Dinas Dinlle, near Caernarfon, North Wales

*Access:* Off the A499 Caernarfon-Pwllheli Road through Dinas Dinlle (about 5 miles)
Tel: Llanwnda (0286) 830220

Passenger-carrying 7¼ in. gauge steam railway, ⅝ mile in length, running from the car park to the Fort.
The railway operates from 1 May to 30 September between 10 am and 5.30 pm daily.
Facilities for visitors include car parking, maritime museum, pleasure cruises to Caernarfon, pleasure flights by light aircraft, cannon firing, pottery, gift shop, refreshments and toilets.
This charming old Fort, situated in secluded and eminently picturesque surroundings, remains a singularly romantic and unspoilt place. Built some two hundred years ago on a small peninsula at the Western entrance to the Menai Straits, Belan is surrounded on three sides by the sea. The Snowdonia range of mountains in the background makes the neighbourhood one of great and varied loveliness.
Very little has changed at Belan for over 200 years, and the Fort, Docks, and cannons have all been maintained in first class working order.
The railway is laid out in a pear-shaped loop configuration running through the sand dunes. Its locomotive is a ¼ full size replica of an original engine built by Bagnalls of Stafford in 1910 for Mexico. Like the original, it has Bagnall-Price patented valve gear and a marine-type firebox.

### Stock
Potts/Bagnall 0-6-0 *El Meson* built 1964-69
Five 5-seat bogie coaches

## 315   Great Orme Tramway                            B

Great Orme Railway, Llandudno Urban District Council,
Transport Department, Builder Street West, Llandudno
Tel. Llandudno 76749

The Great Orme Railway runs from Victoria Station, Llandudno, to just below the summit of the Great Orme headland,
679 feet above sea level.
Authorised in 1898, this 3 ft 6 in. gauge line is in two
sections, passengers changing cars halfway. The lower section, opened on 31 July 1902, is 800 yards long (maximum
gradient 1 in 4.4); the upper, opened on 8 July 1903, is 827
yards long (maximum gradient 1 in 10.3). Both are single
track with a passing loop, although the lower incline has a
portion of double track with a common middle rail.
Cable traction is employed, though an overhead wire is used
for signalling purposes. The cable and pulleys are carried in
a central conduit on the lower (paved) section and above
the ground on conventional sleepers on the upper portion.
Originally steam-driven, the winding and control gear at the
halfway station is now powered by electric induction motors.
The line, which was taken over by Llandudno Urban District
Council from the Great Orme Railway Company on 1 January
1949, opens each summer with a basic 20-minute service,
extra journeys being worked during busy periods.

### Stock
Four six-and-a-half-ton tramcars each seating 48

## 316   Ceudwll Llechwedd (Llechwedd        B
##        Slate Caverns)

Blaenau Ffestiniog, Gwynedd

OS Ref: SH 699468

A 2 ft gauge passenger-carrying partially underground line
operated by Quarry Tours Ltd. Opened in 1972.
The mine is open for visitors and the tramway operates from
10 am to 6 pm daily, 1 March to 30 November, and 10.30 am
to 4 pm on Saturdays and Sundays, December to February.

### Stock
Wingrove and Rogers 4WBE No. 1
Wingrove and Rogers 4WBE No. 2
Wingrove and Rogers 4WBE No. 3
Wingrove and Rogers 4WBE built 1921
Logan 4WBE MBS387 1053 built 1950
Logan 4WBE MBS236 1066 built 1950
Bagnall 0-4-0WE *The Coalition* 1278 built 1890
Twelve Hudson four-seat, four-wheel carriages

The Llechwedd Slate Caverns are part of the Llechwedd
Slate Mines at the northern end of Blaenau Ffestiniog in the
Snowdonia National Park. The veins of slate run deeply
underground and mining, rather than opencast quarrying,
was found to be the most economic method of extracting
the slate. These underground workings extend to a depth
of 900 ft and consist of some 25 miles of tunnels connecting
the vast chambers from which the slate has been removed
over the last 100 years or so.

Visitors to the caverns can take a half-mile return journey
through the mine in specially-designed trains hauled by
battery-electric locomotives. Two trains can operate simultaneously, if required by traffic, as a passing loop is provided
about half-way into the mine. The train conveys visitors to
a slate chamber in which the working conditions of a century
ago have been recreated. Here visitors will see how the vast
caverns were formed by the extraction of slate from the
mountainside. A guide will demonstrate the hand tools used
in bygone days. Back in the slate mill, visitors will be shown
the fascinating process of slate splitting and can try cleaving
a block of slate themselves. Visitors should note that the
temperature underground remains fairly constant throughout
the year at about 50°F (10°C) and that wearing a jacket or
cardigan would be appropriate.
At the time of going to press, a cable worked incline was
being adapted for use as an extension of the passenger line
to give access to two lower levels of the slate mine.

## 317   Welsh Highland Light Railway           B

Porthmadog Depot, Beddgelert Siding, Porthmadog,
Gwynedd
*Access:* Adjacent to BR Porthmadog station.
OS Ref: SH 567393

Passenger-carrying 60 cm gauge railway, ¾ mile in length,
from Beddgelert siding to Pen-y-mount
*Membership Secretary:* E. Hanson, 57 Sheriff Street, Rochdale, Lancashire. Tel. Rochdale 58528
*Subscription:* £2 per annum

The Welsh Highland Railway was the result of many years'
endeavour to build a narrow gauge through route linking the
Porthmadog terminus of the Festiniog Railway with the
LNWR Afon Wen–Caernarfon line. When completed in 1923
it provided an unbroken 35-mile stretch of 60 cm gauge
track between Dinas Junction and Blaenau Ffestiniog. In
actual fact, although the FR and the WHR ultimately came
under the same management, the system was never worked
as one line.
The expense and inconvenience of running the Welsh Highland finally proved too much for the Festiniog and passenger
traffic ceased in 1936. The line was dismantled for scrap
during the war, but miraculously the WHR locomotive *Russell*
survived in industrial service and was preserved in 1955.
For the next ten years it stood outside the Narrow Gauge
Museum at Tywyn until taken over by the Welsh Highland
Light Railway (1964) Ltd, who intend to reinstate part of
the old WHR route.

### Stock
Orenstein and Koppel 0-6-0WT *Fojo* 9239
[3]Orenstein and Koppel 0-6-0WT *Pedemoura* (10808) built
1924
[1]Hunslet 2-6-2T *Russell* (901) built 1906
[2]Barclay 0-6-0T *Gertrude* (1578) built 1918
[4]Peckett 0-4-2T *Karen* 2024 built 1942
Ruston Hornsby 4WDM 327904 (20DL Class) built 1951
Ruston Hornsby 4WDM *Kinnerley* (354068) (40DL Class)
built 1953

Hunslet 0-4-0DM Yard No. P.9260 (2248) built 1940 (2 ft 6 in. gauge)
Ruston Hornsby 4WDM *Cilgwyn* (18/21 HP Class) (175414) built 1936
Friedland–Anklarn Eisenbahn saloon bogie coach No. 960–104 built 1913
Five Snailbeach Railway wagons
Two Isle of Man Railway bogie coaches Nos F3 and F21 (3 ft gauge)
Vale of Rheidol Railway four-wheeled passenger brake van
Two Hudson/WHR bogie coaches
Hudson four-wheeled wagon
Slate wagon

[1]Supplied new to North Wales Narrow Gauge Railways and taken over by the Welsh Highland Railway. Sold to Brymbo Steel Co. Ltd on closure of the WHR and used at Hook Norton Ironstone Mines, Oxfordshire. Sold to Pike Brothers, Fayle and Co. Ltd, Norden Clay Mines, Dorset, in 1948. Preserved by the Birmingham Locomotive Club in 1955.
[2]Ex Stewarts and Lloyds, Bilston, Staffs, in 1960. Loaned to WHLR in 1963 and at present undergoing repairs.
[3]Ex Knebworth West Park and Winter Green Railway, 1975.
[4]Ex Selukee Peak Light Railway, South Africa.

## 318    Pendine Wildlife and Pleasure Park    B

Pendine, Dyfed
OS Ref: SN 244083

A 2 ft gauge passenger-carrying pleasure line.

### Stock
Hudson 4WDM No. 20483 (LX1001) built 1968 (Steam Outline)
Ex Dredging and Construction Co. Ltd, Kings Lynn, Norfolk, 1976.

## 319    Butlins, Pwllheli    B

Pwllheli Holiday Camp, Pen-y-Chain, Gwynedd
OS Ref: SH 434363

A 2 ft gauge passenger-carrying line.

### Stock
Ruston Hornsby 4WDM *Old Sparky* (48DL Class) 487963 built 1963

## 320    Swansea Industrial and Maritime    E
         Museum

Victoria Road, Swansea, West Glamorgan
OS Ref: SS 660928

Open weekdays 10 am to 5 pm
Standard gauge steam locomotive on static display

### Stock
Barclay 0-4-0F No. 1 *Sir Charles* 1473 built 1916

GWR 2-8-0T No. 4270 (42XX Class) built 1919
Ex BP Refinery (Llandarcy) Ltd, 1961
Other exhibits include a Mumbles Railway electric tramcar end (Car No. 7), a section of original Mumbles Railway track, a model of Brunel's Landore viaduct and the beam from one of the original Severn Tunnel pumping engines.

The Museum is adjacent to the operational area of Y Clwb Rheil Cymru (see Group No. 330).
No. 4270 is still at Barry at the time of writing, and the other items were originally restored by club members, although they are museum property.

## 321    Narrow Gauge Railway Museum    E

Tywyn, Gwynedd
OS Ref: SH 586004

Museum established in 1956
Managed by the Narrow Gauge Railway Museum Trust

The Museum adjoins the platform at Tywyn Wharf Station, accommodated in a modern building. Here is displayed a unique collection of equipment from narrow gauge railways all over Britain, ranging in size from steam locomotives – seven in number – wagons and signals, down to uniform buttons and tickets. Slate quarry railways predominate, but there are locomotives from a famous brewery, a gas works and from other industries.
The Museum has considerable educational value and is a popular destination for school parties. Organised and managed by a charitable trust, it relies on volunteer labour for most of the restoration and display work.
*Enquiries to:* Narrow Gauge Railway Museum Trust, Wharf Station, Tywyn, Gwynedd LL36 9EY
*Opening times:* 10 am to 5 pm Easter to October; out of season on request

### Stock
Heywood 0-4-0T *Katie* (4) built 1896 (1 ft 3 in. gauge) (parts only)
Beyer Peacock 0-4-0ST *Dot* (2817) built 1887 (1 ft 6 in. gauge)
[1]LNWR 0-4-0ST *Pet* built 1865 (1 ft 6 in. gauge)
Hunslet 0-4-0ST *Rough Pup* (541) built 1891 (1 ft 10¾ in. gauge)
Sentinel 4WVBTG *Nutty* (7701) built 1929 (2 ft 6 in. gauge) (not on public display; can be seen by special request)
Spence 0-4-0T No. 13 built 1895 (1 ft 10 in. gauge)
De Winton 0-4-0T *George Henry* built 1877 (1 ft 10¾ in. gauge)
Manning Wardle 0-4-0ST *Jubilee 1867* (1382) built 1897 (1 ft 10¾ in. gauge)
Kerr Stuart 0-4-0WT No. 2 (721) built 1901 (2 ft gauge)
Four four-wheeled wagons from narrow gauge industrial railways

[1]Used on the internal system at Crewe Works until withdrawn in 1929 and preserved at Crewe. On display at the Museum of British Transport, Clapham, from 1964 until presented by British Railways Board in 1967.

## 322 National Museum of Wales E

Industrial and Maritime Museum, Bute Crescent, Cardiff, Glamorgan
OS Ref: ST 192745

Locomotives and rolling stock undergoing restoration for display at the museum.

### Stock
Hudswell Clarke 0–6–0ST No. 10 544 built 1900
[1]Hunslet 0–6–0ST No. 18 *Jessie* 1873 built 1937
Ruston Hornsby 4WDM 187100 built 1937 (3 ft gauge)
GWR hand crane
Steam crane

[1]At Splott Park, Cardiff. Presented by Guest Keen Iron & Steel Co. Ltd, East Moors Works, Cardiff, 1965.

Photo: Graham Scott-Lowe

**Almost like a battleship with its surrounding railings to keep its crew on deck is Hunslet 0–6–0ST *Jessie* at Splott Park, Cardiff. Welcome aboard?**

---

## 323 Corris Railway Society E

The Corris Railway Museum, Corris Station Yard, near Machynlleth, Gwynedd

*Access:* Off A487, five miles north of Machynlleth, opposite Braich Goch Hotel.
Static exhibits (2 ft 3 in. gauge).

*Secretary:* 165 Gynsill Lane, Austey, Leicester LE7 7AN.
*Subscriptions:* Adults £1.80; juniors and OAPs 60p; life £18 or three annual payments of £6.50; corporate £1.50.

*Entrance fee (all classes):* 50p (includes copy of 'Index' of relics).

The Society, founded in 1966 to preserve relics of the Corris Railway and to open a museum where they could be displayed to the public, has acquired one of the earliest buildings of this narrow gauge railway – the original motive power depot from the days before steam! This building, in the former station yard at Corris, has been renovated by members, and is in use as the museum. There is still a great deal of work to be done on the building, and new exhibits are being acquired. It is open to the public on Tuesday to Friday during July and August from 1 pm to 5.30 pm. Also on Sundays during the same period from 2 pm to 5 pm and on Bank Holiday weekends. Track is being reinstated on a short length of the old bed adjacent to the museum and a replica of an 1898 bogie coach is being built.
A company is to be formed to limit the liability of members when the demonstration track comes into operation.

### Stock
Motor Rail 4WDM 22258 built 1965, being rebuilt
Slate-slab wagon
Iron-bodied, side-door wagon
Skeleton of bogie coach body built 1898
Brake/Tool van
Four historical wagons in various states of repair
Three non-historical working wagons
Various minor exhibits, photographs, etc.

## 324 Pembrokeshire County Museum E

Dyfed County Council, Scolton House, Scolton, near Haverfordwest, Dyfed
OS Ref: SM 991222

Standard gauge locomotive in store and undergoing restoration.

### Stock
Fox Walker 0–6–0ST *Margaret* (410) built 1878
Locomotive supplied new to North Pembroke and Fishguard Railway, then absorbed into GWR stock as No. 1378. Later it was sold to the Gwendraeth Valleys Railway, finally passing to the Kidwelly Tinplate Co. Ltd in 1923. The locomotive ceased work in 1941 and has been stored ever since.

## 325 National Trust, E
## Penrhyn Castle Museum

Llandegai, near Bangor, Gwynedd
OS Ref: SH 602724

A museum devoted to the history of industrial railways containing locomotives and rolling stock of four different gauges on static display.
Open daily from 1 April to 31 October.

### Stock
Stephenson 0–6–0T *Haydock* (2309) built 1879
Neilson 0–4–0WT No. 1 (1561) built 1870
Hudswell Clarke 0–4–0ST *Hawarden* (526) built 1899

Hudswell Clarke 0–6–0T *Vesta* (1223) built 1916
Black Hawthorn 0–4–0ST *Kettering Furnaces No. 3* (859) built 1883 (3 ft gauge)
Hunslet 0–4–0ST *Charles* (283) built 1882 (1 ft 10¾ in. gauge)
Hunslet 0–4–0ST *Hugh Napier* (855) built 1904 (1 ft 10¾ in. gauge)
Horlock 0–4–0 *Fire Queen* built 1848 (4 ft gauge)
De Winton 0–4–0BT *Watkin* built 1893 (3 ft gauge)
Padarn Railway Velocipede *Arthur* (4 ft gauge)
Penrhyn Railway quarryman's coach (1 ft 10¾ in. gauge)
Penrhyn Railway, Lord Penrhyn's saloon built 1882 (1 ft 10¾ in. gauge)
Four Penrhyn Railway open wagons (1 ft 10¾ in. gauge)

## 326   Narrow Gauge Railway Centre        E

Narrow Gauge Enterprises, Gloddfa Ganol Mountain Tourist Centre, Blaenau Ffestiniog, Gwynedd, North Wales LL41 3NB
*Access:* Off the A470 Blaenau Ffestiniog to Betws-y-Coed road ½ mile north of the town. Turn off at Loco No. 3014!
Nearest station: Blaenau Ffestiniog BR
Tel: Moelwyn (076-689) 500

The largest collection of narrow gauge locomotives in the British Isles, housed in a museum in the world's largest slate mine.

The museum is open daily from Easter to October between 10 am and 5.30 pm. Facilities for visitors include car parking, licensed restaurant, snack bar and grill, toilets, children's playground and playroom, slate works, craft shops, mining museum, preserved quarrymen's cottages, slate grotto and Land Rover tours.
Coach parties especially welcome. Educational parties catered for.
The Narrow Gauge Enterprises collection of locomotives is being concentrated at Gloddfa Ganol. The first phase of the display was opened in summer 1978 and a considerable amount of work remains to be done before the museum is fully complete. Items are continually being added to the collection.

**Progress '79**
In conjunction with the Ffestiniog Mountain Tourist Centre Ltd, Narrow Gauge Enterprises is in the process of setting up their extensive collection of Narrow Gauge Railway exhibits at the highly popular 'Mountain Tourist Centre of North Wales'.
Eventual development into a major (national) NG Museum/Centre is envisaged – complementary to the nearby, established railways in the Principality and elsewhere. The first 46 locos, plus much wagonry and other miscellany, were transferred from storage in various parts of the country over the period May to September 1978. 35 locos are on public show *inside* the new Exhibition Hall recently completed for this purpose; ten others are displayed *outside* the building, plus one (Kerr Stuart 3014) at the main entrance gate. Ex British Railways (Horwich Works) diesel locomotive 'ZM32' and others are available for work, whilst

a further 22 have gone into private storage elsewhere on site.

**Stock**
Hunslet 4WDM 20HP Class 2209 built 1941 2 ft 6 in. gauge
Hudson 4WP/ParM 20HP Class 39924 built *c.* 1931 2 ft gauge
Ruston Hornsby 4WDM 10HP Class 166028 built 1932 2 ft gauge
Bagnall 0–4–0ST 1568 built 1899 2 ft gauge
Baguley 0–4–0PM 10HP Class 646 built 1917 60 cm gauge
Baguley 0–4–0PM 10HP Class 760 built 1918 60 cm gauge
Baguley 0–4–0PM *Oakeley* 20HP Class 774 built 1919 60 cm gauge
Barclay 0–4–0T *The Wee Pug* D Class 984 built 1903 2 ft 6 in. gauge
Bredbury 4WPM *Bredbury* built *c.* 1954 2 ft gauge
BEV 4WBE 551 built 1924 1 ft 6 in. gauge
BEV 4WE *Welsh Pony* 640 built 1926 1 ft 11½ in. gauge
de Winton 0–4–0VBT *Kathleen* built 1877 1 ft 10¾ in. gauge
Deutz 0–4–0DM *Delta* 257081 built *c.* 1930 2 ft gauge
Festiniog Rly. 4WDM *Festiniog* built 1974 1 ft 11½ in. gauge
Hibberd 4WPM Y Class 1881 built 1934 2 ft gauge
Hibberd 4WPM Y Class 3424 built 1949 2 ft gauge
Hudson 4WDM 'GoGo' type 36863 built 1929 2 ft gauge
Hudswell Clarke 4WDM 41HP Class D564 built 1930 2 ft gauge
Hunslet 4WDM 20HP Class 1835 built 1937 60 cm gauge
Hunslet 4WDM 20HP Class 2024 built 1940 60 cm gauge
Hunslet 4WDM 20HP Class 2607 built 1942 60 cm gauge
Kerr Stuart 0–4–0ST *Ashover* 'Wren' class 3114 built 1918 2 ft gauge
Lister 4WPM R Class 3916 built 1931 2 ft gauge
Lister 4W+4WPMR *Whippit Quick* 6502 built 1935 1 ft 3 in. gauge
Baguley 0–4–0PM 736
Lister/Etherinton 4WVBT *Steam Tram* 14005 built 1940 (rebuilt 1970) 2 ft gauge
Locospoor 4WPM No. C37 B7281E 3 ft gauge
BMW/Morris 4–2–0PMR *Rail Taxi* built 1967 2 ft gauge
Motor Rail 4WPM No. 2182 461 built 1917 60 cm gauge
Motor Rail 4WDM H Class 05H006 built 1969 3 ft gauge
Muir Hill 4WP/ParM A Class 110 built 1925 2 ft gauge
Ruston Hornsby 4WDM 10HP Class 164346 built 1932 2 ft gauge
Ruston Hornsby 4WDM 16/20 HP Class 211647 built 1941 60 cm gauge
Ruston Hornsby 4WDM 16/20HP Class 213834 built 1942 2 ft gauge
Ruston Hornsby 4WDM Pen-yr-Orsedd 20DL Class 235711 built 1945 2 ft gauge
Ruston Hornsby 4WDM LBT Class 393327 built 1956 2 ft gauge
Ruston Hornsby 4WDM No. ZM32 LAT Class 416214 built 1957 2 ft gauge
Ruston Hornsby 4WDM LBU Class 432664 built 1959 2 ft gauge
Ruston Proctor 4W ParM 10HP Class 50823 built 1915 Metre gauge
Thakeham 4WPM *Thankeham* built *c.* 1946 2 ft gauge

Wickham 4WPMR 4091 built 1946 3 ft gauge
Wickham 4WPMR 4092 built 1946 3 ft gauge
Brush 4WBE 16306 built 1917 2 ft gauge
de Winton 0-4-0VBT *Llanfair* built 1895 3 ft gauge
Derby & Notts Electric Power Co 4WBE No. 1 *Spondon* built 1926 2 ft gauge
Fowler 4WDM 40HP Class 3930044 built 1950 3 ft gauge
Hibberd 4WPM 10HP Class 1568 built 1927 2 ft gauge
Hibberd 4WPM 10HP Class 1747 built 1931 2 ft gauge
Hibberd 4WDM 2025 built 1937 2 ft gauge
Hibberd 4WDM 2201 built 1939 2 ft gauge
Howard 4WPM S Class 982 built 1931 2 ft gauge
Hudson 4WP/ParM 20HP Class 45913 built 1932 2 ft 6 in. gauge
Hunslet 4WDM 25/32HP Class 2666 built 1942 2 ft gauge
Hunslet 4WDM 21HP Class 6018 built 1961 2 ft gauge
Kerr Stuart 0-6-0T 'Joffre' class 2442 built 1915 60 cm gauge
Kerr Stuart 0-6-0T 'Joffre' class 2451 built 1915 60 cm gauge
Kerr Stuart 0-6-0T 'Joffre' class 3010 built 1916 60 cm gauge
Kerr Stuart 0-6-0T 'Joffre' class 3014 built 1916 60 cm gauge
Lister 4WPM 4 class 6299 built 1935 2 ft gauge
Orenstein & Koppel 4WPM M class 4470 built *c.* 1931 60 cm gauge
Rhiwbach 4WPM 2 ft gauge
Ruhrthaler 0-4-0DM No. LM 11 1082 built *c.* 1936 3 ft gauge
Ruston Hornsby 4WDM 10HP class 164350 built 1932 2 ft gauge
Ruston Hornsby 4WDM LBU class 398102 built 1956 2 ft 4 in. gauge
Wickham 4WPMR No. C13 2449 built 1938 3 ft gauge
Wickham 4WPMR No. C18 4808 built 1948 3 ft gauge
Wickham 4WPMR No. C20 4810 built 1948 3 ft gauge
Wickham 4WPMR No. C23 4813 built 1948 3 ft gauge
Wickham 4WPMR No. C26 4816 built 1948 3 ft gauge
Wingrove & Rogers 0-4-0BE *Little George* 1298 built 1938 2 ft gauge
*Note:* Not all the above items are on display at Gloddfa Ganol yet.

## 327 Conwy Valley Railway Museum          AE

Old Goods Yard, Bettws-y-Coed, Gwynedd LL24 0AL
OS Ref: SH 796565

*Details from:* Allan Pratt, c/o the above address

Museum of locomotives and rolling stock of various gauges. There are displays covering the whole railway scene, with special reference to standard and narrow gauge lines in North Wales. The small exhibits are in a purpose-built museum and there is a collection of standard gauge vehicles and larger exhibits on the site.
The museum is open daily from Easter until mid-September between 11 am and 5.30 pm.
A passenger-carrying 7¼ in. gauge railway, ½ mile in length, was opened as an adjunct to the museum in 1979.

**Museum exhibits**
Kerr Stuart 0-6-0T *Sgt Murphy* 3117 built 1918 1 ft 10¾ in. gauge
GWR fitter's van No. DW14610 (converted from brake van No. 56096) built 1895
LMS 'Stove R' six-wheeled van No. 33016 built 1939
LNER CCT vehicle No. 1370 built 1950
BR Mk1 TSO bogie coach No. 3925 built 1954
SR PMV four-wheeled utility van No. 1070
SR BY four-wheeled parcels brake van No. 407
Pullman camping coach *Emerald* built 1910
LNWR 20-ton goods brake van No. 349

*7¼ in. gauge stock*
Freelance 0-4-0WT *Romulus*
BR Hymek Bo-BoBE

## 328 Buildwell Products          G

Clydach-on-Tawe, Glamorgan
OS Ref: SN 688009

Standard gauge locomotive in store awaiting disposal

**Stock**
Barclay 0-4-0ST *Leaf* 1081 built 1909

Used on works internal system until restored for preservation in 1971.

## 329 Brecon Mountain Railway          F

Pontsticill Junction Station, Powys
OS Ref: SO 063120

This company is constructing an entirely new 60 cm gauge line along a 5½-mile section of the former Brecon and Merthyr Railway between Pant and Torpantau, Powys.
After several years of planning, this exciting new Welsh narrow gauge railway is now under construction. When complete, the line will give passengers an unrivalled 5½-mile ride through the spectacular scenery of the Brecon Beacons. As we go to press, track is being laid southwards from the former B & M Pontsticill Junction Station, past the new carriage sheds towards Pant, a distance of 2 miles. The second phase will involve tracklaying north from Pontsticill a further 3½ miles to Torpantau via Dolygaer.
Construction work is being carried out to a very high standard using 75 lb. flat-bottom rail, and full workshop and servicing facilities are being installed at Pontsticill. It is hoped that a service can be operated over part of the line during 1980.

**Stock**
[1]Baldwin 4-6-2 No. 2 (61269) built 1930
Jung 0-6-2WTT No. 99 3553 1261 built 1908
Hunslet 0-4-0 *Sybil* 827 built 1903
Kerr Stuart 0-4-0T *Diana* 1158 built 1917
Orenstein and Koppel 0-4-0T No. 9 12722 built 1936
Redstone 0-4-0VBT *Redstone* built 1905
de Winton/Hills 0-4-0VBT *Pendyffryn* built 1894
Ruston Hornsby 4WDM 425798 built 1961
Ruston Hornsby 4WDM 425798 built 1961

Ruston Hornsby 4WDM *Phyllis* 444207 built 1961
SAR Bogie covered van
Various construction wagons and components for building
verandah-end 40-seat bogie coaches

[1]Ex Eastern Provinces Cement Co., South Africa, 1974.

The Brecon Mountain Railway Association has been formed
to promote and support the railway. Details of the Association may be obtained from: Mr J.T. Aitchison, 23 Wernlys
Road, Penyfai, Bridgend, Mid Glamorgan.
*Annual Subscription:* Adult £2, Juniors & OAPs £1. A family
membership scheme is also available.

## 330    Y Clwb Rheil Cymru                             D
##         (Railway Club of Wales)

Adjacent to Swansea Industrial and Maritime Museum, Coast
Lines Warehouse, South Dock, Swansea, West Glamorgan

*Access:* A483 or A4067 to Swansea Leisure Centre. Museum
is at rear of Leisure Centre. Nearest BR Station, Swansea
High Street
Tel: 0792 33841
OS Ref: SS 659927

The first steam centre in South West Wales is being established by the Club in association with the Museum. A running
line 500 yards long has been laid where locomotives are
steamed on Sunday afternoons from May to September.
Facilities for visitors include car parking, toilets and sales
stand of railwayana on Steam Days.

*Details from:* 2 Vicarage Lane, Cwmdu, Swansea,
Glamorgan.

### Stock
[1]Sentinel 4WVBTG *Swansea Vale No. 1* 9622 built 1958
[2]Barclay 0-4-0ST *Rosyth No. 1* 1385 built 1914
[3]Ruston Hornsby 4WDM 393302 48DS Class built 1955
GWR 'Toad' 20-ton brake van No. 35978 built 1946

[1]Ex Imperial Smelting Corporation, Vale Works, Llansamlet.
[2]Ex Royal Navy Rosyth Dockyard, RAF Pembroke Dock and
RAF St Athan.
[3]Ex Aluminium Wire & Cable Co., Port Tennant Works,
Swansea.

The Club was formed in 1968 to provide for the varied
interests of railway enthusiasts in Wales by preserving items
of rolling stock, and encouraging an interest in the Principality's railways past, present and future.
The Club's main activity is the operation and maintenance
of its rolling stock at the South Dock Railway, at the Swansea
Industrial and Maritime Museum. Steam Days are held at
Bank Holidays and at other times as advertised. A diesel
service is run on summer Sundays when steaming is not
taking place. For the remaining months of the year, members
are hard at work keeping the locomotives at the highest
possible standard of restoration.
The Club holds fortnightly meetings at the Builders' Arms,
Oxford Street, Swansea. The meetings take the form of
talks, slideshows, quizzes and filmshows. Visits to locations

of railway interest are yet another exciting part of the club
calendar.
'The Red Dragon' is the Club's own *free* quarterly magazine
which takes its name from the important Paddington–South
Wales express of steam days. Members may write articles
on any railway topic for inclusion in the magazine.
Perhaps the most pleasing aspect of the club is that it
maintains a warm, 'family atmosphere' amongst its membership. Any member is free to participate in the club's
activities in any way he or she feels capable.

*Annual Subscription:* Ordinary £1.50, Associate £1.00,
Student/OAP £1.00, Life £15.00. (The Club's magazine is
included in the subscription.)

*Details from:* Railway Club of Wales, 2 Vicarage Lane,
Cwmdu, Swansea, West Glamorgan.

## 331    Conwy and Llanrwst Railway              E
##         Society

Station Yard, Llanrwst, Gwynedd
OS Ref: SH 795623

Collection of standard gauge locomotives and rolling stock
being gathered to form a working transport depot of rail and
road vehicles.
The site is usually open on the first Sunday in each month
and on most Saturdays.
Admission and guide book are free but donations are
welcome!

### Stock
Barclay 0-4-0DM No. 2 *Haunchwood* 349 built 1941
Hibberd 4WDM No. 4007 3147 built 1947
Two Wickham 4WPMR inspection trolleys
Body of Northampton tram No. 21
Lancashire Tar Distillers square tank wagon built 1926
Esso Tank wagon
ICI Salt wagon built *c.* 1890
MOD Flat wagon

## 332    Woodham Brothers Limited             G

Barry Scrapyard, Barry Docks, Glamorgan, South Wales
No public admittance

OS Ref: ST 111670

The following locomotives are stored pending collection and
restoration by various preservation groups. There is no
guarantee that locomotives appearing in the list will, in fact,
be preserved, although this is thought likely in the majority
of cases. A large number of engines at Barry carry painted
slogans alleging they are earmarked for preservation, but it
is wisest to verify individual cases with the societies involved.
Readers are asked not to trespass upon Woodham Brothers'
property or interfere with the locomotives in any way.

### Stock
GWR 2-8-0 No. 2807 (28XX Class) built 1905
GWR 2-8-0 No. 2859 (28XX Class) built 1918

GWR 4-6-0 No. 4936 *Kinlet Hall* built 1929
GWR 4-6-0 No. 4953 *Pitchford Hall* built 1929
GWR 4-6-0 No. 4979 *Wootton Hall* built 1930 (Quainton Railway Society)
GWR 2-6-2T No. 5199 (51XX Class) built 1934
GWR 2-8-0T No. 5227 (5205 Class) built 1924
GWR 2-6-2T No. 5526 (4575 Class) built 1928
GWR 2-6-2T No. 5532 (4575 Class) built 1928
GWR 2-6-2T No. 5538 (4575 Class) built 1928
GWR 2-6-2T No. 5539 (4575 Class) built 1928
GWR 2-6-2T No. 5552 (4575 Class) built 1928
GWR 2-6-2T No. 5553 (4575 Class) built 1928
GWR 0-6-2T No. 5668 (56XX Class) built 1926 (Peak Railway Society)
GWR 4-6-0 No. 5952 *Cogan Hall* built 1935 (Cogan Hall Preservation Group)
GWR 4-6-0 No. 5967 *Bickmarsh Hall* built 1937
GWR 4-6-0 No. 5972 *Olton Hall* built 1937
GWR 4-6-0 No. 6023 *King Edward II* built 1930 (6023 Group)
GWR 0-6-2T No. 6634 (56XX Class) built 1928 (GWR Preservation Group)
GWR 0-6-2T No. 6686 (56XX Class) built 1928
GWR 4-6-0 No. 6984 *Owsden Hall* built 1948
GWR 2-8-2T No. 7200 (72XX Class) built 1934
GWR 4-6-0 No. 7821 *Ditcheat Manor* built 1950
GWR 4-6-0 No. 7828 *Odney Manor* built 1950
GWR 4-6-0 No. 7903 *Foremarke Hall* Built 1949
GWR 4-6-0 No. 7927 *Willington Hall* built 1950
GWR 0-6-0PT No. 9629 (57XX Class) built 1945
GWR 0-6-0PT No. 9682 (57XX Class) built 1949
LSWR 4-6-0 No. 30499 (Urie S15 Class) built 1920 (Urie S15 Preservation Group)
SR 4-6-0 No. 30825 (S15 Class) built 1927
SR 4-6-0 No. 30828 (S15 Class) built 1927
SR 4-6-0 No. 30830 (S15 Class) built 1927
SR 2-6-0 No. 31625 (U Class) built 1929
SR 2-6-0 No. 31638 (U Class) built 1931 (Southern Steam Trust)
SR 4-6-2 No. 34007 *Wadebridge* built 1945
SR 4-6-2 No. 34010 *Sidmouth* built 1945 (Peak Railway Society)
SR 4-6-2 No. 34027 *Taw Valley* built 1946
SR 4-6-2 No. 34028 *Eddystone* built 1946
SR 4-6-2 No. 34046 *Braunton* built 1946
SR 4-6-2 No. 34053 *Sir Keith Park* built 1947
SR 4-6-2 No. 34058 *Sir Frederick Pile* built 1947 (Bournemouth Steam Centre)
SR 4-6-2 No. 34067 *Tangmere* built 1947 (Tangmere Loco Trust)
SR 4-6-2 No. 34070 *Manston* built 1947 (Manston Preservation Group)
SR 4-6-2 No. 34072 *257 Squadron* built 1948
SR 4-6-2 No. 34073 *249 Squadron* built 1948
SR 4-6-2 No. 35006 *Peninsular & Oriental Steamship Navigation Company* built 1941

GWR 2-8-0 No. 2861 (28XX Class) built 1918
GWR 2-8-0 No. 2873 (28XX Class) built 1918
GWR 2-8-0 No. 2874 (28XX Class) built 1918
GWR 2-8-0 No. 2885 (28XX Class) built 1938 (GWR Preservation Group)
GWR 2-8-0 No. 3802 (28XX Class) built 1938
GWR 2-8-0 No. 3803 (28XX Class) built 1939
GWR 2-8-0 No. 3814 (28XX Class) built 1940
GWR 2-8-0 No. 3822 (28XX Class) built 1940
GWR 2-8-0 No. 3845 (28XX Class) built 1942
GWR 2-8-0 No. 3850 (28XX Class) built 1942
GWR 2-8-0 No. 3855 (28XX Class) built 1942
GWR 2-8-0 No. 3862 (28XX Class) built 1942
GWR 2-6-2T No. 4115 (41XX Class) built 1936
GWR 2-6-2T No. 4121 (41XX Class) built 1937
GWR 2-6-2T No. 4156 (41XX Class) built 1947
GWR 2-8-0T No. 4247 (42XX Class) built 1916
GWR 2-8-0T No. 4248 (42XX Class) built 1916
GWR 2-8-0T No. 4253 (42XX Class) built 1917
GWR 2-8-0T No. 4277 (42XX Class) built 1920
GWR 0-6-0PT No. 4612 (57XX Class) built 1942

SR 4-6-2 No. 35009 *Shaw Savill* built 1942 (Wessex Railway Society)
SR 4-6-2 No. 35010 *Blue Star* built 1942
SR 4-6-2 No. 35011 *General Steam Navigation* built 1944
SR 4-6-2 No. 35018 *British India Line* built 1945
SR 4-6-2 No. 35022 *Holland-America Line* built 1948 (Swanage Railway)
SR 4-6-2 No. 35025 *Brocklebank Line* built 1948
SR 4-6-2 No. 35027 *Port Line* built 1948 (Bournemouth Steam Centre)
LMS 2-6-0 No. 42859 (6P/5F Class) built 1930 (Peak Railway Society)
LMS 0-6-0 No. 44123 (4F Class) built 1925 (Peak Railway Society)
LMS 4-6-0 No. 44901 (5MT Class) built 1945 (Peak Railway Society)
LMS 4-6-0 No. 45163 (5MT Class) built 1935
LMS 4-6-0 No. 45293 (5MT Class) built 1936 (45293 Fund)
LMS 4-6-0 No. 45337 (5MT Class) built 1937
LMS 4-6-0 No. 45491 (5MT Class) built 1943
LMS 4-6-0 No. 45699 *Galatea* built 1936 (owners of *Leander*)
LMS 0-6-0T No. 47406 (3F Class) built 1926
LMS 2-8-0 No. 48173 (8F Class) built 1943
LMS 2-8-0 No. 48305 (8F Class) built 1943
LMS 2-8-0 No. 48518 (8F Class) built 1944 (Peak Railway Society)
LMS 2-8-0 No. 48624 (8F Class) built 1943
BR 4-6-0 No. 73096 (5MT Class) built 1955
BR 4-6-0 No. 73156 (5MT Class) built 1956
BR 4-6-0 No. 75014 (4MT Class) built 1951
BR 4-6-0 No. 75079 (4MT Class) built 1956 (reserved)
BR 2-6-0 No. 76077 (4MT Class) built 1956 (reserved)
BR 2-6-0 No. 76084 (4MT Class) built 1957 (reserved)
BR 2-6-0 No. 78059 (2MT Class) built 1956
BR 2-6-4T No. 80072 (4MT Class) built 1953
BR 2-6-4T No. 80080 (4MT Class) built 1954 (reserved)
BR 2-6-4T No. 80097 (4MT Class) built 1954
BR 2-6-4T No. 80098 (4MT Class) built 1954 (Great Central Railway)
BR 2-6-4T No. 80104 (4MT Class) built 1955 (reserved)
BR 2-6-4T No. 80150 (4MT Class) built 1956 (Peak Railway Society)
BR 2-10-0 No. 92085 (9F Class) built 1956
BR 2-10-0 No. 92134 (9F Class) built 1957
BR 2-10-0 No. 92207 (9F Class) built 1959
BR 2-10-0 No. 92214 (9F Class) built 1959
BR 2-10-0 No. 92219 (9F Class) built 1960
BR 2-10-0 No. 92245 (9F Class) built 1958
BR A1A-A1A DH No. D601 *Ark Royal* built 1958
BR Bo-Bo DH No. D6122 built 1959

## 333   BP Chemical International Ltd    I

Sully, Penarth, Glamorgan CF6 2YU
OS Ref: ST 143683

Industrial steam location featuring regular steam working.

**Stock**
Barclay 0-4-0F No. 1 2238 built 1948

## 334   Monsanto Chemicals Ltd    I

Corporation Road, Newport, Gwent
OS Ref: ST 335855

Industrial steam location featuring occasional steam working

**Stock**
Barclay 0-4-0F *Monsanto* 1966 built 1929

## 335   Inco Europe Ltd    I

Clydach-on-Taire, West Glamorgan
OS Ref: SN 696013

Industrial steam location with locomotive in store

**Stock**
Peckett 0-4-0ST MNC No. 1 (W5 Class) 1345 built 1914

## 336   National Coal Board    I

South Wales and Western Areas

Industrial steam locations, many of them featuring regular steam working

**Stock**
Hawthorn Leslie 0-4-0ST *Shakespeare* 3072 built 1914 Bersham Colliery, Rhostyllen
Peckett 0-4-0ST *Hornet* 1935 built 1937 Bersham Colliery, Rhostyllen
Hunslet 0-6-0ST 3829 built 1955 Lady Windsor Colliery, Ynysybwl
Peckett 0-6-0ST (OQ class) 2150 built 1954. Out of use at Mardy Colliery, Maerdy
Hudswell Clarke 0-6-0ST No. 1 1885 built 1955 Mountain Ash depot
Avonside 0-6-0ST *Lord Camrose* 2008 built 1930. Out of use at Mountain Ash depot
RSH 0-6-0ST No. 8 7139 built 1944 Mountain Ash depot
Peckett 0-6-0ST *Sir Gomer* 1859 built 1932 Mountain Ash depot
GWR 0-6-0PT No. 7754 North British Loco 24042 built 1930. Out of use at Mountain Ash depot
Avonside 0-6-0ST *Sir John* 1680 built 1914 Mountain Ash depot
Barclay 0-6-0ST *Llantanum Abbey* 2074 built 1939 Mountain Ash depot
Barclay 0-4-0ST *The Blaenavon Toto No. 6* 1619 built 1919. Dismantled at Blaenavon Washery
Barclay 0-4-0ST *The Blaenavon Nora No. 5* 1680 built 1920. Out of use at Blaenavon Washery
Peckett 0-6-0ST *Meneleaus* (B3 class) 1889 built 1935 Marine Washery, Cwm
Peckett 0-6-0ST (B2 class) 1426 built 1916 Brynlliw Colliery, Gravesend

Peckett 0–6–0ST (B3 class) 2114 built 1951 Brynlliw Colliery, Gravesend
RSH 0–6–0ST No. 71516 7170 built 1944. Out of use at Graig Merthyr Colliery, Pontardulais
Hunslet 0–6–0ST 3846 built 1956. Out of use at Graig Merthyr Colliery, Pontardulais
Bagnall 0–6–0ST 2758 built 1944 Graig Merthyr Colliery, Pontardulais
Hunslet 0–6–0ST *Norma* 3770 built 1952 Graig Merthyr Colliery, Pontardulais
Hunslet 0–6–0ST *Pamela* 3840 built 1956. Out of use at Maesteg depot
Vulcan Foundry 0–6–0ST 5272 built 1945. Out of use at Garw Colliery, Blaengarw

## 337   Holyhead Breakwater Railway          B

Short standard gauge line along Holyhead breakwater, operated by British Railways. Due to its light construction and sharp curves, the line has become the home for the two surviving 01 Class diesel shunters which, despite their new numbering, still sport early BR black livery.
OS Ref: SH 235836

**Stock**
[1]BR 0–4–0DM No. 01 001 Barclay 396 built 1956 (Formerly BR No. D2954)
[1]BR 0–4–0DM No. 01 002 Barclay 397 built 1956 (Formerly BR No. D2955)
Wickham 4WPMR No. TR23 7516

[1]Locomotives used by William Wild & Sons Ltd

## 338   Fairfields-Mabey Limited          G

Engineers and Shipbuilders, Chepstow, Gwent
OS Ref: ST 538938
The following locomotives have been stored out of use for a number of years, but no decision on their future has been made. In view of their historic nature, it is hoped that somebody will preserve them.

No public access

**Stock**
[1]GER 0–4–0ST No. 229 *Neilson* (2119) built 1876
Kerr Stuart 0–4–0WT No. D249 (3063) built 1918

[1]Great Eastern '209' Class saddletank, rebuilt in 1895 and 1906 and withdrawn from service in 1917. The following year it was sold to the Standard Shipbuilding Co. Ltd and subsequently became the property of its present owners. Sister locomotive No. 230 as LNER Class Y5 No. 7230 became works pilot at Stratford Old Works for several years, affectionately known as the 'Coffee Pot', a description that was most apt. The class had long stovepipe chimneys and the characteristic Neilson 'ogee'-shaped saddletank with a flat top, on which the coal supply was kept.

## 339   J. Woodroffe          C

Welshpool, Powys
A private 15in. gauge line, three-quarters-of-a-mile long and being extended to one-and-a-half miles.

**Stock**
Severn-Lamb 0–6–2T *Powys* (20) built 1973
Two bogie coaches

## 340   Croesor Junction and Pacific          C
##         Railroad

A 7¼in. gauge private line under construction by Brian Hollingsworth at his home at Penrhyndeudraeth, Gwynedd. When complete this will be a most ambitious line incorporating spirals and reversing loops with gradients of 1 in 22 due to the terrain over which the line is being built.

**Stock**
East African Railways 4–8–2 + 2–8–4 No. 5928 *Mount Kilimanjaro* 19,340ft (built Coleley-Simkins 1973)
Darjeeling Himalayan Railway 0–4–0STT *Kanchenjunga* (built Coleley-Simkins 1974)
Rio Grande 2–8–2 No. 487 *Queen of Colorado* K36 class built Curwen 1970

## 341   Coney Beach Railway          B

Porthcawl, Glamorgan
OS Ref: SS 821768
A 15in. gauge passenger-carrying line, a quarter of a mile in length connecting Coney Beach with Porthcawl Pier. Operates daily during the holiday season with a very frequent train service.

**Stock**
Freelance 4–6–4PE No. 1935 *Silver Jubilee* built 1935 (steam outline)
Freelance 4–6–4PE No. 1936 *Coney Queen* built 1936 (steam outline)
Open bogie coaches (ex Festival Gardens Railway, Battersea)

## 342   Magic Dragon Railway          B

Gwrych Castle, Abergele, Clwyd
A passenger-carrying 10¼in. gauge line, 400 yards in length. The railway operates to coincide with the Castle opening and trains run as required.

**Stock**
Gwrych Castle Ltd Co-BoD *The Chieftain* built 1954
Six open bogie coaches

## 343 Afan Valley Light Railway          F

Cymmer Afan, Glamorgan
OS Ref: SS 859961

A scheme to construct an entirely new 12¼ in. gauge passenger-carrying steam railway along the trackbed of the former GWR Afan Valley branch between Cymmer and Pontrhydyfen, a distance of 4½ miles. The rolling stock and equipment for the line is that formerly operated on the Reseau Guerledan, Mur de Bretagne, France.

**Stock**
Lister 4WDM 3593 built 1931 (Rebuilt from 2 ft gauge 1978)
Lynton & Barnstaple 2-6-2T No. 1 *Jubilee* built Curwen 1978
Darjeeling-Himalayan Rly 0-4-0TT No. 4 *France* built Milner Engineering 1978
Leek & Manifold Rly 2-6-4T No. 5 *Elaine* built Milner Engineering 1979
Denver & Rio Grande 4-2-0PMR No. 3 *Galloping Goose* built 1978

## 344 Vale of Teifi Narrow Gauge Railway  F

Henllan, Llandyssul, Dyfed
OS Ref: SN 358406

A scheme to construct an entirely new 2 ft gauge passenger-carrying railway along 9 miles of the trackbed of the former Pencader-Newcastle Emlyn branch.
*Details from:* Mr G. Toogood, Old Coach House, Henllan, Llandyssul, Dyfed.

**Stock**
Motor Rail 4WDM No. 1 8683 built 1941
Motor Rail 4WDM No. 35 7126 built 1936
Ten skip wagons

At the time of going to press, a Light Railway Order was being sought.

## 345 Kiln Park Railway          B

Kiln Park, Tenby, Dyfed

Passenger-carrying 2 ft gauge railway consisting of a 600-yard oval track. Formerly operated at Chessington Zoo (see Group No. 86)

The train consists of an accurately conceived model of Stephenson's *Rocket* plus covered carriages.

**Stock**
Stephenson 0-2-2PM *Rocket* (steam outline, BMC 1100cc petrol engine) built 'Group 4' 1970
Bogie covered coaches

## 346 Milton          G

Mr G. Davies, Stevens Green Farm, Milton, near Pembroke, Dyfed
Standard gauge industrial steam locomotive undergoing restoration.

**Stock**
Bagnall 0-4-0ST 2565 built 1936

## 347 Ian Jolly and Friends          G

1 Llewelyn Drive, Bryn-y-Baal, near Mold, Clwyd.
OS Ref: SJ 261647

Private collection of narrow gauge locomotives and rolling stock in store and undergoing restoration.

**Stock**
Motor Rail 4WDM 9547 built 1950 60 cm gauge
Motor Rail 4WDM 20558 built 1955 1 ft 11½ in. gauge
Motor Rail 4WPM 5297 built 1931 1 ft 11½ in. gauge
Motor Rail 4WDM 8723 built 1941 60 cm gauge
Motor Rail 4WPM built c1920 1 ft 11½ in. gauge
Watson/Motor Rail 4WPM built 1918 2 ft 8 in. gauge
Motor Rail 4WPM 6013 built 1931 1 ft 11½ in. gauge
Lister 4WDM 30233 built 1946 1 ft 11½ in. gauge

# AREA H

# West Midlands

Worcestershire
Warwickshire
Staffordshire
Herefordshire
Gloucestershire
West Midlands
Salop

---

### 351   Foxfield Light Railway        ★★★A

Foxfield Colliery, Dilhorne, Blythe Bridge, Stoke-on-Trent, Staffordshire

*Access:* Potteries Motor Traction bus service 86B from either Longton (Stoke-on-Trent) or Cheadle operates in conjunction with the trains on Sundays. A special all-inclusive fare applies; the bus ticket being exchanged for a railway ticket at the Foxfield booking office, whilst the railway ticket acts as the return bus ticket. Passengers alight from the bus at Godley Brook, approximately 200 yards from the railway station.
Tel: Stoke-on-Trent 313920
OS Ref: SJ 976446

Photo: John Gardner

Still in Staffordshire, Hunslet 0–6–0ST *Wimblebury* once hauled coal trains across Cannock Chase. Now she hauls passengers along the Foxfield Light Railway

---

Four mile standard gauge line from Foxfield Colliery to Blythe Bridge (Staffordshire).

The railway was built in 1893 to connect Foxfield Colliery, Dilhorne, with the North Staffordshire Railway at a junction 400 yards west of Blythe Bridge Station. The colliery closed in 1965 and with it the railway, but both were purchased by Tean Minerals Ltd, who now occupy the colliery buildings. The Foxfield Light Railway Society Ltd operate the railway by permission of the owners.

The line climbs steeply away from Foxfield Colliery heading northwards and curves left through Foxfield Wood and Pearcroft Wood to the summit of the line (750 ft). Having curved round to the south-west, the line straightens out through Dilhorne Wood, past the 17th century Stansmore Hall to circle the foot of Blakely Bank Wood and cross the Caverswall–Dilhorne road by a gated level crossing. Continuing downhill, there is a further straight section and deep cutting spanned by the Caverswall–Blythe Bridge road overbridge, and a little further on passengers get a view of the 13th century Caverswall Castle. The railway terminates in a fan of sidings not far from Blythe Bridge BR station.

*Details from:* A. J. Rogers, 100 Drubbery Lane, Blurton, Longton, Stoke-on-Trent, Staffordshire ST3 4BL.
*Subscription:* £2 per year; students £1; juniors £1.
*Facilities:* Train rides and refreshments. All passengers must be members or day members to satisfy insurance requirements.
The railway operates each Sunday between April and October inclusive. Special trains at other times by arrangement.

## Stock

Hunslet 0-6-0ST *Wimblebury* (3839) built 1956
RSH 0-4-0CT *Roker* (7006) built 1940
Manning Wardle 0-6-0ST No. 35 (1317) built 1895
Avonside 0-6-0ST *Robert* (2068) built 1933
Avonside 0-6-0ST *Cranford* (1919) built 1924
Bagnall 0-6-0ST *Topham* (2193) built 1922
Bagnall 0-6-0ST *Lewisham* (2221) built 1927
Bagnall 0-4-0ST *J. T. Daly* (2450) built 1931
Bagnall 0-4-0ST *Hawarden* (2623) built 1940
Peckett 0-4-0ST *Henry Cort* (933) built 1903
Peckett 0-4-0ST No. 11 (2081) built 1947
Barclay 0-4-0F No. 1 (1984) built 1930
Simplex 4WDM *Helen* (2262) built 1923
Sentinel 4WVBTG 9535 built 1952
Ruston Hornsby 4WDM 395305 built 1956
LMS 60 ft vestibuled corridor coach No. 27249 built 1945
Two LMS four-wheeled covered goods vans Nos 7090 and 50085
Three BR Mk 1 bogie coaches
Four LMS bogie scenery vans Nos 37508, 37518, 37519 and 38268 (two converted into observation coaches and another used as refreshment van)
NSR flat wagon No. 11995 built 1916
BR 20-ton goods brake van No. B951789
Seven NCB open coal wagons
Five Wickham 4WPM rail trolleys
CEGB 21-ton all-steel coal wagon built 1937
LNWR coke hopper wagon No. 17420
Tar wagon
LNER tank wagon No. 38386
GWR wagon frame
Smith Rodley steam crane No. 12394
NSR third-class loop-line coach body built *c.* 1875
MR first-class saloon coach body No. 2741 built 1884

*Note:* Some of the above items are privately-owned.

## 352  Severn Valley Railway                A

The Railway Station, Bridgnorth, Salop WV16 5DT

*Access:* Wolverhampton, Stourbridge or Kidderminster BR stations. Thence by West Midlands or Midland Red bus
Tel: Bewdley 403816 or Bridgnorth 4361
OS Ref: SO 793753 (Bewdley) and SO 715926 (Bridgnorth)

Passenger-carrying standard gauge steam railway, 12½ miles in length running from Bridgnorth to Bewdley.
The railway operates at weekends and Bank Holidays from March to October and daily from mid-July to early September.

Facilities for visitors include car parking, railway shops, picnic areas, refreshments and toilets.
*Publicity Manager:* A. G. Bending, 292 Bradford Road, Castle Bromwich, Birmingham B36 9AB. Tel. 021-747 3863
The Severn Valley Railway from Shrewsbury to Hartlebury, 40 miles long, was opened in 1862. It became part of the Great Western Railway in 1872 and that company constructed a spur from Bewdley to Kidderminster in 1878, allowing through running from the industrial West Midlands. Under British Railways ownership, the Severn Valley line was closed to through traffic in 1963. North of Bridgnorth the line was lifted, whilst south of Alveley, coal trains used the line until 1969.
A scheme to preserve the disused but intact section from Bridgnorth to Alveley and to run passenger trains as far as Hampton Loade was first mooted in 1965. The Severn Valley Railway Society was formed in July of that year and after considerable fund-raising efforts and a legal battle with the local councils to obtain Light Railway Orders, the line reopened on 23 May 1970.
In 1972, the Severn Valley Railway (Holdings) Co. was formed and £110,000 was raised by public subscription to enable the railway to be purchased from Alveley to Foley Park (Kidderminster) allowing a 12½-mile passenger run from Bridgnorth to Bewdley. This section was reopened on 18 May 1974.

## Stock

[1]LNER 2-6-0 No. 3442 *The Great Marquess* (Class K4) built 1938
LMR 2-10-0 No. 600 *Gordon* (Riddles Class WD) built 1943
[2]LMS 2-6-0 No. 43106 (Ivatt Class 4MT) built 1951
[5]LMS 2-6-0 No. 46443 (Ivatt Class 2MT) built 1950
LMS 2-6-0 No. 46521 (Ivatt Class 2MT) built 1953
GWR 0-6-0PT No. 3612 built 1939
[10]LMS 2-8-0 No. 8233 (Class 8F) (North British Locomotive Co. No. 24607) built 1940
[9]LMS 0-6-0T No. 47383 (Class 3F) (Vulcan Foundry 3954) built 1926
[11]LMS 2-6-0 No. 2968 (Class 5P/4F) built 1933
[7]BR 4-6-2 No. 70000 *Britannia* (Class 7MT) built 1951
[15]GWR 2-6-0 No. 9303 (Class 43XX) built 1932
[8]GWR 0-6-0ST No. 813 (ex Port Talbot Railway No. 26) (Hudswell Clarke 555) built 1901
[16]GWR 4-6-0 No. 7802 *Bradley Manor* built 1938
[16]GWR 4-6-0 No. 7812 *Erlestoke Manor* built 1939
[17]GWR 2-6-2T No. 4150 (41XX Class) built 1947
[12]GWR 0-6-0PT No. 1501 (Class 15XX) built 1949
[4]GWR 0-6-0 No. 3205 (Class 2251) built 1946
GWR 2-6-2T No. 5164 (Class 5101) built 1930
GWR 0-6-0PT No. 5764 (LT No. L95) (Class 57XX) built 1929
GWR 4-6-0 No. 6960 *Raveningham Hall* built 1944
GWR 2-6-2T No. 4566 (45XX Class) built 1924
[6]LMS 4-6-0 No. 45000 (Stanier 5MT Class) built 1934
[3]LMS 4-6-0 No. 45110 *RAF Biggin Hill* (Class 5MT) (Vulcan Foundry 4653) built 1935
BR 2-6-4T No. 80079 (Class 4MT) built 1954
GWR 2-6-2T No. 4141 (Class 5101) built 1946
GWR 2-8-0 No. 2857 (Class 28XX) built 1918
GWR 4-6-0 No. 7819 *Hinton Manor* built 1939

Photo: Graham Scott-Lowe

A morning mist hangs low over the track as No. 193 *Shropshire* gets to grips with a Boxing Day special from Bewdley

GWR 4-6-0 No. 4930 *Hagley Hall* built 1929
BR 2-6-0 No. 78019 (Class 2MT) built 1954
BR 4-6-0 No. 75069 (Class 4MT) built 1955
GWR 0-6-0PT No. 7714 (Class 57XX) built 1930
Hunslet 0-6-0ST No. 193 *Shropshire* (3793) built 1953
[13]Manning Wardle 0-6-0ST *Warwickshire* (2047) built 1926
[14]Hunslet 0-6-0T *The Lady Armaghdale* (686) built 1898
Peckett 0-4-0ST No. 4 (1738) built 1928
LNWR 2-2-2 No. 173 *Cornwall* built 1847
BR Co-CoDH No. D1013 *Western Ranger* built 1962
BR Co-CoDH No. D1062 *Western Courier* built 1963
Fowler 0-4-0DM No. 17 *Highflyer* 22912) built 1940
Ruston and Hornsby 0-4-0DM 319290 (165DS Class) built 1953
Hudswell Clarke 0-4-0DM *Mary* (D577) built 1932
GWR third-class diner coach No. 9627 built 1932
GWR first-class diner coach No. 9615 built 1932
GWR corridor third bogie coach No. 1116 built 1938
GWR corridor third bogie coach No. 2119 built 1949

GWR corridor third-class bogie coach No. 3930 built 1915
GWR unclassed bogie saloon coach No. 9369 built 1923
LSWR bogie saloon coach No. 11 built 1910
SECR bogie saloon coach No. 177 built 1907
LNWR six-wheeled directors saloon No. 45021 built 1910
GWR corridor composite coach No. 7284 built 1941
GWR Collett third-class saloon coach No. 9103 built 1929
GWR sleeping cars Nos 9082, 9084 and 9085 built 1951
GWR corridor/composite coach No. 6045 built 1928
[17]GNR Gresley family saloon No. 807 built 1912
[19]LMS open third coach No. 27218 built 1945
[15]GWR Churchward brake/third-class saloon No. 9055 built 1912
[15]GWR Hawksworth corridor third bogie coach No. 829 built 1948
[15]GWR Collett corridor third bogie coach No. 1087 built 1938
[15]GWR Collett brake corridor third bogie coach No. 5883 built 1934
[18]GWR Collett corridor third-class bogie coach No. 1146 built 1938
GWR 'Toplight' corridor third coach No. 2426 built 1910
GWR Churchward passenger brake van No. 1145 built 1922

BR corridor composite coach No. M15553 built 1955
BR SK bogie coach No. 24396 built 1953
BR BSK bogie coach No. 34562 built 1955
BR corridor composite coach No. S16202 built 1961
LMS open third bogie coach No. 9355 built 1936
GCR 'Barnum' saloon third bogie coach No. 664 built 1910
LMS corridor composite bogie coach No. 24617 built 1950
LMS brake/third bogie coaches Nos 26921 and 26986 built 1950
LMS third-class open bogie coaches Nos 27220 and 27270 built 1945
BR brake/second open bogie coach No. M9220 built 1955
BR first-class open bogie coach No. W3083 built 1957
[6]GWR buffet car No. 9631 built 1934
LMS corridor third bogie coaches Nos 12992 and 13045 built 1949
BR Mk 1 TSO bogie coach No. SC4054 built 1957
BR Mk 1 TSO bogie coach No. E3785 built 1953
GWR engineers inspection saloon No. DW80969 built 1948
[15]GWR Collett auto coach No. 178 built 1930
[15]GWR Collett brake corridor composite bogie coach No. 6562 built 1938
[15]GWR Collett brake corridor composite bogie coaches Nos 6912 and 6913 built 1934
[20]LMS Open 3rd bogie coach No. 5682 built 1926
LMS Stainer corridor third class coach No. W2300M built 1946
LNER Gresley Buffet car No. 9131 built 1937
LNER Gresley Mess & Tool Van No. 320700
LNER Gresley brake/third class open coach No. 16600
LNER Gresley corridor brake composite coach No. 24068 built 1937
LMS brake/third bogie coach No. 26680 built 1950
GWR corridor/third bogie coach No. 1086 built 1938
LMS open first-class bogie coach No. 7511 built 1934
BR corridor second-class bogie coach No. E24726 built 1953
GWR milk brake van No. 1399 built 1920
LMS six-wheeled 'Stove R' van No. 32919 built 1932
GWR six-wheeled tool van No. 112 built 1904
GWR four-wheeled tool van No. 141 built 1920
GWR four-wheeled riding van No. 89
GWR four-wheeled riding van No. 118 built 1904
GWR four-wheeled tool van No. 143
GWR 'Toad' 20-ton goods brake van No. 17410 built 1940
[15]GWR 'Siphon G' bogie van No. 1257 built 1927
GWR 'Toad' 20-ton goods brake van No. 68669 built 1924
GWR 10-ton banana van No. 82554 built 1927
GWR 'Loriot' 20-ton machinery wagon No. 42343 built 1944
[17]GWR 'Fruit D' van No. W92080 built 1958
[16]GWR 'Fruit D' van No. W92090 built 1958
[16]GWR breakdown tool van No. 66 built 1920
[16]GWR breakdown riding van No. 162 built 1923
[16]LNER bogie pigeon van No. 4236 built 1938
[18]GWR breakdown riding van No. 55 built 1908
[18]GWR sleeper wagon No. 40554 built 1899
[18]GWR steel tool van No. 80982 built 1913
[18]GWR 'Mink' 10-ton covered van No. 93016 built 1918
[18]GWR open wagon No. 97398 built 1921
[18]GWR Signal Department wagon No. 14428 built 1921

[18]GWR 'Mink' 12-ton covered van No. 104621 built 1925
[18]GWR 'Mica B' refrigerated meat van No. 105873 built 1925
[15]GWR 'Macaw B' bogie bolster wagon No. 107291 built 1935
[18]GWR 'Mogo' motor-car van No. 65801 built 1947
[18]GWR 10-ton ballast wagon No. 30903 built 1941
[18]GWR six-ton passenger fruit van No. 2303 built 1898
[18]GWR shunter's 'chariot' No. 41736 built 1913
[18]GWR 'Iron Mink' covered van No. 58725 built 1890
[18]GWR 20-ton 'Toad' goods brake van No. 68501 built 1925
[18]GWR china clay wagon No. 94059 built 1915
[18]GWR 'Vanfit' covered van (plywood body) No. 65620 built 1947
Tar tank wagon No. 76073 built 1914
CR Engineers Wagon No. 300682 cut down from covered van built 1910
LNWR Covered combination truck No. 395273 built 1921
BSC 7-plank open wagon No. 16053 built 1937
LMS 10-ton open wagon No. 14188 built 1934
GWR four-wheeled riding van No. DW9
GWR insulated fruit van A No. 134290 built 1938
GWR 'Mink A' covered van No. 101961 built 1920
LMS 12-ton open wagon No. 257632
LMS 12-ton open wagon *Sycobrite* built 1937
LNER 12-ton open wagon No. 223162 built 1938
LNER 13-ton open wagon No. 225641 built 1938
GWR 'Gane A' bogie bolster wagon No. 60841
GWR balast wagons Nos 80225 and 80603 built 1937
BR 30-ton steam crane No. ADM1091/30 built Cowans Sheldon, 1961
BR match truck No. ADB9998524 built 1961
BR 'Macaw B' bogie bolster wagon
BR horsebox underframes Nos SV14191, 14192 and 14193
BR steam crane No. DW35 built 1949
BR match truck No. DW75 built 1949
Field and Mackay 12-ton open wagon No. 41 built 1936
CR 10-ton covered vans Nos 2080 and 4543 built 1910
Esso oil tank wagon No. 2686 built 1949
Great Western Collieries 13-ton open wagon No. 2717 built 1936
Highley Mining Co. 13-ton open wagon No. 136 built 1946
Lothian Coal Co. Ltd 12-ton open wagon No. 37
GWR 'Fruit D' covered vans Nos 3429 and 3467 built 1950
LMS covered van No. 98543 built 1924
Matesa ballast tamping machine No. PWM4025
BR large tamping machine No. TT65RD
Cadbury all-steel covered van No. 8718
Goodyear Tyre Co. steel mineral wagon No. 1A
Six Wickham petrol rail trolleys

[1]Built at Darlington in June 1938 and withdrawn from Thornton Junction shed in December 1961 as BR No. 61994.

---

**A scene reminiscent of the last days of steam on BR as Ivatt Class 4 2—6—0 No. 43106 draws forward at Bridgnorth on the Severn Valley Railway**

**Photo: John Gardner**

The K4 class, of which only six were built, were the last steam locomotives to be specially designed for the West Highland line from Glasgow to Fort William. On withdrawal, *The Great Marquess* was purchased for preservation by Viscount Garnock and for several years was based in Leeds and worked enthusiasts' special trains.

[2]This design was the last to appear on the LMS prior to nationalisation. Embodying many new features and designed for maximum accessibility of working parts, the locomotives looked impressive and powerful but otherwise were not very pleasing to the eye compared with the older types they were designed to replace. Early examples of the class had double chimneys. Several of the class worked on the former M & GNJR line, in fact the entire class appears to have worked in rather exposed areas where their enclosed cabs and tender shields gave more protection to their crews. No. 43106 was withdrawn from Lostock Hall shed, Preston, in July 1968 and is the only member of the class preserved.

[3]Withdrawn from Lostock Hall shed in August 1968 after working the last steam-hauled standard-gauge BR passenger train. Purchased for preservation in 1969.

[4]Withdrawn from Templecombe (S & DJR) shed in May 1965 as BR No. 3205. The GWR never utilised 0-6-0 tender locomotives to the same extent as other railways, relying on their 2-6-0s for most mixed traffic, intermediate work. The 2251 class was designed to relieve the 'Dean Goods' locomotives of their duties on unrestricted routes in order that these older, smaller engines could be concentrated on the Cambrian section, thus replacing many of the older Cambrian types. One-hundred-and twenty of the 2251 type were constructed and took their turn with passenger work over the longer cross-country routes, the Didcot, Newbury and Southampton line being a typical example.

[5]Withdrawn from Manchester (Newton Heath) shed as BR No. 46443 in March 1967. This class was introduced in 1946 by the LMS to replace an ageing collection of LNWR, Midland and Caledonian class 2F 0-6-0s on lighter work. Simultaneously, a lightweight 2-6-2T version was introduced (see Group No. 151) for corresponding passenger work. Both types were built by BR until the introduction of almost identical standard classes. All finally fell victim to diesel traction, some being withdrawn before types they were intended to displace were extinct. Six of the LMS 2-6-0s and one of the BR design have been preserved and are ideal locomotives for branch line work.

[6]On loan from British Railways Board.

[7]*Britannia* was the prototype British Railways 'Pacific' and the first of the 999 BR standard locomotives to be built between 1951 and 1960. It was also a milestone in British locomotive practice, since it was the first two-cylinder 'Pacific' built for use in this country. The idea of standard designs was to facilitate a reduction in the amount of spare parts required, whilst at the same time producing a range of locomotives capable of working without restriction over the whole British Railways system. Had it not been for the introduction of diesels, there is little doubt that several hundred 'Britannias' would have been built. As it was, only 55 locomotives of the class were constructed and they suffered the fate of other steam engines, the first withdrawal taking place in 1965 after a ridiculously short life of only 14 years. All the survivors had been withdrawn by the end of 1967, with the exception of No. 70013, which was the last steam locomotive to be overhauled by BR at Crewe Works earlier that year. *Britannia* was laid aside after withdrawal for official preservation, but was replaced at the last minute by *Oliver Cromwell*, and it was left to a group of amateur enthusiasts to save this historic engine for posterity. Owned by the Britannia Locomotive Society (*q.v.*).

[8]Sold to Backworth Colliery, Northumberland, as GWR No. 813 in 1934. Purchased for preservation 1968. During the course of overhauls at Swindon, this locomotive was fitted with various standard GWR fittings, making it a prime example of the hybrid products which appeared on the GWR following the grouping. Owned by the GWR 813 Preservation Fund (*q.v.*).

[9]Originally LMS No. 16466. Withdrawn from Westhouses shed in 1967 as BR No. 47383 and purchased for preservation. This engine worked at Williamthorpe Colliery in its later days and was first withdrawn in 1966 when diesel replacements arrived. However, due to repeated diesel failures, No. 47383 was reinstated and worked satisfactorily at the colliery until purchased for preservation. Owned by the Manchester Rail Travel Society (*q.v.*).

[10]Built for War Department service, this locomotive was briefly loaned to the LMS until 1941, after which it was sent to Iran as No. 307, later becoming Iran State Railways No. 41.109, before transfer to Egypt in 1944 as WD No. 70307. Renumbered WD No. 500, it was returned to England in 1952 and served on the Longmoor Military Railway before joining 663 sisters as British Railways No. 48773 in 1957. It was finally withdrawn from Rose Grove shed in 1968 and purchased for preservation. Owned by the Stanier 8F Locomotive Society Ltd (*q.v.*).

[11]The first design of Sir W. A. Stanier following his appointment as CME to the LMSR in 1932 was a batch of 40 2-6-0s built at Crewe Works in 1933/34. A mixed traffic design, the class were deployed and operated throughout the LMSR network and were regularly employed on fast freight and passenger duties. First numbered in the 132XX series, No. 13268 was completed on 24 January 1934 and renumbered 2968 on 20 September 1935 in LMS stock. She eventually became the last working member of the class, being withdrawn as BR No. 42968 from Springs Branch motive power depot, Wigan, on 31 December 1966 as part of the elimination of steam on BR and sold for scrap to Woodham Brothers of Barry on 8 March 1967. Owned by the Stanier Mogul Fund (*q.v.*).

[12]Ex NCB Coventry Colliery, 1971. Owned by the Warwickshire Railway Society (*q.v.*).

[13]The very last locomotive built by Manning Wardle and Co. It was purchased from the Rugby Portland Cement Co. Ltd, New Bilton Works, Rugby, in 1967 and has been immaculately restored in a fully-lined sky-blue livery and named *Warwickshire*. Owned by the Warwickshire Railway Society (*q.v.*).

[14]Ex ICI Dyestuffs Division, Blackley Works, Manchester, 1969. The locomotive formerly worked on the Manchester Ship Canal Railway. Owned by the Warwickshire Railway Society (*q.v.*).

[15]Owned by the Great Western (SVR) Association (*q.v.*).

Photo: Geoff King

Photo: John Gardner

The GWR had a way of doing things in its own impeccable 'manor'! No. 7819 poised ready to go at Bridgnorth is a sight to gladden the hearts of all true Swindon enthusiasts

A proud driver gives a final polish to his gleaming steed, No. 6960 *Raveningham Hall* at Bridgnorth.

[16]Owned by Erlestoke Manor Fund *(q.v.)*.
[17]Owned by 4150 Locomotive Fund *(q.v.)*.
[18]Owned by GWR 813 Preservation Fund *(q.v.)*.
[19]Owned by the Warwickshire Railway Society *(q.v.)*.
[20]Owned by the Historic Rolling Stock Group

## Stanier 8F Locomotive Society Ltd      H

Registered Charity No. 261751

Severn Valley Railway

*Secretary:* A. Violet, 50 Roberts Road, Prestbury, Cheltenham, Gloucestershire
*Subscription:* Ordinary £1.50 per annum, joint husband and wife £2.50; juniors (under 16) and students 75p; pensioners £1; life membership £25
The Society exists to further the continued operation and preservation of Class 8F 2-8-0 No. 8233 as a tribute to these tough and reliable machines, and to the outstanding school of design initiated by Sir William Stanier on the London Midland and Scottish Railway. Members are kept fully informed of all activities through a quarterly illustrated magazine *Black Eight*.

A sight to gladden the hearts of every enthusiast, Great Western or otherwise. Back from the dead comes No. 7812 *Erlestoke Manor* on its inaugural run on 31 August 1979, heading the Cambrian Coast Express along SVR metals

## GWR 813 Preservation Fund      H

Severn Valley Railway, Shropshire

*Aims:* (1) The permanent preservation and restoration to working order of former GWR locomotive 813; (2) the preservation and restoration of a representative collection of items of rolling stock from the former GWR with a special emphasis on goods and other non-passenger vehicles.
*Membership:* Currently about 200 shareholders
*Subscription:* Minimum of two 50p shares (or equivalent in trading stamps), for which a share certificate is issued. No annual subscription stipulated other than a small period contribution for issue of newsletters, etc.

*Secretary:* P. H. Goss, 23 Hatchmere, Thornbury, near Bristol BS12 2EU

The Fund also owns rolling stock housed on the West Somerset Railway (see Group No. 4), The Bristol Suburban Railway (see Group No. 9) and GWS Didcot (see Group No. 456).

## Manchester Rail Travel Society      H

Severn Valley Railway

*Details from:* F. G. Cronin, 12 Chiltern Road, Ramsbottom, Lancashire

*Aims:* The preservation and restoration to working order on the SVR of LMS *Jinty* No. 47383. Steamed late in 1973 after complete overhaul. With the exception of a period in 1976 has worked ever since on the SVR with over 9,000 miles to its credit.

## Britannia Locomotive Society                         H

Severn Valley Railway, Shropshire

*Secretary:* R. L. Kingston, 'Lysander', Merchant Lane, Cranfield, Bedfordshire MK43 0DA
*Annual subscription:* Adults £2; husband and wife £3; OAPs 50p; life membership £20
*Membership:* 225

## Erlestoke Manor Fund                                  H

An independent fund, formed in March 1973, to purchase and restore to working order the former GWR 'Manor' Class 4-6-0 locomotive No. 7812 *Erlestoke Manor*.

*Details from:* The Secretary, Erlestoke Manor Fund, c/o Severn Valley Railway, Bewdley, Worcs. DY12 1BG
*Subscription:* Shares issued in £5 units

The locomotive was purchased from Woodham Bros within a record time of just twelve weeks, and one year later was moved by rail to temporary storage at the Dowty RPS site at Ashchurch.
In April 1976, following a share-holders' referendum, No. 7812 was transferred to Bewdley, on the Severn Valley Railway, where restoration work commenced in earnest. During the following three years, the locomotive was completely dismantled, overhauled, and rebuilt with many newly-fabricated components, finally re-entering service on 1 September 1979.
Sister engine No. 7802 *Bradley Manor* has subsequently been purchased to provide an interchangeable boiler and other 'strategic reserve' spares for No. 7812.

## Stanier Mogul Fund                                    H

Severn Valley Railway, Shropshire
*Secretary:* D. J. Montgomery, 23 Garth Crescent, Ermsford Grange, Coventry CV3 2PP
*Subscriptions:* Restoration certificates issued in £1 units (maximum 250)
Following a successful appeal, No. 42968 was purchased by the Fund in 1973. As the only survivor of her class, the engine has emerged as one of the important preservation schemes of the 1970s, representing the link between Stanier's Swindon training and subsequent LMS and BR practice up to the demise of Steam.

## Great Western (SVR) Association                       H

Bewdley Station, Severn Valley Railway

*Aims:* To acquire and maintain for the Severn Valley Railway rolling stock of GWR origin. To gather under one banner all funds and societies of the SVR and GWR.
*Details from:* C. Howell, 63 Upper Street, Bewdley, Worcs.

## Warwickshire Railway Society                          H

*Headquarters:* Bridgnorth Station, Severn Valley Railway
*Details from:* Pete Kennard, 145 Fulford Hall Road, Tidbury Green, Solihull, West Midlands B90 1QY

## 4150 Locomotive Fund                                  H

*Details from:* D. J. Hall, 33 Gibbs Road, Newport, Gwent NPT 8AR

## 353   Chasewater Light Railway                        A

Chasewater Park, Brownhills, West Midlands

*Access:* Off southbound carriageway of the A5 near junction with A452; entrance is signposted in Pool Road
Tel: Brownhills 5852
OS Ref: SK 034070

Passenger-carrying standard gauge steam railway, 2 miles in length.
Steam-hauled trains operate from 2 pm on the second and fourth Sundays in each month, April to September, and also on Bank Holiday Sundays and Mondays. Timetabled operation is not yet in force.
The Company are willing to co-operate with groups or individuals wishing to hire a steam locomotive plus brake van or coach for trips over the line, providing this does not interfere with normal running.
Facilities for visitors include car parking, refreshments, railway shop and museum of small relics.
The railway is operated by members of the Railway Preservation Society.
The RPS was formed as part of a national movement to preserve historic relics from the railways of Great Britain and to restore them to original condition wherever possible. The Society originally set up a depot at Hednesford, Staffs, to accommodate its acquisitions, but by the summer of 1970 had closed this depot and transferred all the stock to Chasewater Pleasure Park, situated just off the A5 at Brownhills.
The Chasewater Light Railway was first leased by the Society from the NCB in 1965. At the time the line comprised the truncated remains of part of the former Cannock Chase and Wolverhampton Railway built in 1856 and an extension of the Midland Railway's Walsall Wood branch opened in 1884. To run the railway, a company, the Chasewater Light Railway Co. Ltd, was formed and operates under a licence from the RPS. Trains normally run on Sunday afternoons between May and September with pre-grouping stock, usually with steam motive power. The role of the railway in the expanding Chasewater Pleasure Park is a prominent one. Ultimately it is envisaged that vintage steam trains will operate each weekend over the full two-mile length of the line, offering passengers a unique ride through pleasantly varied scenery, including the narrow quarter-mile causeway across the northern end of the lake. Proper station facilities are to be constructed at either end of the line and the track is being brought up to a condition whereby it will withstand heavy continuous use.

*Details from:* Barry J. Bull, 173 Parkeston Crescent, Birmingham B44 0PG

### Stock
Barclay 0-4-0ST *Storm King* (2220) built 1946
[1]Barclay 0-4-0ST *Colin McAndrew* (1223) built 1911
Peckett 0-4-0ST *Lion* (1351) built 1914
[2]Neilson 0-4-0ST No. 11 *Alfred Paget* (2937) built 1882
Peckett 0-4-0ST (R1 Class) 917 built 1902
Hudswell Clarke 0-6-0T No. 10 *Whit No. 4* 1822 built 1949
[3]Hudswell Clarke 0-6-0ST No. 15 (431) built 1895

**History on wheels can be sampled in true light railway style at Chasewater. This vintage ensemble comprises Hawthorn Leslie 0–4–0ST** *Asbestos* **and MS and LR six-wheeled coach**

[4]Hawthorn Leslie 0–4–0ST *Asbestos* (2780) built 1909
Ruston Hornsby 0–4–0DE *Fleet No. DL7* 458641 built 1963
Planet 4WDM No. 1 2914 built 1944
Kent Con/Planet 4WDM No. 20 built 1926
Kent Con/Planet 4WDM No. 21 (1612) built 1929
Simplex 4WPM (L & YR Departmental No. 1) (1947) built 1919
MR four-wheeled full brake coach built *c.* 1880
M & CR six-wheeled coach built 1879
BR bogie saloon DMU trailer coach No. E56301 built 1957
GER six-wheeled full brake coach No. 44 built 1885
MSLR six-wheeled coach built *c.* 1890
LNWR bogie TPO built 1909
[5]LNWR passenger brake van No. DM01836M built 1905
LNWR brake/third bogie coach built 1918
MR four-wheeled flat truck built *c.* 1890
MR four-wheeled box van built 1902
MR four-wheeled 25-cwt hand crane built 1881
L & YR four-wheeled box van built *c.* 1904
CCCR goods brake van built *c.* 1910
NER four-wheeled box van No. 100684 built *c.* 1910

GWR 16-ton goods brake van No. 35831 built 1888
Four-wheeled weedkilling truck built *c.* 1890
Two four-wheeled open wagons built *c.* 1897
Four-wheeled pump-handle trolley (ex-BR)
Smith Rodley diesel rail crane

[1]Ex N. Greening (Warrington) Ltd, Warrington, Lancs, 1966.
[2]Ex Bairds and Scottish Steels Ltd, Gartsherrie Ironworks, Lanarkshire, 1968.
[3]Ex Staveley Minerals Ltd, Desborough Quarry, Northants, 1967.
[4]Presented by Turners Asbestos Cement Co. Ltd, Trafford Park, Manchester, 1968.
[5]Owned by the London and North Western Society (*q.v.*).

**London and North Western Society**      **H**
Chasewater Light Railway

*Details from:* J. C. James, 4 Longview Drive, Huyton, Liverpool L36 6EE

Formed in January 1974 as a registered charity to preserve and exhibit for the benefit of the public, items of London and North Western Railway origin. In furtherance of the above but not otherwise:
(a) The acquisition of historic relics from the London and North Western Railway together with associated research.
(b) Restoration to original condition of such historic relics wherever possible and their display to the public in suitable museums in Great Britain.

(c) Modelling of items of London and North Western Railway origin for display in suitable museums in Great Britain.

*Membership details:* Entrance Fee 50p, Annual Subscription 50p. Minimum age limit, 12 years of age
*Membership:* 17


## 354   Birmingham Railway Museum        AD

Tyseley Motive Power Depot, Warwick Road, Birmingham

*Access:* By rail to Tyseley Station (note: this station is closed on Sundays when the Museum is open). By bus routes 37 and 44 from City Centre. By car along the Warwick Road adjacent to the BR depot
OS Ref: SP 105841

Standard gauge steam railway preservation centre and workshops.
The museum is open every Sunday (except Christmas and New Year) from 2 pm to 5 pm and at other times by prior arrangement. Steam days on the first Sunday of each month from April to December from 11 am to 5 pm, plus some steam weekends and special trains as advertised.
Facilities for visitors include car parking (except on steam days), museum and workshop, railway shop, refreshments including Pullman meal service by arrangement.
The Birmingham Railway Museum was formed in 1969 to cater for the increasing need for a specialised steam workshop and in 1975 the West Midlands County Council became a one-third partner in the project. Now, this appropriately located museum is one of the best equipped steam restoration and maintenance workshops in Britain, with many unique pieces of machinery of considerable industrial archaeological interest.
In addition, the museum has gained wide public support for its policy of restoring, maintaining and exhibiting steam locomotives and equipment in first class working order, fully capable of hauling loads for which they were designed over British Rail's tracks. Five of the museum's locomotives have already been restored to the high engineering standards that will ensure this will be one of the finest collections of working steam locomotives in the country.
The museum also possesses a collection of historically interesting rolling stock, including sufficient Pullman coaches to form a superbly comfortable vintage train. Other exhibits include railway equipment, scale models, model railways dating back to the 1890s and the Cattell collection of railwayana which was donated to the City of Birmingham expressly for display at Tyseley. Plans are currently in preparation for the re-erection of part of the locomotive roundhouse as an exhibition hall and small exhibits museum as funds become available.
*Workshop equipment:* Noble & Lund wheel lathe built 1947, Ransome & Rapier wheel drop (ex Ipswich), 6 ft 6 in. double head planing machine, special purpose running shed combination machine, Lang centre lathe, Short bed Deane Smith & Grace centre lathe, Hendy Norton centre lathe, No. 4 Herbert capstan lathe, Cincinnati No. 2 vertical drilling machine, Herbert drilling machine (all in machine shop) and various other lathes, milling and drilling machines in tool room

**Stock**
[5]GWR 4-6-0 No. 4983 *Albert Hall* built 1931
[10]GWR 4-6-0 No. 5043 *Earl of Mount Edgcumbe* built 1936
[10]GWR 4-6-0 No. 5080 *Defiant* built 1939
[4]GWR 4-6-0 No. 7027 *Thornbury Castle* built 1949
[2]GWR 4-6-0 No. 7029 *Clun Castle* built 1950
[6]GWR 0-6-2T No. 5637 (56XX Class) built 1925
[1,7]GWR 0-6-0PT No. 7752 (LT No. L94) (57XX Class) built 1930
[8]GWR 0-6-0PT No. 7760 (LT No. L90) (57XX Class) built 1930
[9]GWR 0-6-0PT No. 9600 (57XX Class) built 1945
GWR 2-6-2T No. 4160 (41XX Class) built 1948
[3]LMS 4-6-0 No. 5593 *Kolhapur* (BR No. 45593) built 1934
Peckett 0-4-0ST *Rocket* (1722) built 1926
Peckett 0-4-0ST No. 1 (2004) built 1942
Pullman first-class cars *Ibis* and *Ione* built 1925-28
Pullman bar car *Pegasus*
Pullman second-class car No. 54 built 1923
GWR engineers saloon coach No. W80972 built 1948
LNWR six-wheeled goods brake van
LNWR royal saloon No. M806 built 1903
GWR semi-Royal Saloon coach No. 9001
LNER Gresley buffet car No. E9123 built 1937
Two GWR 'Fruit D' vans Nos W2342W and W92076
Shell Oil tank wagon (ex GER) No. A498 built 1902
GWR 'Toad' 20-ton goods brake van No. 35938
Cowans-Sheldon 30-ton steam crane No. 139 built 1960
GWR 6-ton Hand Crane
Fifteen-ton match trucks Nos ADW42194 and ADB998526
GWR 6-wheel Mess & Tool van
Two GWR standard 5-plank wagons
GWR standard box van
Pensnett Railway 7-plank wagon

[1]Approved by British Rail for main line running
[2]One of the final batch of 'Castles' (7028-37) built at Swindon under BR auspices in May 1950. Withdrawn from Gloucester shed on 31 December 1965 as BR No. 7029 and purchased for preservation by 7029 Clun Castle Limited. In common with a number of its class, 7029 was later fitted with a double chimney and in this condition worked the last steam train out of Paddington. The engine finished its days in BR service as Gloucester station pilot.
[3]'Jubilee' class three-cylinder 4-6-0 built by the North British Locomotive Co. Ltd (Works No. 24151). Withdrawn from Leeds (Holbeck) in November 1967 and purchased for preservation. First introduced in May 1934, all the 191 locomotives comprising the class were in traffic by the end of 1936. Many of the class worked on the Midland section of the LMS, most of which was banned to larger locomotives.
[4]No. 7027 was built by British Railways in 1949, although originally scheduled for construction in 1939 by the GWR. Unlike No. 7029, she retains the single chimney and blast-pipe, so that Tyseley now has a representative engine of both types. No. 7027 was purchased from Woodham Brothers at Barry in August 1972 as a source of spares for No. 7029. However, preliminary examination has proved she is in sound mechanical order and that the tolerances are on

**Returning to its birthplace, No. 7029** *Clun Castle* **gets ready to set off home to Tyseley**

the top size. In due course – when time and finances permit – she will be restored to become a working companion to No. 7029. *Thornbury Castle* spent a large part of her working life running between Worcester and London, and, like No. 7029 *Clun Castle*, often worked the crack train over that section – the 'Cathedrals Express'.

[5]The Great Western 'Hall' class was developed from the earlier two-cylinder 'Saints' designed by G. J. Churchward in the early part of the century. In 1931, No. 4983 was one of the first batches of engines, originally built with a 3,500 gallon tender, which she now carries. 'Halls' ran over most of the Great Western system, and were 'the maids of all work', being used on any job from an express to a freight train. No. 4983 spent a large part of her working life in South Devon and South Wales where she ended her active days. She carries a standard boiler which received a heavy repair shortly before withdrawal, but it is interesting to note that this boiler once adorned a 'Saint' giving No. 4983 a true link with Churchward. By the time the decision was taken to acquire a genuine GWR tender engine there was no choice outside Woodham Brothers at Barry.

[6]A detailed mechanical inspection decided the purchase of this locomotive from Barry scrapyard. Ultimately, it will fulfil a need for a suburban trip engine. Restoration will be a long-term job.

[7]No. 7752 spent most of her working life in South Wales. She was withdrawn from Tondu and sold to London Transport in 1959. She had the distinction of working the last steam train on LT lines and arrived at Tyseley during the summer of 1971.

[8]No. 7760 was withdrawn from Oxford and sold to London Transport in 1961. Ten years later it was sold to a London scrap merchant from whom it was purchased for Tyseley. Neither of these engines was used for passenger traffic on London Transport, but were acquired solely for goods and maintenance trains. Both were built in 1930 by the North British Locomotive Company on the instruction of the GWR.

[9]No. 9600 is a later design of pannier tank, being constructed at Swindon in 1945. She was purchased from the National Coal Board in South Wales and is at present undergoing a complete overhaul.

[10]Retained for spares only.

The membership side is called **Birmingham Railway Museum Association**

*Annual Subscription:* Association membership £3 ordinary, £1.50 child/OAP, £5 Family
*Membership:* 500
*Details from:* Philip J. Wright, Birmingham Railway Museum, PO Box 29, Solihull, West Midlands

H. P. Bulmer Ltd (Cider Makers), Whitecross Road, Hereford

*Access:* ½ mile from city centre on A438 Brecon road.
Nearest BR station Hereford
Tel: Hereford 6182
OS Ref: SO 505402

Standard gauge steam railway preservation centre.
The centre is open for static display every weekend from
April to September inclusive. Steam days on the last Sunday
in each month; also Easter, Spring and Summer Bank
Holidays.
Facilities for visitors include car parking, souvenir shop,
refreshments and toilets.

### Stock
[1]GWR 4-6-0 No. 6000 *King George V* built 1927
[2]SR 4-6-2 No. 35028 *Clan Line* (Bulleid MN Class) built
1948
[4]LMS 4-6-2 No. 6201 *Princess Elizabeth* built 1933
[5]GWR 0-6-0PT No. 5786 built 1930
[6]Kitson 0-6-0ST No. 47 *Carnarvon* (5474) built 1934
[8]Hunslet 0-6-0DM No. 2 *Cider Queen* (6999) built 1955 (BR
No. D2579)
[7]Peckett 0-4-0ST *Pectin* (1579) built 1921
[7]Fowler 0-4-0DM No. 1 *Woodpecker* (2287) built 1939
[7]Pullman car *Ruth* (refitted as a members' clubroom); formerly a kitchen composite car (ex 6PUL) built 1933
[7]BR Mk 1 CK bogie coach No. 15879 built 1957 (new SHL
99205)

**The majesty of steam. Stanier Pacific No. 6201 looks
every inch a Princess as she departs from Hereford
with an enthusiasts' special**

[7]BR Mk 1 BSK bogie coach
[7]LNER Gresley buffet coach No. E9115
[7]GWR 20-ton PW brake van No. 40732 built 1893
[7]GWR 'Toad' 20-ton goods brake van No. 35923
[7]PO 12-ton flat wagon
[3]BR Mk I BSK bogie coach No. S35028
[10]GWR Covered goods van No. W96835 built 1921
[9]LMS 'Stove R' six-wheeled van No. 32918 built 1932
[8]Pullman FK coach *Aquila* built 1951
[8]Pullman brake parlour third *Morella* built 1926
[8]Pullman parlour third *Christine* built 1928
[8]Pullman parlour third *Eve* built 1928
[8]Pullman parlour third *Prinia* built 1930

[1]Withdrawn from Old Oak Common shed in 1962 as BR
No. 6000 and stored until presented to Swindon Borough
Council and moved to Swindon in 1966. Loaned to H. P.
Bulmer Ltd and restored to BR livery by A. R. Adams Ltd,
Newport, in 1968. *King George V* was the first locomotive
to inaugurate a 'Return to Steam' on BR tracks in October
1971.
Designed specifically for hauling the very heaviest express
passenger trains, the 'Kings' were the largest and most
powerful 4-6-0s ever built. No. 6000 visited America in
1927 for the Baltimore and Ohio Railroad Centenary celebrations and has carried its presentation plaque and bell ever
since.
[2]Bulleid 'Merchant Navy' Class locomotive, the most powerful class every built for the Southern Railway. As constructed, they incorporated many of Oliver Bulleid's
unorthodox features such as the 'air-smoothed' streamline
casing, chain-driven valve gear working in an enclosed oil-
bath and BFB cast steel wheel centres. From 1956 onwards
the entire class was rebuilt by BR with outside Walschaert's
valve gear and with the air-smoothed casing removed. In
their new guise the class did much excellent work, recording
speeds in excess of 100 mph on several occasions. *Clan
Line* was so rebuilt in 1959 and withdrawn from Nine Elms
shed on the last day of Southern steam, 9 July 1967. Owned
by the Merchant Navy Locomotive Preservation Society Ltd
(*q.v.*).
[3]Owned by the Merchant Navy Locomotive Preservation
Society Ltd (*q.v.*).
[4]Nos. 6200 and 6201 were the first 'Pacifics' built for the
LMS and the first major Stanier design. During the course
of a test run on the 16/17 November 1936, *Princess
Elizabeth* hauled a load averaging 240 tons from Euston to
Glasgow and return, a distance of 802.8 miles, at an average
speed of 69 mph. This remains a world record for continuous
high-speed travel with steam traction. The locomotive was
finally withdrawn from Carlisle Kingmoor shed in 1962 as
BR No. 46201 and purchased for preservation. It has been
painted in LMS livery, the boiler completely retubed, plus
other work, and attended the S & D 150th Anniversary
Celebrations at Shildon in 1975. Owned by the Princess
Elizabeth Locomotive Society (*q.v.*).
[5]Sold to London Transport in 1958, becoming No. L92.
Purchased for preservation 1969 and restored to GWR livery
at Bewdley. Moved to Hereford in 1970. Owned by the
Worcester Locomotive Society Ltd (*q.v.*).
[6]Ex Stewarts and Lloyds Minerals Ltd, Gretton Brook, Corby,

Northants, 1969. Owned by the Worcester Locomotive Society Ltd (q.v.).
[7]Owned by Steam in Hereford Ltd (q.v.).
[8]Owned by H. P. Bulmer Ltd.
[9]Owned by the Princes Elizabeth Locomotive Society (q.v.).
[10]Owned by the Worcester Locomotive Society Ltd (q.v.).

### Steam in Hereford Ltd                                    H

The 6000 Locomotive Association
(stewards to GWR locomotive 6000 *King George V* restored by Bulmers Cider)

*Details from:* D. C. Layton, Membership Secretary, 31 Blaydon Crescent, Hereford HR1 2TX
*Subscriptions:* £5 family; £4 adults; £2 juniors and senior citizens
*Membership:* 300

### Merchant Navy Locomotive Preservation          H
### Society Ltd

Registered as a charity

Bulmers Railway Centre, Hereford

*Details from:* John Harvey, 1 Ponsonby Road, Roehampton, London SW15
*Subscription:* £3.25 per year. Members receive four issues of the illustrated magazine *Southern Express*
*Membership:* Approx 450

The MNLPS was formed in 1965 and purchased *Clan Line* for £2200. Initially the Society stored the loco on the Longmoor Military Railway. From August 1971 the loco was resident at Ashford, Kent, and it was during this period that she worked her first 'Return to Steam' Special, between Basingstoke, Salisbury and Westbury. In April 1975 she moved to the Bulmer Steam Centre at Hereford, her present home. In the last 6 years she has worked many railtours and must be one of the most consistent performers of all preserved locos. During August 1975, she formed part of the cavalcade for the Rail 150 celebrations.
No Society can exist without its members. This Society is unusual in that it is not backed by big names, or sponsored by big money. It is a grouping of enthusiasts who, together with professional railwaymen, carry out the essential tasks of maintenance and coachwork. The Society maintains its links with members via its quarterly magazine (produced in association with the Bulleid Society), Hereford Open Days, Railtours and social evenings.

### Princess Elizabeth Locomotive Society           H

Bulmers Railway Centre, Hereford

*General Secretary:* V. Smart, 7 Pine Close, Thornbury, Avon
*Membership Secretary:* Mrs J. Allen, 56 Springfields Avenue, Sandiacre, Nottingham

---

**Presenting another regal picture from the Hereford stable. With the famous bell to the fore GWR No. 6000 gets ready for the road**

**Photo: Rex Coffin**

*Subscriptions:* Full member £5, husband and wife £7, Junior 50p, OAPs £1

### Worcester Locomotive Society Ltd                 H

Bulmers Railway Centre, Hereford

*General Secretary:* David R. G. Nowell, 1 Ronelagh Street, Hereford
*Facilities:* Meetings monthly in Worcester, Gloucester, Birmingham and Hereford, and occasionally in other towns. Tours to BR installations and systems, industrial and preservation locations, and continental tours to most European countries. Also film shows and exhibitions. Own publications ranging from books to Christmas cards and calendars and printed magazine. Work on Society's locomotives and rolling stock at weekends at H. P. Bulmer Ltd railway centre in Hereford.
*Annual subscription:* Adults £1.50; under-16 50p; OAPs 50p
The Society exists to cater for the interests of all average railway enthusiasts throughout Great Britain, especially in the areas where membership is most concentrated. It is not our policy to duplicate the coverage given by other more specialist societies, but enthusiasts with a deeper interest find membership of the Worcester Locomotive Society useful to supplement other organisations.

The WLS also owns the following rolling stock housed at Morton-on-Lugg, Herefordshire, where access is currently restricted to Society members:
Motor Rail 4WPM 4217 built 1931
GWR covered goods van No. W95750
GWR covered goods van No. W16295
Wickham petrol-driven gang trolley 6645 built 1953

## 356   Dean Forest Railway                        DF
##        Society Ltd

Norchard Depot, near Lydney, Forest of Dean, Gloucestershire

*Access:* Norchard is on the B4234 road from Lydney. BR Gloucester–Newport service to Lydney. National Welsh bus No. 40 passes the site
Tel: Lydney (05944) 3423
OS Ref: SO 629044

Standard gauge steam railway preservation centre offering short steam-hauled rides over ¼ mile of track.
The depot is open every Saturday and Sunday throughout the year from 11 am to 5 pm. Facilities for visitors include car parking, museum of small relics, souvenir shop, refreshments and toilets.
The Dean Forest Railway Society Ltd was formed by railway enthusiasts in 1970 when the goods-only branch railway from Lydney Junction to Parkend, in the Forest of Dean, first came under threat of closure. The Society has built up a collection of railway equipment close to this line so that it could be in a position to operate steam passenger trains should British Rail decide to dispose of it. At Norchard, just outside Lydney, a steam centre has been developed. Here

**It's not just an enthusiast's dream. The spirit of the Great Western is beginning to take solid form on the Dean Forest Railway**

Hunslet 0–4–0DM 2145 built 1940
[3]GWR brake/third No. 1649 built 1938
GWR auto-trailer No. 167 built 1928
GWR 'Mica B' insulated meat van No. 79636 built 1913
GWR 'Toad' 20-ton goods brake van No. 56835 built 1906
LMS 'Stove R' 6-wheel passenger brake van No. 32978
GWR 'Toad' 20-ton goods brake van No. 17294
[2]GWR shunter's truck No. 41152 built 1942
[3]GWR breakdown train van No. 161 built 1923
GWR 'Mica B' wagon underframe No. 105928 used as a flat wagon
GWR 'Fruit D' van No. W3411 built 1950
GWR Smith, Rodley 10-ton steam crane No. TS 5027 built 1953
Two GWR open wagons
Five LMS vans
Four flat wagons
Two Shell tank wagons
Wickham 4WPMR 8774 built 1961
Wickham 4WPMR 4254 built 1947

*Signal boxes*
GWR 13-lever, formerly at Mileage Yard, Gloucester
LMS (Midland Railway) 30-lever, formerly at Charfield
LMS (Midland Railway), formerly at Barnwood (building only)

[1]Withdrawn as BR No. 5541 in July 1962 and sold to Woodham Brothers, Barry, for scrap. Purchased for preservation and moved to Parkend in 1972. Owned by the Forest Prairie Fund (q.v.).
[2]Owned by the Forest Pannier Tank Fund (q.v.).
[3]Owned by individual members or groups of members.

### Dean Forest Railway Society Ltd     H

*Details from:* P. Skinner, 58 Grimsbury Road, Kingswood, Bristol BS15 2SD
*Subscriptions:* Annual adult £2.50, annual corporate £3.50, annual OAP 75p, junior (14–18) £1, life membership £25. For full voting membership (adults only) purchase of at least one £1 share is required.
*Membership:* Approx 400

### Forest Prairie Fund     H

Parkend Station, Dean Forest Railway Preservation Society, Gloucestershire

*Details from:* John Harris, 21 Chandos Street, Hereford

Since 1972 members of the Fund have completed restoration of the engine, including a successful boiler hydraulic pressure test, complete refitting of motion, tank repairs, ashpan renewal and reinstatement of cab and pipework fittings. A successful steam test took place in November 1975 and the engine was in use at some steam days at Parkend during 1976.
Visitors to the Dean Forest Railway Society should find No. 5541 in steam at Norchard. Restoration has been made possible by a loan, still partly outstanding, and shares at £1 are still available in the locomotive.

### The Forest Pannier Tank Fund     H

*Details from:* J. Hatton, 23 Robinson Road, Gloucester GL1 5DL

track has been relaid, buildings and facilities are being provided to offer the public the opportunity to inspect the preserved rolling stock and take short steam trips in attractive woodland surroundings. This centre will become a depot for the complete branch line.
The line climbs from the Cardiff–Gloucester line at Lydney, on the Severn Estuary, through a wooded valley, passing Norchard and the village of Whitecroft, into the Dean National Forest Park, terminating at Parkend.
The Society is restoring stock and equipment to the former GWR/LMS (MR) condition, preserving the history of the original Severn and Wye Railway where appropriate.

**Stock**
[1]GWR 2–6–2T No. 5541 (Class 4575) built 1928
[2]GWR 0–6–0PT No. 9681 (Class 8750) built 1949
Hunslet 0–6–0ST (3806) built 1953
[3]Peckett 0–4–0ST *Uskmouth 1* (2147) built 1952

## 357 Dowty Railway Preservation Society    DE

*Secretary:* c/o Dowty Sports and Social Society, Ashchurch, near Tewkesbury, Gloucestershire GL20 8JR

*Access:* ½ mile from motorway exit off M5 along the A438 towards Evesham.
OS Ref: SO 925335

The Dowty Railway Preservation Society was formed in 1962 to cater for the needs of railway enthusiast members of the Dowty Sports and Social Society – the sports and social club of the Dowty Group of engineering companies (based in Gloucestershire).
Non-employees may join as associate members.
The Dowty RPS occupies five sidings adjacent to one of the factory buildings at Ashchurch. Restoration work on the Society's vehicles proceeds every weekend and for a small fee visitors can inspect progress on Sunday afternoons. From time to time special open days are held when there are usually one or two locomotives in steam and rides are given. Although not having the grand aims of groups hoping to open full railways, the Dowty RPS has no shortage of work in hand and, free of the distractions of having to raise vast sums of money, sees advantages in more modest operations where all facets of railway preservation can be undertaken in a convivial atmosphere.

### Stock
Avonside 0–4–0T *Cadbury No. 1* (1977) built 1925
Barclay 0–4–0ST No. 2 (2221) built 1946
Barclay 0–4–0F (2126) built 1942
Barclay 0–4–0ST *Drake* (2086) built 1940
GWR restaurant car No. 9635 built 1935
GWR special saloon carriage No. 9044 built 1881
L & YR covered van built 1894
MR six-wheeled brake van No. 1060 built 1904
GWR three-ton manual crane No. 538 built 1903
GWR 'Coral A' glass wagon No. 41723 built 1908

### Narrow gauge stock
Hunslet 0–4–0ST *George B* (680) built 1898 (1 ft 11½ in. gauge)
Jung 0–4–0WT *Justine* (939) built 1906 (60 cm gauge)
Lister 4WDM No. 2 (34523) (2 ft gauge)
Motor Rail 4WPM No. 3 (4565) built 1928 (2 ft gauge)
Motor Rail 4WPM *Spitfire* (7053) built 1937 (2 ft gauge)
Ruston Hornsby 4WDM No. 802 (221645) built 1944 (2 ft gauge)
Ruston Hornsby 4WDM No. L5 (181820) built 1936 (2 ft gauge)
Ruston Hornsby 4WDM No. 1 (166010) built 1932 (2 ft gauge)
Ruston Hornsby 4WDM 354028 built 1953 (2 ft gauge)
Hudson bogie carriage
Hudson all-steel bogie wagon
Hudson wooden-bodied drop-side four-wheeled wagon
Three Hudson tipping skips
Two four-wheeled coaches on skip chassis
Four unsprung four-wheeled flat wagons
One tipping skip (continental origin)

Also a comprehensive collection of signalling, station and lineside equipment

## 358 Churnet Valley Steam Railway Museum    DF

North Staffordshire Railway Co (1978) Ltd, Cheddleton Station, Station Road, Cheddleton, near Leek, Staffordshire

*Access:* Off the A520 Leek–Stone road at Cheddleton, then follow signposts. PMT or Berrisfor''s Buses operate to Cheddleton from Leek and Hanley. Nearest BR Station, Stoke-on-Trent
Tel: Churnet Side 360522
OS Ref: SJ 983519

Standard gauge railway preservation centre which is the first phase of the scheme to reopen a passenger railway in the Churnet Valley. The station buildings have been converted into a museum reflecting the original North Staffordshire Railway Company, 'Owd Knotty'. Short train rides are available at the museum on Sundays and Bank Holidays hauled by steam or diesel locomotives.
Facilities for visitors include souvenir shop, refreshments, museum and toilets.
The museum is open daily from April to September and on Sundays only from October to March.
The Churnet Valley is renowned for its natural beauty and visitors to the station can readily sample the pleasant scenery and places of interest within a short radius of the museum. In fact the picturesque Cauldon Canal runs parallel to the railway and is only a short walk away from the station. The passenger carrying narrow boat 'Royal Jubilee' operates along the Cauldon Canal throughout the Summer Season – enquiries re booking should be made at Cheddleton Station. A well restored flint mill and church (St Edward's) are located in Cheddleton village, with Coombes Valley nature reserve nearby; the area is honeycombed with pleasant walkways and the station is situated on the Staffordshire County Council leisure drive.
The well-known tourist attractions of Alton Towers and Rudyard Lake are within easy driving distance of the museum. The station building at Cheddleton is both beautiful and imposing, built in the Jacobean style, reputedly by the famous architect Pugin and is protected as a listed building (grade 2) by the Department of the Environment. An attractive souvenir shop and museum rooms are situated at platform level in the main building with the railway offices above. Light refreshments are available from either the shop or one of the carriages located in the bay-platform area. Snacks are provided at the nearby 'Boat Inn' and hot meals are available at the 'Travellers Rest' (Leekbrook). Cheddleton is being restored to represent a typical country station of the old 'Knotty' railway and the museum contains authentic relics and items of interest from the original North Staffordshire Railway.

### Stock
[1]LMS 0–6–0 No. 4422 (BR No. 44422) Fowler Class 4F built 1927
Hunslet 0–6–0ST *Josiah Wedgwood* 3777 built 1952
BR 2–6–4T No. 80136 Riddles Class 4 MT built 1956

Ruston Hornsby 4WDM RSH 0-4-0DM 6980 built 1940
BR Fitted freight vans Nos B73059 and B75443
BR Mk 1 bogie coaches Nos M15207 and M15208 built
Metro-Cammell 1953
Two NSR coach bodies

[1]No. 4422 was completed at Derby in October 1927 and
spent much of her working life in the Midlands and later the
south-west of England.
During her time with the London, Midland and Scottish
Railway she was shedded at Leicester, Wigston, Bristol and
Bath. She later worked from Penzance during BR days and
was often seen on the Somerset and Dorset line before her
withdrawal in June 1965.
The company plans to operate in conjunction with British
Rail a DMU train service between Stoke-on-Trent and Cheddleton in the picturesque Churnet Valley. Further development would involve relaying the track from the line's current
terminus at Oakamoor into the restored station at Alton
Towers which is adjacent to the famous gardens of the same
name. It is intended that the train service between Alton
Towers and Oakamoor will be steam-hauled.

## 359   Walsall Steam Railway                                  A

Arboretum Park, Walsall, West Midlands

*Access:* off Broadway North, Double gates by Grange
Playhouse
15 minutes walk from Walsall BR station.
Tel: Walsall 30078 or 22544

Passenger carrying, 7¼ in. gauge steam railway, ⅝ mile in
length featuring double-track running.
The railway operates every Saturday, Sunday and Bank
Holiday from Easter to October.
Facilities for visitors include car parking, toilets, putting
greens and boating on the lake.
Walsall Arboretum Railway was opened Easter 1976 with
single track and passing loops at each end. Loco power was
provided by the 4-6-2 Steam Loco *Princess Elizabeth*
together with two Cromar White Battery Electric Locos. The
following year saw double track installed throughout, Loco
shed erected, and two new steam locos, *A. H. Peppercorn*
and *Duchess of Buccleugh*, together with a Bo-Bo battery
Electric Railcar. For the 1979 season the track was extended
a further 200 yards and a new Terminal Station with 3 bays
built.

*Details from:* C. M. Cartwright, 58 Charlemont Road, Walsall,
West Midlands.

**Stock**
LMS 4-6-2 No. 6201 *Princess Elizabeth* built Glaze
LMS 4-6-2 No. 6230 *Duchess of Buccleugh* built Monk
1978
LNER 4-6-2 No. 525 *A. H. Peppercorn* built Glaze 1977
BR 2-10-0 No. 92203 *Black Prince* built 1979
LMS 4-6-0 Stanier class 5MT under construction 1979
Cromar White Bo-BoBER No. E7051 built 1977
Cromar White 4WBE No. S12
12 'Sit-astride' bogie coaches
2 Works mineral wagons

## 360   Hilton Valley Railway                                   A

Weston Park, Weston-under-Lizard, Shropshire

*Access:* With the growing network of motorways Weston
Park is well situated for easy access from a great number
of the English counties. The Park is seven miles west from
the M6/A5 interchange (Junction 12) on the A5 at Weston-
under-Lizard. The nearest railway station is at Shifnal and
public bus services run to Tong and Weston-under-Lizard.
Tel: Weston-under-Lizard 207 or 385

This extensive and well-known 7¼ in. gauge system was
moved in its entirety from its original site at Hilton, near
Bridgnorth during the winter of 1979/80. Advantage is
being taken of the new location to lay the line out with
future development in mind. Existing operational features
are retained, such as crossing loops controlled by colour
light signals, interlocked with the train 'staff' system.
Weston Park is open at the following times:
Mid-April–31 July: Daily, except for Mondays and Fridays,
open Bank Holidays. Additionally open Mondays in May,
June and July for school parties only.
August: Daily. September: Weekends only. Closed on 30
September.
The Park is open from 11 am to 7.30 pm, and the House
from 2 pm to 6 pm. Last admissions 5.30 pm.
There is ample free parking space for cars and coaches.
Particular arrangements are made to ensure comfort for the
aged and physically handicapped, including the provision of
special lavatory facilities.
A cafeteria and restaurant offer excellent catering facilities
from snacks to full meals. The emphasis is on home-baking,
estate produce and traditional fare.
Prior booking for large parties wishing to have meals is
essential.
Fully licensed catering facilities for special events, confer-
ences, promotional events etc. in The Old Stables, the House
or the Temple of Diana throughout the year.
Every year more and more coach parties find Weston Park
an enjoyable venue. Around 30% reduction available on
coach parties. These terms apply for parties of 20 or more
in coaches only. Special evening visits can be made on the
first and last Wednesday of every open month, and every
Wednesday in June. Prior booking is essential.
Full details of all party booking arrangements are available
on request.
Other facilities for visitors include Woodland Adventure
Playground, British Wildlife collection, Aquarium and pottery.

**Stock**
Shaw 4-6-2 No. 1 *Lorna Doone* built 1925, rebuilt 1969
Liversage 2-6-0 No. 2 *Hilton Queen* built 1950, rebuilt 1968
Guest/Lloyd 4-8-4 No. 3 *Francis Henry Lloyd* built 1959,
rebuilt 1970
Freelance Bo+2 BE No. 4 built 1958
Freelance 4WBE No. 5 built 1960
Freelance Bo+2 PE No. 6 built 1965, rebuilt 1971
GWR/Freelance 2-6-2 No. 7 built by Monk, rebuilt Glaze
1969
Cromo Bo+2 DM No. 8 rebuilt 1970

Glaze 2-8-0 No. 9 *Michael Charles Lloyd MBE* built 1975
Two enclosed bogie saloon coaches built 1972
Thirteen open bogie coaches
Open bogie wagon
Open four-wheeled wagon built 1968


## 361   Leek and Manifold Railway          A

Rudyard Station, Staffordshire

A 10¼ in. gauge passenger-carrying line built on the trackbed of the former North Staffordshire Railway, Leek–Manchester line. The railway is operated by Waterhouses School and at present extends for a distance of 400 yards alongside Rudyard Lake. Operation of the line extends from May to September at weekends only.
The idea behind this project stems from a desire to provide the pupils in the school, who are affected by the raising of the school leaving age, with a long-term, man-sized project which has a real practical objective in view and providing the opportunity for the pupils to experience a wide range of educational activities, ranging from surveying, planning, railway construction and operation, to conservation and environmental work, etc.
It was not possible, unfortunately, to use the site of the former Leek and Manifold Railway for the project as had been hoped. Instead the new line perpetuates the name and spirit of its 2 ft 6 in. gauge ancestor in miniature on the site of a former 'Knotty' line.
The railway was opened on 27 June 1978 and plans exist to extend it to over 2 miles in length.

### Stock
Coleby-Simkins 2-6-4T *E. R. Calthrop* built 1974 (replica of the Leek and Manifold Railway locomotive of the same name).
Blackhurst 2-6-4T *J. B. Earle* under construction 1979
LMS 4-6-0 No. 6100 *Royal Scot*
Twelve articulated bogie coaches
On 27 June 1974 the engine was officially named by Brian Hollingsworth, a director of the Romney, Hythe and Dymchurch Railway, at a luncheon to commemorate the 70th anniversary of the opening of the Leek–Manifold Valley Light Railway.
It is felt that the educational opportunities of this project are limitless. Almost every subject which one can think of can be covered by the work involved – mathematics, English, science, geography, history, commerce, business management, art and handicraft and catering – all have major parts to play. It affords a real-life challenge, providing the opportunity for the children to learn from first-hand experience and see, in practical terms, the results of their labours.


## 362   Echills Wood Railway          A

A 7¼ in. passenger-carrying miniature railway adjacent to the Royal Agricultural Society's showground at Stoneleigh, Warwickshire. The railway only operates in conjunction with events at the showground and is closed and the rolling stock removed at intervening times. Construction of an extension to the line was started in 1975 and has now been completed. This comprises a circular line round Echills Wood itself, with a length of about 830 ft., and a major remodelling of Harvesters Station at the other end of the system to provide a locomotive/rolling stock holding road, a servicing bay and a turntable. These additions permit continuous running from Harvesters back to Harvesters, with or without additional circuits of the wood, giving a minimum run of about 2,500 ft.; continuous running in the wood with a shuttle service over the line from Harvesters; or a combination of both.
When running for the public locomotives will now run forwards at all times, an important aid to safety. Additional rolling stock, similar to the four high-capacity wagons already in service, is also under construction, while it is hoped that a few new locomotives will appear each year to augment the regular stud.
Please note, the EWR is wholly contained within the boundaries of the RASoE showground. It therefore follows that visits can only be made during open periods at the showground. Unfortunately the railway is not empowered to authorise visits to its workshops and depot. However, arrangements can be made for individuals given reasonable notice – written permission is essential for any visits.
The railway is operated by members of the 7¼ in. Gauge Society who provide the motive power. This is usually all-steam and typically includes the following locomotives.

### Stock
Walters 0-4-0ST No. 1 *Rosabel* built 1971
Oughton 0-4-0WT No. 2 *Romulus* built 1975
MGR 0-4-0WT *Remus* built 1976
MGR 0-4-0ST *Penrhyn* built 1970
MGR 4-4-0 *Zebedelia* (58) built 1974
MGR 0-4-0ST *Jacky* (52) built 1974
Marsh 0-4-0ST No. 7 *Dolbadarn* built 1970
Marsh 0-4-2T *Tinkerbell* built 1968
Drury 0-4-0ST *Topsy* built 1975
Evans/BR 4-6-2 *Duke of Gloucester*
Strickland 0-6-0ST *Andes* built 1976
Richardson/GWR 0-4-0T No. 1106 built 1976
Haydock 4WPM No. 1 built 1975
James/GWR 0-6-0T No. 1509 built 1972
Haydock 4WPM No. 2 built 1974
Peraton Bo-BoBE No. 1111 built 1974


## 363   Telford Town Tramway          A

Telford Development Corporation, Telford Town Park, Telford, Salop

*Access:* Adjacent to Telford Town Centre. Pedestrian access from car park near sports field in Town Park
Tel: Telford 619393 (not weekends)

60 cm gauge passenger-carrying steam tramway under construction along ½ mile stretch of the former LNWR Coalport branch. Construction work on this interesting new line com-

menced in 1978. Since the New Towns Act forbids a Corporation to operate a railway, the mode of operation will be determined following the Railway Inspector's report. To date the track has been laid solely in the Town Park on the original LNWR Coalport Route, but there is scope for expansion both in the Park and outside it.

Construction has been undertaken by TDC Forestry Dept, Work Experience teams and also boys from Phoenix School and supervised from the Landscape Dept. It is hoped to learn enough from operating trials during 1979 to extend the route and operate a regular service in 1980. It will be the only steam tramway in the British Isles.

**Stock**
Kierstead-Pontis 4WVBTG No. 1 built 1979
4-wheel balcony-end 16-seat coach built 1979
PW Flat wagon
Tipper wagon

A supporting Society is in the course of formation.
*Details from:* Doug Skinner, TDC Landscape Dept, Priorslee Hall, Telford, Salop.


## 364   Alton Towers Railway                                    B

Alton Towers, near Leek, Staffordshire

2 ft gauge passenger-carrying line

OS Ref: SK 075437

In the grounds of Alton Towers, long noted for their beauty, runs a 2 ft gauge line, some 750 yards long. It operates from Easter to the end of October.

**Stock**
Baguley 0–4–0DM *Altonia* (1769) built 1929 (steam outline)
Six 4-wheel open coaches
Also on view is a 15 in. gauge steam locomotive on static display
[1]Barnes 4–4–2 *John* 103 built 1924
[1]Ex Marine Lake Miniature Railway, Rhyl


## 365   Trentham Gardens                                        B
Miniature Railway

Trentham Gardens, a few miles south of Stoke-on-Trent and formerly owned by the Dukes of Sutherland, have long been a favourite resort of the inhabitants of the Potteries. They are administered by a limited company, of which the present Duke is chairman.

A 2 ft gauge line was added to the attractions in 1935. Built under the supervision of the engineer to the Stafford Coal and Iron Co. Ltd, it runs for about a mile through woodland scenery alongside the lake. The station and engine shed are situated in the children's playground on the west side of the lake. The passenger service begins daily at 2 pm, a four-coach train being normally run. On Sundays and Bank Holidays two six-coach trains depart at seven-minute intervals, if required.

OS Ref: SJ 864406

*Fares:* No charge on production of Gardens admission ticket

**Stock**
Baguley 0–4–0PM *Brora* (1797) built 1930
Baguley 0–4–0DM *Golspie* (2085) built 1934
Baguley 0–6–0DM *Dunrobin* (3014) built 1938
Twelve open 'Toastrack' 12-seat coaches

All locomotives have steam outline.


## 366   Bromyard and Linton                               C
Light Railway '

W. Morris, Broadbridge House, Bromyard, Herefordshire

A 2 ft gauge line constructed along the track-bed of the former GWR Worcester–Bromyard branch, half-a-mile long, to be extended to one mile

OS Ref: SO 657548

**Bromyard and Linton Light Railway Association**

*Details from:* R. F. Walland, 1 Hereford Road, Leominster, Herefordshire

**Stock**
Peckett 0–6–0ST *Mesozoic* (1327) built 1913
Ruston Hornsby 4WDM 213848 (16/20 HP Class) built 1942
Ruston Hornsby 4WDM 246793 (30DL Class) built 1947
Ruston Hornsby 4WDM 229656 built 1944
Ruston Hornsby 4WDM No. 6 *Princess* (229655) (20DL Class) built 1944
Ruston Hornsby 4WDM No. 3 *Nell Gwynne* (229648) (20DL Class) built 1944
Ruston Hornsby 4WDM No. L10 (198241) (25/30 HP Class) built 1939
Ruston Hornsby 4WDM 187101 (16/20 HP Class) built 1937
Ruston Hornsby 4WDM 195849 built 1939
Motor Rail 4WDM 102G038 built 1972
Motor Rail 4WDM No. 7 (20082) built 1953
Motor Rail 4WDM 9676 built 1952
Motor Rail 4WDM 9677 built 1952
Motor Rail 4WDM 9382 built 1948
Baguley 4WDM 3406 built 1953 (2 ft 6 in. gauge)
Wickham 4WPM 3030
Wickham 4WPM 3034


## 367   Herefordshire Waterworks Museum  B

Broomy Hill Waterworks Museum, Hereford

OS Ref: SO 497394

*Curator:* J. Townsend

A 300-yard, 2 ft gauge line under construction
Leaving a shed/workshop via a curve, in which the inner rail has a radius of only about 7 ft, the line crosses a short section which is only laid on running days, being normally

removed for the passage of contractor's vehicles, and then enters the meadows rising at about 1 in 30. Steepening to less than 1 in 20 the railway reaches a summit and then falls until the end of the line is reached after about 100 yards.

**Stock**

Lister-Blackstone 4WDM 52886 built 1962
Motor Rail 4WPM 1381 built 1918
Three coaches
Tipper wagons

The museum itself has two vertical steam engines as well as many small exhibits and displays, including a special section on waterworks railways.

## 368   The Royal Air Force Museum          E

RAF Cosford, Shropshire

60 cm gauge locomotive on static display in aircraft museum.

**Stock**

Ruston Hornsby 4WDM 48DL Class 370571

Formerly operated on the service railway at RAF Masirah in the Middle East. Flown back to England in February 1977 for restoration for museum display.

## 369   Shugborough Hall          E

Staffordshire County Council Industrial Museum, Great Haywood, Stafford

OS Ref: SJ 992215

Standard gauge steam locomotives on static display.

**Stock**

[1]LNWR 0-4-0ST No. 1439 built 1865
[2]NSR 0-6-2T No. 2 built 1922
[3]NSR 4WBE No. 2 built 1917
[4]Baguley 0-4-0PM No. L86 (800) built 1920
[5]R. Heath 0-4-0ST No. 6 built 1896
[6]Kerr Stuart 0-4-0ST *Moss Bay* (4167) built 1920
Section of Oxford, Worcester and Wolverhampton Railway 0-6-0 (GWR No. 252) built by E. B. Wilson and Co. in 1855. The engine was reduced to the leading four coupled wheels and frames, complete with cylinders and motion, to serve as an instructional model at Stafford Road Works, Wolverhampton, in 1904.

[1]Successively renumbered 1985 and 3042, this engine was withdrawn in 1919 and sold to Kynochs Ltd, Birmingham. Kynochs eventually became part of ICI (Metals Division), and when No. 1439 was no longer required it was presented to BR for preservation. After being kept in Crewe paintshop for some years, the locomotive was moved to Shugborough.
[2]Withdrawn in 1937 as LMS No. 2271 and sold to Walkden Collieries, Manchester, where it was named *Princess* and continued in service until 1966. During 1958, the locomotive was repainted in NSR maroon livery and sent to Stoke-on-Trent to participate in an exhibition. On retirement, No. 2

was moved to Shugborough.
[3]Battery electric locomotive designed by J. A. Hookham and built by Thomas Bolton and Sons. Never included in either service or capital stock, the number 2 was its sole identity, and it spent several years shunting at Thomas Bolton's sidings at Oakmoor, Staffordshire. Finally taken out of service in 1964.
[4]Ex London Brick Co. Ltd, Gildenburgh Works, Cambridgeshire, 1968. This locomotive is painted in a rather startling white livery!
[5]Ex NCB, Staffordshire Area, Norton Colliery, near Biddulph, 1969. This engine was rebuilt by Cowlishaw Walker Engineering Co. Ltd, Biddulph, in 1934.
[6]Ex South Eastern Gas Board, Waddon Marsh Gas Works, Croydon, Surrey, 1968.

## 370   Ironbridge Gorge Museum          E

Ironbridge Gorge Museum Trust Ltd, Blists Hill Industrial Museum, Ironbridge, Telford, Shropshire

Standard gauge steam locomotive and rolling stock on static display

*Access:* Ironbridge stands on the River Severn in Telford, Shropshire, south of the A5, west of the A442, thirty minutes from the M6. Visitors should follow signposts leading to Telford.
Nearest BR stations Wellington and Shifnal. Buses thence to Ironbridge.
Facilities for visitors include car parking, museum shop, refreshments and toilets.

OS Ref: SJ 694033

The Ironbridge Gorge was the scene of the remarkable breakthrough which led Britain to become the first industrial nation and the workshop of the world. The area still retains much of the atmosphere of those momentous times.
Here, the ironmaster Abraham Darby first smelted iron using coke as fuel. This paved the way for the first iron rails, iron bridge, iron boat, iron aqueduct and iron-framed building. In tribute to these achievements the Ironbridge Gorge Museum is being created around a unique series of industrial monuments spread over three miles of the Severn Valley.
At Blists Hill Open Air Museum stand steam engines and pit-heads, with examples of clay-working, iron-making and early transport methods, all on a 42-acre woodland site.
Ironbridge lies in the heart of England, an hour's drive from Birmingham, two from Manchester and three from London. On sale at our three main locations are a wide variety of museum publications and products. At Blists Hill you may also visit a working pottery.

The Museum Site is open daily from 10 am to 6 pm April to October inclusive, 10 am to 5 pm November to March inclusive. Closed Christmas Day.
For further information on the Museum and its activities contact: The Ironbridge Gorge Museum Trust, Ironbridge, Telford, Shropshire TF8 7AW.
Tel: Ironbridge (095-245) 3522 (weekdays); Ironbridge (095-245) 3418 (weekends)

**Stock**
[1]Barclay 0–6–0ST *Peter* (782) built 1896
Motor Rail 4WPM 6031 built 1936 (2 ft gauge)
MR goods brake van (ex Cannock Wood Colliery)
Five 6-plank mineral wagons

[1]Presented by Lunt Comley and Pitt Ltd, Shut End, Pensnett, Staffordshire, 1970.

## 371 Coalbrookdale Works Museum E

Ironbridge Gorge Museum Trust Ltd, Coalbrookdale, Shropshire

Standard gauge steam locomotives on static display.

*Access:* Ironbridge stands on the River Severn in Telford, Shropshire, south of the A5, west of the A442, thirty minutes from the M6. Visitors should follow signposts leading to Telford

OS Ref: SJ 668044

Here, in 1709 the Quaker ironmaster Abraham Darby first smelted iron using coke as a fuel instead of the traditional charcoal. This was a major breakthrough in ironmaking and one of the most significant events in Britain's early progress towards industrialisation. In the succeeding century the Coalbrookdale Company which Darby established was in the forefront of iron technology, producing in the 1720s the first iron steam engine cylinders, in 1767 the first iron rails on which iron wheels ran and in 1779 the world's first iron bridge.
In 1959 the original Darby furnace, excavated and restored, was opened to the public by its then owners Allied Iron-founders together with a museum of ironfounding.
The furnace and museum are now administered by the Ironbridge Gorge Museum Trust which was set up in 1968 to conserve for all time the unique range of industrial monuments in the Ironbridge Gorge.
*Opening times:* The Furnace Site and Museum are open daily from 10 am to 6 pm April to October inclusive, 10 am to 5 pm November to March inclusive. Closed Christmas Day.

For further information on the Museum and its activities contact: The Ironbridge Gorge Museum Trust, Ironbridge, Telford, Shropshire TF8 7AW
Tel: Ironbridge (095-245) 3522 (weekdays); Ironbridge (095-245) 3418 (weekends)

**Stock**
[1]Coalbrookdale 0–4–0ST No. 5 built *c.* 1865
[2]Coalbrookdale 0–4–0VBTG built 1865
[3]Sentinel 0–4–0VBTG 6155 built 1925

[1]Presented by Bardon Hill Quarries (Ellis and Everard Ltd), Coalville, Leicestershire, 1959.
[2]Re-built by Sentinel as their 6185 of 1925 from a Coalbrookdale 0–4–0ST of 1865.
[3]Awaiting removal for restoration. Rebuilt from a Manning Wardle 0–4–0ST

A supporting organisation for all the Ironbridge Gorge Museum Sites is known as the Friends of Ironbridge Gorge Museum Trust. Details are available from all museum sites and from the address above.

## 372 Birmingham Museum of Science and Industry E

Newhall Street, Birmingham B3 1RZ

OS Ref: SP 064874
Tel: 021-236 1022

Open Monday–Friday 10 am–5 pm; Saturdays 10 am–5.30 pm, Sundays from 2 pm to 5.30 pm
First Wednesday in each month 10 am–9 pm.
Steam locomotives on static display.
Admission free
The Museum also houses a collection of locomotives, cars, bicycles, steam-engines and other transport items. Live steam events take place periodically.
Facilities for visitors include museum shop and toilets. Car parking nearby.

**Stock**
[1]LMS 4–6–2 No. 46235 *City of Birmingham* built 1939
Bagnall 0–4–0ST No. 1 *Leonard* (2087) built 1918 (2 ft gauge)
Kerr Stuart 0–4–0ST No. 56 *Lorna Doone* (4250) built 1922 (2 ft gauge)
[2]Bellis and Seekings 0–6–0WT *Secundus* built 1874 2 ft 8½ in. gauge

[1]Capable of being moved by external power unit along a short length of track. *City of Birmingham* was built as a streamlined 'Coronation' Class Pacific to Sir William Stanier's design at Crewe. In 1946, the streamline casing was removed and the class performed well in their unstreamlined form at the head of the heaviest Anglo-Scottish expresses. From 1960, the introduction of diesel locomotives meant the 'Coronation' Pacifics being relegated to parcels and secondary duties. All were withdrawn by the end of 1964 and No. 46235 gained a well-earned retirement in the city whose name it carries.
[2]Ex Pike Brothers, Fayle and Co. Ltd, Furzebrook, Dorset. Purchased and presented by Abelson and Co. (Engineers) Ltd and the Birmingham Locomotive Club in 1955.

## 373 The Bass Museum E

Horninglow Street, Burton upon Trent, Staffordshire

OS Ref: SK 248234

*Details from:* The Bass Museum, c/o Bass Production, High Street, Burton upon Trent, Staffs. Tel: 0283 45301 (office hours) 0283 45707 (all other times)
*Admission:* Adults 30p, children and OAPs 15p, party rates and guided brewery tours by prior arrangement
*Opening times:* Weekdays 10.30 am to 4.30 pm. Saturday, Sunday and Bank Holidays 11 am to 5 pm.
*Refreshments:* Snacks and light meals always available, party lunches by arrangement.

*Shop:* Reprints of early accounts of the brewery and its railway system; general industrial archaeological literature; brewery advertising material.

The Museum is situated at the entrance to Bass's Brewery and is housed in what was formerly the company's joiners shop and its surrounding buildings.
Bass's fleet of 11 locomotives once operated over 26 miles of track and much emphasis is given in the exhibition to Burton's Victorian railway boom.
On display is Bass No. 9 – an 0–4–0 saddle tank locomotive built in Glasgow in 1901 – and the directors coach built in 1889 by the Ashby Railway Carriage and Iron Co. Ltd, Manchester. Also on display are a Robey horizontal compound engine and a late 19th-century experimental brewery.

**Stock**
Neilson Reid 0–4–0ST No. 9 5907 built 1901
Burton Brewery Rly 4-wheel saloon coach built 1889

## 374   Winchcombe Railway Museum          E

*Details from:* T. R. Petchey, 23 Gloucester Street, Winchcombe, Gloucestershire
*Opening dates:* Easter, Spring and Summer Bank Holidays, Sunday and Monday; certain Sundays June to September inclusive. Open 2.30 pm until dusk.
Admission free

The Winchcombe Railway Museum specialises not in locomotives and rolling stock but in other delights, such as signalling equipment, lineside fixtures, horse-drawn road vehicles, tickets and all kinds of paperwork, lamps and even a couple of railway gas meters! There are indoor and outdoor displays in pleasant garden surroundings.

## 375   LCP Fuels Ltd          E

Pensnett Trading Estate, Shut End, Dudley, West Midlands
OS Ref: SO 901897

Standard gauge steam locomotive on static display
Diesel locomotive undergoing restoration

**Stock**
Manning Wardle 0–6–0ST *Winston Churchill* (2025) built 1923
Ruston Hornsby 4WDM 215755 built 1942

## 376   Stafford          E

Victoria Gardens (outside Stafford BR Station)
OS Ref: SJ 919229

2 ft gauge steam locomotive on static display
**Stock**
Bagnall 0–4–0ST *Isabel* (1491) built 1898
Presented by English Electric Co. Ltd, for display, 1963.

## 377   City of Birmingham Corporation          E

Great Francis Street Playground, Aston, Birmingham
OS Ref: SP 087877
Standard gauge steam locomotive on static display

**Stock**
Manning Wardle 0–6–0ST *Abernant* (2015) built 1921
Ex Austin Motor Co. Ltd, Longbridge, Birmingham, 1964.

## 378   Gloucester Railway Carriage          G
and Wagon Company

Bristol Road, Gloucester

Standard gauge vehicle preserved in works
**Stock**
London Transport 'G'-class third-class motor car No. 4184 built 1923

## 379   Lichfield District Council          E

Beacon Park, Lichfield, Staffordshire
OS Ref: SK 110097
Standard gauge locomotive on static display

**Stock**
Hibberd 4WDM 3809 built 1963
Ex Rom River Reinforcements Co Ltd, Lichfield 1973.

## 380   Rocester          E

Standard gauge steam locomotive on static display in children's playground at Rocester, Staffordshire
OS Ref: SK 108394

**Stock**
Barclay 0–4–0ST No. 67 (2352) built 1954
Ex CEGB, Goldington Power Station, Bedford, 1973.

## 381   Cambrian Railways Society Ltd          F

This Society is promoting a scheme for the formation of a living museum of Cambrian Railways relics centred on Oswestry, Salop.

OS Ref: SJ 294297

*Details from:* Stephen C. Edwards, 'Sheldan', Chirk Road, Gobowen, Oswestry, Salop SY11 3LB

The Society aims to be a major participant in the restoration of the Oswestry station building from its present dilapidated state. The building, an imposing Victorian structure, was the administrative headquarters of the Cambrian Railways until the Grouping, and a divisional HQ for GWR and BR after that. The Society is negotiating for occupation of part of the building and feels that it could contain passenger facilities, a museum and shop, while the remaining space should be let commercially.

**Stock**
[3]GWR 4-6-0 No. 7822 *Foxcote Manor* built 1950
Peckett 0-4-0ST *Adam* 1430 built 1916
Barclay 0-6-0ST No. 8 885 built 1900
Hunslet 0-6-0DM No. 3 3526 built 1947
Hudswell Clarke 0-4-0DM built 1954
Peckett 0-4-0ST No. 6 (2131) built 1951
[1]Beyer Peacock 0-4-0ST 1827 built 1879
[2]Planet 4WDM No. 322 (3541) built 1952
GWR auto-trailer coach built 1928
Two Burmah-Castrol oil tank wagons
Port of Sunderland Authority 3-plank open wagon

[1]Ex Beyer Peacock and Co. Ltd, Gorton Foundry, Manchester, 1966.
[2]Ex Fletcher and Stewart Ltd, Masson Works, Derby, 1973.
[3]Owned by the Foxcote Manor Society.

## 382  North Staffs and Cheshire        G
## Traction Engine Club

Draycott-in-the-Clay, Staffordshire

OS Ref: SK 156289

1 ft 11½ in. gauge locomotive undergoing restoration.

**Stock**
FR/George England 0-4-0STT *Palmerston* built 1864

## 383  Telford (Horsehay) Steam Trust        G

Adamson-Butterley Ltd, Horsehay, Shropshire

OS Ref: SJ 675073

Standard gauge steam locomotives undergoing restoration. *Details from:* N. Cossons, 'Southside', Church Hill, Ironbridge, Telford, Shropshire.

**Stock**
[1]GWR 0-6-2T No. 5619 (Class 56XX) built 1925
LNWR 0-8-0 No. 485 (BR No. 49395) built 1921

[1]Withdrawn from service as BR No. 5619 and sold for scrap to Woodham Brothers, Barry. Purchased for preservation and moved to its present location in 1973.

## 384  Croda Ltd        I

Four Ashes, Staffordshire

OS Ref: SJ 917085

Industrial steam location featuring occasional steam working.

**Stock**
Barclay 0-4-0F No. MP1 1944 built 1927

## 385  CEGB, West Midlands        I

Industrial steam locations featuring occasional steam working.

**Stock**
Peckett 0-4-0ST No. 1 (W6 Class) (1803) built 1933
(Ironbridge Power Station OS Ref: SJ 654042)
Peckett 0-4-0ST No. 3 (W7 Class) (1990) built 1940
(Ironbridge Power Station OS Ref: SJ 654042)
RSH 0-6-0T No. 9 (7151) built 1944
(Hams Hall Power Station OS Ref: SP 193920)

## 386  MODAD, Long Marston        I

Ministry of Defence Central Engineering Park, Long Marston, Warwickshire

OS Ref: SP 153473

Industrial steam location featuring occasional steam working.

**Stock**
Hunslet 0-6-0ST No. 98 *Royal Engineer* (3798) built 1953

## 387  Brookfield Foundry and        G
## Engineering Company

California Works, Stoke-on-Trent, Staffordshire

OS Ref: SJ 882444

Standard gauge steam locomotives in store in the former Kerr Stuart locomotive works. No public access.

**Stock**
Kerr Stuart 0-4-0ST 4388 built 1926
Bagnall 0-6-0PT 2613 built 1940

## 388  J. and H. B. Jackson Ltd        E

Scrap Merchants, Coventry, West Midlands

OS Ref: SP 343804

Standard gauge industrial locomotive preserved as a static exhibit on a short length of track by the entrance to the yard.

**Stock**
Hudswell Clarke 0-4-0DM *Southam* D604 built 1936

## 389  Birds Commercial Motors Ltd        G

Scrap Merchants, Long Marston, Warwickshire

OS Ref: SP 154458

Standard gauge steam locomotive in storage pending scrapping.

**Stock**
Barclay 0-4-0F No. 1 (1772) built 1922

## 390 Titanic Steamship Company     G

Mark Bamford and J. Goodman, Crab Key, Ellastone, Staffordshire

A private collection of standard gauge industrial locomotives operating on a ½ mile line.

**Stock**
Hunslet 0–6–0ST *King George* (2409) built 1942
RSH 0–6–0ST 7086 built 1942
Hunslet 0–6–0ST *Arthur* (3782) built 1953
Peckett 0–4–0ST 1438 built 1916
Peckett 0–4–0ST 1976 built 1939
Hudswell Clarke 0–6–0DM No. D1.D615 built 1938
Three BR Mk I Suburban bogie coaches.

## 391 Umberslade Light Railway     C

J. Marshall, 38 Spring Lane, Hockley Heath, Warwickshire
OS Ref: SP 152725

Private 2 ft gauge light railway. Occasional open days are organised.

**Stock**
Marshall 4WVBTG No. 1 *Oddson* built 1970
Hunslet 4WDM No. PWG 5 2207 built 1941

## 392 Oldberrow Light Railway     C

A. D. Smith, Oldberrow House, Henley-in-Arden, Warwickshire
OS Ref: SP 121659

2 ft gauge portable light railway.

**Stock**
Bagnall 0–4–0ST *Lady Luxborough* (2088) built 1918
Ex Birmingham Tame and Rea District Drainage Board, Minworth, 1961.

## 393 'The Spot Gate'     E

Ind Coope Restaurant, Hilderstone, Staffordshire

**Stock**
Pullman Car No. 75 built 1928
Pullman Car *Ursula* built 1928

Vehicles in use as a 'Pullman steak bar'.

## 394 Courtaulds Ltd     G

Coventry, West Midlands
Industrial Museum under construction.
OS Ref: SP 336808

Standard gauge steam locomotive in store.

**Stock**
Hawthorn Leslie 0–4–0ST *Henry* (2491) built 1901

## 395 Dudley Zoo Miniature Railway     B

A passenger carrying 15 in. gauge line operated by W & T (Leisure) Ltd, commencing in the grounds of Dudley zoo and extending for over ⅓ mile round Castle Hill on a wooded ledge which includes four short viaducts. The line was opened in 1938 on the 10¼ in. gauge and converted to 15 in. gauge after World War II. For many years, the line's motive power was provided by G & S Light Engineering of Stourbridge with steam locomotives of Trevor Guest's design. These were ultimately sold to various miniature lines, notably the Fairbourne Railway (Group No. 309), and the Dudley line was acquired by new owners using new stock.

OS Ref: SO 947911

**Stock**
Guest Bo-BoPM built 1953
Guest Co-BoPM built 1960
Minirail 4WDMR
Twelve open bogie coaches

## 396 Drayton Manor Park     B
##        Miniature Railway

Drayton Manor Park, Fazeley, near Tamworth, Staffordshire

A 10¼ in. gauge line comprising almost a mile of track running round the main lake in this well-appointed inland pleasure resort of 160 acres. Apart from the miniature railway, its attractions include alpine aerial cars, an amusement park, fleets of boats, a sternwheeler paddle boat seating 36 and a well-known zoo.

The park is open daily from Easter to September between 10.00 am and 7.00 pm. The railway operates daily during this period from 2.00 pm to 6.30 pm.

**Stock**
Severn Lamb 2–8–0 Bo-Bo PH No. 278 built 1970 (Steam outline)
Three open bogie coaches
Three closed bogie coaches

## 397 Ledbury Light Railway     C

Ledbury County Secondary School, Ledbury, Herefordshire

Private 7¼ in. gauge passenger carrying line, 500 yards in length running round the school grounds. Plans exist to extend the line to 1 mile.

**Stock**
Freelance 4WPM *Primus* built 1979
Four-seat bogie coach
4-wheel brake van

## 398 The Downs School C

Colwall, near Malvern, Worcs

Private 8½ in. gauge passenger carrying steam railway, ¼ mile in length in the school grounds. Plans exist for the line to be extended.

**Stock**
Bassett Lowke 4–4–2 *George* built 1910
Curwen 0–4–0T *Brock*
Downs School 4WPM *Tubby*

## 399 Bewdley Wildlife Park Railway B

West Midlands Safari and Leisure Park, Bewdley, Worcs.

Passenger-carrying 15 in. gauge railway

**Stock**
Severn Lamb 2–8–0DH 15–2–79 built 1979 (Steam outline)

## 400 Steam Cinema

Railway film-makers and exhibitors

*Details from:* Roger Crombleholme, 140 New Road, Netherton, Dudley, West Midlands DY2 9AY

Whilst not a railway preservation organisation as such, 'Steam Cinema' looks upon film as a preservation medium, recording events for posterity in a kind of 'time capsule'. So much has passed away on the railway scene in the last 30 years that in comparison the vast amount of admirable work performed by preservation societies is a mere drop in the ocean. For what has passed, we must rely on our own memories or on the wealth of published photographs covering this particular period. Better still, for a representation of an event that mere still photographs cannot portray, we can look at films.

Steam Cinema's' objective is to bring together as much footage as possible from a variety of sources to form a national archive collection. A start has already been made, and over 180 films covering the period since 1950 have been brought together to form the nucleus of the collection. Further films are constantly being added to our repertoire and these will be available for screening at railway society and public film shows throughout the coming season. For 'Steam Cinema' does not function as a mere film library. Instead it acts as a travelling cinema service available to clubs and societies providing an evening's entertainment on film with programme content to the choice of the booking organisation.

'Steam Cinema's' charge for its services is £5 plus 10p per mile return travelling expenses from our Dudley headquarters.

# AREA

# East Midlands

Leicestershire
Derbyshire
Nottinghamshire
Northamptonshire

## 401    Cadeby Light Railway                    A

A 2 ft gauge passenger-carrying line

*Details from:* The Rev. E. R. Boston, Cadeby Rectory, Cadeby, Hinckley, Leicestershire
*Access:* On the A447, one mile south of Market Bosworth
The railway is in operation on the second Saturday of each month from April to November and an advertised timetable is operated, though of necessity trains run with a wide recovery margin.
A collection box is available to cover fuel costs and for local church restoration. At the Cadeby end of the line there is a small steam museum containing a 1903 Aveling Porter steam roller and a 1927 Foster traction engine. There is also a 4 mm scale model Great Western Railway layout measuring 20 ft by 40 ft with about 50 representative locomotives.
Interested persons are welcome at any time, but are advised

to telephone Market Bosworth 290462 before 9 am any morning to ascertain whether the line is open.
OS Ref: SK 426024

**Stock**
[1]Bagnall 0–4–0ST No. 1 *Pixie* 2090 built 1919
[2]Hunslet 0–4–0ST *Margaret* 605 built 1894
Orenstein & Koppel 0–4–0WT No. 2 7529 built 1914
[3]Baguley 0–4–0PM 1695 built 1928
Lister 4WPM *New Star* 4088 built 1931
Motor Rail 4WDM No. 20 8748 built 1942
Motor Rail 4WDM No. 42 7710 built 1939
Motor Rail 4WDM 3874 built 1929
Motor Rail 4WDM 5609 built 1931
Motor Rail 4WDM No. 24 5853 built 1934
Hundswell Clarke 4WDM D558 built 1930
Penrhyn Quarries coach 'O'
Two wooden-sided wagons
Four Fullersite wagons
Two flat trucks
Three open trucks
Platelayers trolley

[1]Ex Staveley Minerals Ltd, Cranford Quarries, Northants, 1962.
[2]Ex Penrhyn Quarries Ltd, Bethesda, Caernarfonshire, 1968. (In store.)
[3]Ex Lilleshall Abbey and Woodland Railway, Shropshire, 1967 (steam outline).

The Cadeby Light Railway is probably the smallest steam-worked narrow gauge railway in the world. The line exists because of people who are fascinated by steam locomotives and the complications of a railway system and who thoroughly enjoy themselves working out the problems involved. Largely, it is the brainchild of the well-known steam enthusiast and Rector of Cadeby, the Rev. 'Teddy' Boston, who bought *Pixie* from Cranford Ironstone Quarry, Northants, in 1962 and laid about 400 yards of 2 ft gauge track round the perimeter of the Rectory garden on which to run her.
The railway has stations at each end of the line known as Sutton Lane and Cadeby respectively. At a point about halfway along the route, where the line runs in the trees parallel to the main A447, is Hinckley Road Halt. At Cadeby there are sidings leading to the motive power sheds and to the road transfer dock near the church.
The motive power is predominantly steam, though both petrol and diesel locomotives are used on works trains and the winter services.

## 402    Market Bosworth Light Railway         A

Shackerstone Station, near Market Bosworth, Leicestershire

*Access:* Turn right at Twycross on the A444 Nuneaton–Burton road, then take unclassified road through Cougerstone
OS Ref: SK 379066

Passenger-carrying standard gauge steam railway, 2¾ miles in length, running from Shackerstone to Market Bosworth.

**Photo: Geoff King**

While impatient passengers look on, the crew of Hunslet 0–4–0ST No. 11 coal up the engine by hand. One lump, or two? It's a good thing that present-day passengers on the Market Bosworth light railway now travel with a roof over their heads

The railway operates at weekends and Bank Holidays from Easter to the end of October.
Facilities for visitors include car parking, museum, shop, refreshments and toilets.

**Stock**
BR 2–6–0 No. 78018 Riddles Class 2MT built 1954
[1]Borrows 0–4–0WT *The King* 48 built 1906
Hunslet 0–4–0ST *NCB No. 11* 1493 built 1925
Hudswell Clarke 0–6–0T 1857 built 1953
Hawthorn Leslie 0–6–0ST No. 21 3931 built 1938
Bagnall 0–6–0ST No. 2 3059 built 1953
BR/Drewry 0–6–0DM DVLR No. 2 (BR No. D2245) 2577 built 1956
Peckett 0–4–0ST *Dunlop No. 7* 2130 built 1951
[2]RSH 0–6–0T No. 3 7537 built 1949
[2]RSH 0–6–0T No. 4 7684 built 1951
Peckett 0–4–0ST *Herbert* 2012 built 1942
Ruston Hornsby 4 WDM *Peeping Tom* 235513 48DS Class built 1945
Hibberd 4WDM *C. P. May* 2895 built 1944
BR Mk I BCK coach No. E21031 built 1954
BR Mk I FK coach No. 13125 built 1954
BR/Park Royal Observation car No. M50397 built 1957
BR/Park Royal Observation car No. M56160 built 1957
RCT Mobile Workshop
[3]BR 16-ton mineral wagon No. B276232 built 1956
[4]Shell/BP tank wagon No. 5029 built 1938
LMS flat wagon No. M45605 built 1926
LMS brake van No. M732195 built 1946
Two LMS 12-ton open wagons
Smith 6-ton steam crane No. 21085 built 1953

Grafton steam crane 1618 built 1917
Jones 4WDM 6-ton shunting crane

[1]Ex United Glass (England) Ltd, Charlton, London, 1967. Purchased for preservation by the Industrial Locomotive Preservation Group and stored at Robertsbridge, K & ESR, until 1969 when it was resold to the Shackerstone Railway Society.
[2]Ex CEGB, Nechells Power Station, Birmingham, 1972.
[3]Presented by Cravens of Sheffield.
[4]Donated by Shell-Mex BP.

## 403  Great Central Railway  A

Loughborough Central Station, Great Central Road, Loughborough, Leicestershire

Tel: Loughborough 216433
OS Ref: SK 543194

Passenger-carrying standard gauge steam railway, 5½ miles in length running from Loughborough Central to Rothley Station.
The railway operates at weekends and Bank Holidays from Mid-March. Facilities for visitors include car parking, museum, souvenir shop, refreshments and toilets.

**Stock**
[1]LMS 4–6–0 No. 5231 *3rd Volunteer Battalion, The Worcestershire and Sherwood Foresters Regiment* (Class 5MT) Armstrong Whitworth 1286 built 1936
[2]SR 4–6–2 No. 34039 *Boscastle* (Bullied WC Class) built 1946
[3]GWR 4–6–0 No. 6990 *Witherslack Hall* built 1948
[4]LNER 4–6–0 No. 61264 (Class B1) built 1947
LNER 4–6–0 No. 1306 *Mayflower* Class B1 built 1948
[9]LNER 0–6–2T No. 4744 (Class N2) (NB Locomotive 22600) built 1921
GWR 2–8–0T No. 5224 5205 Class built 1924
BR 2–10–0 No. 92212 Riddles Class 9F built 1959
[10]BR 4–6–2 No. 71000 *Duke of Gloucester* Riddles Class 8P built 1954
[5]GCR 4–4–0 No. 506 *Butler Henderson* (BR No. 62660) Class 11F built 1919
NSB 2–6–0 No. 377 *King Haakon VII* (Nohab) built 1919
[6]Bagnall 0–6–0ST *Lamport No. 3* 2670 built 1942
Hunslet 0–6–0ST *Robert Nelson No. 4* 1800 built 1936
Manning Wardle 0–6–0ST *Littleton No. 5* 2018 built 1922
RSH 0–6–0T No. 39 6947 built 1938
[7]NER 0–4–0T No. 985 (LNER Class Y7) built 1923
[8]Hawthorn Leslie 0–4–0ST *Marston No. 3* 3581 built 1924
Peckett 0–4–0ST *Hilda* built 1938
Wickham 4WPM rail inspection trolley
Fowler 0–4–0DM No. D4279 *Arthur Wright* 4210079 built 1952
LNER Gresley buffet car No. NE1852E built 1938
GCR 'Barnum' open third-class bogie coach No. 664 built 1910
BR Mk 1 FO bogie coach No. S3042 built 1958
BR Mk 1 CK bogie coaches Nos E15096 and E15611 built 1953 and 1955

BR Mk 1 BSK bogie coaches Nos E34393 and E34738 built 1955
LNER Gresley buffet car No. E9124E built 1937
LNER Gresley Brake/3rd coach No. E16520E built 1939
LNER Non-Gangwayed 6 wheel full brake No. E70654 built 1950
LMS 20-ton goods brake van No. 2 built 1924
MR Covered van
NSB four-wheeled Konductorvogn No. 547 built by Strommens, Vaersted, 1912
NSB four-wheeled brake/third No. 1001 built by Strommens, Oslo, 1915
Thomas Smith and Sons (Rodley) self-propelled steam crane
BR 'Catfish' ballast hopper wagon No. DB983393
Shell/BP tank wagon (LMS No. 164253) in 'Vickers Oils' livery built 1943
Three NCB wooden coal wagons
LMS 12-ton open wagon No. DM742591

[1]LMS Stanier *Black Five* withdrawn from Carnforth shed in 1968 as BR No. 45231 and kept at Steamtown, Carnforth, following preservation until moved to Loughborough in 1973.
[2]Withdrawn from service as BR No. 34039 in 1967 and sold to Woodham Brothers, Barry, for scrap. Purchased for preservation and moved to Loughborough in 1973.
[3]Withdrawn from service in November 1965 and sold to Woodham Brothers, Barry, for scrap. Purchased for preservation by the Witherslack Hall Society and moved to Loughborough in 1975.
[4]Withdrawn from service as BR Eastern Region Departmental Locomotive No. 29 in November 1965 and sold to Woodham Brothers of Barry for scrap. Purchased for preservation by

the Thompson B1 Locomotive Society in 1975.
[5]Robinson 'Director' Class locomotive withdrawn from Sheffield (Darnall) as BR No. 62660 in 1960. This fine locomotive is the sole survivor of the GCR passenger classes and was housed in Clapham Museum until its closure in 1973.
[6]Ex-Staveley Minerals Ltd, Lamport, Northants, 1969.
[7]Formerly BR No. 68088. Withdrawn as Departmental Locomotive No. 34 in 1952. Sold to NCB and purchased for preservation in 1964. Twenty-two of these locomotives were built, many being sold for further work after withdrawal. No. 985 worked at Tyne Dock until June 1948, after which it was sent to Stratford as works shunter.
[8]Ex Marston, Thompson and Evershed Ltd, Burton-on-Trent, Staffs, 1967. This locomotive was housed on the Foxfield Light Railway until the end of 1972.
[9]Originally GNR No. 1744 and withdrawn from Peterborough shed in 1962 as BR No. 69523. Purchased for preservation in 1963 and moved to the Keighley and Worth Valley Railway in 1965. One hundred and seven of these locomotives were constructed and were principally used on the Kings Cross suburban services. For working in the Metropolitan tunnels, these engines were fitted with condensing gear consisting of large diameter pipes for carrying exhaust steam from the smokebox to the top of the side tanks. Owned by the Gresley Society (*q.v.*).
[10]No. 71000 *Duke of Gloucester* was Britain's last Class 8 'Pacific' locomotive. Built in 1954 at Crewe Works, it hauled

---

**Nostalgia for a passenger who no doubt can recall the days when the Great Central ran all the way to London. At the head of this train is LMS *Black Five* No. 5231**

Photo: Bill Squires

express trains on the London Midland Region until 1962, when it was withdrawn for preservation by British Rail, probably because of its unique cylinders and valve gear (the latter being an improvement of the British Caprotti type) which were the most efficient on any simple expansion steam locomotive in history. However, after some considerable time, British Rail changed their mind and decided to scrap the locomotive, but on doing this in 1967, removed one of the outside cylinders, complete with valve gear, and placed it (sectioned) on display in the Science Museum at Kensington. Eventually the locomotive appeared in the scrapyard at Barry, South Wales, minus the other outside cylinder. It remained there until 1973, when it was purchased by members of the present Trust who then took it to Main Line Steam Trust at Loughborough, Leicestershire (part of the former Great Central Railway). The locomotive is now being restored to its former condition. Owned by the Duke of Gloucester Steam Locomotive Trust Ltd (q.v.).

**The Gresley Society** H
Loughborough Central Station, Leicestershire

*Details from:* Mr P. Holmes, 9 Broadmead, Willow Wong, Burton Joyce, Nottingham

**Duke of Gloucester Steam Locomotive Trust Limited (formerly the 71000 Preservation Society)** H

Loughborough Central Station, Leicestershire

At present the Trust has approximately 180 members and membership is now available on a two-tier system: full membership at £3 per annum, which gives all privileges and benefits available from the Trust; and associate membership at £1.50 per annum, which is really only intended for those who wish to keep informed of the events within the Trust. Further membership details are available from Mr C. Hazlehurst, 138 Fernhill, Harlow, Essex.

## 404   Dinting Railway Centre      D

Dinting Lane, Glossop, Derbyshire

*Access:* Dinting Lane, off A57 road, 1 mile from Glossop. Dinting BR station
Tel: Glossop 5596
OS Ref: SK 021946

Standard gauge steam railway centre, featuring short steam-hauled train rides over ¼ mile of track.
Dinting Railway Centre is open daily except Christmas and Boxing Days from 10.30 am to 5 pm. Locomotives in steam each Sunday from March to October inclusive.
Facilities for visitors include car parking, museum, shop, refreshments, toilets, picnic area and miniature steam railway.
In 1968 the Committee of the Bahamas Locomotive Society began to search for a home for their newly restored locomotive *Bahamas*. Dinting was ideal and with generous assistance from a Society member and encouragement from Glossop Council the site was purchased from British Rail. Since that time a great deal of work has been undertaken

to improve the services offered. An Exhibition Hall, capable of housing up to nine main line locomotives has been constructed, a picnic area created, road access, car park facilities, refreshment and shop areas built. There is also an extensive steam operated miniature railway which has been constructed by members of the Buxton Model Engineering Society.

*Details from:* Mr K. J. Tait, 15 Priestnall Road, Heaton Mersey, Stockport, Cheshire SK4 3HR
*Subscription:* £1.50 per year; lady members and juniors aged 12–17 75p; life membership £15.75
*Membership:* 950

### Stock
[1]LMS 4–6–0 No. 5596 *Bahamas* (Stanier Class 5XP) built 1935
[9]LNER 4–6–2 No. 532 *Blue Peter* (Peppercorn A2/3 Class) built 1948
[10]LNER 4–6–2 No. 19 *Bittern* (Gresley A4 Class) built 1937
[2]LMS 4–6–0 No. 6115 *Scots Guardsman* (Stanier Class 7P) built 1927
[3]SR 4–4–0 No. 30925 *Cheltenham* (Maunsell Class 'V') built 1934
[8]GCR 2–8–0 No. 102 (BR No. 63601) (04 Class) built 1911
[4]LNWR 0–6–2T No. 1054 (BR No. 58926) built 1888
RSH 0–4–0CT *Southwick* (7069) built 1942
RSH 0–6–0ST No. 150 *Warrington* (7136) built 1944
Hudswell Clarke 0–6–0T *Nunlow* (1704) built 1938
Avonside 0–6–0ST 1883 built 1923
Barclay 0–4–0ST *Tiny* (2258) built 1949
[5]Beyer Peacock 0–4–0VB tram locomotive 2734 built 1886
[6]Baguley (McEwan Pratt) 0–4–0PM *Jacob* (680) built 1916
[7]Avonside/Rolls Royce 0–4–0DH No. RS8 (1913) built 1923
[11]LMS medical officer's saloon 45017 built 1923
BR Mk 1 BSK bogie coach No. 34460 built 1953
MSCR open wagon No. 6115
SR bogie brake van No. S56287 built 1936
BR brake van No. B950690

[1]'Jubilee' Class locomotive built by the North British Locomotive Co. Ltd (Works No. 24154). Withdrawn from Stockport shed as BR No. 45596 in August 1966. This locomotive was fitted with a double chimney during the course of its career, apart from which it is identical with No. 5593 at Tyseley and its shed mate No. 5690. Given a complete overhaul by the Hunslet Engine Co. Ltd, Leeds, during 1968 and repainted in original LMS maroon, *Bahamas* has since taken part in many 'Return to Steam' rail tours. The locomotive is at present undergoing extensive repairs, for which purposes a special appeal fund has been launched.
[2]Three-cylinder 'Royal Scot' Class locomotive built by the North British Locomotive Co. Ltd (Works No. 23610). Rebuilt with taper boiler at Crewe in 1947 and withdrawn from Carlisle (Kingmoor) as BR No. 46115 in December 1965. *Scots Guardsman* was the last of its class in service and made a number of excursions with enthusiasts' special trains immediately prior to its withdrawal. The locomotive was preserved privately and housed initially on the K & WVR before moving on to Dinting.
[3]On loan from BRB. Withdrawn from Basingstoke shed in

Let's hope the northern rails will soon echo to the sound of another Jubilee! No. 5596 *Bahamas* is currently undergoing an extensive boiler refit at Dinting

---

1962 and set aside for preservation in the official collection. The locomotive has been stored at several locations, including Preston Park and Tyseley, until moved to Dinting in 1972. The 'Schools' class was the final development of the 4-4-0 type in Great Britain, being designed principally for the London–Hastings line where high power was required within a confined loading gauge. The class subsequently proved superior to the older 'King Arthurs' on the Bournemouth expresses and were used on passenger duties right up to their demise.

[4]On loan from The National Trust, Penrhyn Castle Museum (Group No. 325).

[5]On loan from Manchester Museum of Science and Technology.

[6]On loan from the North of England Open Air Museum (Group No. 165).

[7]Rebuilt from 0-4-0ST in 1957 by ICI Ltd at Tunstead, near Buxton, Derbyshire, from whom the engine was purchased in 1974.

[8]On loan from the National Railway Museum.

[9]Built as BR No. 60532 and withdrawn from Dundee shed in 1966. Purchased for preservation in 1968 and restored in LNER livery in 1969. *Blue Peter* was, in fact, the first new locomotive built at Doncaster Works to bear a number in the BR series. In view of its LNER lineage, its new owners have restored it as No. 532.

[10]Originally LNER No. 4464. Withdrawn from Aberdeen (Ferryhill) shed in 1966 as BR No. 60019 and restored for working special trains.

[11]Owned by the Historic Rolling Stock Group. (See Group No. 352.)

## 405  Midland Railway Centre                          DF

Butterley Station, near Ripley, Derbyshire

*Access:* On A61 road, 1½ miles north of Ripley
OS Ref: SK 403520

Standard gauge steam railway preservation centre devoted to the Midland Railway and its successors. When fully operational, trains will run over 3¼ miles of track.

Through the lens of a modern day camera is captured the living, breathing spirit of the Midland Railway as it was at the turn of the century. This unique scene at Butterley has been made possible by the Midland Railway Trust

---

The Midland Railway Centre is open daily throughout the year with steam Open Days at intervals as advertised. Facilities for visitors include limited car parking, souvenir shop and refreshments.
The Midland Railway project will historically portray the Midland Railway and early LMS by means of a static museum and a working length of line. This is on part of the ex-Midland line from Ambergate to Pye Bridge, in particular the section from Hammersmith to Pye Bridge, a distance of 3 miles 22 chains. The main museum exhibits and amenities area is incorporated, along with the main station, locomotive workshops, carriage sidings, etc, at Butterley.
The basic operating railway will consist of a double-track line between Butterley station, and Swanwick Colliery Junction, with its associated sidings and museum site, workshops and servicing facilities, with a single line running from Swanwick Colliery Junction via Ironville Junction to a station in the vicinity of the former Pye Bridge Station. This single line could eventually be doubled if necessary and would be shared with Butterley Engineering, who at present lease the

section from BR. There will be two short branch lines feeding into the 'main line' at Swanwick Junction.

## Stock

BR 4-6-0 No. 73129 (Class 5MT Caprotti) built 1956
[1]LMS 4-6-2 No. 6203 *Princess Margaret Rose* built 1935
[2]MR 2-4-0 No. 158A built 1866
[3]MR 4-2-2 No. 673 built 1890
LMS 0-6-0 No. 4027 (BR No. 44027) built 1924
LMS 0-6-0T No. 47564 (Class 3F) (Hunslet 1580) built 1928
LMS 0-6-0T No. 47327 (Class 3F) (NB Loco 23406) built 1926
LMS 0-6-0T No. 16440 (BR No. 47357) (Class 3F) (NB Loco 23436) built 1926
LMS 0-6-0T No. 47445 (Class 3F) (Hunslet 1529) built 1927
[4]MR 0-6-0T No. 1708 (Class 1F) built 1880
Hunslet 0-6-0ST No. 3193 built 1944
Markham 0-4-0ST *Gladys* (109) built 1894
Barclay 0-4-0CT *Stanton No. 24* (1875) built 1925
Peckett 0-4-0ST *Victory* (1547) built 1919
Nasmyth Wilson 0-4-0ST No. 4 built 1894
BR 0-6-0DE No. 12077 built 1950
Simplex 4WDM No. RS9 (2024) built 1921
Simplex 4WDM No. RS12 (460) built 1917
Fowler 0-4-0DM *Andy* (16038) built 1923
Drewry 0-6-0DM No. 2271 (2615) built 1957
BR compartment bogie coach No. E46097 built 1954
BR brake/second compartment coach No. E43186 built 1954
L & YR first-class family saloon coach No. 995 built 1911
LMS third-class sleeping car No. M612 built 1952
LMS dynamometer car No. 1 (BR No. M45050) built 1913
MSJ & AR bogie composite coach No. M29663M built 1931
GWR auto-trailer No. 38 built 1907
LMS inspection saloon No. DM395222 built 1930
LD & ECR staff van No. DE950249 built 1898
MR bogie composite coach No. DM195955 built 1910
MR six-wheeled passenger brake van No. DM198587 built 1902
MR six-wheeled passenger brake van No. DM297290 built 1898
MR six-wheeled third/brake coach No. 7243 built 1884
MR clerestory passenger brake van built 1902
MR clerestory brake/composite No. 198829 built 1905
MR four-wheeled motor car van No. 8272 built 1916
MR six-wheeled ballast brake van No. 291 built 1916
MR 10-ton covered goods van No. WD47135 built 1915
MR 20-ton goods brake van No. 11 built 1921
MR bogie tool van No. DM198715 built 1905
MR 10-ton covered goods van No. WD47872 built 1915
MR 10-ton covered goods van No. WD47961 built 1915
BR four-wheeled horsebox No. M42608 built 1949
LMS 12-ton cattle wagon No. M292063 built 1933
MR square-tank tar wagon No. 72110 built 1913
MR gas tar tank wagon No. 18712 built 1895
MR Pullman car body *Midland* built 1874
MR third-class composite brake coach No. DM395525 built 1921

Photo: John Gardner

**And here's proof of the standard set by the Midland Railway Trust with this perfect restoration of LMS *Jinty* No. 16440**

MR six-wheeled brake van built *c*.1900
Two NER tar wagons built 1895 and 1913
AD flat truck No. 60007 built 1901
Twelve-ton low-sided wagon No. 11 built 1926
LNWR three-ton hand crane built 1897
Hudswell Clarke 0–4–0ST *Handyman* (573) built 1900 (3 ft gauge)
Fowler 2–4–0DM No. 2 (20685) built 1935 (3 ft gauge)

[1]Withdrawn from Carlisle (Upperby) in 1962 as BR No. 46203. Restored to LMS livery at Crewe and placed on display in 1963. The class worked Anglo-Scottish expresses until 1937–8, after which they were favourites on the Liverpool–London trains for a number of years.

[2]This locomotive survived successive renumberings and reboilerings to enjoy an exceptionally long life in service, not being withdrawn until 1947. This is all the more remarkable since the rest of its class became extinct in the 1930s. Originally used on express passenger work, it is almost certain that its declining years would have been spent on station or shed pilot work, with maybe the odd excursion now and then. On withdrawal, the LMS restored it to its pre-1923 condition as No. 158A.

[3]Johnson Class 115 locomotive later renumbered 673 and withdrawn from service in 1928. Restored to MR livery at Derby in 1929 and stored until presented for display in Leicester Museum. The Midland 'Spinners' were considered by many to be one of the most graceful designs of locomotive ever to run in this country. They were introduced right at the end of the 'single' era, since the invention of steam sanding gear made them a practical proposition for hauling the moderate loads of that time. No less than 95 were built, but the greatly increased loads which became the order of the day from 1914 onwards spelt doom for them and all were withdrawn by 1922, with the exception of No. 673 which was retained and restored as MR No. 118.

[4]Withdrawn as BR No. 41708 in 1966. This engine, together with four other members of its class, was retained for shunting duties at Staveley Ironworks under the terms of a 100-year agreement entered into by the Midland Railway in 1866. All five engines were withdrawn immediately the agreement expired and No. 41708, being in the best condition, was purchased for preservation in 1967. A total of 240 of these locomotives were built between 1878 and 1899 and from the design was developed the standard LMS shunting type. Owned by the 1708 Locomotive Preservation Trust Ltd. (q.v.).

### 1708 Locomotive Preservation Trust Ltd    H

*Details from:* G. S. Mimms, 64 Elmwood Crescent, Luton, Bedfordshire.
The Trust also own the following locomotive, currently being overhauled at APCM Dunstable Works, Bedfordshire.

Hunslet 0–6–0ST *Cunarder* (1690) built 1931
Ex APCM Ltd, Harbury, Warwickshire, 1969.


## 406   Northamptonshire Ironstone    F
## Railway Trust Limited

Hunsbury Hill, Northampton

OS Ref: SP 735584
Nearest BR station: Northampton

The Trust was formed to put together a museum of ironstone relics in order to preserve something of the county's heritage. The intended site for the railway exhibits is the trackbed of the former ironstone tramway serving Hunsbury furnaces, which lies within the bounds of the proposed Hunsbury Hill Park.
The site is open to visitors at weekends, May to September inclusive.
*Details from:* Alan Clayton, 30 Fulford Drive, Northampton, Northants.

**Stock**
Manning Wardle 0–4–0ST No. 14 *Brill* (1795) built 1912
Sentinel 4WVBTG *Musketeer* (9365) built 1946
Sentinel 4WVBTG *Belvedere* (9369) built 1946
Hunslet 0–4–0DM 2087 built 1940
Ruston Hornsby 4WDM 235511 built 1945
Peckett 0–6–0ST No. 85 *Banshee* (1870) built 1934 (metre gauge)
[1]Peckett 0–6–0ST No. 86 (1871) built 1934 (metre gauge)
[1]Peckett 0–6–0ST No. 87 (2029) built 1942 (metre gauge)
[2]Lister 4WPM 14006 built 1940 (2 ft gauge)
Motor Rail 4WDM 9711 built 1952 (2 ft gauge)
Motor Rail 4WDM 8969 built 1945 (2 ft gauge)
Motor Rail 4WDM 8731 built 1941 (2 ft gauge)
Wickham 4WPMR 6887 built 1954 (metre gauge)
Also the station buildings from Yelvertoft and Lilbourne

[1]Ex Stewarts and Lloyds Minerals Ltd, Wellingborough Quarries, 1967.
[2]Stored at Richmond Terrace Pumping Station, Northampton.


## 407   Papplewick Pumping Station    A

Longdale Lane, Ravenshead, Nottinghamshire

*Access:* 7 miles north of Nottingham

Passenger-carrying 7¼ in. gauge steam railway, 800 ft in length. The railway is in operation when the pumping engines are steamed, i.e. Bank Holidays, etc.
The railway was opened at Easter 1978 and is operated by members of the Chesterfield and District Model Engineering Society.

**Stock**
CMES 0–4–0WTT *Percy* ('Romulus' type) built 1978
Two open bogie coaches

Papplewick is worthy of a visit in its own right. There is preserved a complete Victorian steam pumping station complete with working beam engines. The elegant pumping station building is set in attractively landscaped grounds with ornamental lakes.


## 408   Stapleford Miniature Railway    A

Stapleford Park, Melton Mowbray, Leicestershire
OS Ref: SK 813182

A 10¼ in. gauge line opened in 1958, now extending to just under one mile in length. Operating in Stapleford Park, home of Lord and Lady Gretton, this is one of the finest miniature railways in the country, having three stations, a tunnel, an automatic level crossing and colour light signalling. An unusual feature of the line's operation is the boat train to Lakeside Station where passengers can join the *Northern Star* and *Southern Cross*, models of the Shaw Savill line ships of the same names, for voyage on the lake.
An extension to the railway was opened in 1977 serving a new station, 'Chestnuts'.
The railway operates when the house and grounds are open to visitors: Easter Sunday and Monday, Spring Bank Holiday Monday and Tuesday and Late Summer Holiday Monday; also every Sunday, Wednesday and Thursday afternoons from May to September (inclusive) from 2.30 to 6.30 pm.

**Stock**
Curwen 4–4–2 No. 751 *John of Gaunt* built 1948
Curwen 4–4–2 No. 750 *Blanche of Lancaster* built 1948
Coleby-Simkins 2–8–4 No. 752 *The Lady Margaret* built 1971
LMS 4–6–0 No. 5565 *Victoria* built 1948–75
Curwen Bo-Bo PM No. D100 *The White Heron* built 1962
Three articulated bogie coaches
Twelve open bogie coaches


## 409   Thoresby Hall Miniature Railway    A

Thoresby Park, Ollerton, Newark, Notts.
OS Ref: SK 6371

A 10¼ in. gauge line, 750 yards long, opened in 1969 and still being developed. It runs alongside the River Medan and the smaller of two lakes in the park, which is in the centre of Sherwood Forest. A locomotive shed is at one end of the line and a temporary platform is situated at the other, so present operation is 'push-pull'. Further extensions of track are planned for both ends of the route.

Operation is on Sunday afternoons and Bank Holidays from Easter until September.

**Stock**
LNER 4-6-2 No. 4498 *Sir Nigel Gresley* (A4 Class) built Kirkland 1967
Three articulated bogie coaches

## 410 Hall Leys Miniature Railway          A

Hall Leys Pleasure Gardens, Matlock, Derbyshire. Operated by L & S Miniature Railway Co. Ltd
Tel: Matlock 55976

A 9½ in. gauge passenger-carrying line, 220 yards in length, originally opened in 1947.
Facilities for visitors include car parking, refreshments and toilets.
The railway operates from Easter to the end of September (weather permitting).

**Stock**
Batteson 4-6-2 (LNER Pacific type) built 1948
Allcock/Coleby-Simkins 0-6-0DH built 1975
Two 'sit-astride' bogie coaches
Children's open bogie coach

## 411 Manor Miniature Railway          B

Manor Park, Glossop, Derbyshire

A 7¼ in. gauge passenger-carrying line operated by Mr K. Beeley and opened in 1970. The line forms a circuit round a wooded park, crossing a stream in two places.

**Stock**
Cromar White Bo-BoPM No. 7001 *Hymek*
Three sit-astride bogie coaches

## 412 Wicksteed Park Lakeside Railway          B

Wicksteed Park, Kettering, Northants
OS Ref: SP 883770

A 2 ft gauge passenger-carrying line, one-and-a-half miles long laid out in a circuit of the park. The railway operates from Easter to the end of September.

**Stock**
Baguley 0-4-0DM *King Arthur* (2042) built 1931
Baguley 0-4-0DM *Lady of the Lake* (2043) built 1931

Motor Rail 4WDM *Cheyenne* (22224) built 1966
Ten open four-wheeled coaches with rustic-type garden seats built 1931
Four covered toastrack bogie coaches built 1966

Wicksteed Park is an attractive expanse of over 150 acres bordering the main A6 road between Kettering and Barton Seagrave. The park was created for the public by the late Charles Wicksteed who was a pioneer of the steam plough. This enterprising engineer first visited Kettering in 1871 and established the engineering works which bears his name. The minature railway was the last of Wicksteed's enterprises before his death in 1931.
Entrance to the park is free.
All the locomotives have a steam outline.

*Also at Wicksteed Park*
Standard gauge steam locomotive on static display
OS Ref: SP879773
Barclay 0-4-0ST No. 9 (2323) built 1952
Presented by South Durham Steel and Iron Co. Ltd., Irchester Quarry, 1969. On display at Wollaston Road recreation ground, Irchester, until 1979

## 413 Billing Miniature Railway          B

Billing Aquadrome, Billing, Northampton
OS Ref: SP808615

A 2 ft gauge passenger-carrying line three-quarters-of-a-mile long around the Willow Lake and fishing area. Billing Aquadrome is a 350-acre expanse of lakes, lawns, woods and parkland set in the rich Northamptonshire countryside. Besides providing caravan and camping sites, the Aquadrome is an attractive resort for the day visitor and with its railway is open from March to October each year.

**Stock**
Ruston Hornsby 4WDM 242887 (20DL Class) built 1946 (American steam outline)
Five articulated open bogie coaches

## 414 Overstone Solarium Light Railway          B

Overstone Park, Sywell, Northamptonshire
OS Ref: SP819654

A 60 cm gauge passenger-carrying line 1,300 yards long operated by Overstone Solarium Ltd, Ecton Lane, Sywell, Northampton NN6 0BD. Tel. Northampton 42241

The railway operates (weather permitting) on Saturdays, Sundays and Bank Holidays from April to September. Also on weekdays in July and August

**Stock**
Simplex 4WDM No. 22 (8727) built 1941
Three bogie coaches

The trackage of the railway totals some 800 yards, laid as a single main line from the station (which is near the swimming pool and funfair) along the edge of the park and then into the wood. In the woods, the line is looped to return trains to the station, giving a total run of some 1,300 yards. Every effort has been made to capture the narrow-gauge image on this railway, which opened in 1969.

## 415   Tramway Museum Society                    B

Crich, near Ambergate, Derbyshire DE4 5DP

*Access:* Trent bus 240/241 from Matlock, Alfreton, Alfreton & Mansfield Parkway. B.R. ½-hour uphill walk from What-standwell (BR); Trent 151 bus from Derby or Bakewell to Crich Market Place.
Tel: 077-385-2565
OS Ref: SK 345549

One mile long standard gauge electric tramway.
Open Saturdays, Sundays and Bank Holidays, April–October, 10.30 am to 5.00 pm; Tuesdays, Wednesdays and Thursdays, May, June, July and August only, 10 am to 4.30 pm. Also Mondays in July and August.
A regular service is operated on these dates by the largest collection of tramcars in Europe. The Museum has a unique collection of over 40 trams, of which the majority are in working order. Apart from British vehicles, the collection includes examples from Czechoslovakia, Portugal and South Africa, as well as a former New York streetcar which last ran in Vienna.
Other special features of the Museum include Edwardian street project; façade of Assembly Rooms – Ancient Monument from Derby re-erected at Museum. Lead Mining display by Peak District Mines Historical Society.

*Amenities:* Car and coach park; museum shop for tramway and light railway books, films and souvenirs; cafe, toilets and picnic area.

*Details from:* D. J. H. Senior, 23 South Road, Twickenham, Middlesex.

The Tramway Museum was established in 1955 to preserve and operate a representative collection of trams and tramway equipment. In 1959 the Museum was established in part of a limestone quarry which had been served by a narrow gauge mineral railway built by George Stephenson. Depots and workshops have been built and the electric tramway has been progressively extended to give visitors scenic views over the Derwent Valley. Over 40 trams have been collected and many restored to their original condition and full working order. The collection includes horse and electric cars and a steam tramway locomotive.

### Stock
Beyer Peacock 0-4-0VB Tram No. 2 2464 built 1885
English Electric 4WE 717 built 1927
Ruston Hornsby 4WDM *Rupert* 223741 (20DL Class) built 1944, rebuilt TMS 1964
Ruston Hornsby 4WDM *GMJ* 326058 (48DL Class) built 1952, rebuilt TMS 1969
Ruston Hornsby 4WDM 373363 (48DL Class) built 1954 (metre gauge)

### Tramcar Fleet List
Blackpool No. 1 built 1884
Derby No. 1 built 1904
Douglas Southern Electric Tramways No. 1 built 1896
London Transport No. 1 built 1931
Blackpool & Fleetwood No. 2 built 1898
Gateshead & District No. 5 built 1927
Oporto No. 9 built 1873
Hill of Howth (Dublin) No. 10 built 1902 (5ft 3in. gauge)
Grimsby & Immingham No. 14 built 1915
Sheffield No. 15 built 1874
Cheltenham & District No. 21 built 1921
Glasgow No. 22 built 1922
Blackpool & Fleetwood No. 40 built 1914
Blackpool No. 40 built 1926
Southampton No. 45 built 1903
Sheffield No. 46 built 1899
Blackpool No. 49 built 1926
Gateshead & District No. 52 built 1901
[1]Blackpool No. 59 built 1902
Johannesburg No. 60 built 1905
Paisley District No. 68 built 1919
Leicester No. 76 built 1904
Newcastle No. 102 built 1902
Hull No. 132 built 1910
Blackpool No. 166 built 1927
Blackpool No. 167 built 1928
Leeds No. 180 built 1931
Prague No. 180 built 1905
Sheffield No. 189 built 1934
Sheffield No. 264 built 1937
Metropolitan Electric Tramways (London) No. 331 built 1930
Leeds No. 345 built 1921
Leeds No. 399 built 1926
Sheffield No. 510 built 1950
Leeds No. 600 built 1931
Leeds No. 602 built 1953
Glasgow No. 812 built 1960
Glasgow No. 1100 built 1927
Glasgow No. 1115 built 1929
Glasgow No. 1282 built 1940
Glasgow No. 1297 built 1948
[2]New York No. 674 built 1939
Leeds No. 2 (Tower Car) built 1932
Sheffield No. 330 (Rail Grinder) built 1919
Glasgow No. 1 (Cable Layer) built 1905
Glasgow No. 21 (Tool Van)
Blackpool No. 2 (Generator) built 1927
Cardiff No. 131 (Water Car) built 1905

[1]Currently on loan to Blackpool Corporation.
[2]Purchased for preservation as Vienna No. 4225.

## 416   Lound Hall Mining Museum                  BE

National Coal Board, Lound Hall, Haughton, Bevercotes, near Retford, Nottinghamshire

*Access:* On B6387 Retford–New Ollerton Road
OS Ref: SK 700728

Museum open 2 pm–5.30 pm (April–October); 2 pm–dusk (winter) on the first Sunday of each month.

*Enquiries to:* Industrial Relations Officer, National Coal Board, Edwinstowe, Mansfield, Nottinghamshire.

Standard gauge steam locomotives on static display.

**Stock**
Manning Wardle 0–6–0ST *The Welshman* 1207 built 1890
Yorkshire Engine Co. 0–6–0ST No. 9 2521 built 1952

Also a passenger-carrying 2 ft gauge railway, 1 mile in length.

**Stock**
Ruston Hornsby 4WDM LAT class 375347 built 1954

## 417   Nottingham Industrial Museum          E

Wollaton Park, Nottingham

*Access:* A609 from Nottingham, via main park entrance in Wollaton Road
Tel: Nottingham 284602

Standard gauge steam locomotive on static display.
The Museum is open from April to September on Mondays to Saturdays 10 am to 7 pm, and Sundays 2 pm to 5 pm. October to March on Thursdays and Saturdays 10 am to 4.30 pm and Sundays 1.30 pm to 4.30 pm.

**Stock**
Chaplin 0–4–0VBTG 2368 built 1885
Taken out of service *c.*1950 and preserved at Northampton Gas Works from *c.*1955 until presented by the East Midlands Gas Board for display in 1966.

## 418   Millgate Folk Museum          E

Newark, Nottinghamshire

Standard gauge steam locomotive on static display

**Stock**
Hudswell Clarke 0–6–0ST No. 54 *Julie* 1682 built 1937
Ex British Sugar Corporation, Kelkham Factory, Newark, 1979.

## 419   Leicester Transport Museum          E

Abbey Lane Pumping Station, Corporation Road, Leicester

*Access:* Bus route 54 from Charles Street. (Shows 88 returning)
Tel: Leicester 61330
OS Ref: SK 589067

Operated by: Leicester Museums and Art Galleries.

Open:   Mondays–Saturdays   10 am–5.30 pm.   Sundays 2 pm–5.30 pm.
Facilities for visitors include car parking and museum shop.

**Stock**
[2]RSH 0–4–0ST *Mars II* 7493 built 1948
[1]Brush 0–4–0ST No. 6 314 built 1906
Barclay 0–4–0F No. 2 1815 built 1924
Simplex 4WPM 52600 built 1931 2 ft gauge

[1]Originally Powlesland and Mason No. 6. Taken over by the GWR in 1924, becoming No. 921. Sold to Sugar Beet and Crop Driers Ltd, Eynsham, in 1928 and resold to Berry Wiggins and Co. Ltd, Kingsnorth, Kent, in 1931. Purchased for preservation 1968.
[2]Ex East Midlands Gas Board, Aylestone Road Gasworks, Leicester, 1970. Adopted by the Leicester Railway Society for restoration as a working exhibit.

## 420   Daventry Borough Council          E

New Street Children's Playground, Daventry, Northants

*Access:* No. 311 bus from Northampton. BR Station
OS Ref: SP 574624

Standard gauge steam locomotive on static display.

**Stock**
Bagnall 0–6–0ST *Cherwell* 2654 built 1942
Ex Byfield Ironstone Co. Ltd, Byfield, Northants, 1966.

## 421   Welland Valley Vintage          E
##         Traction Club

Wellfield Street, Market Harborough, Leicestershire
OS Ref: SP 742868

Three-foot gauge static exhibits

**Stock**
Manning Wardle 0–6–0ST *Kettering Furnaces No. 8* (1675) built 1906
Kettering Ironstone tramway side-tipping wagon
Presented by Kettering Iron and Coal Co. Ltd, 1963.

## 422   Woodlands Railway          B

Gullivers Kingdom, Temple Road, Matlock Bath, Derbyshire.

Passenger-carrying 7¼ in. gauge railway, 100 yards in length running round a model village. The railway was opened in 1978 and conveys children only.

**Stock**
Cromar White 4WBE No. E7040
Three 4-wheel coaches
Long 4-wheel goods wagon

## 423　Corby, Northants　　　　　　　　E

West Glebe Park, Cottingham Road, Corby, Northants

Standard gauge industrial steam locomotives on static display at opposite ends of the park.

**Stock**
[2]Hawthorn Leslie 0-6-0ST No. 14 (3827) built 1934
[1]Hunslet 0-6-0ST No. 24 (2411) built 1941

[1]Ex British Steel Corporation, Corby Works, 1972. Preserved by Corby & District Model Railway Club. OS Ref: SP 892893
[2]Ex British Steel Corporation, Corby Works, 1971. Preserved by Corby District Council. OS Ref: SP 886890

## 424　Riber Castle Wild Life Park　　　E

Near Matlock, Derbyshire
OS Ref: SK 308590

Standard gauge steam locomotive on static display.

**Stock**
Peckett 0-4-0ST 1555 built 1920
Ex Derbyshire Stone Quarries Ltd, Cawdor Limestone Quarries, Matlock, Derbyshire, 1971.

## 425　British Celanese Limited　　　　E

Spondon, Derby
OS Ref: SK 410350

Standard gauge steam locomotive on static display alongside company sports-ground.

**Stock**
RSH 0-4-0ST *George* (7214) built 1945
Used on works internal system until preserved, 1967.

## 426　Market Overton Industrial　　　　D
　　　Railway Association

Market Overton, Leicestershire
OS Ref: SK 889176

Standard gauge industrial railway preservation centre, where a growing collection of steam locomotives is demonstrated at intervals as advertised, using a short section of the former British Steel Corporation ironstone quarry railway.

*Details from:* Peter Layfield, 'Westgate', Old Lincoln Road, Caythorpe, Grantham, Lincs.

**Stock**
Peckett 0-4-0ST No. 8 (2110) built 1950
Avonside 0-4-0ST No. 2 *Dora* (1973) built 1927
Barclay 0-4-0ST 1931 built 1927
Peckett 0-4-0ST *Elizabeth* 1759 built 1928
Peckett 0-4-0ST *Uppingham* 1257 built 1912
Hawthorn Leslie 0-4-0ST *Singapore* 3865 built 1936

Barclay 0-4-0ST *Sir Thomas Royden* 2088 built 1940
Hunslet 0-6-0ST *Coal Products No. 6* 2868 built 1943
Ruston Hornsby 4WDM 305302 built 1951
Hibberd 4WDM 3887 built 1958
Stewarts & Lloyds 4-plank open wagon No. 3046

## 427　Peak Railway Society Ltd　　　　F

Matlock Railway Station, Matlock, Derbyshire.

Shop and Office open every weekend and public holiday 10.30 am–5.30 pm

*Access:* On A6, 18 miles north of Derby.
Tel: Derby 515861
OS Ref: SK373336

Standard gauge railway preservation centre.
The Society was formed in 1975 with the object of reopening the former Midland Railway main line between Matlock and Buxton for the full range of services, including steam operated weekend services. The line, which passes through Rowsley and Bakewell, is best remembered for the magnificent viaducts at Monsal Dale and Millers Dale and for the outstanding scenic beauty of the route, which for the major part of its distance passes through the Peak District National Park.

*Details from:* Mrs M. B. Royle, 62 Uttoxeter Road, Mickleover, Derby.
*Membership:* 2,500
*Annual Subscription:* Adults £1.50, Junior (under 18) £1.00, OAP £1.00, Family £3.00, Associate £5.00

**Stock**
S.R. 4-6-2 No. 34101 *Hartland* (Bulleid WC Class) built 1947
In store at Derby undergoing renovation.
Additionally, a number of locomotives have been reserved at Barry scrapyard. (See Group No. 332.)

**Progress Report**
The initial planning application for the railway submitted by the Society was rejected by the local planning authorities for a number of reasons. Now a new planning application is to be submitted by the proposed operating company, Peak Rail Operations Ltd, which it is anticipated will bring success. Meanwhile the Society have leased the former station buildings at Matlock from British Rail and have completed the renovation of these for use as a shop and information office. It is hoped that acquisition of part of the goods yard will allow some railway operations to be mounted at Matlock in 1980.
Negotiations are also under way with British Rail and High Peak Borough Council for the establishment of a steam centre and railway museum at the former Buxton (Midland) station site and 1980 will see the first steps being taken in erecting new buildings and workshops on this site. Work already underway in the field of sponsorship and fund raising will hopefully mean that the locomotives awaiting purchase at Barry will be acquired and moved to Buxton for restoration to commence, as well as permitting static display. 1979 saw the Society, in association with BR and Peak Rail

Operations Ltd, operate a pilot diesel service on a Sunday between Derby and Matlock. This experiment proved successful and, subject to agreement with BR it is the intention of Peak Rail and the Society to operate this charter service every summer Sunday in 1980, Society members helping to staff the train, sell tickets, etc. It is believed that such a service will be unique and could be the first steps towards future steam services operating south of Matlock, perhaps even to Derby if operational problems can be overcome!

## 428  Boots Pure Drug Company                    I

Beeston, Nottingham
OS Ref: SK 545363

Industrial steam location featuring occasional steam working.

**Stock**
Barclay 0-4-0F No. 2 (2008) built 1935
Ruston Hornsby 0-4-0DE No. B7211 384139 built 1955

## 429  National Coal Board                         I

Cadley Hill Colliery, Church Gresley, near Burton-on-Trent
OS Ref: SK 279193

Industrial steam location featuring regular steam working.

**Stock**
RSH 0-6-0ST *Progress* (7298) built 1946
Bagnall 0-6-0ST *Empress* (3061) built 1954
Hunslet 0-6-0ST *Cadley Hill No. 1* (3851) built 1962
Hunslet 0-6-0ST 2857 built 1943
Hunslet 0-6-0ST No. 65 (3889) built 1964

## 430  CEGB, Castle Donington Power Station        I

Castle Donington, Leicestershire
OS Ref: SK 433284

Standard gauge industrial steam location featuring occasional steam working.

**Stock**
RSH 0-4-0ST No. 1 (7817) built 1954
RSH 0-4-0ST No. 2 (7818) built 1954
Barclay 0-4-0DM No. 3 415 built 1957
Barclay 0-4-0DM No. 4 416 built 1957

Photo: Geoff King
Completely at home in its authentic surroundings as a characteristic power station shunter is this little Stephenson's and Hawthorn's 0-4-0ST at Leicester generating plant

## 431  Newbold Verdon                               C

Mr J. Vernon, Church Farm, Newbold Verdon, Leicestershire
OS Ref: SK 442038

Short 1 ft 10¾ in. gauge private line

**Stock**
[1]Hunslet 0-4-0ST *Pamela* (920) built 1906
[1]Hunslet 0-4-0ST *Sybil Mary* (921) built 1906
Vernon 4WBE built 1972
Ruston Hornsby 4WDM No. 24 (382820) (40DL Class) built 1955

[1]Both ex Penrhyn Quarries Ltd, Bethesda, Caernarfonshire, 1966.

## 432   Hunt & Co. (Hinckley) Ltd          G

London Road Works, Hinckley, Leicestershire
OS Ref: SP 437937

Standard gauge steam locomotive in store

**Stock**
Bagnall 0–6–0ST *Huntsman* (2655) built 1942
Ex Stavely Minerals Ltd, Cranford Ironstone Quarries,
Northamptonshire 1970. Formerly named *Loddington No. 2.*


## 433   Tom Brooks          G

Nottingham Scrap Metal Co. Ltd, Plimsol Road, Basford,
Nottingham
OS Ref: SK 554416

Standard gauge steam locomotive in store

**Stock**
Barclay 0–4–0ST *Holwell No. 17* (1651) built 1919
Ex British Steel Corporation, Holwell Works, Nottingham,
1973.

Planning permission has been obtained to use one mile of
the former LNWR/GNR joint line at Harby and Stathern,
Leicestershire.


## 434   Melton Mowbray Miniature Railway   B

Sports Ground, Leicester Road, Melton Mowbray,
Leicestershire

Passenger-carrying 10¼ in. gauge railway, ¼ mile in length.

**Stock**
Wilcox 4WPM
Ex Hamworthy Miniature Railway.


## 435   Derwent Gardens Miniature Railway B

South Parade, Matlock Bath, Derbyshire

Passenger-carrying 10¼ in. gauge railway, 75 yards in
length, laid out in a horseshoe pattern.

**Stock**
Freelance 4WBE
Two 4-wheel passenger coaches


## 436   Queens Park Miniature Railway          B

Queens Park, Chesterfield, Derbyshire

A 10¼ in. gauge passenger-carrying line situated on the
trackbed of a former BR line and extending for a quarter of
a mile.

**Stock**
Shepperton Bo-BoPM
Three bogie coaches built by Cromar-White


## 437   Buxton Miniature Railway          B

Pavilion Gardens, Buxton, Derbyshire

Passenger-carrying 10¼ in. gauge railway, 320 yards in
length, running round a small lake.

**Stock**
Fenlow Bo-BoDM *Borough of Buxton* built c1972.
Three articulated bogie coaches


## 438   Twycross Zoo Miniature Railway          B

Twycross, Leicestershire

Passenger-carrying 12 in. gauge railway, ¾ mile in length.
Operates to coincide with the Zoo opening.

**Stock**
Cromar White Bo-BoPM No. D7011 built 1969
Open bogie coaches

# AREA J

# Home Counties

Oxfordshire
Berkshire
Hertfordshire
Buckinghamshire
Bedfordshire
Greater London

---

## 451   Leighton Buzzard Narrow          A
        Gauge Railway

The Railway Workshops, Mile Tree Road, Leighton Buzzard
LU7 91A

*Main Station:* Pages Park Station, Billington Road, Leighton
Buzzard, Beds. Tel. Leighton Buzzard (0525) 373888

*Access:* From M1, follow the signs from junction 11 or 13
to the A5 and follow signs on the A5 for Leighton Buzzard
which is well signposted. From Leighton Buzzard follow
'Narrow Gauge Railway' signs from Town Centre, The Railway lies on the east side of Billington Road, the A4146 to
Hemel Hempstead.
OS Ref: SP 929242

Passenger-carrying 2 ft gauge railway, 1¾ miles in length
from Pages Park to Vandyke Road over the tracks of the
former Leighton Buzzard Light Railway.

The railway operates on Sundays from the end of March to
the end of September from 11 am to 5 pm, also on Bank
Holidays and Saturdays (at Bank Holiday periods) from 2 pm
to 5 pm.

Facilities for visitors include car parking, railway shop,
refreshments and toilets (200 yds).

The Leighton Buzzard Light Railway was opened in 1919 to
carry sand quarried in the north-east of the town to exchange
sidings on the LNWR Luton–Dunstable line in the south. It
was built without statutory powers by two of the principal
companies of sand merchants. In 1963 the railway came
under the sole ownership of its principal user, sand merchants
Joseph Arnold and Sons Ltd, and until 1978 the northern
end of the line was still used for sand traffic using small
internal combustion locomotives. The LBNGRS reached
agreement with Arnolds to use the southern portion of the
line and its first train ran in March 1968.

The railway is operated by members of the Leighton Buzzard
Narrow Gauge Railway Society Ltd.

*Details from:* LBNGRS Ltd, Pages Park Station, Billington
Road, Leighton Buzzard, Bedfordshire LU7 8TN

*Membership:* Shares £4; Subscription, members and asso-
ciates £4; Juniors under 14 £2; Corporate Members (open
to Companies, Societies, etc) £4 plus share; Life membership
£50 plus share.

**Stock**
[1]De Winton 0–4–0T No. 1 *Chaloner* built 1877
[2]Kerr Stuart 0–4–0ST No. 2 *Pixie* (4260) built 1922
Baguley 0–4–0T No. 3 *Rishra* (2007) built 1921
[3]Barclay 0–6–0T No. 4 *The Doll* (1641) built 1919
Orenstein and Koppel 4WDM No. 7 *Falcon* (8986) built 1939
[4]Orenstein and Koppel 0–6–0WT No. 5 *Elf* (12740) built
1936
Motor Rail 4WDM No. 43 (10409) built 1954
Motor Rail 4WDM No. 44 (7933) built 1941
Motor Rail 4WDM No. 10 *Haydn Taylor* (7956) built 1945
Lister 4WDM No. 16 *Thor in Oakenshield* (11221) built 1939
Orenstein and Koppel 0–4–0WT No. 11 *P. C. Allen* (5834)
built 1912
Motor Rail 4WPM No. 12 *Carbon* (6012) built 1930
Motor Rail 4WDM No. 6 *Caravan* (7129) built 1938
Hunslet 4WDM No. 14 (3646) built 1946
Hibberd 4WDM No. 15 (2514) built 1941
Ruston Hornsby 4WDM No. 8 (20DL class) 217999 built
1942
Motor Rail 4WDM No. 131 5613
Five passenger coaches
Two passenger brake-coaches
Three bogie flat trucks
Several 1½ and 1 cu yd skips
Several assorted permanent way vehicles

[1]Ex Penyrorsedd Slate Quarry Co. Ltd, Nantlle, Caernarfon-
shire, 1960. Loaned to the LBNGRS in 1968 by its owner,
Mr A. Fisher, and at present on display in the National
Railway Museum.

Photo: Roger Crombleholme

A lively light railway scene at Leighton Buzzard as enthusiasts gather round the only working de Winton 0–4–0T in the country. *Chaloner* is at present on loan to the National Railway Museum

[2]Ex Devon County Council, Wilmanstone Quarry, Tavistock, 1957, for preservation by the Industrial Locomotive Society. Loaned to the LBNGRS in 1968.
[3]Ex Stewarts and Lloyds Ltd, Bilston, Staffordshire, 1960. Sold to Alan Bloom for use at Bressingham in 1966 and resold to LBNGRS Ltd in 1969. Undergoing extensive rebuild at present.
[4]This wood-burning locomotive is owned by A. Fisher, who rescued it from darkest Africa in 1973.

## 452   Whipsnade and Umfolozi Railway      A

Passenger-carrying 2 ft 6 in. gauge line through the animal paddocks at Whipsnade Zoo Park, Dunstable, Bedfordshire.
Tel: Whipsnade 872995 (Zoo: 872171).
OS Ref: TL 004172

Operated by Pleasure Rail Ltd, Buchanan House, 24/30 Holborn, London EC1

*Facilities:* Car parking and refreshments

The railway was opened on 26 August 1970 as a public attraction and a means of seeing some of the larger species of animals at close quarters. Much of the line's equipment and rolling stock came from the Bowaters Railway at Sittingbourne. The line forms a continuous three-mile circuit incorporating several sharp gradients, a number of bridges and a short tunnel. In this form, the line was officially opened by Princess Margaret on 2 August 1973.
The railway operates daily from Easter to the end of September and is normally steam worked. Also runs on winter weekends and school holidays.
Visitors should note that a diesel pay-train may operate before 1 pm.

### Stock
Manning Wardle 0–6–2T No. 1 *Chevallier* (1877) built 1915
Kerr Stuart 0–4–2ST No. 2 *Excelsior* (1049) built 1908
Bagnall 0–6–2T No. 3 *Conqueror* (2192) built 1922
Kerr Stuart 0–6–2T No. 4 *Superior* (4034) built 1920

[1]Fowler 0–6–0DM No. 9 *Victor* (4160005) built 1951
Fowler 0–6–0DM 4160004 built 1951
Motor Rail 4WDM No. L116 (5606) built 1931
Wingrove and Rogers 4WBE No. 7 1393 built 1939
Wingrove and Rogers 4WBE 1616 built 1940
Wingrove and Rogers 4WBE 1801 built 1940
Ten 30-seat passenger bogie coaches rebuilt from Bowater bogie pulp wagons in 1970

[1]Ex Welshpool and Llanfair Light Railway 1972.

*3 ft 6 in. gauge static exhibits*
Zambesi Sawmills Railway 4–8–0 No. 390 (Sharp Stewart 4150) built 1896
Rhodesia Railways balcony-ended clerestory first/second-class sleeping car No. 1808 (Gloucester Carriage and Wagon Co. Ltd) built 1927
Ford 8 motor car mounted on rail wheels for use as an inspection trolley

## Historical note
In 1973, David Shepherd was presented by the Government of Zambia with two steam locomotives and a coach, and the 12,000 mile journey of one engine and the coach from Zambia to Whipsnade was the subject of the BBC TV film *Last Train to Mulobezi*. The rolling stock has now been given a home at Whipsnade, courtesy the Zoological Society of London and Pleasurerail, until such time as funds and space permit transfer to the East Somerset Railway at Cranmore. The second locomotive, ex-Rhodesia Railways Class 10 4–8–2 (Sharp Stewart 1922), remains in Bulawayo until funds are available for her return home. The Class 7 has reverted to her original number of 390, with new brass cabside plates. This was her number when exported in 1896 to the Cape Government Railway. She was renumbered 993 when taken into South African Railways stock, and she was the last Class 7 in their lists, working as Johannesburg station pilot, when purchased for work on the Zambesi Sawmills Railway in Zambia in 1971. When this system was taken over by Zambia Railways, the rolling stock became redundant and the coach and engines were given to David Shepherd.
On 6 August 1976 an exhibition of early photographs recording the 78 years of life in Africa of No. 390 was opened in the coach by Zambia's High Commissioner to London. On this occasion also, the Chairman of Ford, Great Britain, presented to David Shepherd a 1938 Ford 8, in working order – an exact replica of the cars used as inspection trolleys on the Zambesi Sawmills Railway in the 1930s. The car has been adapted for railway operation by 27 Command Workshops, REME.

## 453   Knebworth West Park and   A
Winter Green Railway

A one-and-a-quarter mile, 1 ft 11½ in. gauge passenger-carrying line in the grounds of Knebworth House near Stevenage, Herts.
*Access:* Knebworth House is permanently signposted on all major surrounding roads. Nearest BR station: Knebworth.

OS Ref: TL 228208
Tel: Stevenage 812661

Operated by Pleasure Rail Ltd, Buchanan House, 24/30 Holborn, London EC1

The railway operates daily from Easter to the end of September. Steam operation on Saturdays, Sundays and Bank Holidays and on one weekday during the school holidays, otherwise a diesel service is run.

### Stock
[1]Bagnall 4–4–0T No. 23 *Isibutu* (2820) built 1946
Orenstein and Koppel 0–6–0WT *Sao Domingos* (11784)
Peckett 0–6–0ST *Triassic* (1270) built 1911
Avonside 0–4–0T *Sezela No. 4* (1738) built 1916
Hunslet 0–4–0ST *Lilla* (554) built 1891
Hunslet 0–4–0ST No. 1 *Lady Joan* (1429) built 1922
Motor Rail 4WDM No. 2 (8993) built 1946 (steam outline)
Ruston Hornsby 4WDM 354043 built 1953
Motor Rail 4WDM 40S273 built 1966
Nine bogie coaches
Two four-wheeled brake vans

[1]Ex Tongaat Sugar Co., Natal, South Africa 1972

## 454   Blenheim Park Railway   A

Woodstock, Oxfordshire
Tel: Woodstock 811805
OS Ref: SP 444163

A 15 in. gauge passenger-carrying line ½ mile in length running through the grounds of Blenheim Palace operated by Pleasure Rail Ltd.

### Stock
Guest/G & S 4–6–2 No. 5751 *Sir Winston Churchill* (9) built 1946
Guest/G & S 2–6–2TPM *Tracy-Jo* (20) built 1964
Minirail Bo-BoDE *Doctor Diesel* built 1966
Batty 2–6–4DE built *c.* 1955
Two train sets each of four bogie coaches
Eaton Hall Railway brake van built by Sir Arthur Heywood

## 455   Quainton Railway Centre   AD

Quainton Railway Society Ltd, The Railway Station, Quainton, near Aylesbury, Bucks. HP22 4BY
Registered Charity No. 263669

*Access:* By road – take A41 from Aylesbury, turn off after 6 miles at Waddesdon. Follow Quainton signs. No buses or rail access.
Tel: St. Albans 54904
OS Ref: SP 739190

Standard gauge steam railway preservation centre, featuring steam-hauled rides in vintage coaching stock over ½ mile of track.
The centre is open on Easter Monday, Spring and August Bank Holidays and on the last Sunday of every month from Easter till October between 10 am and 6 pm.

Facilities for visitors include free car parking, museum, shop, refreshments and toilets.

The Quainton Railway Society was formed in 1969 and aims to form a working railway museum of locomotives and other rolling stock and equipment of all kinds such as was used on the railways before modernisation in the 1950s. The Society arose out of the London Railway Preservation Society, formed in 1962. It is now a registered charity, a full member of the ARPS and affiliated to the Transport Trust. It is run entirely by volunteers.

Quainton is of interest as being the place where the Great Central Railway and Metropolitan met, and is the reason for the extensive sidings on both sides of the line, which is now used by BR for freight only; the Society using the sidings. There are some 40 locomotives and interesting rolling stock, some owned by the Society and some privately. Many of the engines and rolling stock reflect the Great Central and Metropolitan interest, but there are also other main line and industrial engines, it being the aim to make the collection as comprehensive as possible.

*Details from:* A. T. G. Lyster, Hon. Publicity Officer, 42 Watling Street, St. Albans, Herts AL1 2QB.

*Subscriptions:* Shares at £5 each; shareholders annual subscription £2; associate members £2.50. For details of membership, family, OAP, etc, write to Hon. Membership Secretary, Mrs B. Sell, 9 Hastoe Park, Aylesbury, Bucks
*Membership:* 550

## Stock

[1]GWR 0–6–0PT No. 7715 (LT No. L99) (Class 57XX) (Kerr Stuart 4450) built 1930
GWR 0–6–0PT No. 9466 (94XX Class) built 1952
[5]GWR 4–6–0 No. 6024 *King Edward I* built 1930
GWR 4–6–0 No. 6989 *Wightwick Hall* built 1949
[3]LSWR 2–4–0WT No. 0314 (BR No. 30585) (Beyer Peacock 1414) built 1874
[4]Metropolitan Railway 0–4–4T No. 1 (LT No. L44) built 1898
[7]LMS 2–6–0 No. 46447 (Class 2MT) built 1950
[8]LMS 2–6–2T No. 41298 (Class 2MT) built 1951
[10]LMS 2–6–2T No. 41313 (Class 2MT) built 1952
[9]Hunslet 0–6–0ST *Juno* (3850) built 1958
Yorkshire Engine Co. 0–6–0ST *Chislet* (2498) built 1951
Hunslet 0–6–0ST No. 66 (3890) built 1964
Hudswell Clarke 0–6–0T *Sir Thomas* (1334) built 1918
Hudswell Clarke 0–4–0ST *Millom* (1742) built 1946
Hawthorn Leslie 0–4–0ST No. 3 (3717) built 1928
Hunslet 0–4–0ST *Trym* (287) built 1882
Peckett 0–4–0ST *Hornpipe* (1756) built 1928
Peckett 0–4–0T (1900) built 1936
Peckett 0–4–0ST 2104 built 1948
Peckett 0–4–0ST 2105 built 1948
Bagnall 0–4–0ST *Scott* (2469) built 1932
NB Locomotive Co. 0–6–0T *Coventry No. 1* (24564) built 1939
Barclay 0–4–0ST *Swanscombe* (699) built 1891
Barclay 0–4–0ST *Punch Hull* (776) built 1896
Barclay 0–4–0ST *Alexander* (1865) built 1926
Barclay 0–4–0ST *Tom Parry* (2015) built 1935
Barclay 0–4–0F No. GF3 (1477) built 1916
Barclay 0–4–0F 2243 built 1948

Aveling Porter 4WTG *Sydenham* (3547) built 1895
Sentinel 4WVBTG No. 2 *Isebrook* (GWR No. 12) (6515) built 1926
Sentinel 4WVBTG No. 7 (9376) built 1947
Sentinel 4WVBTG No. 11 (9366) built 1945
Kerr Stuart 0–4–0DM K4428 built 1929
Fowler 0–4–0DM *Osram* (20067) built 1933
Hibberd 4WDM *Tarmac* (3765) built 1955
Peckett 0–4–0ST *James* (2129) built 1952
BR Mk 1 BSK bogie coach No. S34947 built 1956
BR Mk 1 CK bogie coach No. M15319 built 1953
BR Mk 1 SK bogie coach No. E24993 built 1956
LMS Stove R six-wheeled passenger brake van No. M33014 built 1939
LNWR 12-wheeled sleeping car (now cinema coach) No. DM395017M built 1907, rebuilt 1937
LNWR first-class kitchen/dining car No. 77 built 1901
LNWR six-wheeled passenger full brake No. DM279982 built 1891
LCDR first-class four-wheeled coach built 1880
LNER Gresley BSK coach No. 41384 built 1936
[11]LNWR bogie brake second coach No. 22736 built 1921
[11]LMS bogie third-class sleeper No. 592 built 1933
[11]LNWR six-wheeled CCT No. 580 built 1912
[11]MSLR six-wheeled third class coach No. 1076 built 1890
[11]GCR first-class bogie coach No. 957 built 1906
GWR BG No. W64 built 1938 (In use as refreshment coach)
[11]LNWR Corridor Composite coach No. ADM 395136 built 1920
[11]LMS Open 3rd class coach No. 271762 built 1945
GNR six-wheeled brake/third coach No. 1470 built 1895
GNR six-compartment third-class coach No. DE900178 built c. 1881
LNWR six-compartment brake/third coach No. 22736 (BR No. TDM395209) built 1921
LMS third-class sleeping car No. 592 (BR No. DM395922) built 1933
GWR 'Toad' 20-ton goods brake van No. 68624: built 1923
BR four-wheeled horsebox No. S96403 built 1958
MR box van No. 34676 built 1922
MR brake van No. 1692 built 1923
MR open wagon No. M18300 built 1912
LBSCR 10-ton open wagon No. AD46054
LSWR box van No. 47253
AD box van No. 47683
MR eight-ton box vans Nos. 47251 and 47271
[2]SR four-wheeled PMV No. S1108S built 1947
[6]GWR six-wheeled milk tank wagon No. W2536
LMS box van No. SNSO807
GNSR 4-wheel coach frame (was 6-wheel) date unknown. Will be used for LNWR observation coach body No. 68 built 1860
LNER open wagons Nos. AD46021 and AD46378
H & BR open wagon No. 85 built 1885

---

**Portrait of a centenarian. Steaming on in active retirement at Quainton Road is LSWR *Beattie* well tank No. E0314**

Photo: John Gardner

'Laporte' open industrial wagon
Met. & GCR hand crane and match truck Nos. 1 and 3282
built 1914
Wickham 4WPM rail inspection car
Wickham 4WPM railcar No. 9040
Wickham 4WPM rail trolley
MR road crane built 1890

[1]Collett 57XX Class pannier tank sold to London Transport
in 1963, becoming No. L99. Purchased for preservation in
1970.
[2]Owned by the 6024 Preservation Society Ltd (q.v.).
[3]Beattie well tank, originally LSWR No. 0314. Successively
rebuilt throughout its long active life, it was one of three
survivors of its class retained for working the Wenford Bridge
mineral branch in Cornwall. Withdrawn in 1962, it was
purchased for preservation in 1964 and stored at Bishop's
Stortford until 1969.
[4]Metropolitan Railway 'E' Class locomotive built at Neasden
to haul Aylesbury line passenger trains. The class were
confined to freight work after 1937 and this particular
locomotive was renumbered L44 in the following year.
Withdrawn in 1964 after taking part in the Metropolitan
centenary parade at Neasden. Stored at Luton until 1968.
[5]Withdrawn as BR No. 6024 in 1962 and sold to Woodham
Brothers, Barry, for scrap. Purchased for preservation and
moved to Quainton Road in 1973. Owned by the 6024
Preservation Society Ltd (q.v).
[6]Donated by Unigate Dairies Limited 1973 and moved to
Quainton Road. Owned by the 6024 Preservation Society
Ltd (q.v.).
[7]Withdrawn as BR No. 46447 and sold to Woodham
Brothers, Barry, for scrap. Purchased for preservation in
1972. Owned by the Ivatt Locomotive Trust (q.v.).
[8]Withdrawn as BR No. 41298 from Nine Elms shed on the
last day of Southern steam, 9 July 1967. One of a batch of
30 locomotives built at Crewe Works to Ivatt's LMS design
for use on the Southern Region to replace older 0–4–4T
types. These locomotives differed from the rest of their class
by having taller, tapered chimneys. Owned by the Ivatt
Locomotive Trust (q.v.).
[9]Ex Stewarts and Lloyds Minerals Ltd, Buckminster Ironstone
Quarries, Lincolnshire, 1969. Owned by the Ivatt Locomotive
Trust (q.v.).
[10]Owned by the Ivatt Locomotive Trust (q.v.).
[11]Owned by the Great Central Railway Coach Group (q.v.).

## 6024 Preservation Society Ltd       H
Quainton Railway Centre

*Details from:* W. A. Wilkinson (Secretary), 12 Tudor Square,
Hayes End, Middlesex UB3 2QT
*Membership rates:* Life £15; shareholder £2; associate (under
21 and over 65) £1; joint membership of husband and wife
£2. Shares of £1 each are available (limited to 5,000 per
member); shares are transferable.
*Membership:* 246

The Society purchased *King Edward I* No. 6024 in January
1973 from Barry, where she had lain since 1962, being the
best of the two Kings there, for restoration to full running

order. Removal took place in the last few days of March
1973 to Quainton Road Museum, arriving there on 1.4.73.
The Society was registered as a Charity in 1976 and became
a registered Society on 30 September 1976 (No. 21746R
– London). An appeal has been launched for the raising of
£25,000, to be raised hopefully by fund raising. A group has
been formed and it is hoped through the sale of shares,
increased membership and general sales that this figure is
reached.

## Ivatt Locomotive Trust       H
Quainton Road Station, near Aylesbury, Bucks
Registered Charity No. 262075

*Trustees:* P. I. Clarke and R. B. Miller, 'Ducal', 25 Loudham
Road, Little Chalfont, Amersham, Bucks

## Great Central Railway Coach Group       H
Quainton Road Station, near Aylesbury, Bucks.

*Secretary:* J. S. Parsons, 8 Grendon Way, Bierton, Aylesbury,
Bucks HP22 5DD
The Group was formed in 1971 to purchase, finance and
promote interest in coaches of GCR origin and to ensure
where possible that they would return to former GCR lines.
The Group's interest has changed to include other coaches
of historical interest. To date 6-wheeled 1057 is carrying
passengers at Quainton Road after a 30 year retirement and
GCR *Barnum* No. 664 has been sold to the Great Central
Railway at Loughborough and hopefully will be running on
the GCR main line soon.
Restoration continues at Quainton Road and it is hoped that
GCR No. 957 will be the next coach to be completed.

## 456    Great Western Society Ltd       AD

Didcot Railway Centre, Didcot, Oxfordshire

*Access:* Through Didcot BR station
OS Ref: SU 524906

Standard gauge steam railway preservation centre devoted
specifically to the Great Western Railway. Steam-hauled
rides are available on open days over ¼ mile of track.
Steaming days at Didcot Railway Centre are held on the
first and last Sunday of each month, on Bank Holiday
weekends and all Sundays in August.
Facilities for visitors include car parking, museum, souvenir
shop, refreshments, toilets, miniature railway and model
railway.
The Great Western Society was formed in 1961 to ensure
that as far as possible the Great Western Railway did not
disappear entirely in the era of rapid modernization of British
Railways. At Didcot Railway Centre it now has the largest
collection of GWR locomotives and rolling stock housed in
the original engine shed and complementary buildings. A
demonstration line has been laid on which a GWR train
operates on steaming days, giving rides to the public. A
second demonstration line is planned; a signal box from

Radstock in Somerset has been re-erected to control the signalling on this line.

*Membership details from:* Great Western Society, Didcot, Oxfordshire.

*Membership:* 3,500

**Stock**

GWR 4-6-0 No. 5029 *Nunney Castle* built 1934
GWR 2-8-0 No. 3822 (28XX Class) built 1940
[1]GWR 4-6-0 No. 5051 *Earl Bathurst/Drysllwyn Castle* built 1936
[2]GWR 4-6-0 No. 4942 *Maindy Hall* built 1929
GWR 4-6-0 No. 5900 *Hinderton Hall* built 1931
[3]GWR 4-6-0 No. 6998 *Burton Agnes Hall* built 1949
[4]GWR 4-6-0 No. 7808 *Cookham Manor* built 1938
[5]GWR 2-6-0 No. 5322 (Class 43XX) built 1917
GWR 2-8-2T No. 7202 (Class 72XX) built 1934
GWR 2-6-2T No. 4144 (Class 51XX) built 1946
GWR 2-6-2T No. 5572 (Class 4574) built 1927
[6]GWR 2-6-2T No. 6106 (Class 61XX) built 1931
[7]GWR 0-6-2T No. 6697 (Class 56XX) built 1928
GWR 0-6-0PT No. 3650 (Class 57XX) built 1939
GWR 0-6-0PT No. 3738 (Class 57XX) built 1937
[12]GWR 0-6-0ST No. 1363 (Class 1361) built 1910
GWR 0-4-2T No. 1466 (Class 48XX) built 1936

A regular feature from the Great Western Society at Didcot is an impressive line-up of Great Western motive power. And here we proudly present this year's Swindon selection

**Photo: GWS**

[8]GWR 0-4-0ST No. 1340 *Trojan* (ex Alexandra Docks and Railway) (Avonside 1386) built 1897
Wantage Tramway 0-4-0WT No. 5 *Shannon* (George England) built 1857
[9]SR 4-6-2 No. 21C 151 (BR No. 34051) *Winston Churchill* (BB Class) built 1946
[10]BPGVR 0-6-0ST No. 2 *Pontyberem* (Avonside 1421) built 1900
GWR Diesel railcar No. 22 built 1941
[11]RSH 0-4-0ST *Bonnie Prince Charlie* (7544) built 1949
[11]RSH 0-6-0ST No. 47 (7800) built 1954
Hunslet 0-6-0DM No. DL26 5238 built 1957
[13]BR Bo-Bo DH No. D7018 (Beyer Peacock 7912) built 1961
Ruston Hornsby 4WDM 224353 built 1945
GWR Collett full brake No. 111 built 1934
GWR auto-trailer No. 92 built 1912
GWR auto-trailer No. 190 built 1933

GWR auto-trailer No. 212 built 1936
GWR auto-trailer No. 231 built 1951
GWR four-wheeled composite No. 290 built 1902
GWR four-wheeled brake third No. 416 built 1891
GWR all-third corridor No. 536 built 1940
GWR TPO sorting van No. 814 built 1940
GWR full brake No. 933 built 1898
GWR corridor brake/third No. 2202 built 1950
GWR compartment brake/third Nos. 3755 and 3756 built 1921
GWR corridor brake/third No. 5787 built 1933
GWR six-wheeled tri-composite No. 6824 built 1887
GWR corridor composite No. 7285 built 1941
GWR corridor brake/composite No. 7976 built 1924
GWR four-wheeled all-third No. 975 built 1902
GWR all-third corridor No. 1111 built 1938
GWR bow-ended full brake No. 1184 built 1930
GWR excursion third No. 1289 built 1937
GWR clerestory third No. 1357 built 1903
GWR clerestory third No. 1941 built 1901
GWR six-wheeled family saloon No. 2511 built 1894
GWR 'Siphon G' No. 2796 built 1937
GWR all-third 'Dreadnought' No. 3299 built 1905
GWR bow-ended corridor third No. 4553 built 1925
GWR bow-ended corridor third No. 5085 built 1928
GWR corridor third No. 5952 built 1935
GWR corridor composite No. 7313 built 1940
GWR corridor brake/composite No. 7362 built 1941
GWR corridor brake/composite No. 7371 built 1941
GWR corridor brake/composite No. 7372 built 1948
GWR Dean composite diner clerestory built 1903
GWR medical officers saloon No. 1159 built 1925
GWR special saloon No. 9002 built 1940
GWR special saloon No. 9005 built 1930
GWR first-class sleeping car No. 9083 built 1951
GWR 'Ocean' saloon No. 9112 *Queen Mary* built 1932
GWR 'Ocean' saloon No. 9113 *Prince of Wales* built 1932
GWR 'Ocean' saloon No. 9118 *Princess Elizabeth* built 1932
GWR 'Toplight' brake tri-composite (now staff van) No. 7538 built 1907
Cambrian Railways four-wheeled tri-composite No. 238 built 1895
BR composites S15565 and S15577 built 1955 (used as dormitory coaches)
GWR mess and tool vans Nos 47 and 135 built 1908
GWR 12-ton hand crane and match truck No. 205 built 1894
GWR five-plank end-door china clay wagon No. 92943 built 1913
SR six-wheeled milk tank No. S4409
GWR five-plank open wagon No. 553
GWR mess van No. 263 rebuilt 1952
GWR motor-car van *Python* (565) built 1914
GWR special cattle truck No. 752 built 1953
GWR six-wheeled 'Ro-tank' No. 3030 built 1947
GWR open wagon No. 24203 built 1915
GWR 'Crocodile F' well wagon No. 41934 built 1909
GWR well wagon 'Hydra D' No. 42193 built 1917
GWR locomotive coal wagon No. 63066 built 1946
GWR tea van No. 79933 rebuilt 1938

**A little engine with a big heart. No. 1363 made the long journey up from the West Country to become a regular working member of the Didcot stud**

**Photo: GWS**

Charles Roberts Tar Wagon No. 1 (adapted for weedkilling)
ICI Salt Wagon No. 45 built 1910
GWR 'Bloater' Fish Van No. 2671 built 1925
GWR 'Grano' Grain Van No. 42239 built 1927
GWR 'Toad' 16 ton brake van No. 56100 built 1895
GWR 'Toad' 20 ton brake van No. 68684 built 1924
GWR Banana van No. 105599 built 1930
[14]GWR tool van No. 1 built 1908
[14]GWR riding van No. 56 built 1912
[14]GWR 'Toad' 20-ton goods brake van No. 58092 built 1948
[15]GWR iron 'Mink' van No. 11152 built 1900
Smith, Rodley 5 ton shunting steam crane No. 23059 built 1954
GWR 'Grampus' sleeper wagon No. 80668 built 1937
GWR shunters truck No. 100377 built 1921
GWR 10-ton van 'Mink A' No. 101720 built 1926
GWR insulated van 'Mica B' No. 105860 built 1926
GWR 20-ton van 'Mink G' No. 112843 built 1931
GWR motor-car van 'Asmo' No. 116954 built 1930
GWR ten-ton van 'Fruit B' No. 2356 built 1925
FR Esso 'Royal Daylight' tank wagon No. 745 built 1912
TVR seven-plank end-door open wagon No. 10153
BR 'Aardvark' 4WPM motor trolley.
Three-wheeled 'Velocipede'.

[1]Withdrawn as BR No. 5051 in 1963 and sold to Woodham Brothers, Barry, for scrap. Purchased for the Great Western Society and moved to Didcot in February 1970.
[2]Withdrawn as BR No. 4942 and sold to Woodham Brothers, Barry, for scrap. Purchased for conversion into a 'Saint' class 29XX series 4–6–0 in 1973.
[3]6959 or 'Modified Hall' Class built at Swindon under BR auspices. Withdrawn from Oxford shed on 31 December

1965 and purchased by the GWS. The 'Halls' had their beginning in 1925 when a 'Saint' 4-6-0 was rebuilt with smaller driving wheels. Commencing in 1928, some were built in practically every year until 1952. The modified type appeared in 1944 and was a much superior machine. Altogether 330 of the class were constructed, the second largest class on the GWR. They worked on express passenger and ordinary freight work as required and many of the class were still in service when steam finished on GWR lines on the last day of 1965.

[4]Withdrawn from Gloucester shed in December 1965 and purchased for preservation. The 'Manors' were the smallest of the GWR 4-6-0s. Only 30 were built and they operated over the most severely restricted routes. Many were used on the former Cambrian main line between Shrewsbury and Aberystwyth, mainly on passenger work. They were the last GWR class to remain intact.

[5]No. 5322 has had a varied career, having worked in France during World War I and subsequently over most of the GWR system. It was withdrawn from Pontypool Road in 1964 and rescued from Barry scrapyard in 1969. It was the first Society engine purchased from Barry to be steamed.

[6]Withdrawn from Southall shed in December 1965 as BR No. 6106. There were several GWR classes of large 2-6-2T built for suburban passenger work, the 6100 Class being the final development and most powerful of its type. For many years the whole class of 70 engines worked entirely in the London division, the vast majority of them from Southall, Slough and Paddington sheds. Introduced to replace the ageing 4-4-2 and 2-4-0 tanks, the 6100 engines proved highly successful and several of the class survived until the last day of steam traction on the Western Region.

[7]Withdrawn from Croes Newydd shed, Wrexham, in May 1966 and purchased for preservation by the GWS, being stored initially at the Dowty RPS depot at Ashchurch. The GWR inherited a miscellany of 0-6-2 tanks at the grouping, mostly from the South Wales railways. Many of these were due for replacement and the 56XX Class was introduced in 1924 as a result. A total of 200 were built by the end of 1928 and the class remained intact until 1962. Most spent their entire working lives in the South Wales valleys where they handled both passenger and coal trains with ease.

[8]This diminutive engine was built for Messrs Dunn and Shute Ltd, the shunting contractors at Newport Docks. It was purchased by the Alexandra Docks and Railway Co. in April 1903 and absorbed by the GWR in 1922, becoming No. 1340 and retaining its name. It was withdrawn from traffic in July 1932 and stood outside Swindon Works until sold to the Victoria Colliery Co. of Wellington, Shropshire, in June 1934. It was hired to the Netherseal Colliery, Burton-on-Trent, and in 1947 was sold to Alders Paper Mill, Tamworth, where it worked until purchased for preservation and moved to Didcot.

[9]On loan from National Collection.

[10]The only surviving ex Burry Port and Gwendraeth Valley Railway engine. Sold out of service in 1914 to Llewellyn (Nixon) Ltd (later Mountain Ash Colliery) before the BPGVR was absorbed into the GWR in 1923. Purchased for preservation from NCB, Penrikyber, 1972.

[11]Owned by the Salisbury Steam Locomotive Preservation Trust (q.v.).

[12]No. 1363 is one of five saddletanks of the 1361 class, a modernised version of a Cornwall Mineral Railway design; the class spent their whole lives in the West Country on dock shunting and similar duties. They were the last saddletanks built for the GWR and No. 1363 is the oldest operational locomotive of GWR origin.

[13]Owned by the Diesel and Electric Group (see Group No. 4).

[14]Located at GWS Taunton Group Depot, Taunton, Somerset.

[15]Located at GWS Swindon Group Depot, W. D. & H. O. Wills private siding, Swindon, Wilts.

**Salisbury Steam Locomotive Preservation Trust**　　**H**
Didcot MPD, Oxfordshire

*Details from:* E. J. Roper, 33 Victoria Road, Wilton, near Salisbury, Wilts SP2 0OZ
*Subscription:* £1 per annum
*Membership:* 25

## 457　King's Arms Miniature Railway　　A

A 9½ in. gauge passenger-carrying miniature railway in the garden of the King's Arms public house, Cardington, Bedfordshire. The line, which was opened in 1962, is a quarter-of-a-mile in length and services run on Sundays only throughout the season.
*Operator:* Mr C. Surridge

**Stock**
Bassett-Lowke 4-4-2 *Ruby* built *c.* 1914
Three 'sit-astride' bogie coaches

## 458　Prince of Wales Miniature Railway　　A

A 7¼ in. gauge passenger-carrying railway in the garden of the Prince of Wales public house, Arlesey, Bedfordshire
*Operator:* Mr Allan Ford

**Stock**
Hunslet 0-4-0STT *Prince of Wales* built Milner Engineering Co., 1976

## 459　East Herts Miniature Railway　　A

Van Hage Garden Centre, Great Amwell, near Ware, Herts

*Access:* On A1170 road about ½ mile north of the junction with the A414 between Hoddesdon and Ware, Herts
Tel: Cuffley (Herts) 3561

Passenger-carrying 7¼ in. gauge steam railway, 670 feet in length, operated by the Lee Valley Live Steam Society.
The railway operates every Sunday from Easter to the last Sunday in October from 11 am to 5.30 pm.
Facilities for visitors include car parking, toilets and the Garden Centre.

The East Herts Miniature Railway came into being when a number of members of another East Herts Railway Club became tired of the miniature track at that club being a constant target for local vandals. After negotiations with the proprietor of the Van Hage Garden Centre, building commenced on the first Sunday in March 1978. The initial circuit of 670 feet, complete with tunnel (35 ft), station and workshop (Terrapin hut) was opened to the public on 30 July 1978. By the last Sunday in October, 12,811 passengers had been carried. By Easter Sunday 1979, when the new season commenced, a third rail had been laid in to add 5 in. gauge to the original 7¼ in. and work continues on building a further (inner) circuit, turntable, ash pits and many other improvements. A fare of 5p per ride is charged.

The Van Hage Garden Centre is a very go-ahead concern, much larger than average with a 'mini-farm' which is free to visitors where many animals and birds can be seen. There is a permanent camping exhibition and a number of other attractions.

*Details from:* Mr V. G. Ives, 32 Colston Crescent, Goffs Oak, Waltham Cross, Herts EN7 5RS

### Stock

Hunslet 0–4–0ST *Jackie* built Milner Engineering 1978
Two enclosed bogie coaches
'Sit-astride' bogie coaches
Also various 7¼ in. and 5 in. gauge locomotives owned by members, mostly steam but one petrol powered.

## 460    Cotswold Wild Life Park                      B

Burford, Oxfordshire
OS Ref: SP 237084

A 2 ft gauge passenger-carrying line, 1 mile in length, operated by Leisuretrack Ltd.

### Stock

Motor Rail 4WDM *Oliver* 9869 built c. 1954 (steam outline)
Motor Rail 4WDM *Adam* 9978 built 1954 (steam outline)
Ruston Hornsby 4WDM 229631 (20DL Class) built 1944
Motor Rail 4WDM 9976 built 1954
Six enclosed bogie coaches

## 461    Woburn Abbey Railway                         B

Woburn Abbey, Bedfordshire

A 2 ft gauge passenger-carrying line opened in 1973 by Track Supplies and Services Ltd, Wolverton, Bucks.

### Stock

Ruston Hornsby 4WDM *Duchess* (223749) (20DL Class) built 1944 (steam outline)
Ruston Hornsby 4WDM 239381 (40DL Class) built 1946 (steam outline)
Four open coaches

## 462    London Transport Museum                      E

Old Flower Market Hall, Covent Garden, London

Nearest Underground station: Covent Garden
OS Ref: TQ 3182

London Transport has set up a permanent home for road and rail vehicles spanning nearly 150 years of public transport in the London area. Most of the exhibits were previously at the Museum of British Transport, Clapham, and then at Syon Park, Brentford, Middlesex.

### Stock

[1]Metropolitan Railway 4–4–0T No. 23 ('A' class) (Beyer Peacock 710) built 1866
Metropolitan Railway Bo–Bo E No. 5 *John Hampden* built 1922
Wotton Tramway 0–4–0TG (Aveling Porter 807) built 1872
District Railway Q23 stock motor coach No. 4248 built 1923
Metropolitan Railway milk van built 1896
C & SLR underground coach built 1890
[2]Body of City and South London Railway coach No. 163 built 1907
Also London buses, trolleybuses and trams, posters, signs, tickets and other exhibits.

[1]One of the Metropolitan 'A' class tanks which used to work the Inner Circle line before electrification in 1905. No. 23 was rebuilt several times and in its final guise was the regular passenger engine on the rustic Brill branch in Buckinghamshire. When finally withdrawn as LTE No. L45, the engine was restored to its 1903 condition at Neasden and moved to Clapham Museum in 1961. On the closure of Clapham Museum in 1973, No. 23 was moved to Syon Park.
[2]Preserved by the London Underground Railway Society.

## 463    Science Museum                               E

Exhibition Road, South Kensington, London SW7

*Access:* LT Underground, buses. Parking is metered
Tel: 01-589 3456
OS Ref: TQ 368793

Facilities for visitors include museum shop, refreshments and toilets.
Open weekdays 10 am–6 pm, Sundays 2.30 pm–6 pm. Admission free.

### Stock

Hunslet 0–4–0DM 3469 built 1951 (1 ft 11½ in. gauge)
Wylam Colliery 4W *Puffing Billy* built 1813 (5 ft gauge)
L & MR 0–2–2 *Rocket* built 1829
L & MR 0–4–0 *Sanspareil* built 1829
St Helens Railway 0–4–0 *Novelty* (replica built 1929)
C & SLR 4WE No. 1 (Mather and Platt/Beyer Peacock) built 1890
GWR 4–6–0 No. 4073 *Caerphilly Castle* built 1923
English Electric Co-Co DE *Deltic* 2007 built 1955
Black Hawthorn 0–4–0ST *Bauxite No. 2* 305 built 1874
LPTB underground coach No. 3327 built 1927

## 464    GWR Preservation Group    G

Private Goods Station, Bridge Road, Southall, Middlesex

*Details from:* R. A. Gorringe, 16 Grange Close, Heston, Middlesex TW5 0HW
Locomotives being purchased for preservation from Woodham Brothers, Barry and elsewhere.

**Stock**
[1]GWR 2–8–0 No. 2885 (28XX Class) built 1938
GWR 2–6–2T No. 4110 (41XX Class) built 1936
[2]AEC 4WDM built 1938

[1]Not yet moved to Southall.
[2]Ex British Leyland, Southall 1979.


## 465    Pymmes Park Miniature Railway    B

Pymmes Park, Enfield, Greater London

Passenger-carrying 7¼ in. gauge railway, 200 yards in length running alongside the lake in the park. The line was opened in 1976.
*Operator:* Mr Max Hampson
The railway operates daily in August and on Sundays at other times.

**Stock**
Cromar White 4WBE No. E7047 built 1976
Two open coaches built 1976


## 466    Fancott Railway    B

Fancott Arms Public House, Fancott, near Toddington, Bedfordshire

*Access:* On B579 road south of Toddington
OS Ref: TL 022278

Passenger-carrying 10¼ in. gauge railway, 150 yards in length opened in 1975.
The line operates on Sundays throughout the year.

**Stock**
Harper 0–4–0PM (steam outline)
Two covered 4-wheel coaches


## 467    CEGB, Home Counties    I

Industrial steam locations featuring occasional steam working.

**Stock**
Barclay 0–4–0ST *Little Barford* (2069) built 1939. Acton Lane Power Station, Harlesden NW10
RSH 0–4–0ST *Birkenhead* (7386) built 1948. Acton Lane Power Station, Harlesden NW10
Barclay 0–4–0ST No. ED4 *Edmundsons* (2168) built 1943. Little Barford Power Station, St Neots, Bedfordshire


## 468    Fawley Hill Railway    C

Private standard-gauge line owned by Mr W. H. McAlpine, Dobson's Farm, Fawley, near Henley-on-Thames, Bucks
OS Ref: SU 755861

Shades of *The Titfield Thunderbolt*! The piston flies, the flywheel spins, the motion is just a blur, but the geared driving wheels of *Sirapite* go, oh, so slowly. This is one of the joys of travel on Bill McAlpine's Fawley Hill Light Railway

Photo: Mike Wood

**Stock**
[1]Aveling Porter 0–4–0TG *Sirapite* (6158) built 1906
[2]Avonside 0–4–0ST *Elizabeth* (1865) built 1922
Hudswell Clarke 0–6–0ST No 31 (1026) built 1913
Baguley 0–4–0DM No. 5 (3027) built 1939
GWR 'Toad' 20-ton brake van
GWR shunters 'chariot'

[1]Ex Richard Garrett Engineering Works Ltd, Leiston, Suffolk, 1966. Restored at McAlpine's Duston-on-Tyne yard and moved to present site in 1970.
[2]Ex South Eastern Gas Board, Waddon Marsh Gasworks, Croydon. Purchased for preservation by Mr J. B. Latham in 1969 and moved to Fawley Hill.

## 469   Goodman Brothers                          G

Scrap Dealers, Wolverton, Bucks
OS Ref: SP 832413

Standard gauge steam locomotives stored in scrapyard

**Stock**
Hawthorn Leslie 0–6–0ST No. 3138 built 1915
Barclay 0–6–0ST No. 2138 built 1941

## 470   Ware, Hertfordshire                       G

Mr Malcolm Saul, Wengeo Lane, Ware, Herts
OS Ref: TL 346153

Standard gauge steam locomotive undergoing restoration.

**Stock**
Hunslet 0–6–0ST *Newstead* (1589) built 1929
Ex NCB, Woolley Colliery, Darton, Yorkshire, 1973.

## 471   City Industrial Limited                   G

Finsbury Park, London

**Stock**
SR Pullman kitchen/first No. 282 *Doris* built 1932
Ex 'Brighton Belle'.

## 472   Didcot                                     G

Mr R. Hilton, 'Poplars', North Moreton, Didcot, Oxfordshire
OS Ref: SU 552904

Narrow gauge locomotives in store

**Stock**
[1]Bagnall 0–4–0ST No. ED10 (1889) built 1911 (3 ft gauge)
[2]Bagnall 0–4–0ST *Kidbrooke* (2043) built 1917 (1 ft 11½ in. gauge)

[1]Ex BR, Beeston Sleeper Works, Nottinghamshire, 1962.

[2]Ex Oakeley Slate Quarries Co. Ltd, Blaenau Ffestiniog, 1961. Stored at Minffordd on the Festiniog Railway until 1971.

## 473   Alan Keef Limited                          G

Light Railway Engineers
Cote Farm, Bampton, Oxfordshire OX8 2EG
Tel: 099-385 260
OS Ref: SP 351030

Narrow gauge locomotives for restoration and resale.
Due to the frequency with which locomotives arrive and depart from Cote Farm, it is impracticable to give a meaningful list of current stock, though at any one time this may amount to some 30 locomotives of several different gauges.

## 474   Bletchley                                  G

40 Wye Close, Bletchley, Buckinghamshire.

Private collection of 2 ft gauge locomotives owned by Mr A. Cocklin and Mr J. Thomas
OS Ref: SP 852345

**Stock**
Orenstein & Koppel 4WDM No. 1 (6705)
Orenstein & Koppel 4WDM No. 2 (7600)
Orenstein & Koppel 4WDM 7371
Orenstein & Koppel 4WDM 4805
Lister 4WDM 4288 built 1931
All ex Oxted Greystone Lime Co. Ltd.

## 475   Watford Miniature Railway                  B

Cassiobury Park, Watford, Herts

A 10¼ in. gauge miniature railway approximately one-third-of-a-mile in length laid out in oval formation and situated alongside the River Gade. The line is in operation every weekend and daily during school holidays from Easter until the end of September.

**Stock**
BR 0–6–0DM (based on '08' class diesel shunter design)
Three open articulated bogie coaches

## 476   Bedfordshire County Council                E

Dovery Down County Primary School, Heath Road, Leighton Buzzard, Beds
2 ft gauge locomotive on static display

**Stock**
Motor Rail 4WDM No. 30 (8695) built 1941
Ex Joseph Arnold, Leighton Buzzard.

## 477   Windsor Safari Park                                          E

Windsor, Berkshire

**Stock**
SR Pullman coach No. 289 built 1932
Ex 'Brighton Belle'. Formerly sited at the Little Mill Inn, Rowarth, Stockport, Cheshire, where it was known as 'The Derbyshire Belle'.

## 478   H & G Car Parks Limited                                      E

Sterne Street, Shepherds Bush, London W12

The company owns Southern Railway coach No. S12613S, which it uses as a transport cafe.
No. S12613S was built as a restaurant car to run in '4RES' electric unit No. 3072, introduced for the electrification of the Portsmouth direct line in 1937. In 1954 it was badly damaged by fire and rebuilt as a buffet car, the layout being experimental to see if it was suitable for the new BR buffet cars.
Unit No. 3072 was reclassified '4BUF'. It was withdrawn from service in April 1971.

## 479   The 'Denham Express' Inn                                     E

Ind Coope Limited. Coach used as a restaurant on the North Orbital Road, Denham, Bucks

**Stock**
Italian wagon-lit coach No. 2757 built Reggio, Emilia, 1926

## 480   Ian Allan Limited                                            G

Shepperton, Middlesex

**Stock**
Pullman kitchen/first *Malaga* built 1921

## 481   Thames Water Authority                                       C

Metropolitan Water Division, Charlton Road Depot, Shepperton, Middlesex
OS Ref: TQ 083694

Passenger-carrying 2 ft gauge portable railway 100 yards in length which makes public appearances, usually at waterworks open days in the TWA area, throughout the year.

**Stock**
Hibberd 4WPM *Ivan* 3317 built 1957
Orenstein & Koppel 4WDM 6504
Two 4-wheel passenger coaches

# AREA K

## Ireland

**501  Railway Preservation Society  AD**
**of Ireland**

Whitehead Excursion Station, Co. Antrim

*Operations Officer:* Denis Grimshaw, 14 Craigdarragh Park
East, Craigavad, Co. Down. Tel: Holywood 3816
*Secretary:* Tony Ragg, 58 Abbey Drive, Bangor, Co. Down
*Membership:* 619

The RPSI was formed in 1964 to obtain some examples of
Ireland's steam locomotives and to restore and maintain
them in working order. The Society's base is at Whitehead
Excursion Station, built by the LMS (NCC) in 1903 to cope
with the day trip traffic from Belfast. The facilities include
a long platform and water tower, together with the original
two-road engine shed and the recently added three-road
extension built by the members. The Society carries out its
own minor repairs, painting and cleaning.
Each year the Society operates several main line railtours
over the NIR and CIE systems. RPSI tours are designed for
the enthusiast with plenty of photographic and tape-record-
ing opportunities with special stops, runpasts, lineside buses
and train-splitting on two-engine tours.

**Stock**
[1]GNR (I) 4-4-0 No. 171 *Slieve Gullion* (Class S) built 1913
[2]LMS (NCC) 2-6-4T No. 4 (Class WT) built 1947
[3]GS & WR 0-6-0 No. 186 (Class J15) built 1879
[4]GSWR 0-6-0 No. 184 (Class J15) built 1899
[5]GNR (I) 4-4-0 No. 85 *Merlin* (Beyer Peacock 6733) built
1932
DSER 2-6-0 No. 15 (Beyer Peacock 6112) built 1922
[6]SL & NCR 0-6-4T *Lough Erne* (Beyer Peacock 7242) built
1949
[7]Hudswell Clarke 0-4-0ST No. 3 *Guinness* (1152) built 1919
[8]Avonside 0-6-0ST LP & HC No. 3 *R. H. Smyth* (2021) built
1928
[9]Planet 4WDM No. 23 built 1928
GSWR 12-wheeled 'Rosslare Express' brake/composite
coach No. 861 built 1906
GNR (I) directors' saloon No. 50 built 1911
GSR Bredin corridor bogie coaches Nos 1327, 1328, 1333
and 1335 built 1935-37
GNR (I) dining car No. 88 built 1938
GSWR corridor compartment coach No. 4012 built 1914
GNR (I) BUT railcar brakes Nos 562 (first-class) and 594
(second-class) built 1946-48
GNR (I) K15 open seconds Nos 98 and 176 built 1941
GNR (I) AEC non-powered driving trailer open second No. 586
built 1954
LMS-NCC brake second 'North Atlantic' No. 91 built 1934
LMS-NCC corridor seconds Nos 340, 342 and 358 built
1921-24
Two GNR (I) bogie grain wagons
Irish Shell tank wagon
GNR (I) six-wheeled goods brake van
Inglis bread container and wagon

[1]Clifford 'S' Class rebuilt in 1938 by Glover. This locomotive
is the last example of the five 'Mountain' Class 4-4-0s and
is a typical Edwardian express engine. These locomotives
pulled the principal trains on the Belfast to Dublin and
Londonderry lines. Restored in Great Northern sky blue
livery. Owned by the Northern Ireland Transport Holding
Company and leased to the RPSI.
[2]No. 4 was one of 18 Class WT engines which were used
extensively by the Ulster Transport Authority, later Northern
Ireland Railways. Their last task was the hauling of the 20-
wagon two-engine spoil trains on the Belfast-Larne line, and
when No. 4 was bought by the Society in 1971 for £1,275
she was the last steam engine still in company service in the
British Isles.
[3]This engine is an example of Ireland's largest class
of locomotives. In all 111 of this type were built from
1866 onwards at Inchicore to the design of MacDonnell.
These locomotives were typical examples of the
Ramsbottom/Webb Crewe tradition and were to be found
throughout the Great Southern system. They were very
successful machines and were mainly used for freight and
local passenger workings, with a top speed in the low 60s.
Built in 1879 by Sharp Stewart principally for goods trains,
186 is now the oldest working steam engine in Ireland.
Livery is unlined black.
[4]A sister engine of No. 186, this engine is the saturated

The lure of steam in Ireland is personified by the elegant sky blue 4–4–0 No. 171 *Slieve Gullion* seen here at Londonderry Waterside on an RPSI rail tour

steam version of the J15 class. Until the 1940s this locomotive was fitted with the old type of double smokebox doors. Some years ago No. 184 was used in the making of the film *Darling Lili*. Both J15s have since had starring roles in the Michael Crichton film *The First Great Train Robbery*.

[5]The handsome 'V' Class 4–4–0s were the ultimate development of the Smith/Deeley Midland compound. Designed by G. T. Glover, five locomotives were built and it was possible to accelerate the Belfast to Dublin expresses immediately they entered traffic. They became well-known in the post-war years for their haulage of the 'Enterprise' express. *Merlin* passed to the CIE in 1958 on the dissolution of the GNR (I) and was withdrawn in 1963.

[6]The last surviving locomotive of the Sligo, Leitrim and Northern Counties Railway, which had been operated principally by 0–6–4Ts since 1882. It was the last conventional steam locomotive built for any Irish railway and passed to the UTA on closure of the Sligo line. It was purchased privately for preservation in 1970.

[7]No. 3 was used by the brewery of Arthur Guinness, Son and Co., for short workings between the brewery in Dublin, along streets to Kingsbridge goods yard. She became redundant in 1965 and was presented to the Society, along with spare parts, by Guinness's. Formerly she carried no nameplate, but this was added by the Society as thanks to the brewery. She is the favourite engine for the Sunday afternoon steam train rides at Whitehead during the summer.

[8]The Society's latest steam acquisition worked with the Londonderry Port and Harbour Commissioners until the late 1950s when she became redundant and was bought by a clergyman. He sold her to the Society for a penny in 1972 and since then the Whitehead locomotive maintenance team have been working hard on overhauling her.

[9]Presented to the Society via the Irish Steam Preservation Society from Irish Shell and BP in 1973. Reckoned to be the smallest standard-gauge engine ever used in Ireland. The engines, except Nos 85, 184 and 186, are all kept at Whitehead, the base for all the tours and scene of the Sunday afternoon steam train rides in July and August.

Photo: Charles Friel

Fresh from its exploits in the film of *The Great Train Robbery,* **J15 No. 186** provides vintage broad gauge motive power at the RPSI Whitehead depot

### Activities

The Society is the only body in Ireland operating main line steam engines, and enjoys close co-operation with the Irish railway companies CIE and NIR. No restrictions are placed on routes over which steam can run, and the Society's tours are exclusively steam-hauled. The annual tour programme usually comprises one-day outings from Dublin and then Belfast in the spring, followed by the big one – a two-day two-engine all steam tour from Dublin in June over part of the CIE system. The summer is the time for the season of four 'Portrush Flyer' steam excursion trains – an accurate recreation of the Ulster excursion train to the seaside. Then, to round things off, another one-day tour is operated in Northern Ireland in September.

Steam train rides are operated at Whitehead on Sunday afternoons in July and August. Work goes on there every weekend.

The Society runs a number of film shows and meetings in Belfast during the winter.

Details of membership are available from Laurence Morrison, 9 Dunraven Drive, Belfast 5.

The annual subscription is £4 for adults.

## 502    Irish Steam Preservation     A
         Society Limited

Stradbally, Co. Laois, Ireland

*Access:* Stradbally is eight miles from Athy, Co. Kildare, and six miles from Portlaoise, Co. Laois, the nearest CIE buses on the Dublin–Kilkenny route, but this service is unsuitable for day visits, except on Sundays. Intending visitors should contact the Society's Secretary, Mrs Olive Condell, Main Street, Stradbally, Co. Laois (Telephone 0502/25136), for appointments to visit the museum and for details of other operating dates for the railway. Work parties are generally there on the first Saturday each month, when visitors would be specially welcome.

This Society operates a 3 ft gauge railway ½ mile in length in the grounds of Stradbally Hall, Stradbally, Co. Laois, by kind permission of Mr A. P. S. A. Cosby.

In addition to the railway, the Society has a steam museum in the town of Stradbally, which is opened on request at any time, by prior appointment. Each year, the railway is a major attraction during the National Traction Engine Rally held in the grounds of Stradbally Hall at the beginning of August. It is also hoped to operate the line for open days on the other days, particularly if there are any other suitable functions in the town.

*1980 Open Days:* August 2, 3 & 4, October 26 and 27
*Details from:* R. C. Flewitt, 6 Waterloo Avenue, Dublin 3, Ireland
*Subscriptions:* Gentlemen £1; ladies 75p; juniors (14–17 years inclusive) 50p

### Workable Stock
Barclay 0–4–0WT No. 2 2264 built 1949
Hunslet 4WDM No. 1 2280 built 1941
Wickham 4WPM railcar No. C39 6861 built *c.*1955
One bogie toastrack coach, 45 seats
Ballast wagon

### Other Stock
Drewry 4WPM railcar No. 5 1495 built 1927 (5 ft 3 in. gauge)
Spence 0–4–0T No. 15 built 1895 (1 ft 10 in. gauge)
Kennon 0–6–0 built 1955 (1 ft 9 in. gauge)
Spence 0–4–0T No. 21 built 1905 (f ft 10 in.) gauge)

The Society was founded in 1965 by some local traction engine enthusiasts. The present 3 ft gauge railway was started in 1969 and has been gradually extended since then as far as limited finance and voluntary labour has allowed. The Society organises the National Traction Engine Rally each year and the railway represents the only steam ride available to the public.

## 503   Shane's Castle Railway

Shane's Castle, Antrim, Northern Ireland

One-and-a-half mile, 3 ft gauge passenger-carrying line operated by The Lord O'Neill

*Access:* On the A6 Antrim–Randalstown road, 1 mile out of Antrim
Tel: Antrim 3380

Facilities for visitors include car parking, railway shop, refreshments, toilets and nature reserve.

The Shane's Castle Light Railway opened in May 1971 and is currently the only narrow gauge steam operated railway in regular use anywhere in Ireland. The railway runs from the terminus on the edge of Antrim through a largely wooded setting to the ruins of Old Shane's Castle. The area is also a nature reserve, which is jointly managed with the Royal Society for the Protection of Birds. The system operates on Sundays and Bank Holidays in April and May, on Saturdays, Sundays and Bank Holidays in June, on Wednesdays, Saturdays and Sundays in July and August and on Sundays in September. Opening hours, 12 noon to 6 pm.

### Stock
Peckett 0–4–0T No. 1 *Tyrone* 1026 built 1904
Simplex 4WDM No. 2 *Rory* 11039 built 1956
Barclay 0–4–0WT No. 3 *Shane* 2265 built 1949
Planet 4WDM No. 4 *Nippy* 2014 built 1936
Avonside 0–6–0T *Nancy* 1547 built 1908
Wickham 4WPMR 7441
Charleroi Tramway trailer cars
Seven four-wheeled covered coaches
Four four-wheeled open coaches
Four-wheeled brake/saloon coach
B & NCR coal wagon
BAC (Larne) open wagon converted into a spray truck
L & LSR three-plank open wagon
L & LSR mobile crane truck

*Static Exhibits (owned by the North West of Ireland Railway Society)*
Nasmyth Wilson 2–6–4T No. 6 *Columbkille* 830 built 1907
CDRJC 0–4–0+4WDMR No. 12 built 1934
CDRJC 0–4–0+4WDMR No. 18 built Walker Brothers, 1940
CDRJC bogie composite coach No. 14 built 1893
CDRJC railcar wagon
Five CDRJC bogie coach underframes

The Shane's Castle Railway was conceived in the late sixties and opened to the public in May 1971. Essentially a tourist attraction, it complements the other points of interest at Shane's Castle. However, it is currently the only place in Ireland where 3 ft gauge steam locomotives can be seen in regular use during the summer months. Recently, the stock of the North West of Ireland Railway Society has moved on to the system and plans are under discussion about future developments which could lead to a more ambitious 3 ft gauge museum arising.

## 504   Coras Iompair Eireann                           E

Static exhibits on display at locations named

### Stock
[1]GSWR 2–2–2 No. 36 (Bury Curtis and Kennedy) built 1846: Cork (Kent)
GNR (I) 4–4–0 No. 131 *Uranus* built 1901: Dundalk
[3]GSWR 0–6–0T No. 90 built 1880: Mallow
[4]West Clare Railway 0–6–2T No. 5 (Dubs 2890) built 1892 (3 ft gauge): Ennis

[1]This locomotive is a passenger version of the Bury design with 5 ft 8 in. wheels and bar frames. It is worthy of comparison with the ex Furness Railway 0–4–0 *Coppernob*. There were 20 of these engines on the Great Southern and Western and this was the last in service in 1881.
[3]This is one of three similar engines built to the design of J. A. F. Aspinall for light lines in Ireland. They ran on the Castletown and Mitchelstown to Fermoy branches, though

No. 90 ended its days on the Timoleague and Courtmacsherry Light Railway. In working order it weighed a mere 22 tons and had a tractive effort of 5,160 lb.

[4]Originally named *Slieve Callan* and withdrawn as CIE (West Clare Section) Class INI No. 5C in 1959. Used during filming of *The Rising of the Moon* then stored at Inchicore Works, Dublin, until restored in 1961. This engine has been kept not only for its interest as a West Clare locomotive but as a memorial to the late Percy French who immortalised the idiosyncrasies of the line in his song, 'Are ye right there, Michael?'

## 505   Belfast Transport Museum               E

Witham Street, Belfast 4, Northern Ireland

Static exhibits
*Open:* Weekdays 10 am–6 pm (9 pm on Wednesdays)

**Stock**
*5 ft 3 in. gauge*
[1]B & CDR 4–4–2T No. 30 (Beyer Peacock 4231) built 1901
[2]GNR (I) 2–4–2T No. 93 built 1895
[3]GNR (I) 4W diesel railcar 'E' built 1934
[4]NCC 4–4–0 No. 74 *Dunluce Castle* (Class U2) (NB Loco. 23096) built 1924
[5]GSR 4–6–0T No. 800 *Maeve* built 1939
Stephenson 0–6–0T No. 1 (2738) built 1891
[6]GNR (I) Fintona horse tram No. 381

*3 ft gauge*
CDRJC 2–6–4T No. 2 *Blanche* (Nasmyth Wilson 956) built 1912
CDRJC Drewry petrol railcar No. 3 built 1926
CDRJC Ford petrol railcar No 1 built 1906
CDRJC 0–4–0D No. 11 *Phoenix* (Atkinson Walker 114) built 1928
Clogher Valley Railway diesel railcar No. 1 built 1932
Cavan and Leitrim Railway 4–4–0T No. 3 *Kathleen* (Stephenson 2613) built 1887
Peckett 0–4–0T No. 2 (1097) built 1906
Portstewart Tramway 0–4–0 tram locomotive No. 2 (Kitson T84) built 1883

*1 ft 10 in. gauge*
Spence 0–4–0T No. 20 built 1905

The museum houses part of the Ulster Folk Museum collection and covers all aspects of transport. Over 100 vehicles, including railway and tramway examples, also models, equipment and records.

[1]This is a typical Beyer Peacock design developed from earlier 2–4–2T engines. The class was responsible for the bulk of B & CDR passenger train haulage. This locomotive became UTA No. 30 and was stored from 1956 to 1961, when it was restored to its original livery and placed on display. Officially withdrawn in 1962.
[2]Clifford Class JT. Restored and presented by the GNR (I) board in 1955. Originally named *Sutton*.

[3]Originally known as 'Railcar E'. Withdrawn by the UTA in 1966.
[4]Designed by Sir Henry Fowler, this locomotive can be described as an Irish version of his LMS Class 2P 4–4–0s. Withdrawn as UTA No. 74 in 1961 and restored to NCC livery in 1962. Placed on display in 1963.
[5]Bredin Class BIA locomotive withdrawn as CIE No. 800 in 1957. This locomotive and its two sisters were the crack locomotives of Ireland. Apart from the GWR 'King' class they were probably the most powerful 4–6–0s in Western Europe and were introduced with a view to speeding up the Dublin–Cork services. The magnificent bronze nameplates were inscribed in Erse after ancient queens of Ireland, and the spelling 'Maeve' is the English rendering. Restored at Inchicore Works, Dublin, in 1963 and presented for display in the following year by the CIE.
[6]This vehicle became a celebrity in its own right and ran on the half-mile Fintona Junction to Fintona Town branch in connection with the main line trains. It was withdrawn (and the horse retired) when the main line service ceased. The tram carried first, second and third class passengers, though these distinctions were largely ignored!

## 506   Arthur Guinness Son and               E
         Company (Dublin) Limited

St James Gate Brewery, Dublin 8

Static exhibit (1 ft 10 in. gauge)
Open daily 11 am–4.15 pm; admission free

**Stock**
Spence 0–4–0T No. 17 built 1902

## 507   Ulster Folk Museum                     E

Cultra, County Down

Passenger-carrying 2 ft gauge railway opened in 1976 featuring gradients up to 1 in 30.

**Stock**
Hunslet 4WDM 3127 built 1943
Motor Rail 4WPM 246 built 1916
Hibberd 4WDM
Four 12-seat passenger coaches
Giant's Causeway Tramway trailer car No. 2 (3 ft gauge) static exhibit

## 508   Galway Miniature Railway               B

Galway, Eire

A 10¼ in. gauge passenger-carrying line

**Stock**
Severn-Lamb 2–8–0PH No. 278 *Rio Grande* built 1975 (steam outline)

## 509   Doctor Ralph Cox                              G

Strabane Station, Country Tyrone

3 ft gauge former County Donegal Railways rolling stock in store at Strabane. The future of these acquisitions is unknown, but since much of the collection has been heavily vandalised and now lies derelict, it is doubtful whether it will remain in existence for much longer.

**Stock**
Nasmyth Wilson 2–6–4T No. 4 *Meenglas* (828) built 1907
Nasmyth Wilson 2–6–4T No. 5 *Drumboe* 829 built 1907
CDRJC bogie composite coaches Nos. 12, 15, 16 and 17 built 1893
CDRJC passenger van No. 23 built 1893
All the above coaches have been reduced to underframes and bogies only.


## 510   Belfast and County Down              F
Railway Museum Trust

Ballynahinch Junction Station, County Down

The Trust is undertaking the establishment of a working railway museum based at Ballynahinch Junction on the former Belfast and County Down Railway. The project entails the relaying of five-and-a-half miles of line between Rowallane Gardens at Saintfield, the National Trust property, and Ballynahinch Town. The project has been put before Down District Council and has received full council backing, and the council are hopeful of getting the Trust a grant in the region of £200,000 to get the scheme under way. It is hoped to make the Trust into a Charitable Trust, at the same time establishing a limited company to undertake the working of the railway, etc. Secretary of the Trust is Mr R. J. Pue, 8 Woburn Drive, Millisle, County Down BT22 2HU.

**Stock**
Orenstein & Koppel 0–4–0T 12475 built 1934
Orenstein & Koppel 0–4–0T 12662 built 1935


## 511   Tramore Miniature Railway              B

Tramore, County Waterford, Eire

A 15 in. gauge passenger-carrying line

**Stock**
Severn-Lamb 2–8–0PH No. 278 *Rio Grande* (22) built 1973 (Steam outline)


## 512   Rosminian Fathers                         B

Upton, Innishannon, County Cork

A 2 ft gauge passenger-carrying line formerly operated by the St John of God Brothers at Drumcar, County Louth

**Stock**
Ruston & Hornsby 4WDM 264244 (Class 13DL) built 1949